K. Golden Bitting Collection on Gastronomy

The New American Cook Book

containing thousands of recipes, practical suggestions and methods for the

household, contributed by celebrated chefs and more than two hundred

experienced housekeepers

K. Golden Bitting Collection on Gastronomy

The New American Cook Book
containing thousands of recipes, practical suggestions and methods for the household,
contributed by celebrated chefs and more than two hundred experienced housekeepers

ISBN/EAN: 9783337121419

Printed in Europe, USA, Canada, Australia, Japan

Cover: Foto ©Andreas Hilbeck / pixelio.de

More available books at **www.hansebooks.com**

THE NEW

AMERICAN

COOK BOOK

CONTAINING THOUSANDS OF RECIPES, PRACTICAL SUGGESTIONS AND
METHODS FOR THE HOUSEHOLD, CONTRIBUTED BY CELEBRATED
CHEFS AND MORE THAN TWO HUNDRED EXPERIENCED HOUSE-
KEEPERS, WHO ARE RECOGNIZED AUTHORITIES IN THE
CULINARY ART, AND COVERING EVERY BRANCH
OF COOKERY; WITH SPECIAL DIRECTIONS FOR
SERVING AT TABLE; ALSO PRESERVING,
PICKLING, CANDY-MAKING, ETC.;

Presenting the Most Healthful, Palatable, Economical
and Approved Use of the Foods of
the Twentieth Century.

HUNDREDS OF FINE ILLUSTRATIONS.

———

PUBLISHED BY
MAST, CROWELL & KIRKPATRICK,
SPRINGFIELD, OHIO.

THE RECIPES IN THIS COOK BOOK WERE CONTRIBUTED BY MORE
THAN TWO HUNDRED PRACTICAL AND EXPERIENCED
HOUSEKEEPERS, BESIDES THE FOLLOWING

CELEBRATED CHEFS

.....AND.....

PROMINENT WOMEN,

WHO ARE RECOGNIZED AS AUTHORITIES IN THE CULINARY ART.

PAUL RESAL, ... WASHINGTON, D. C.
Chef of White House (Executive Mansion).

LOUIS C. ZEREGA, ... ST. AUGUSTINE, FLA.
Chef of Hotel Ponce de Leon.

GUSTAVE BERAUD, ... CHICAGO, ILL.
Chef of Calumet Club, formerly Chef of William Astor, New York City.

A. GALLIER, ... NEW YORK CITY.
President "Societe Culinaire de New York," and Chef of Hotel Brunswick.

LOUIS MARCHE, ... CINCINNATI, OHIO.
Chef of Burnet House.

EUGENE STUYVESANT HOWARD, ... LOUISVILLE, KY.
Member of the "Universal Cookery and Food Association," London, England,
and Chef de Cuisine, "Louisville Hotel."

5

A. J. PILLAUET, ...   MINNEAPOLIS, MINN.
Chef of West House.

MISS HARRIOTT T. WARD, ...   BOSTON, MASS.
Scientific and Special Teacher of Cooking.

MISS ANGELINE M. WEAVER,   .   .   .   BOSTON, MASS.
Instructor Hyde School Kitchen.

MISS IDA M. FOSTER, ...   WILKESBARRE, PA.
City Hospital.

MISS AMABEL G. E. HOPE, ...   BOSTON, MASS.
Teacher of Cookery, Boston School Kitchen No. 1.

MISS CORNELIA CAMPBELL BEDFORD,   .   .   .   NEW YORK CITY.
Superintendent New York Cooking School.

MRS. S. T. RORER, ...   PHILADELPHIA, PA.
Author of "Mrs. Rorer's Cook Book," and Principal Philadelphia Cooking School.

MRS. ALTHEA SOMES, ...   BOSTON, MASS.
Teacher of Cookery, Manual Training School.

MRS. GESINE LEMCKE, ...   BROOKLYN, N. Y.
Principal German-American Cooking College.

MISS EMILY E. SQUIRE, ...   WESTFIELD, MASS.
Author of "Woronoco Women's Wisdom."

MISS MARION L. CAMPBELL,   .   .   .   CLEVELAND, OHIO.
Friendly Inn Cooking School.

MRS. G. L. GREEN, ...   CONCORD, N. H.
Formerly Principal Boston Y. M. C. A. School of Cookery,
now Teacher of Cooking in the Concord High School.

MRS. A. E. KIRTLAND, ...   MONTGOMERY, ALA.
Author of "Mrs. Kirtland's Cook Book."

CONTENTS

[For complete Index see last 12 pages of the book.]

PAGE

CHAPTER I.

STOCKS FOR SOUP, GRAVY, ETC., . . . 9

CHAPTER II.

SAUCES, ... 11

SWEET SAUCES, FOR PUDDINGS, ETC., . . 24

CHAPTER III.

GARNISHES, PUREES, FARCES, ETC., . 30

CHAPTER IV.

SOUPS, ... 37

CHAPTER V.

OYSTERS AND FISH, ... 49

CHAPTER VI.

POULTRY AND GAME, ... 75

CHAPTER VII.

MEATS, ... 111

CHAPTER VIII.

VEGETABLES, ... 142

CHAPTER IX.

BREAD, BISCUIT, ETC., ... 157

CHAPTER X.

EGGS, OMELETS, BREAKFAST AND TEA DISHES, . . 173

CHAPTER XI.
RELISHES, ... 187

CHAPTER XII.
SALADS, ... 209

CHAPTER XIII.
PIES AND PUDDINGS, ... 215

CHAPTER XIV.
CUSTARDS AND DESSERTS, . . . 235
ICES, CREAMS, SHERBETS, ETC., . . 262
PASTES, ICINGS, ETC., ... 269

CHAPTER XV.
CAKES, COOKIES AND FRITTERS, . . . 275
SMALL CAKES, ... 296

CHAPTER XVI.
PICKLES AND CATSUPS, ... 301

CHAPTER XVII.
PRESERVES AND JELLIES, ... 311

CHAPTER XVIII.
BEVERAGES, . . . 317

CHAPTER XIX.
CANDIES, ... 321

CHAPTER XX.
INVALID COOKERY, ... 325

CHAPTER XXI.
PRACTICAL SUGGESTIONS TO YOUNG HOUSEKEEPERS, . 331

BILLS OF FARE FOR FAMILY DINNERS, . . . 335
BILLS OF FARE FOR SPECIAL DAYS, . . . 337
STATE DINNERS, ... 338
GLOSSARY OF COOKING TERMS, ... 341
NECESSARY KITCHEN UTENSILS, . . . 344
NAPERY, ... 346
SUGGESTIONS ON CARVING, . . . 349
WEIGHTS AND MEASURES, . . . 355
LAUNDRY-WORK, ... 356
HOUSEHOLD HINTS AND RECIPES, . . . 360
GARNISHED SKEWERS, ... 366
MOLDS FOR CREAMS AND ICES, ... 369

THE
AMERICAN COOK BOOK.

STOCKS FOR SOUP, GRAVY, ETC.

CHAPTER I.

Stock in some shape or other is the foundation of soups, gravies, etc., and on its quality depends almost entirely the excellence of any cuisine. It may be briefly described as the solution in water of the juices of the meat, etc., used in its composition, by a long and gentle process of simmering; and this essence, variously flavored, is the basis of all gravies, sauces, soups, etc. Stock can be made from almost anything—fish, flesh or vegetable; but in all cases the process is the same, and its cost depends entirely on the requirements and the management of its maker.

Roughly speaking, stock may be divided into two sorts—white and brown; the former made chiefly from white meat, such as veal, rabbit, poultry, etc.; the latter from beef, game, etc.

For ordinary purposes a very good stock can be made of broken-up bones, cooked or raw, and the trimmings, giblets, etc., of poultry (with or without the addition of a little soup-meat), simmered gently for several hours in the stock-pot. But for high-class cookery, where distinct and delicate flavors are indispensable, each kind, as white, brown or game, should be made separately, and if possible of uncooked meat, bones, etc.

Sauces and gravies of various kinds, of which the stocks mentioned above are the bases, are the indispensable adjuncts of nearly every dish, and must be well made to insure its success. Entrees and made dishes depend in great measure on the sauces that accompany them.

In addition to savory sauces, there are also sweet ones, used in conjunction with certain meats, and various sweet entremets, specimens of which will be found duly given.

The materials employed in the composition of savory sauces are stock, milk, cream, flour, butter, eggs, water, seasonings, etc., and from these are formed the standard sauces, which form part or more or less of all the others.

ECONOMIC STOCK FOR SOUP, GRAVY, ETC.

Take odds and ends, such as about three or four pounds of cooked or raw bones, the rind of bacon that has been scraped, and the necks, cleaned feet, gizzards and livers of chickens, chop these up, put with them one or two sliced onions, a little sliced carrot, turnip, celery, and leek if you have any, and a few herbs, such as thyme, parsley, bay-leaf, and a few peppercorns, into a saucepan,

9

first putting a tablespoonful of fat in the bottom of the pan; close these down in the saucepan and let them fry until the contents at the bottom are quite brown; then cover up the bones with cold water, add a little salt, let it come gently to a boil, then skim off all the scum, and let it simmer steadily for three or four hours; be sure it does not boil quickly. When it is done, strain off, and when cool, take off the fat, which can be boiled up in water and clarified for other purposes. This gravy should always be kept ready, and requires to be boiled up every day during warm weather. The meat taken to clarify stock can be used again to make a good, clear, light stock by covering it, when strained, with cold water and boiling it gently. The bones can be boiled two or three times for light stock. (See clear soup.)

FISH STOCKS.

Take the bones of any white fish, such as soles, whiting, cod, etc., whether raw or cooked, with any fish trimmings, lobster-shell, shrimps' heads and tails, etc., and lay them in a pan, with a dessert-spoonful of lemon-juice, one or two sliced onions, a bunch of herbs, a few peppercorns and a pinch of salt; cover it with cold water, one quart for each pound of fish-bones. Simmer it all gently for about an hour, skimming it when it comes to a boil. For fish sauces or bisques, this stock will only require to be freed from fat, and strained; for clear fish stock, it must be clarified in the usual way, with the whites and shells of four eggs to each quart of stock. For clear brown fish soups, fry the onions and herbs together in a little butter, then lay in the fish-bones (well and carefully dried in a cloth), and let all fry together for fifteen minutes; it should then be covered with cold water, and finished off like the clear fish stock given above.

GAME STOCK.

Take any kind of poultry or game bones, fresh or roast; fresh are best. Put two ounces of butter or fat into a stew-pan, with two onions cut up into little dice shapes, one large leek, one carrot, a little celery, one turnip, a good bunch of herbs (thyme, parsley, bay-leaf, basil and marjoram), two or three fresh mushrooms if you have them, and a pinch of mignonette pepper. Place the bones on this, cover the pan, and fry the contents all together for about twenty to thirty minutes, taking care they do not burn. Then cover them well with stock (any stock from veal, rabbit or chicken, such as above, can be used), let it come to a boil, then strain, and let it simmer gently for two or three hours. Strain off when cold, remove any fat, and use. Clarify the stock with either rabbit, hare or beef, allowing half a pound of raw beef and four whites of eggs to each quart of stock. The meat should be chopped fine and mixed with the whites before being put into the soup, stir together occasionally till it boils, then simmer gently for about an hour, and strain.

WHITE STOCK.

Take about twenty-five cents' worth of veal-bones, or the bones of rabbit or chicken, put them into a pan, with two or three sliced onions, a pinch of salt, small bunch of herbs—thyme, parsley and bay-leaf—about six peppercorns, black and white, and two cloves. Cover with cold water; let it come to a boil, then skim, and cover up the pan, and boil gently for about one hour and a half, strain off, remove the fat, and use.

Sauces

CHAPTER II

AMERICAN SAUCE.

Put half a pound of game or poultry bones into a stew-pan, with one ounce of butter, half a sliced onion, one or two bay-leaves, six crushed peppercorns, one sliced tomato and one fresh mushroom; cover up, and let these fry on the stove for about twenty minutes; then add one wine-glassful of white wine, a few drops of carmine and a pint of brown sauce; let it boil for fifteen to twenty minutes, keeping it skimmed during the boiling; then strain through the tammy, and mix in it a dessert-spoonful of chopped fresh mushrooms and a dust of red pepper; boil up, and serve.

ANCHOVY CREAM.

Wash and bone six anchovies, and pound them, with one yolk of hard-boiled egg, one tablespoonful of salad-oil, a dust of red pepper and a few drops of carmine; when smooth, add half a gill of liquid aspic jelly, and rub through a tammy. Mix this purée with a gill of stiffly whipped cream, and use when ice-cold.

ANCHOVY SAUCE FOR FISH.

Take the bones from four anchovies, and pound them in a mortar to a paste, with one ounce of butter. Set on the stove in a saucepan sufficient butter to make half a pint when melted, stir into it the pounded anchovies, a sprinkle of pepper and the juice of half a small lemon; boil one minute, and send to the table very hot. Serve with turbot or soles.

APPLE SAUCE.

Pare one dozen best apples, stew until tender, stir in one tablespoonful of butter, one teacupful of sugar, the juice of one lemon and a little grated nutmeg.

11

ARTICHOKE SAUCE.

Put a piece of butter the size of an egg into a saucepan, let it melt, put into it a sliced onion, half a head of celery, a tablespoonful of chopped ham, a pinch of powdered cinnamon, a salt-spoonful of salt and a little cayenne; stir the ingredients constantly over a fire gently for a quarter of an hour, adding more butter, if necessary; then add to them a pound of Jerusalem artichokes, boiled and beaten to a pulp, and a pint of milk, boil all together until the sauce is rather thicker than cream; strain, boil again, and serve hot. Boil the ingredients together ten minutes. Sufficient for rather more than a pint of sauce.

ASPARAGUS SAUCE.

Boil one bunch of asparagus; when tender, cut in pieces; stew in a teacupful of cream, with salt and pepper; thicken with butter rolled in flour. To be served with any delicate fish.

ASPIC CREAM.

Take half a pint of liquid aspic jelly, one gill of thick, fresh cream, then add a dessert-spoonful of tarragon vinegar; tammy, and use when cooling for masking chicken, etc.

ASPIC JELLY.

Take a handful of aromatic herbs, such as burnet, chervil and tarragon, boil them in white vinegar; when the vinegar is well scented, pour into the stew-pan some consomme of fowl, reduced; season well before you clarify. When the aspic is highly seasoned, break the whites of four eggs into an earthen pan, and beat them with an osier rod; throw the aspic into the whites of eggs, and put the whole on the fire in a stew-pan; keep beating or stirring till the jelly gets white; it is then very near boiling. Put it on the corner of the stove, with a cover over it, and a little fire on the top of it. When quite clear and bright, strain it through a bag, or sieve, or napkin, to be used when wanted. Or if this is wanted for a mayonnaise, or as a jelly in molds, make sure of its being stiff enough. Then put a knuckle of veal in a small stock-pot, a small part of a knuckle of ham and two calf feet, some trimming of fowl or game. Season this with onions, carrots and a bunch of herbs well seasoned, and moisten with good broth; let it boil gently for four hours, then skim away all the fat, and drain it through a silken sieve; put that into a stew-pan, with two spoonfuls of tarragon vinegar and four whites of eggs, salt and pepper, to clarify; keep stirring it over the fire until the whole becomes very white, then put this on the side, with a little fire over the cover; when you find it clear, drain it in a cloth or jelly-bag, and use it for aspic; if not, do not put in any vinegar; jelly for pie or galantine does not require acid.

BAIN-MARIE SAUCE OR STEW PAN.

The bain-marie is a shallow vessel, generally made of copper, which is used for keeping sauces, stews, etc., hot when they are already sufficiently cooked, and when it is not convenient that they should be immediately served. It will be found most valuable in those families where regularity and punctuality in meals cannot be depended upon, as it affords the best means of keeping dishes hot without destroying their flavor or burning them. When it is to be used, the bain-marie should be filled with boiling water, and the pans containing the sauces or entrees should be put into it closely covered. It should then be put upon a hot plate, or by the side of the fire, to keep up the heat of the water without allowing it to boil, and should there remain until the dishes are wanted. The principle of the bain-marie may be adapted for keeping sauces and gravies warm when a proper pan is not at hand. Instead of retaining the compound slowly simmering by the side of the fire in the pan in which it was made, by which means it would, in all probability, be either smoked, burned or rendered flavorless, put it into a basin or jar, cover it closely, and place it in a pan of boiling water. If the water is allowed to boil, the sauce or gravy will become too thick.

BECHAMEL SAUCE (CREAMY).

Put one and a half ounces of fine flour and the same of butter to fry together without discoloring, then mix with it a half pint of milk flavored as in recipe for thick bechamel, stir together till it boils, then add a gill of single cream and a little seasoning, tammy, and use. This sauce is excellent for serving with boiled chicken, etc.

BECHAMEL SAUCE (THICK).

Half a pint of milk boiled with a little mace and half a shallot; mix onto two ounces of flour which have been lightly fried with two ounces of butter, stir until it boils, add a little red pepper and salt, tammy, and use.

BEARNAISE SAUCE.

Three tablespoonfuls of tarragon vinegar, the yolks of two eggs and one half pound of butter; put the vinegar into a small saucepan over a moderate fire, let it boil until reduced to one spoonful, then put in the yolks and a small piece of butter, stir continually with a wooden spoon or small egg-whip. As soon as the first piece of butter is melted, take from the fire; put in a second piece, and stir until melted; continue this until the whole amount of butter is melted; put over the fire again for one minute, add a teaspoonful of fresh tarragon, chopped fine. You must be careful in doing this sauce, for it will break very easily; in case of breaking, add a little cold water, drop by drop, until the sauce comes right again. Care must be taken not to cook the yolk, as it will cause the sauce to break. This sauce may be served with steak.

A. J. Pillauet, Chef West Hotel, Minneapolis, Minnesota.

BORDEAUX SAUCE.

2 gallons of cabbage, cut fine,	1 ounce of ground ginger,
1 gallon of green tomatoes, sliced,	1 ounce of ground black pepper,
1 dozen sliced onions,	½ pound of white mustard-seed,
1 ounce of turmeric-powder,	1½ pounds of white sugar,
1 ounce of celery-seed,	1 gill of salt,
1 ounce of whole allspice,	1 gallon of vinegar.
1 ounce of cloves.	

Mix all, and boil fifteen or twenty minutes.

Laura M. Logan, Shirland, Pennsylvania.

BREAD SAUCE.

One cupful of stale bread-crumbs, one onion, two ounces of butter, pepper, salt and mace. Cut the onions very fine and boil in sweet milk, then strain on the bread, and let stand half an hour; put into a saucepan, with onion, pepper, salt and butter; boil. Serve with goose, duck or any kind of game.

BROWN CHESTNUT SAUCE.

This is made in the same way as white chestnut sauce, excepting brown gravy is used instead of milk; this is usually served with roasted fowl, and seasoned rather more highly than the white sauce.

BROWN ONION SAUCE.

Fry the onions in butter and a dash of sugar to a nice brown; thicken a little with "brown roux" or flour, and add enough strong beef gravy to make a thick sauce. Season with cayenne or black pepper, and rub through a sieve. Very nice with roasted goose or pork.

RUBBING SAUCES THROUGH THE TAMMY.

BROWN SAUCE.

Fry four ounces of flour, four ounces of butter and four ounces of tomatoes till a good brown color; then add two quarts of good-flavored stock made from cooked meat-bones, stir till it boils, and let it boil till reduced one fourth, keeping it well skimmed; then, when quite free from fat, tammy. This sauce may always be kept ready for use by being boiled up once or twice a week.

BROWN SAUCE.

Melt and stir one ounce of butter over the fire until brown, thicken with a tablespoonful of flour and mix smooth, thin with half a pint of boiling stock; add one finely chopped onion, a small carrot, a sprig each of parsley, thyme and sweet marjoram, a blade of mace, a little black pepper and salt. Simmer for ten minutes, then strain, and stir in a tablespoonful of Worcestershire sauce, a tablespoonful each of tomato, mushroom and walnut catchup, with the juice of one lemon, stir until thoroughly mixed. Serve with beefsteak, mutton chops and warmed-over meats.

CAPER SAUCE (BROWN).

Take some thick brown sauce, adding the vinegar the capers are pickled in; season it highly with cayenne and salt. Put capers to the sauce just before serving; and they must be used liberally. Nasturtium buds or seeds are sometimes used as a substitute.

CAPER SAUCE (WHITE).

Put whole capers into melted butter, adding a little of the vinegar they are pickled in, a pinch of salt, and sufficient cream to make it white. This is used principally for boiled mutton.

CELERY SAUCE.

Chop the celery fine, and boil it until tender; use only a little water; season with one half cupful of cream, one tablespoonful of butter, and salt and pepper to suit the taste.

Mrs. Louisa Ash, Mt. Vernon, Ohio.

CHAPONAY SAUCE.

Put two peeled shallots into a stew-pan, with a sliced tomato, a bunch of herbs, one mushroom chopped fine, a little piece of bacon-bone, half a pound of bones from any birds, one tablespoonful of clarified butter or salad-oil, pinch of mignonette pepper, and fry all together for about fifteen minutes. Then add one ounce of glaze and three quarters of a pint of good brown sauce; boil all together for about a quarter of an hour, and keep skimmed while boiling; tammy, and mix in twelve shredded turned olives, a few drops of carmine and a quarter of a pint of champagne just before serving. This is an excellent sauce for serving with larks, quails, etc.

CHAUDFROID (BROWN).

Three quarters of a pint of aspic, quarter of a pint of tomato sauce, a few drops of carmine, half a wine-glassful of sherry, half an ounce of glaze and a dust of red pepper; reduce one quarter, keep skimmed while boiling, then tammy, and use when somewhat cool.

CHAUDFROID (WHITE).

Put together a quarter of a pint of veloute sauce, a quarter of a pint of thick cream, half a pint of aspic jelly, and boil till reduced one quarter, keeping it well skimmed; tammy, and use when cooling.

CHILLI SAUCE.

18 ripe tomatoes, cut fine,	1 cupful of sugar,
1 green pepper, cut fine,	1 tablespoonful of salt,
1 onion, cut fine,	2 cupfuls of best vinegar,
2 tablespoonfuls of all kinds of spices, pulverized.	

Boil, and bottle for use.

Cousin Lizzie, Girardtown, West Virginia.

CLARET SAUCE.

Boil one cupful of sugar and one fourth cupful of water until it thickens slightly; cool a little, and add three tablespoonfuls of claret.

Mrs. Althea Somes, Teacher of Cookery, Manual Training School, Boston, Mass.

CLARIFIED BUTTER.

For serving with boiled fish, globe artichokes, asparagus, etc. Put half a pound of good butter into a stew-pan and stand on the side of the stove; let it boil very gently, keep it continually skimmed while boiling, but do not allow it to discolor; then, when it presents the appearance of clear salad-oil, carefully pour it off from the sediment at the bottom of the pan, and serve in a sauce-boat. This is also very good for frying cutlets, etc., in. It will require about half an hour to clarify, and the above quantity is sufficient for six to eight persons.

CRANBERRY SAUCE.

Wash a quart of cranberries, put into a preserve-kettle, with water to cover, and stew until the berries break; then strain through a colander, return to the kettle, add one and one half pounds of sugar, and stir until it boils; turn out to cool.

CREAM SAUCE.

Put two tablespoonfuls of hot water and a teacupful of sweet cream into a saucepan, stir in one tablespoonful of butter and a little chopped parsley; set the saucepan into a kettle of boiling water, add a little strained soup stock, let boil, take from the fire, and add a tablespoonful of butter. Then pour around the hot fish.

CREAM SAUCE.

In New York, where salmon is dressed to perfection, cream sauce is a frequent accompaniment. The cream is made very hot, but not brought quite to a boil, seasoned to taste, sometimes with shrimp or anchovy essence, sometimes with chopped parsley. If for baked salmon, the liquor from the can is strained and stirred into it; it requires no thickening. It will be found an admirable sauce for fish of almost any kind; capers chopped and added will be excellent with codfish—a thoroughly French combination.

CURRANT SAUCE.

5 pounds of currants,	1 tablespoonful of cloves,
3 pounds of sugar,	1 tablespoonful of allspice,
1 pint of vinegar,	1 tablespoonful of pepper,
1 tablespoonful of cinnamon,	1 teaspoonful of salt.

Boil one half hour, and bottle. If preferred, omit the vinegar.
Mrs. H. H. Himian, Battle Creek, Michigan.

DEVIL SAUCE.

Four tablespoonfuls of cold gravy; that from a joint, or, if not to be had, use brown stock.

1 teaspoonful of loaf-sugar,	½ of a lemon, the juice of,
¼ teaspoonful of mustard,	1 ounce of fresh butter.
1 dessert-spoonful of good mush-room catchup,	Salt and pepper to suit the palate.

The pepper should be added cautiously at first; it varies so much in strength, it is almost impossible to state the exact quantity. This may be varied considerably; Worcestershire or any other good sauce can take the place of the catchup, and vinegar, plain or flavored with herbs, may be used instead of the lemon-juice.

DRAWN-BUTTER SAUCE.

One quarter of a pound of butter, with two teaspoonfuls of flour well mixed with it, put into a saucepan, with one half a pint of water or stock, cover it, and set the saucepan into a larger one filled with boiling water; shake it constantly until thoroughly melted; take it off as soon as it comes to a boil. Season with salt and pepper.

DUTCH SAUCE.

This sauce is in high repute in France and America; it is served with various kinds of fish and vegetables, especially artichokes. It sounds extravagant, but no one needs much of it, and it is very delicious. To make it, put the yolks of only two eggs into a jar or jug, and two ounces of fresh butter, with a small glassful of water and a little salt and grated nutmeg; set this in a saucepan of boiling water over the fire, and stir until it is thick, but do not let it boil. Add, off the fire, a dessert-spoonful of lemon-juice. When for serving with calf's head, with which it is very nice, substitute veal gravy for the water. A few drops of strong white vinegar may be used instead of lemon-juice.

EGG SAUCE.

We tasted recently a delicious egg sauce, in which the yolks were pounded, and the whites chopped as usual. A little parsley, chopped fine, had been added, and it looked, as well as tasted, very good. The lady who made it sometimes uses fennel instead of parsley.

ESPAGNOL SAUCE.

Mix three quarters of a pint of brown sauce with one ounce of glaze or a teaspoonful of extract of meat, one or two fresh mushrooms, one wine-glassful of sherry, a few drops of carmine and a pinch of castor-sugar; reduce one fourth, keep it skimmed while boiling, then tammy, and use.

EXCELLENT FISH SAUCE.

Put one tablespoonful of chopped parsley into a bowl and pound it until reduced to a pulp, then add to it the yolks of three eggs; mix thoroughly, season with a dash of cayenne pepper, half a teaspoonful of salt, thin with one tablespoonful of vinegar, mix in gradually half a pint of olive-oil and a tablespoonful of finely chopped gherkins. Serve with boiled or broiled fish.

FISH SAUCE.

½ pint of walnut pickle,	1 dozen shallots,
½ pint of mushroom catchup,	¼ pint of soy,
1 dozen anchovies,	½ teaspoonful of cayenne pepper.

Put all the ingredients into a saucepan, having previously chopped the shallots and anchovies very fine; let simmer fifteen minutes, strain, and when cold, bottle for use, and seal.

FOWL SAUCE.

Take scraps of veal, the necks and feet of fowls, put into a saucepan, with a blade of mace, a few peppercorns, one head of celery, a bunch of sweet herbs, the juice of one lemon; put all into a quart of water and boil one hour; strain, and thicken with half a pound of butter rolled in flour. Mix in a teacupful of fresh or canned mushrooms, the beaten yolks of two eggs, with a teacupful of cream and half a nutmeg, grated. Shake over the fire until ready to serve.

FRENCH BECHAMEL SAUCE.

That popular French white sauce is very easy to make in even ordinary households where economy is practised. For instance, in making this on a large scale, a whole fowl would probably be boiled down for it, together with a knuckle of veal and a piece of lean ham. Proceed, however, as follows: Put into a saucepan the bones of a boiled or a roasted fowl, broken small, with any scraps of fresh veal and a bit of raw lean ham, or the bones from a piece of boiled bacon; add

A bit of carrot,	A few button mushrooms,
A slice of onion,	1 pint of cold water,
A tiny bit of mace,	A sprig of thyme and parsley,
A few white peppercorns.	

Simmer until there is only half a pint of liquid, or even less, and if it does not taste rich, put in a teaspoonful of gelatin. Stir until that is dissolved, then strain the sauce. In a separate saucepan bring to a boil half the measure of cream mixed with a small teaspoonful of arrow-root; mix the white stock gradually with this, let the whole boil for a few minutes, then serve, adding, off the fire, a few drops of lemon-juice or white vinegar, and a little salt. If the stock can be allowed to cool before mixing with the cream, the fat will be more effectually removed. We have dwelt at some length on this recipe, by way of illustrating the fact that people often deprive themselves of nice dishes simply because the quantities given in recipes are too great for their needs, and they are not sufficiently practical to reduce or alter them to meet their modest requirements. We may mention that if the meat and vegetables are allowed to stew first in a little butter, the sauce will taste much better.

FRENCH SALAD SAUCE.

Put half a teaspoonful of salt and pepper each into a bowl, add gradually three tablespoonfuls of olive-oil, rub and mix thoroughly, then stir in the vinegar by degrees, and it is ready for use.

GREEN-PEA SAUCE (FOR FISH).

Cook in a double boiler for ten minutes, one cupful of milk, one half teaspoonful of onion and one little piece of celery; melt one half teaspoonful of butter, add one tablespoonful of flour, and hot milk a little at a time. Strain back into the double boiler, add one fourth of a teaspoonful of salt, a little pepper and one half cupful of cold cooked peas. Just before serving, add to it one beaten yolk.

Miss Marion L. Campbell, Friendly Inn Cooking School, Cleveland, Ohio.

HALIBUT SAUCE.

Take a quart of soup stock, thicken very little, add the juice of a lemon, one tablespoonful of tomato catchup and Worcestershire sauce, pepper and salt. Send to the table in a gravy-boat, to be served with boiled halibut.

HOME-MADE WORCESTERSHIRE SAUCE.

Add to one quart of vinegar

3 mashed anchovies,	2 heads of garlic, chopped,
3 teaspoonfuls of allspice,	2 blades of mace,
½ ounce of cayenne pepper,	2 teaspoonfuls of ground cloves,
½ teaspoonful each of cinnamon and ginger.	

Let stand twenty-four hours. Strain; add the juice of one lemon. Cork, and set aside for ten days; pour into a crock, skim, bottle and seal.

HORSE-RADISH SAUCE.

2 tablespoonfuls of grated horse-radish,	1 egg, the yolk of,
2 tablespoonfuls of cider vinegar,	1 tablespoonful of butter,
1 cupful of cream,	Salt to taste.

Cover the horse-radish with water, let boil half an hour; drain off the water, add the vinegar, butter, one half teaspoonful of sugar and the salt, mix them; beat the egg and cream, and add just before sending to the table. Serve with oysters or cold fish.

ICED CHAMPAGNE SAUCE.

Grated rind and juice of one orange,	¾ of a cupful of water,
1½ cupfuls of granulated sugar,	1 pint of champagne.

Put the sugar and water over the fire and boil for five minutes; pour half on the orange rind and juice, return the remainder to the fire for three minutes, then pour it over the whites of two eggs whipped to a stiff froth with two tablespoonfuls of powdered sugar, beat well while mixing, and strain into it the orange-syrup mixture. When cold, add the champagne, and freeze to the consistency of sorbet.

Miss Cornella Campbell Bedford, Superintendent New York Cooking School, New York.

IRLANDAISE SAUCE (HOT).

Put a pint of good brown sauce into a stew-pan, with a wine-glassful of port wine, one good tablespoonful of red-currant jelly, the juice of one lemon, one bay-leaf, six crushed peppercorns, a dust of red pepper, a small sprig of thyme,

one sliced tomato, a few drops of carmine and half a shallot, chopped fine; boil
gently for about ten minutes, keeping it skimmed; pass it through the tammy-
cloth, make hot in the bain-marie, and serve hot.

LEMON SAUCE.

Cut three slices of lemon into very small dice, and put them into drawn
butter. Let it come just to a boiling-point, and pour over boiled fowls.

LOBSTER SAUCE.

Boil a little mace, cloves and cayenne pepper in a pint of water, strain, and
melt half a pound of butter into it; cut the lobster in small pieces, and stew
until very tender; squeeze in the juice of one lemon.

MAITRE D'HOTE SAUCE.

Add to one cupful of freshly made drawn butter the juice of one lemon, a
tablespoonful of chopped parsley, half of a small onion, minced, and a teaspoonful of powdered thyme, cayenne pepper and salt; set on the stove, and beat
while simmering. Serve with fish.

MAYONNAISE ASPIC.

Take half a pint of aspic jelly that is not quite set, and mix it into three large
tablespoonfuls of thick mayonnaise sauce, stirring well together till it begins to
thicken, then use. To make this softer and better blended, it is advisable to pass
it through the tammy-cloth before using.

MAYONNAISE SAUCE.

For half a pint of mayonnaise sauce, put one raw yolk of egg into a basin, a
salt-spoonful of English and same of French mustard, a pinch of salt and white
pepper and a tiny dust of red pepper. Mix with salad-oil, with a wooden spoon,
just dropping in the oil carefully, drop by drop; when this is as thick as butter,
add a teaspoonful of tarragon vinegar, four or five drops of chilli vinegar and
eight drops of lemon-juice. The sauce should be kept quite stiff.

MELTED-BUTTER SAUCE.

First, the one sauce which we are supposed to make, and that not well!
How often is it to be met with on the one hand like bill-stickers' paste, on the
other, a slop which swims the plate and looks like thin gruel! And as this is
the foundation of so many sauces, sweet and savory, it is certainly worth while
to know the correct way to make it. We are nothing if not practical, so it will
not serve our purpose to enlighten our readers as to the method adopted when
the richest melted butter is required; we may say that it is almost all butter,
and those who can afford it will no doubt have cooks competent to produce it.
Unquestionably, the surest way to avoid lumps is to first melt the butter in a
small stew-pan, then add the flour very gradually, next the water or milk,
also, little by little, stirring unceasingly until it boils, and for one minute afterward, when it is ready to serve. As to quantities, the happy medium is hit,
and a nice, smooth sauce the result, by using an ounce of butter and half an
ounce of flour to each half pint of water or milk. When the latter is used, add

the salt last; it is apt to curdle new milk if put in with it. When a richer sauce is desired, allow an extra ounce of butter, and reduce the water a little. Many of the best cooks approve of the addition of a slice of butter stirred in after the sauce is taken from the fire; a spoonful of cream is another improvement. This, as most of our readers are presumably aware, forms the basis of an almost endless variety of sauces, such as parsley, egg, onion, and fish sauces innumerable. In some cases it is an improvement to use veal stock or gravy instead of water, and fish sauce—when the fish is filleted—should receive all the goodness and flavor of the bones, which need slow stewing in the water used for making the sauce. We want chiefly to impress the correct proportions of flour, butter and liquid upon our readers' minds; they can then alter, or deviate from, any recipes they may meet with.

WRINGING SAUCES THROUGH THE TAMMY.

MUSHROOM SAUCE.

Prepare the mushrooms by cutting off the stalks, and throw them into boiling water. Season very sparingly with salt, pepper and butter. Boil until tender, and thicken the gravy with a tablespoonful of flour and a piece of butter the size of a butter-bean, and pour it over the meat. Some use a little lemon-juice to add to the flavor.

MUSTARD SAUCE.

2 eggs, the yolk of,	1 teacupful of vinegar,
1 small glassful of jelly,	2 tablespoonfuls of mustard,
1 tablespoonful of butter,	1 small teaspoonful of salt.

Cook until thick. When cold it is ready for use.

M. L. Hann, Wellington, Kansas.

OYSTER SAUCE.

What a popular dainty is a tureen of oyster sauce, and how often is it spoiled by the common practice of letting the oysters boil in it! The proper way is to strain the liquor, and boil that with the flour and butter, adding a dash of cayenne, lemon-juice, nutmeg and anchovy essence, and the oysters the last thing, long enough for them to become hot through, removing the sauce from the fire so that it shall not boil after they are put in. Follow this plan either for canned or fresh oysters; when the last-named are used, the beards should be stewed in the oyster liquor until their flavor is fully extracted. Many cooks recommend mace for almost all white sauces, but one fears to mention it, for it is a spice that is so overpowering in flavor that a trifle too much renders anything uneatable. In the hands of a skilled cook it is certainly valuable, though nutmeg can, in almost every case, be used as a substitute.

PARSLEY SAUCE.

Wash a bunch of parsley in cold water, then boil in salt-water ten minutes, add a tablespoonful of flour, same of butter; let boil, and serve.

PEPPER SAUCE.

Three dozen peppers, two heads of cabbage, one root of horse-radish, with mustard-seed, cloves and sugar. Boil in two quarts of vinegar. Strain.

ROMAN SAUCE.

Put one teacupful of water and one of milk over the fire to scald, stir in a tablespoonful of flour and three well-beaten eggs; season with pepper and salt, two ounces of butter and a tablespoonful of vinegar. Boil four eggs, slice, and lay in the dish. Serve with boiled tongue, venison or large game.

SALMIS SAUCE.

One and a half ounces of good butter put into a pan, with an onion that is cut up in dice shapes, a slice or two of tomato, one or two fresh mushrooms, a little thyme, parsley, pinch of mignonette pepper, and the bones of any birds chopped up; fry all together for about fifteen minutes with the cover on the pan, then add about an ounce of flour, a wine-glassful of port wine or sherry, an ounce of glace or a teaspoonful of extract of meat, a pint of brown sauce, a dust of red pepper and a few drops of carmine; boil all together for about fifteen minutes, keep skimmed, remove the bones, then tammy, and use. The bones can be afterward put in the stock-pot.

SALSIFY SAUCE.

Scrape and wash two roots of salsify, rub them with lemon, and throw them into cold water till wanted; boil the roots till perfectly tender in lightly salted water; drain them, cut them into small pieces, stir them into half a pint of melted butter, simmer a few minutes, and serve. Time, one hour and a quarter.

SAUCE.

One cupful of butter well creamed with two cupfuls of sugar, beat in the yolks of two eggs and one half cupful of water, let come to a boil; remove, and flavor with wine and nutmeg, or anything preferred.

Mrs. A. E. Kirtland, author of "Mrs. Kirtland's Cook Book," Montgomery, Alabama.

SAUCE.

Beat to a cream two tablespoonfuls of butter and ten tablespoonfuls of confectioners' sugar, then beat in gradually one half cupful of cream. Flavor with vanilla.

Mrs. Althea Somes, Teacher of Cookery, Manual Training School, Boston, Mass.

SHAD-ROE SAUCE.

Wash two shad roes, put into a saucepan, add one tablespoonful of salt, cover with boiling water, let simmer for twenty minutes; take up, skin, and mash fine; make rich drawn butter, add the roe, stir, let boil. Serve with boiled or baked shad.

SNOWFLAKE SAUCE.

One cupful of white coffee-sugar, creamed with one heaping tablespoonful of butter; thicken one cupful of boiling milk with one tablespoonful of corn-starch wet with a little cold milk, cook five minutes, stirring constantly; when cold, add two tablespoonfuls of maraschino, the creamed butter and sugar, then cut and fold in the white of one egg beaten very stiffly.

Miss Emily E. Squire, author of " Woronoco Women's Wisdom," Westfield, Mass.

SUPREME SAUCE.

Two ounces of butter and two ounces of flour lightly fried, then mixed with three quarters of a pint of veal or chicken stock; stir till it boils. Add a gill of cream and a few fresh white mushrooms, their peels and stalks; cook on the stove for about ten minutes, add a pinch of salt, tammy, and use.

TARTARE SAUCE.

The yolks of two eggs beaten in a gill of salad-oil, a tablespoonful of good vinegar, a teaspoonful of mustard, a tablespoonful of gherkins, with pepper and salt, beat all together in a bowl. Serve with cold meats.

TOMATO BUTTER.

Put two or three tomatoes in a stew-pan, with two ounces of butter, quarter pint of light gravy, the juice of half a lemon and one eighth of an ounce of arrow-root that is mixed with a tablespoonful of cold gravy, season with a little salt and a pinch of red pepper, add a few drops of carmine, and draw down on the side of the stove for about fifteen to twenty minutes, then rub through the tammy, rewarm, and use.

TOMATO SAUCE.

Stew one dozen tomatoes in a pint of soup stock, with one onion, a bunch of parsley, salt and pepper; boil soft, and rub through a fine sieve; thicken with butter rolled in flour. Serve with mushrooms, macaroni, etc.

VELOUTÉ SAUCE.

One and a half ounces of fine flour, one and a half ounces of butter; mix well, and let it fry gently on the side of the stove till a very pale color; then mix it with three quarters of a pint of nicely flavored stock, either veal, rabbit or chicken. Stir till it boils; add a quarter of a pint of cream, a pinch of salt and three or four drops of lemon-juice; keep boiling for about five minutes; keep skimmed, tammy, and use. The thick, creamy veloute may be made by reducing this one quarter.

VINAIGRETTE SAUCE.

Put three tablespoonfuls of salad-oil into a basin, with a tablespoonful of tarragon vinegar, a salt-spoonful of chilli vinegar, a teaspoonful of fresh tarragon and chervil, finely chopped, a salt-spoonful of mignonette pepper, a dust of red pepper and a good pinch of salt. Mix well, and serve in a boat. This sauce is very good served with hot asparagus, brains, calf's head, etc.

WHITE CHESTNUT SAUCE.

This is an excellent accompaniment to boiled fowl, and would form a pleasant change from parsley sauce, usually served with it. Boil or bake a score of chestnuts until tender, then pound the white part in a mortar to a smooth paste, with a couple of ounces of butter, a pinch of white sugar and half a teaspoonful of salt. Mix slowly with it half a pint of cream and milk mixed; stir the liquid over the fire until it boils.

WHITE SAUCE.

Take one cupful of butter and salt, shake in three tablespoonfuls of flour, add one quart of sweet milk, stir until it boils. Serve with boiled meats.

WORCESTERSHIRE SAUCE.

½ bushel of tomatoes,	¼ pound of allspice,
1 quart of cider vinegar,	1 pound of salt,
1 pound of brown sugar,	10 lemons,
1 ounce of ground cloves.	

Cook all together and strain through a sieve. Add juice of one lemon. Cork tight while hot, and seal up.

Howard F. Carey, College Hill, Ohio.

SWEET SAUCES, FOR PUDDINGS, ETC.

ANGELIC SAUCE.

Put four peeled and sliced onions into a stew-pan, with enough cold water to cover them; just bring them to a boil, then strain them and return to the stew-pan, with four washed and finely chopped, fresh white mushrooms and a bunch of herbs; cover with one and a half pints of chicken stock, the strained juice of one lemon and a fourth of a pint of mushroom liquor; boil for one hour, mix in one and a half ounces of fine flour that has been fried, without discoloring, with the same quantity of butter; stir again until it boils, add a quarter of a pint of cream and a pinch of salt; tammy. Use with cutlets, rabbit, chicken, etc.

APRICOT OR JAM SAUCE.

Half a potful of apricot or any other jam, two tablespoonfuls of castor-sugar, four tablespoonfuls of water; boil for ten minutes, then pass it all through a tammy or sieve; add a little carmine, a wine-glassful of white rum and a wine-glassful of maraschino or noyeau syrup.

CHEESE CREAM SAUCE.

Take four ounces of good Cheddar or Gryere cheese, cut up into very fine slices, put it into a stew-pan, with one and a half gills of cream, a quarter of a pint of bechamel sauce and a dust of pepper; stir these ingredients over the fire until they melt, then use at once for croutons, cauliflower, macaroni, etc.

COURTE SAUCE.

Put into a stew-pan the juice of one lemon and one orange, four tablespoonfuls of good-flavored brown sauce, half an ounce of glaze and two finely chopped shallots; bring to a boil, skim, add a wine-glassful of port and claret and a dust of castor-sugar; serve very hot, with teal, widgeon, pheasant or other birds, roast, grilled or braised.

CUSTARD SAUCE.

1 pint of milk,	½ cupful of sugar,
4 eggs, yolks of,	Set over fire and stir until thick.

CZARINA SAUCE.

Put a few bones from larks, quails or other birds into a stew-pan, with half a pint of white wine, a wine-glassful of sherry and two finely chopped shallots; boil together for about fifteen minutes, then pour off the liquor or wring it through the tammy, add it to three fourths of a pint of veloute sauce and eight to ten fresh button mushrooms that have been washed and finely chopped; boil all together for fifteen minutes, add half a gill of cream and one or two chopped truffles. Use with entrees, sweetbreads, farced birds, such as roast pheasant, chickens, etc.

DRAWN-BUTTER SAUCE.

½ cupful of butter,	½ teaspoonful of vanilla or the juice of one lemon,
1 pint of hot water,	1 tablespoonful of flour or corn-starch made to a
½ cupful of sugar,	smooth paste.

Turn into the rest and let it boil five minutes; add a little grated nutmeg.
    Christie Irving.

DUCHESS SAUCE.

Boil two ounces of grated chocolate in one half pint of milk five minutes; strain on yolks of two eggs beaten with one half gill of cream and one half cupful of sugar; strain, return to fire, stir until thick as honey; remove, and add one teaspoonful of extract of vanilla.

FINANCIÈRE SAUCE.

Put into a stew-pan two wine-glassfuls of sherry, a dust of pepper, three well-washed fresh mushrooms and the liquor from a bottle of truffles; reduce to half the quantity, then add three fourths of a pint of good espagnol sauce; boil up all together, tammy, and use for entrees and meats, chickens, etc., as a hot sauce. If this sauce is to be used for braised meats, take the liquor from the braise, free it from the fat, and add it to the sauce with the espagnol sauce.

GERMAN SAUCE.

Set on the fire in tin pail placed in a stew-pan half full of boiling water, one cupful of cream and one cupful of milk; when it reaches the boiling-point, add sugar and the yolks of four eggs, with a pinch of salt; whisk very quickly until it has the appearance of thick cream very frothy. Just before serving, add a tablespoonful of butter, one teaspoonful each of extract of nutmeg and vanilla.

HARD SAUCE.

Beat one cupful of sugar and one half cupful of butter to a white cream; add the whites of two eggs, beat a few minutes longer; add a teaspoonful of extract of nutmeg. Put on ice until needed.

HARD SAUCE FOR PUDDING.

Stir together one cupful of butter and three cupfuls of powdered sugar. When light, beat in the juice of a lemon, or vanilla. When cold, serve.

     H. B. A., Plainfield, Connecticut.

HUBERT SAUCE.

Put into a stew-pan the chopped bones from any birds, such as pheasant, partridge, grouse, a few strips of celery, two sliced onions, a bunch of herbs, the peels and stalks of a few fresh mushrooms, a wine-glassful of sherry and white wine, the juice of a lemon, and enough cold water to cover; bring to a boil, skim, and simmer for half an hour; strain, and mix three fourths of a pint of this gravy in two ounces of butter and an ounce and a half of fine flour that has been fried without discoloring; stir together until boiling, then tammy, and mix with a gill of whipped cream; just before serving, add a teaspoonful of chopped truffle. Use with game entrees.

HYGIENIC CREAM SAUCE.

½ pint of milk,	1 tablespoonful of buckwheat dissolved
½ pint of cream,	in a little milk.
1 egg, yolk of,	Large pinch of salt.

Bring milk and cream to a boil in thick, well-lined saucepan; add to it buckwheat dissolved in milk, stirring rapidly to prevent lumping; allow it to boil five minutes; remove from the fire, beat in the yolk of egg diluted with a tablespoonful of milk. This is better and far more healthful (especially for children) than so much butter and syrup. Syrup minus butter is well enough, but the use of butter with hot cakes cannot be recommended.

LEMON SAUCE.

2 eggs, the yolks of,	½ cupful of butter,
1 cupful of sugar,	1 tablespoonful of corn-starch.

Beat the eggs and sugar until light; add the grated rind and juice of one lemon. Stir the whole into three gills of boiling water, and cook until it thickens sufficiently for the table.

LEMON SAUCE.

Boil one cupful of sugar and one cupful of water together fifteen minutes, then remove; when cooled a little, add one half a teaspoonful of extract of lemon and one tablespoonful of lemon-juice.

MAGENTA SAUCE.

Take the bones and skins from any birds, chop them, and put them into a buttered saute-pan, with two or three fresh mushrooms, two sliced tomatoes, a bunch of herbs (such as thyme, parsley and bay-leaf), a piece of bacon-bone and a pinch of mignonette pepper; place the cover on the pan, and fry the contents for about fifteen minutes; then add a wine-glassful of sherry, one teaspoonful of any good extract of meat, one pint of good brown sauce and a few drops of liquid carmine; bring to a boil, reduce one fourth, keep well skimmed while boiling, then remove the bones, pass the sauce through a tammy, add a little raw chopped parsley or truffle, and use with roast or braised birds, etc.

MAPLE SYRUP.

¼ pound of maple sugar,   1 pound of cut sugar,
3 pints of water.

Break maple sugar small, place over the fire with cut sugar and water; boil five minutes, skim, then cool.

NESLE SAUCE.

Take one ounce of glaze, half a pint of brown sauce, two tablespoonfuls of white wine and the same of sherry, one teaspoonful of French mustard, one dessert-spoonful of chopped chutney, two finely chopped shallots, two washed and finely chopped mushrooms; boil all together for about fifteen minutes, add a teaspoonful of chopped parsley. Use with roast meats or poultry.

ORANGE SAUCE.

Put into a stew-pan one and a half gills of thick brown sauce, one ounce of glaze, a dust of pepper, the strained juice of a lemon, a pinch of castor-sugar, the strained juice of three oranges; boil all together, then thicken with half an ounce of arrow-root that has been mixed with a wine-glassful of sherry; stir until the sauce reboils, then pass through a tammy-cloth. Cut the quarters from two oranges into fine slices, free them from pith and pips and add to the sauce; make quite hot in the bain-marie; take the peel of an orange that is freed from pith and cut into Julienne strips, put into cold water, with a pinch of salt, and bring to a boil, then strain, rinse in hot water, and add to the sauce. Serve with wild duck, teal, turkey, braised ham, etc.

PEACH SAUCE.

Pour peach-juice from a can into a small saucepan, add equal volume of water, a little more sugar and eight or ten raisins; boil this ten minutes, strain, and just before serving, add eight drops of bitter almonds.

PUDDING SAUCE.

4 tablespoonfuls of fine, white sugar,   2 tablespoonfuls of butter,
1 tablespoonful of flour.

Stir them together to a cream. Beat the white of an egg to a stiff froth, and add it; then pour into the dish a gill of boiling water, stirring very fast. Flavor with lemon or vanilla.

Mrs. L. H. Hart, Dresden, Texas.

RAGUSE SAUCE.

Take the bones from raw hare, chop finely, and put them into a stew-pan, with two or three green capsicums, a bunch of herbs (basil, marjoram, bay-leaf, thyme and parsley) and one ounce of butter; fry with the cover on the pan for about fifteen minutes, then add two raw, fresh mushrooms or a few peels of the same, two ounces of lean raw ham, one dessert-spoonful of red-currant jelly, one teaspoonful of any extract of good meat, half a pint of claret, one fourth of a pint of mushroom catchup and one and one half pints of brown stock; let these simmer together on the side of the stove for about half an hour, keeping well skimmed while boiling, then strain off the liquor; mix in another stew-pan one ounce of butter and one and one half ounces of arrow-root, then add a pint of the liquor from the bones, stir until it boils again, tammy, and use after adding a few drops of liquid carmine; serve with hare either roasted or braised, or with entrees. The bones will make good gravy stock by being reboiled.

REXFORD SAUCE.

Dissolve one teaspoonful of corn-starch in a little water, add it to one cupful of boiling water, with two thirds of a cupful of brown sugar, boil ten minutes; remove from the fire, add one half cupful of scalding-hot vinegar, yolks of two eggs and one large tablespoonful of good butter.

RUBANEE SAUCE.

Take one wine-glassful of sherry, the same of port wine, six Christiania anchovies rubbed through a sieve, one teaspoonful of extract of meat, two fresh mushrooms, two chopped capsicums, two raw tomatoes, the juice of one lemon, a dust of pepper and one pint of thick brown sauce; reduce one fourth, keep skimmed while boiling, tammy, and use for entrees of birds, meats, etc.

SAUCE AUX QUATRE FRUITS.

Remove, very thinly, one third of the rind of one lemon and one orange; remove remainder with the thick white skin very close to pulp; then cut each into small dice, removing seeds; peel, core and cut into dice two sour apples; simmer until tender; then add one cupful of seedless raisins, lemon and orange dice, with lemon and orange peel cut into shreds, and boil in very little water, which add to sauce to flavor. When about to serve, add one teaspoonful of extract of almonds.

SAUCE FOR PUDDINGS.

1 egg.   ½ cupful of flour,
1 cupful of sugar,   1 pint of milk.

Boil until it thickens, and flavor to suit the taste.

Mrs. L. A. Ashley, Springfield, Ohio.

SPICED SAUCE.

Set on the fire three fourths of a pint of water, one cupful of sugar; boil twenty minutes, remove from fire, and add one teaspoonful each of extract of cloves and ginger.

SUÈDOISE SAUCE.

Take half a pint of very stiff mayonnaise sauce, and mix into it two table-spoonfuls of finely grated horse-radish, two tablespoonfuls of freshly peeled, finely chopped cucumber, one finely chopped shallot, one teaspoonful of chopped capers, then add one fourth of a pint of stiffly whipped cream, and put aside on ice until wanted. Serve with hot or cold fish, either grilled or boiled, arti-chokes, asparagus, etc.

SUGAR SAUCE.

Beat to light cream one half cupful of sugar flavored with one half teaspoon-ful of extract of lemon and one half cupful of butter; add the yolks of two eggs, and place on ice until wanted.

VANILLA SAUCE.

Put one half pint of milk into a small saucepan over the fire; when scalding hot, add the yolks of three eggs; stir until as thick as boiled custard; add, when taken from the fire and cooled, one tablespoonful of extract of vanilla and the whites of the eggs whipped stiff.

VINEGAR SAUCE.

1 cupful of water,	A pinch of salt,
1 spoonful of butter,	1 tablespoonful of flour.
1 cupful of brown sugar.	1 spoonful of vinegar,

Beat all well together, pour boiling water over them, let them come to a good boil, and serve.

WELLINGTON SAUCE.

Slice one or two peeled onions, and put them into a stew-pan, with an ounce of butter; fry them until a nice golden color, then add one tablespoonful of French vinegar, two sliced tomatoes, three boned and pounded Christiania anchovies, one teaspoonful of French mustard, one and one half gills of brown sauce and one fourth of a pint of good gravy; boil together for about twenty minutes, then rub through a tammy, rewarm in the bain-marie, add a few drops of liquid carmine, and use with fish or steak, etc.

WHITE MUSHROOM SAUCE.

Put half a pound of well-washed, fresh white button mushrooms with their peels and stalks (or preserved button ones), chop them fine, and put them into a saucepan, with a quart of good-flavored white stock (as chicken, veal or rabbit), the strained juice of one lemon, a pinch of salt; simmer gently on the stove for about half an hour, keeping skimmed; stir one pint of the liquor onto two ounces of butter and the same of fine flour that have been fried together without browning, until it reboils, then add a pinch of salt, a half wine-glassful of sherry and a gill of thick cream; stir again until boiling. Use for entrees of meat, as sweetbread, cutlets of chicken, boiled chicken, rabbit, pheasant, etc.

GARNISHES, PURÉES, FARCES, ETC.

[Farces required for borders must be made stiffer than if required for masking or stuffing; this is effected by using proportionally more panard and eggs. Any farce left from an entree can be converted into a nice soup by the addition of stock.]

CHAPTER III.

ASPARAGUS PEAS.

For garnishing soups and purées.

Scrape, and then cut off the points of some fresh asparagus, put them into boiling water, with a little salt and a tiny bit of soda, and gently boil for fifteen minutes; then strain and use. Cut the tender part of the stalks into little lengths of about one fourth of an inch; cook these in the same manner as the points in a separate stew-pan, and use.

BEEF FARCE FOR BORDER.

For one ordinary-sized border-mold take eight ounces of panard, eight ounces of lean neck of beef, and pound separately until smooth; then mix with one ounce of butter, a few drops of carmine, a pinch of salt and red pepper and two and one half eggs; rub through a coarse wire sieve, put into a buttered border-mold, and poach for fifteen minutes in boiling water. Veal farce border can be prepared in a similar manner.

BEEF FARCE, FOR STUFFING OR MASKING.

5 ounces of beef,	2½ raw yolks of egg.
5 ounces of panard,	A little pepper, salt and red pepper.
1 ounce of butter,	A few drops of carmine.

First pound the meat well, then pound the panard separately; now pound these together, then mix in the seasoning and yolks, and pass through a sieve. Veal farce can be prepared in the same way.

BRAISED OLIVES.

Turn about a dozen and a half olives, put them into a stew-pan, with sufficient stock to cover them, add half a wine-glassful of sherry, and braise for about half an hour on the side of the stove with the pan covered.

CAUL.

Put it into cold water, with a little salt; by changing the water occasionally it will keep some days. Twelve cents' worth will be sufficient for two or three entrees.

CUCUMBER PEAS.
For soup, etc.

Peel the cucumber, and by means of a pea-cutter scoop out into pea shapes; put these into cold water, with a pinch of salt, and gently boil until tender— for about fifteen minutes—then strain, and use. Potato peas are prepared in a similar way.

FARCE OR PURÉE OF CHESTNUTS.

Cut off the tops of a pound and a half of nuts and roast them for fifteen minutes; then take off the outer and inner skins, and put them to cook in a pan, with sufficient light stock to cover them, and cook for three quarters of an hour, with buttered paper over, when they should be quite dry; pass them through a wire sieve, then mix with them a little cream or milk, a pat of butter, a little pinch of salt and sugar, a good tablespoonful of anisette, and color with liquid carmine to a pale salmon shade; add a dust of red pepper, warm, and use for garnishing entrees. It may also be used cold.

RUBBING THE PURÉE THROUGH THE SIEVE.

FINANCIÈRE GARNISH.

This is prepared in bottles. It consists of truffles, mushrooms, cockscombs, etc.

FISH FARCE.

Pound ten ounces of raw whitefish, free from skin and bone, until quite smooth; pound eight ounces of panard, season with a little salt, one ounce of butter, a little white pepper; then mix, and add three whole eggs by degrees, and pass through a wire sieve. Butter the mold in which the farce is to be cooked, and sprinkle it over with coral, put in the farce by means of a forcing-bag and a large, plain pipe, knock it down well on the table to set firm in the mold, poach for about fifteen minutes, placing it into a stew-pan on a fold of paper, and then covering it with boiling water; watch the water reboil, then draw to the side and poach until firm.

FISH FARCE.

For pies.

Take one and one half pounds of fresh raw whiting, haddock or cod, twelve ounces of panard, one and one half ounces of butter, one salt-spoonful of salt, one dessert-spoonful of anchovy essence, a dust of pepper; pound the fish and panard separately until smooth, then mix, add the other ingredients and seasonings, and work until smooth; mix with four raw eggs and two wine-glassfuls of white wine, rub through a fine wire sieve, and use.

GREEN MAYONNAISE.

Two tablespoonfuls of mayonnaise sauce, two tablespoonfuls of liquid aspic jelly, a little sap-green, to make a pale green color; mix all, tammy, and pour into a saute-pan to about a quarter of an inch thick. When it is firm, cut it out into the required shapes.

LIVER FARCE, FOR STUFFING BIRDS, ETC.

Cut into small dice shapes eight ounces of game, poultry or calf's liver, four ounces of fat bacon, four ounces of lean veal, rabbit or chicken, and half a small onion; put all together into a saute-pan, with one ounce of butter or fat, two bay-leaves, two or three sprigs of thyme, a sprig of parsley, a good pinch of mignonette pepper and a little red pepper and salt, and fry for about five minutes. Then, while it is hot, pound it in a mortar and rub through a sieve; mix with the puree one raw yolk of egg and two or three chopped button mushrooms or truffles, place it in a forcing-bag with a plain pipe, and fill the birds with it. This is sufficient for four pigeons, and other birds in proportion to their size.

MAITRE D'HOTEL BUTTER.

Have two ounces of fresh butter mixed with a tablespoonful of chopped parsley and a tablespoonful of lemon-juice.

MONTPELIER OR GREEN BUTTER.

Blanch together three or four sprigs of fresh tarragon and of chervil, parsley and fennel, with one shallot; strain dry, and add

3 yolks of hard-boiled eggs,	2 tablespoonfuls of salad-oil,
12 fillets of anchovies,	¾ of a pound of fresh butter,
A tablespoonful of capers,	A little salt,
4 gherkins,	A little sap-green,
A very little red pepper.	

Pound all together and pass through a hair-sieve; set in a cool place before serving, so that it may become quite firm. This is nice for garnishing cold trout, salmon, etc.

POTATO BORDER.

Peel and boil the potatoes, taking care that they do not become soft in the cooking, as for this purpose they require to be very dry when cooked; season with a little salt and pass through a wire sieve. For three ordinary-sized potatoes add one ounce of butter, one raw yolk of egg and a tiny dust of red pepper. Make it into the border (using as little flour as when rolling paste); beat up an egg, and glaze the border with it; mark the potato with the knife for ornament, bake a nice golden color, and use.

PURÉE OF MUSHROOMS.

Wash well one pound of fresh mushrooms, dry them, chop fine, and put them into a saute-pan, with one and one half ounces of butter; draw down on the side of the stove for seven or eight minutes, then mix with two tablespoonfuls of freshly made bread-crumbs; season with salt and a little red pepper; add one tablespoonful of brown sauce, boil up, mix in a teaspoonful of chopped parsley, and use.

PURÉE OF POTATOES.

Peel and plainly boil three or four large potatoes; when cooked and quite white, rub them through a wire sieve, put them into a clean stew-pan, and mix in one ounce of butter, a tiny pinch of salt, a tiny dust of red pepper and two or three tablespoonfuls of cream, make quite hot, and use.

QUENELLES OF CHICKEN, VEAL OR RABBIT.

Take ten ounces of raw meat, six ounces of panard, two tablespoonfuls of thick bechamel sauce, one ounce of butter, two and one half eggs; season with red pepper and a very little salt. Pound the meat until quite smooth, then pound the panard separately and complete as in the above farces, and after passing through the sieve, mix in two tablespoonfuls of cream and form into shapes with spoons.

SHAPING QUENELLES.

RICE FOR BORDERS.

Put a pound and a half of Carolina rice into enough cold water to cover it; bring to a boil, wash it, and place it in the stew-pan, and just cover it again with clean, cold water; cover it with a buttered paper, let it come to a boil, and simmer it in the oven or on the side of the stove for two and a half to three hours, during which time occasionally add a little more water—about a pint in all; when quite cooked and dry, pound it until smooth, and work it with the hand into a ball, dipping the hand into cold water occasionally to prevent it sticking. Remove any moisture from it by pressing it in a clean cloth, place it in a plain, round, buttered mold, and keep it under pressure until quite cold, then turn it out and use, or cut it into any desired shape.

RICE FOR CURRY.

Put one pound of Patna rice into a stew-pan, with enough cold water to cover it, and a pinch of salt; bring to a boil, strain, and wash the rice in cold water; put it into about three quarts of boiling water, and cook for twelve to fifteen minutes; strain it off into a colander, pour a little hot water over it, put a cloth over the colander, and put the rice to dry in the screen for two or three hours. If properly prepared, every grain will be separate.

TOMATO ASPIC.

Pound three large, ripe tomatoes until smooth, and mix with one and one half gills of aspic jelly and a dust of red pepper; color with a few drops of carmine, and rub through a tammy-cloth into a saute-pan to about a quarter of an inch in depth. Let it set, then cut out in blocks, as described above, and use.

TOMATOES.
For garnishing.

Cut some ripe tomatoes into slices about one fourth of an inch thick, season with a little pepper and a little salt, put into a buttered saute-pan, and cook in a moderate oven, with a buttered paper over, for about ten minutes. Use for fillets of beef, sweetbread, etc.

TOMATO PURÉE.

Boil together for about ten minutes four tablespoonfuls of tomato sauce, four small or two large sliced tomatoes, a little red pepper, a few drops of carmine and one ounce of butter; then rub through the tammy, warm in the bain-marie, and use. A dessert-spoonful of French vinegar may be added, if liked.

TONGUE PURÉE.
For masking cold meats, etc.

Pound one fourth of a pound of tongue until quite smooth; mix it well into two tablespoonfuls of bechamel sauce, two tablespoonfuls of cream, a few drops of liquid carmine, a dust of pepper and one half pint of liquid aspic jelly; pass the whole through the tammy, and use.

VEAL, RABBIT OR CHICKEN FARCES.

Prepare these in the same way as beef, substituting one of these meats for the beef.

Forcemeat, to use as a dressing to other meats, can be made from any of the following recipes:

ALMOND FORCEMEAT.

Beat up the yolks of three eggs with a fourth of a pint of good cream, and flavor with a little nutmeg. Blanch and pound in a mortar three ounces of sweet almonds, using white of egg to moisten; add these, with three fourths of a pound of light bread-crumbs and three ounces of butter broken into small bits, to the egg mixture; stir in, lastly, the whites of the eggs whisked to a solid froth, and fill either capon or turkey.

CHESTNUT FORCEMEAT.

Remove the outer skin from some chestnuts (they should be ripe and sound), boil them for two or three minutes to get off the inner skin; peel them, and to preserve their color throw them into cold water; drain and weigh them; stew six ounces of them gently for about twenty minutes in veal gravy, let them get cold, pound them until smooth, with an equal quantity of butter or half their weight in fat bacon, and add two ounces of bread-crumbs and a little salt, lemon-rind and nutmeg; bind the mixture together with the unbeaten yolks of two eggs. If this forcemeat is formed into cakes, these should be dipped into flour before being fried. Time to fry, fifteen minutes.

CURRY FORCEMEAT BALLS.

Pound together bread-crumbs, yolks of hard-boiled eggs, a small quantity of butter and a seasoning of curry-powder and salt; make into small balls. Time to fry, two or three minutes.

EGG FORCEMEAT BALLS.

Pound the yolks of half a dozen hard-boiled eggs, with some chopped parsley, a teaspoonful of flour, a little pepper, salt and cayenne; moisten with egg, and make the paste into small balls; boil for two minutes before using in soup or other dishes. Sufficient for one tureen of soup.

FORCEMEAT BALLS.

Chop a fourth of a pound of beef suet, a little lemon-peel and parsley, mix with a basin of bread-crumbs, and flavor with pepper, salt and nutmeg; moisten with the yolks of two eggs, roll in flour, and make up into small balls; bake in a hot oven till crisp. This recipe will do for fowls. The addition of a little ham, chopped or pounded, will be found a considerable improvement.

FORCEMEAT BALLS, BRAIN.

Clean and soak the brains in lukewarm water for three hours, then boil; when cold, pound them in a mortar, with a little flour, some chopped parsley, salt and pepper; bind with raw egg, and make into small balls; fry a light brown, and drop them into the tureen. Time, ten minutes to boil.

FORCEMEAT FOR BAKED PIKE.

Prepare three ounces of bread-crumbs from a stale loaf, shred two ounces of suet, and mince eight or ten bearded oysters; put together into a stew-pan, with a flavoring of mace (pounded), salt and pepper; moisten with the liquor from the oysters and six tablespoonfuls of thick cream, bind with the yolks of two eggs, and stir over the fire till the forcemeat thickens; stuff this forcemeat into the pike, and sew the fish up securely. Time to thicken forcemeat, four or five minutes; to bake pike, one hour, more or less. Sufficient for one pike.

FORCEMEAT BALLS FOR MOCK-TURTLE SOUP.

Panada, the delicate French preparation, will, if used in the composition of these balls, be found a great improvement. Prepare it thus: Soak the crumbs of two or three rolls, put it into a small saucepan by the side of the fire, with enough pale, rich gravy to cover it; when sufficiently boiled, squeeze off the moisture, put the panada into an enameled saucepan, and stir with a wooden spoon till dry; then mix with it the yolks of two unbeaten eggs, and let it cool for use. Pound in a mortar four ounces of veal, free from gristle, bone and skin; add the panada to this, with three ounces of fresh butter; season with nutmeg, mace, salt and cayenne. If liked, a little lean ham and more seasoning may be used. Roll into balls, and boil before adding to the soup. Time, twelve minutes to boil.

FORCEMEAT OF BEEF.

Take cold mashed potatoes, some slices of beef minced fine, a few savory herbs, pepper and salt, mix with two eggs to a paste, make into balls, and fry in butter a rich brown; garnish with fried parsley.

FORCEMEAT OF FISH.

Clear away the skin and bone from turbot, brill or any solid fish; mince one pound of the flesh very fine. Stew an onion in butter, and when tender, pound it in a mortar, with four ounces of butter broken into bits; add six ounces of bread previously soaked in milk and squeezed dry, a couple of well-beaten eggs, pepper, salt and nutmeg, and when all is well mixed, stir in the fish, and make up into balls to be fried or boiled. Previous to mixing the fish with the other ingredients it should be passed through a wire sieve.

FORCEMEAT OF GAME.

Clear the meat from the bones, and mince it with one fourth of a pound of fat bacon to each pound of game; flavor with shallot, capers, lemon-peel and a very few leaves of tarragon, all of which should be minced very fine. Soak some bread, and press out all the moisture; add it, with the yolks of three eggs. If the bacon be salt, be careful not to oversalt the forcemeat; pepper to taste, and stir in the frothed whites of eggs before using.

FORCEMEAT OF SAUSAGE.

Prepare sausage meat, in the proportion of two parts of lean pork to one of fat; take equal quantities of this and bread-crumbs, add two ounces of butter, a seasoning of salt, pepper and a dram of mace, pound all together in a mortar, and bind with the yolks of two eggs.

FORCEMEAT OF VEAL.

Chop clean veal, free from skin or fat, and then pound it in a mortar; add a third of its weight of butter or suet and the same of fine bread, which should be first soaked in cold milk and squeezed dry; pound all in the mortar; flavor with salt, pepper and nutmeg, bind with the yolks of two eggs, and make the paste into little balls, or use it as a stuffing.

OYSTER FORCEMEAT.

Three cupfuls of bread-crumbs, one pint of oysters, one even teaspoonful of pepper, one and one half tablespoonfuls of finely chopped parsley, one half teaspoonful of salt, one tablespoonful of butter and yolks of three eggs; strain the oyster liquor over the bread-crumbs, chop the oysters fine, and add them, with the ingredients, to the bread-crumbs; mix all, and lastly add the butter, which should be previously melted.

Mrs. Gesine Lemcke, of the German-American Cooking College, Brooklyn, N. Y.

CHAPTER IV.

The quantity of water in making soup should be proportioned to the quantity of meat used. Allow a quart of water to a pound of meat. In making soup from fresh meat, always put it on to cook in cold water. To keep the quantity, fill up from water in tea-kettle, which should be boiling, so as not to stop your soup boiling.

If you wish a vegetable soup, cook the vegetables separately, and add them to your soup shortly before removal.

If soup is desired frequently, stock for making it quickly can always be on hand. With your meat-cleaver, cut up all the bones left from your roasts and beefsteaks, and keep them in a covered stone jar. When you have sufficient, put them on and boil for three hours; strain this into an earthen vessel, and set aside to cool. A thick top of grease will rise to the surface, which can be taken off and used for frying purposes. The meat-juice beneath, which sometimes is a thick jelly, can be diluted if not wanted strong. With the addition of some cooked vegetables, soup can readily be made from this.

The grease should always be skimmed from all soups. Long and slow boiling is necessary to extract the strength from the meat. If boiled rapidly over a very hot fire, the meat becomes hard and tough, and will not give out its juices. The

37

cook should season soup slightly, as more can be added if necessary, while it is impossible to remove it.

For flavoring soups, bay-leaves, sweet marjoram, thyme, celery-tops and parsley are used, as suits the taste.

If a purely vegetable soup is desired, three or four vegetables combined is sufficient; namely, cabbage, potatoes, turnips and onions. If tomatoes are desired, use a little onion only.

Never use rice, pearl barley or noodles in the same soup.

Pearl barley should be cooked by itself, and then added to the soup.

The best soup is made by cooking the stock the day previous, and adding the cooked vegetables to this, heated the second day.

All soup should be well skimmed, as often there is a scum rising to the surface of all boiling meats.

Never set away soups or gravies in a vessel of tin or copper; and it is best to use a wooden spoon.

There are two kinds of soups—brown and white. To make the brown, use beef; the white, veal.

To color soups, use scorched flour or burnt sugar.

Though celery may be obtained at all times of the year, it may be well to know that celery-seed is an excellent substitute.

Vermicelli and macaroni for soups can be bought of the grocer; also prepared bean and pea flour for thickening soups.

BEEF SOUP.

Take five or six pounds of beef, and put it into a large kettle, with two gallons of cold water and one tablespoonful of salt. Put it to cooking soon after breakfast, and when it boils, skim off all the scum that rises. Let it boil slowly until one hour before dinner, then add

2 large onions,	1 root of celery, chopped fine,
½ head of cabbage,	8 potatoes, quartered,
2 carrots,	Some parsley-leaves.

When the vegetables are done, put a piece of butter in a skillet, with two tablespoonfuls of flour, and stir it to a nice brown. Add this to the soup, and season with pepper and salt.

Mrs. R. Jaeger, Cleveland, Minnesota.

BISQUE OF MUTTON.

Wash, and cut into pieces one neck of mutton, put it into a kettle, with two quarts of cold water, simmer gently for two hours, then add

1 small onion,	4 cloves,
1 bay-leaf,	½ cupful of rice.

Simmer gently for thirty minutes, strain, and press the rice through a sieve; return the soup and rice to the kettle and bring to the boiling point; add a pint of milk or thin cream and a palatable seasoning of salt and pepper, and it is ready to serve. This makes one of the daintiest of luncheon soups, and is exceedingly beneficial for convalescing patients.

Mrs. S. T. Rorer, Principal Philadelphia Cooking School.

BOUILLON.

To three pounds of raw meat, chopped fine, add three quarts of cold water, let it hardly warm for the first hour, then increase the heat and let it gently simmer for six hours, stirring it occasionally; turn it into an earthen vessel, salt to taste, and cover till cool; skim off all the fat, squeeze the meat hard as you remove it from the liquid, return the liquid to the fire, and boil rapidly for a few moments, then strain carefully through a thin cloth. Do not squeeze it, as it should be a clear amber color. For entertainments, serve hot in cups; for family use, either hot or cold, as preferred.

BREAD SOUP.

Take toasted bread and break into pieces, put into a dish, with a little salt, and pour boiling water over it; season with a tablespoonful of sweet cream.

Carrie E. Money, North Royalton, Ohio.

CHICKEN SOUP.

Take one well-dressed chicken, cut it into small pieces, and put into a stew-pan nearly full of water; add

1 large tomato,	½ pod of red pepper, cut fine,
1 large onion,	½ cupful of rice.

Salt to suit the taste. If the chicken is not fat, add a bit of butter.

Mrs. J. T., Dublin Depot, Virginia.

CLAM SOUP.

Open fifteen strawberry clams; put them into an enameled kettle, with one quart of boiling water; boil, removing all scum that rises. Stir one tablespoonful of corn-starch into a cupful of milk, with a little salt, pepper and a small piece of butter; pour on the clams, and let boil until done, as the starch requires cooking. Beat up one egg with a little milk, and remove your kettle from the fire; stir in your beaten egg carefully, else it will be stringy; send to the table.

Dora V. Harvey, Amsterdam, New York.

CLEAR SOUP.

Take one quart of flavored stock, made either from bones or fresh meat, skim it, and pour without sediment into a stew-pan; while it is cold, stir in one half pound of beef without either fat or sinew, and cut very small, one carrot scraped to pulp, one turnip and one leek cut into dice; keep stirring until the liquor is on the point of boiling, then draw the stew-pan back, skim, and let simmer for twenty minutes; strain slowly through a jelly-bag until clear. The soup will become cloudy if allowed to stand long before being used. If liked, it can be clarified with white of egg, but white of egg impoverishes soup, while beef enriches it.

CLEAR SOUP (MADE FROM BONE).

Take the bones of a piece of roast beef, which should weigh, before cooking, seven or eight pounds; or if this is not at hand, one pound of fresh bones; break them into small pieces, and put into a stew-pan, with three quarts of cold water; let the liquor boil, then draw the stew-pan to the side of the fire and let simmer gently for six hours; carefully remove the scum as it rises, strain, and leave it until the next day. Remove every particle of fat, and put it into a stew-pan (being careful to leave any sediment at the bottom); add one large carrot cut into slices, one turnip, one onion and one half dram of bruised celery-seed tied in muslin; let simmer for one and one half hours. If the liquid is very much reduced, add a little cold water, so as to keep up the quantity to three pints. Season it while boiling with pepper, salt and a small lump of sugar; strain again, and skim it carefully from time to time. In order to make it quite clear and bright, whisk the whites of two eggs with one half pint of water, and stir briskly into the soup when it is just warm; let it boil, and gently lift off the scum as it rises; draw the stew-pan back a little, and keep boiling gently for one half hour; let it stand to settle, and strain through a jelly-bag two or three times if necessary. It requires the white of one egg to each pint of soup. Add one teaspoonful of extract of beef, and a little browning if the color is too light, but care must be taken in this. This soup may be varied to any extent; carrots, turnips, onions, celery, green peas, asparagus, vermicelli or macaroni may be added. Macaroni and vermicelli should be boiled separately, or they will spoil the clearness. Sufficient for three pints.

CLEAR WHITE CHICKEN BROTH, WITH TAPIOCA.

[Favorite soup of Madame Adelina Patti, as served at the Louisville Hotel, Louisville, Kentucky.]

The day before the broth is required, disjoint one fowl, put into a stew-pan, and cover with water; add

1 veal-bone, and salt it,	A little whole white pepper,
1 bay-leaf,	1 stalk of celery,
1 onion,	½ stalk of leek,
A little garlic,	1 parsley-root,
1 blade of mace,	1 small carrot.

Boil slowly for five hours, strain through a cloth, and set aside to cool; then set in the ice-box until the next day; remove all the grease. Chop one pound of lean veal, mix with the whites and shells of four eggs, add the stock, and whip thoroughly; put over a moderate fire, and boil slowly until clarified; then strain, and add the boiled tapioca. Serve with small, round pieces of toast on a separate plate.

To Boil Tapioca.—Cover four ounces of tapioca (pearl) with plenty of boiling water, and stir until it becomes transparent; wash it in plenty of cold water, and add to the broth.

Eugene Stuyvesant Howard, member of the Universal Cookery and Food Association, London, England, and Chef de Cuisine, Louisville Hotel, Louisville, Kentucky.

CONSOMMÉ.

Chop six pounds of lean beef (shin or round), put into a soup-pot, and add

1 carrot,	4 cloves,
1 onion,	1 blade of mace,
1 stalk of leek,	1 teaspoonful of whole black pepper,
A little celery,	6 raw eggs, whites and shells of.

Cover this with two gallons of cold white stock, stir well, and place on a hot range, stirring it occasionally; slice one onion, put on range-top to brown, and add to the liquid, which will give the consomme a nice color. Chicken bones or wings and tomato cuttings can also be added if on hand. Salt to suit the taste, and boil slowly for four hours; when clear, strain it through a cloth, remove all grease that may have accumulated, and serve. Hot, it may be served in plates or cups; cold, only in cups. To hot consomme we add garnishings, such as vermicelli, green peas, macaroni cut into small pieces, tapioca, etc.

Eugene Stuyvesant Howard, Member of the Universal Cookery and Food Association, London, England, and Chef de Cuisine, Louisville Hotel, Louisville, Kentucky

CORN SOUP.

Take one half dozen ears of corn, and with a sharp knife cut open each row of grain, then cut them off the cobs; put the cobs into one quart of boiling water, and let them boil about ten minutes; take them out, and put in the corn, and let it boil for fifteen or twenty minutes; add one pint of milk and a lump of butter the size of an egg, and let it come to a boil; season with pepper and salt to suit the taste.

CREAM OF PEARL BARLEY À LA PRINCESS.

Use white consomme of game in preparing the cream of barley, the puree being finished according to the usual method. When about to send the soup to the table, pour it into a tureen containing scallops of the fillet of three young red-legged partridges, roasted a few minutes previously for the purpose.

Louis C. Zerega, Chef Hotel Ponce de Leon, St. Augustine, Florida.

CRECY SOUP, WITH WHOLE RICE.

Wash, blanch, and boil in consomme half a pound of Carolina rice; add this to a sufficient quantity of crecy or carrot soup, either prepared for the occasion or reserved from the previous day's dinner, mix these gently, and take care not to break the grains of the rice nor to serve it too thick.

NOTE.—This may be varied by substituting macaroni, vermicelli or any kind of Italian paste for the rice. This rule is applicable to puree of vegetables in general.

Louis C. Zerega, Chef Hotel Ponce de Leon, St. Augustine, Florida.

ENGLISH HOTCHPOTCH.

Put one pint of peas into one quart of water, and boil them until they are so tender as to be easily pulped through a sieve; take of the leanest end of a loin of mutton three pounds, cut it into chops, and put into a stew-pan, with one gallon of water, four carrots and four turnips cut into small pieces, season with salt and pepper, and boil until all the vegetables are quite tender; put in the pulped peas, one head of celery and one sliced onion; boil fifteen minutes, and serve.

GIBLET SOUP.

Take the feet, neck, pinions and giblets of three chickens or two geese, one and one half pounds of veal, one half pound of ham and three quarts of water; crack the bones, cut up the giblets, and cut the meat into slices; put all together over the fire, with a bunch of herbs and a pinch of allspice; stew slowly for two hours; pick out the giblets, and set aside in a pan where they will keep warm; take up a teacupful of the soup, and stir into it a large tablespoonful of flour which has been wet with cold water, and two tablespoonfuls of butter; return to the pot, and boil fifteen minutes; season to taste, and add the giblets.

GIBLET SOUP (GERMAN).

Put one quart of haricot-beans into cold water the day before the soup is wanted, and let soak over night; drain them, boil until tender, and press one half of them through a coarse sieve. Stew the giblets with two quarts of stock and seasoning; when the giblets are tender, cut them into small pieces, strain the soup, and mix it smoothly with the beans, both mashed and whole; add the giblets, let them get hot once more, and serve. The soup should be as thick as cream. A variation may be made by boiling very small potatoes instead of beans in the soup until tender, but unbroken. Time, two and one half hours to prepare the soup. Sufficient for six persons.

GREEN-PEA SOUP.

Wash a small quantity of lamb in cold water, and put it into a soup-pot, with six quarts of cold water; add two tablespoonfuls of salt, and set it over a moderate fire; let it boil gently for two hours, then skim it clear; add one quart of shelled peas and one teaspoonful of pepper; cover it, and let boil one half hour; then, having scraped the skins from a quart of small, young potatoes, add them to the soup; cover the pot, and let it boil one half hour longer; work four ounces of butter and a dessert-spoonful of flour together, and add to the soup ten or twelve minutes before taking it off the fire. Serve the meat on a dish with parsley sauce over it, and the soup in a tureen.

GUMBO SOUP.

Six pounds of fresh beef; allowing a little less than a quart of water for each pound, boil one hour; add two quarts of finely minced okras, one dozen ripe tomatoes, one half pint of Lima beans, four leaves of finely cut parsley, two thinly sliced turnips; season to taste. Cook one and one half hours longer.

JENNY LIND'S SOUP.

Make about three quarts of stock, and strain through a fine sieve into a middle-sized stew-pan; add three ounces of sago, and let it boil gently for twenty minutes, and skim; just previous to serving, break four fresh eggs, place the yolks, entirely free from the whites, in a basin, beat well with a spoon, and add one gill of cream; take the soup from the fire, pour in the yolks, and stir quickly for one minute; serve immediately. Do not let it boil after adding the eggs or it will curdle, and would not be fit to be partaken of. The stock being previously seasoned, it only requires the addition of one half teaspoonful of sugar, a little more salt, pepper and nutmeg; thyme, parsley and bay-leaf will agreeably vary the flavor without interfering with the quality.

MILK SOUP.

1 quart of cold water.	1 tablespoonful of butter.
1 pint of milk.	2 boiled and mashed potatoes.
2 tablespoonfuls of tapioca.	

Let this mixture boil before adding the tapioca, and then boil ten minutes. An onion may be added, if preferred.

Mrs. J. B. A., Georgetown, Delaware.

MOCK-TURTLE SOUP.

Put two ounces of butter into a saucepan, and set over the fire; when melted, add a tablespoonful of flour, stir, and when turning brown, add three pints of broth (either beef broth or broth made by boiling a calf's head); boil five minutes, and then add about four ounces of calf's head cut into dice, mushrooms and truffles cut into dice; boil five minutes. Cut two hard-boiled eggs and half a lemon into dice, and put into the tureen and turn the soup over.

MONGOLE SOUP.

Place a saucepan with half a pint of dried peas over the fire, cover with cold beef stock, boil until tender, and then pass through a sieve. Cut one medium-sized, well-cleaned carrot into thin slices, lay several slices over one another, and cut into strips like straws; cut one white onion the same way, and add to this one leek cut fine. Place the vegetables over the fire, with one tablespoonful of butter; cook ten minutes, then cover with one pint of boiling meat stock, and cook until tender. Stew one half of a can of tomatoes, with

½ tablespoonful of butter,	¼ teaspoonful of pepper,
½ teaspoonful of salt,	1 teaspoonful of sugar,

For twenty minutes, and then strain. As soon as the vegetables are done, add the pea puree, the strained tomatoes and one quart of good stock; cook for a few minutes, season to taste, and serve.

Mrs. Gesine Lemcke, Principal German-American Cooking College, Brooklyn, N. Y.

MUTTON SOUP.

Cut a neck of mutton into four pieces, put it aside; take a slice of the gammon of bacon and put it into a saucepan, with a quart of peas, with enough water to boil them; let the peas boil to a pulp, and strain them through a cloth; put them aside; to boil the mutton, add enough water to that in which the bacon and peas were boiled; slice three turnips, as many carrots, and boil slowly for an hour; add sweet herbs, onions, cabbage and lettuce, chopped small, stew a quarter of an hour longer, sufficient to cook the mutton, then take it out; take some fresh green peas, add them, with some chopped parsley and the peas first boiled, to the soup, put in a lump of butter rolled in flour, and stew till the green peas are done.

NOODLES FOR SOUP.

Take two eggs, a little salt, and beat them thoroughly; add flour enough to mold; roll it out very thin, sprinkle the top of the crust with flour, and beginning at one edge, roll up in a long roll, then with a sharp knife cut up into as fine shreds or strips as possible; after sprinkling flour over each piece, shake it off through the fingers, and it will straighten the noodles out. Lay them on the pie-board, and set where they will dry hard; then they are ready for the soup. Let them boil in it for twenty minutes, and serve hot.

NOODLE SOUP, WITH POTATOES.

Put one half pint of butter, with a little salt, into a kettle of boiling water. Drop into this one dozen sliced potatoes; when done, add noodles prepared from the above recipe.

OKRA SOUP.

Fry one pound of round steak cut into bits, two tablespoonfuls of butter and one sliced onion until very brown; put this into three quarts of water in a soup-kettle, and boil slowly one hour; then add one pint of sliced okra, and simmer two hours; season with salt and pepper; strain, and serve.

Mrs. T. B. J., Tuscumbia, Alabama.

OX-TAIL SOUP (CLEAR).

Cut a fine, fresh ox-tail into pieces one inch long, and divide the thick part into four; wash these pieces, and throw them into boiling water for fifteen minutes, then drain, and wipe them with a soft cloth; put into a stew-pan, with two carrots, one onion stuck with three cloves, a sprig of parsley, a small piece of thyme, two or three sticks of celery, one half blade of mace, one teaspoonful of salt, six or eight peppercorns and one quart of water or clear stock; boil, remove the scum carefully as it rises, then draw the stew-pan to the side of the fire, and let simmer very gently until the meat is tender; lift out the pieces of ox-tail, strain the soup, and if it is not clear and bright, clarify it according to the directions given in clear soup. Turn three carrots and two turnips into any small shapes that may be preferred, or into thin shreds one inch long, being careful only that they are all of the same size. Other vegetables may be used as well as turnips and carrots—such as French beans, green peas, asparagus, celery, onions, etc. Put these into a saucepan, pour the clarified stock over them, and simmer gently until the vegetables are tender. Heat the pieces of ox-tail, pour the soup over them, and serve as hot as possible. Time, about three hours to simmer the ox-tail. Sufficient for six to eight persons.

OYSTER SOUP.

Pour one pint of water over one quart of oysters, pick over the oysters carefully, and drain; strain the liquor, and put over the fire to boil; skim well, add the oysters, and cook thirty minutes; rub through a sieve. Put one quart of milk, one small slice of onion and a bit of mace into a double boiler; cook one half hour. Melt four tablespoonfuls of butter, add three tablespoonfuls of flour, and mix well. Add the hot milk slowly, and then add the oyster liquor. Season with salt, pepper and celery salt. The milk can be cooking in the double boiler while the oysters are being prepared.

Mrs. Althea Somes, Teacher of Cookery, Manual Training School, Boston, Mass.

OYSTER SOUP.

½ pint of water,   The liquor from one quart of oysters,
3 quarts of sweet milk,   ½ pound of butter.
Salt and pepper to suit the taste.

Let it come to a boil. Then add the oysters, and add one and one fourth pounds of rolled crackers, and let it all boil a few minutes. The addition of half a dozen grains of whole allspice to oyster soup gives a very nice flavor.

Mrs. Carrie Bell, Eminence, Kentucky.

PEA SOUP.

Take four pounds of knuckle of veal, to which add one pound of bacon; cut them into pieces and put into a soup-kettle, with a sprig of mint and five quarts of water; boil and skim well; when the meat is boiled to rags, strain, and to the liquor add one quart of young green peas; boil until the peas are entirely dissolved. Have ready two quarts of green peas that have been boiled in another pot, with a sprig of mint and two or three lumps of white sugar; add these to your soup liquor.

PEPPER POT.

Put four cow-feet and four pounds of tripe to boil with water to cover them, and a little salt; when simmered to pieces, take them out, and skim and strain the liquor; cut up the tripe, put it into the pot, and pour the liquor over it; add sliced onions, potatoes and herbs, also small dumplings made with flour and butter, and season with salt and pepper. A little butter rolled in flour is an improvement. When done, serve in a tureen.

POTAGE À LA ROYALE.

Melt one tablespoonful of butter; add to it one tablespoonful of corn-starch, and pour over it slowly three cupfuls of white stock; add one teaspoonful of salt, one salt-spoonful of pepper, one salt-spoonful of celery salt, one half cupful of green peas and one half cupful of carrot dice, and cook for ten minutes; then add one cupful of cream and one well-beaten egg.

Miss Ida M. Foster, City Hospital, Wilkesbarre, Pennsylvania.

POTAGE DE SAUTÉ (SOUP OF HEALTH).

Pick, wash and cut up some sorrel and a little cicely; boil it down in a little butter, moisten with consomme (meat jelly), and let it cook ten minutes; as a thickening, add the yolks of one or two eggs. Put into the soup some asparagustops, season to taste, and serve.

Louis Marche, Chef of Burnet House, Cincinnati, Ohio.

POTAGE JULIENNE.

Cut some carrots and turnips (more carrots than turnips) into thin slices one and one half inches long; also cut some cabbage, leek and one onion. Put a morsel of butter into a stew-pan, and let melt slowly; then put the cut vegetables into the pan, adding a little salt and a pinch of sugar; parboil the vegetables, stirring them from time to time without breaking them, until they are slightly browned; moisten with consomme (meat jelly), and let the whole cook for two hours; skim the soup, add some boiled green peas, and serve.

Louis Marche, Chef of Burnet House, Cincinnati, Ohio.

POTAGE PARMENTIER.

Take some large potatoes, and pick, wash and cut them into pieces; put them into a stew-pan, with a piece of butter and a little salt; add a large handful of cress, one onion cut into fourths, and the white of a leek; moisten with water sufficient to cook the vegetables into a soup, then pass the whole through a strainer; mix with the soup some consomme (meat jelly) so as to give it the proper consistency; finish with a little butter, and pour the soup into a tureen over some crusts that have been fried in butter.

Louis Marche, Chef of Burnet House, Cincinnati, Ohio.

POTATO SOUP.

Pare and cut into dice four or six good-sized potatoes, put on to boil in three pints of cold water. The potatoes should cook entirely fine. Then add one pint of milk, a lump of butter, a very little salt and one well-beaten egg. If not disagreeable to the taste, one dozen whole allspice greatly improves this. In all cases the quantity of liquid must be kept up by adding hot water.

PURÉE OF GREEN PEAS À LA VICTORIA.

Just before dinner-time roast two plump spring chickens; as soon as they are taken off the spit, cut the breast and legs into small members, put them into a soup-tureen, with two dozen small quenelles of fowl, and then pour over the whole a purée of green peas nearly boiling and prepared in the usual manner, and send to the table.

Louis C. Zerega, Chef Hotel Ponce de Leon, St. Augustine, Florida.

PURÉE OF SPRING HERBS.

1 double handful of sorrel,	3 cabbage-lettuces,
1 handful of chervil.	A little balm,
1 handful of dandelion,	A little borage.

Wash these thoroughly, and put into a stew-pan, with two ounces of fresh butter, and set on the stove to simmer, stirring them quickly all the time, then add three pints of good consomme of veal or fowl. Allow the soup to boil gently for half an hour, and just before sending to the table, finish the soup by mixing into it gradually a seasoning of the yolks of six eggs, one half pint of cream, a pat of butter, a little grated nutmeg and pounded sugar; put some duchess crusts into a tureen, pour the soup over them, and serve. Be careful to not allow the soup to boil after the eggs are added, as in this case the eggs would curdle, and thereby render the soup unsightly, if not unpalatable.

Louis C. Zerega, Chef Hotel Ponce de Leon, St. Augustine, Florida.

QUENELLES.

Quenelles are small balls made of delicate French forcemeat, composed of panada, calf's udder and the flesh of veal, poultry or fish, thoroughly pounded, then seasoned and moistened with egg. They take their names from the meats of which they are composed. Great care and patience are required in making them, and these must be directed principally to pounding the ingredients thoroughly, first separately and afterward together. Quenelles are served either in soups or with rich sauce, as a ragout, or they may be dipped in egg and breadcrumbs, fried in hot fat, and served as croquettes. When the forcemeat is made, it is always best to test a little piece before poaching or frying the whole of the preparation. To do this, a small ball should be molded and thrown into fast-boiling water. If, when it is taken out, the quenelle is light, firm and well seasoned, no alteration is necessary; if it is too firm, a little water may be added, and if not firm enough, the yolk of an egg will, in all probability, make it of the proper consistency.

QUENELLES FOR WHITE AND CLEAR SOUPS.

Melt one ounce of butter in a stew-pan over a gentle fire; beat it up with a little flour and some thick cream, as much as will make a smooth paste; add two ounces of boiled macaroni, two ounces of grated Parmesan cheese, a little salt, pepper and grated nutmeg; beat the mixture over the fire until it is smooth and firm, and leaves the sides of the stew-pan with the spoon. Mold it into quenelles with a teaspoon which has been dipped into hot water, and poach them in boiling gravy until they are done through; lift them out with a skimmer, and put them into the tureen with the soup.

RICE SOUP.

Take white stock, season it, and either whole rice boiled till very tender, or the flour of rice may be used; one half pound will be sufficient for two quarts of broth.

TOMATO SOUP.

Take one dozen ripe tomatoes or one can of tomatoes, and put over the fire in one quart of water; when thoroughly cooked, strain, and add one pint of milk or cream, a lump of butter the size of an egg, salt to taste and a very little thickening of flour. Serve hot.

TOMATO SOUP.

Take one can of tomatoes and put on to boil in a soup-pot; add one pint of water at the end of one half hour's boiling, keeping liquid enough so it will not burn; add one quart of milk, a lump of butter the size of an egg, and salt and pepper to taste; when this comes to a boil, add one level tablespoonful of soda. Serve with crackers.

TURTLE SOUP.

Kill the turtle the night before it is to be used, and hang up to bleed. In the morning, separate the shells, taking care not to break the gall; put the eggs, fins and flesh into cold water, removing carefully the black skin from the fins. Put the turtle to boil in twice as much water as you wish soup, to allow for boiling away; let it boil for two hours, skimming it well; then add six slices of nice ham and one fourth of a pound of fresh butter, and let it boil three hours more. About an hour before it is done, add one gill of rice, one gill of flour creamed with a heaping tablespoonful of butter, one finely minced onion, two stalks of chopped celery, a little bunch of thyme, half a teaspoonful each of cloves and allspice; cook for one hour more.

VEAL BROTH (BROWN).

Slice one or two onions, and fry them in hot fat until they are browned, but not at all burnt; cut one pound of veal into slices, and break the bone belonging to it into small pieces; take up the onions with a slice, and brown the meat in the same fat; pour three pints of stock or water over the meat; add the bones with any bones and remains of cold roast beef or poultry that may be at hand; let it boil, skim carefully, and simmer quickly until the gravy is sufficiently strong. Flavoring vegetables may be stewed with it or not, and a spoonful of catchup may be added if liked. Time to simmer the stock, about two hours.

VEGETABLE SOUP.

Take three carrots, four onions, four potatoes and one pint of cabbage, cut fine, and put to stew, with just enough water to cover, until the ingredients are tender; then fill up the stew-pan with boiling water; twenty minutes before serving, add one pint of milk, one tablespoonful of butter and two beaten eggs; stir thick with flour, add a little yeast-powder, and boil for a few minutes.

VENISON SOUP (BROWN).

Cut about one and one half pounds of the breast of venison into small pieces, and stew them with a small piece of fresh butter for one half hour; turn them about occasionally, and be careful that they do not burn. Mix one quart of cold water with one fourth of a pint of the blood; put the liquor into a separate stew-pan, and stir until it boils; put the stew into it, and add six or eight black peppercorns, one minced onion and the grated red part of one carrot; then simmer gently for from one and one half to two hours; strain the soup, and add brown thickening; put the meat into it again, make it thoroughly hot, and serve. When the blood is objected to, beef or mutton stock may be substituted for it and the water. French beans cut into diamonds, and carrots and turnips cut into dice, may be served with this soup.

VERMICELLI SOUP.

Take one fourth of a pound of vermicelli, break it, and blanch in boiling water to dispel the taste of dust; strain, and throw it into boiling broth, otherwise it would stick together, and could not be separated unless crumbled into a thousand pieces. Remember that the vermicelli must be boiled in broth before being mixed with puree, and take care to break it before blanching. Sufficient for eight persons.

WHITE SOUP.

Cut a knuckle of veal into three or four pieces, one fourth pound of lean ham, one large or two small onions, one half teaspoonful of thyme, one half dozen whole cloves and a piece of mace; put into a pot and cover with cold water; let it boil until the meat leaves the bone; remove from the fire and strain through a sieve; when cold, remove the fat that comes to the top; add to this stock four ounces of pounded blanched almonds; let it boil slowly, and half an hour before serving, thicken it with one half pint of sweet cream and one well-beaten egg; set it where it will keep warm, but not boil.

CHAPTER V.

In selecting a fish, see that the flesh is firm when pressed by the finger, and the eyes full. If the fish is at all stale, the flesh will be flabby and the eyes sunken.

To remove the earthy or muddy taste, soak in strong salt-water a short time before cooking.

To clean fish, lay it on a board outdoors, take a dull knife, and holding the fish by the tail, with the knife held nearly flat, scrape toward the head, then thoroughly rinse, and wipe dry. Cut off the head and fins and remove the entrails. If there are any eggs, cook them with the fish.

Always cook your fish the same day you buy.

Fresh mackerel spoil quicker than almost any other.

To freshen salt fish, lay it skin side up, and always in an earthen vessel, never in tin.

In frying fish, have your lard very hot; lay in the fish, and as soon as browned on one side, turn over; when that side is brown, move the skillet to the back of the stove, cover closely, and let it cook slowly. In this way it retains its sweetness.

Garnishes for fish are sliced beets, parsley, lettuce-leaves and hard-boiled eggs.

In shredding codfish, or other salt fish, use a small, three-tined steel fork.

You must use plenty of lard in frying fish, never butter.

If you have not a fish-kettle in which to boil fish, it must be carefully tied up in thin swiss or cambric, to preserve the shape.

Oysters are considered in season only from October 1st until the last of March.

BROWNED CODFISH.

Soak salt codfish in cold water for two days, changing the water frequently; dry, and cut into pieces for serving; season with salt and pepper, dip into dried sifted bread-crumbs, into beaten egg, and into crumbs again; fry in deep fat until a delicate brown—about eight minutes—and drain on paper.

    Miss Marion L. Campbell, Friendly Inn Cooking School, Cleveland, Ohio.

BREAD STUFFING FOR FISH.

Take about one half pound of stale bread and soak in water, and when soft, press out the water; add a very little chopped suet, pepper and salt, a large tablespoonful of minced and fried onion, and if preferred, a little minced parsley; cook a trifle, and after removing from the fire, add a beaten egg.

CHARTREUSE OF FISH À LA HAVRAISE.

Chartreuse de Poisson à la Havraise.

Take the fillets of a sole, put them to press until cool, then cut them out with a plain, round cutter; ornament half of them with chopped tarragon, chervil or parsley, and the remaining half with truffle, setting the garnish with a little liquid aspic jelly. Line a mold with aspic jelly, and arrange the rounds of sole all over it, as shown in the engraving; set this with aspic, then fill up the center

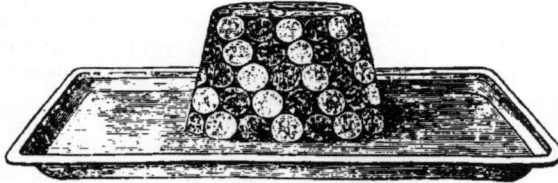

with the mixture below; put the mold aside until this is set, then dip the mold into hot water, turn out the form onto a cold dish. Serve for a luncheon or second-course dish. The dish may be garnished with any nice salad, such as lettuce or endive, mixed with a little salad-oil, tarragon, chilli vinegar and chopped tarragon.

MIXTURE FOR CHARTREUSE OF FISH A LA HAVRAISE.—Take one half pint of cleansed, picked shrimps, the trimmings from the sole cut into dice shapes, two peeled tomatoes, four cooked artichoke bottoms and twelve raw bearded sauce oysters, all similarly cut up; add a little tarragon and chervil, mix with one half pint of liquid aspic jelly and two large tablespoonfuls of mayonnaise sauce, stir all together on ice until beginning to set, then pour into the mold as directed.

FRIED FISH.

The proper method of frying fish is simply boiling in lard. French cooks never use butter in frying, as the color is not good, but give the preference to beef fat. The great secret of success is to have the fat the proper temperature before putting in the fish. Experienced cooks know just when the boiling-point is reached, but for those not so expert, a good test is to drop in a piece of dough or a bit of bread; if it browns in a minute, the fat is at the proper heat.

TO BOIL FRESH FISH.

Clean and wash well, and tie up in a cloth; put it into a kettle of boiling water with a tablespoonful of salt in it, and boil it from one half to three fourths of an hour. Then take

6 finely chopped, hard-boiled eggs,	1 teaspoonful of salt,
2 tablespoonfuls of butter,	½ teaspoonful of mustard,
1 teaspoonful of pepper,	

The fish eggs, if any, and milk enough to make a gravy; boil this mixture, and pour it over the fish after it is taken from the bag and laid on the platter. This sauce is nice for any kind of fish.

Mrs. Carrie Bell, Eminence, Kentucky.

MARINADED HERRINGS À LA RAVIGOTE.

Take some marinaded fillets of herrings and stamp them out with a plain round cutter about one and one fourth inches in diameter; place these on a plate, sprinkle them with a little salad-oil, and mask them alternately with yolk and white of hard-boiled egg that has been rubbed through a wire sieve, and finely chopped, fresh green parsley; then arrange them on slices of hard-

boiled egg that are sprinkled with chopped French gherkin; place in the center of each a little cucumber salad cut in shreds and mixed with a little oil and salt; place a little ball of caviar in the center of the cucumber, and dish up on small, fancy plates, if for hors-d'oeuvre, allowing one to each person; or if required to be served for a savory, dish them on a paper.

TO DRESS ALL KINDS OF FISH.

Dredge well with flour, salt and pepper, fry brown in boiling-hot lard. Take half a pound of butter and put into another pan, slice into it ripe tomatoes and one small onion. When fried, add one teacupful of cream, half a dozen pounded cloves, a tablespoonful of vinegar and a teacupful of mushroom catchup. Put the fish into this gravy.

MACKEREL.

Wash and soak the fish over night, or six hours, and then pour on boiling water enough to cover; let it stand a minute or two without boiling, then pour off all the water, and put the fish, outside down, into a well-buttered pan; pour on one half of a teaspoonful of sweet cream, and a little pepper if desired; set it in the oven, and let it brown a little, then serve.

Mrs. A. L. Marion, Pennsylvania.

BLACK BASS, WITH SAUCE.

Clean a good-sized black bass, cut the tail, remove the skin from both sides, and sprinkle a little salt over it; melt in a pan or deep pie-plate a piece of butter the size of an egg, add well-chopped onions or shallots, put the bass into it, cover with a piece of well-buttered white paper, and bake for thirty minutes in a moderate oven; when done, take the bass up on a platter, taking care not to break it, and keep it covered with the paper; mix a piece of butter the size of an egg and one tablespoonful of flour, put it into the pan in which the bass has been cooked, add one half pint of chicken or veal broth, put over a brisk fire, and boil for five minutes, stirring well; add a few drops of lemon-juice and a tablespoonful of chopped parsley, pour the sauce over the bass, season to taste, and serve as hot as possible.

A. J. Pillauet, Chef West Hotel, Minneapolis, Minnesota.

FILLETS OF HERRING À LA ROWEN.

Take some croutons of fried bread, in lengths about three inches and one and one fourth inches wide, on each place one of the prepared fillets of herring, and garnish by means of a forcing-bag and small rose-pipe with anchovy butter,

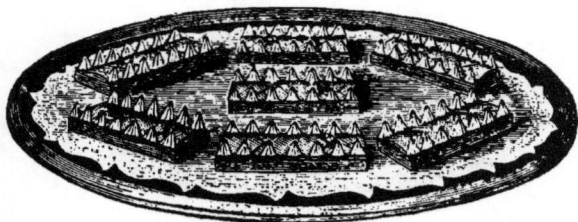

and little strips of French gherkin and white of hard-boiled egg. Dish up on a paper, and garnish with yolk of hard-boiled egg that has been rubbed through a wire sieve, and small, red French chillies, and serve one to each person for savory or hors-d'oeuvre.

SALT MACKEREL.

Soak one salt mackerel in cold water for forty-eight hours, the skin side up; boil it, skin side down, until done; put it into a skillet, and cover with fresh cream and one half ounce of butter, boil for four minutes, and serve with a few slices of lemon and a little hashed parsley on top. Specially nice as a Lenten dish.

Eugene Stuyvesant Howard, member of the Universal Cookery and Food Association, London, England, and Chef de Cuisine, Louisville Hotel, Louisville, Kentucky.

＊ FISH CROQUETTES.

Pick into pieces, taking out all the bones, one pound of any cold fish; heat two ounces of butter, stir in two tablespoonfuls of sweet milk, thicken with flour; when cooked, add one beaten egg, the minced fish, pepper, salt, a little chopped parsley and the juice of half a lemon; spread out to cool; form in croquettes, dip into grated bread-crumbs, and fry in hot lard.

ANCHOVY BUTTER.

Take three ounces of fresh butter, two yolks of hard-boiled eggs and six boned Christiania anchovies, pound together, then rub through a sieve; add a few drops of liquid carmine, the juice of half a large or one small lemon, mix, and use cold for fish or meats.

SARDINE SANDWICHES.

Take a boxful of sardines and chop them fine; add two hard-boiled eggs, chopped, and seasoned with one half teaspoonful of French mustard and one half teaspoonful of grated horse-radish; mix well, and spread between thin slices of buttered bread or cold biscuits.

MARINADED FILLETS OF HERRING ON TOAST.
Filets de Harengs Marinés sur Croûtes.

Take a slice of stale, thin bread and toast it; spread it over with butter, and then place on it some of the prepared fillets of herrings, in white wine. Sprinkle over with a little red pepper, then place the toast on a baking-tin,

and cover it over with a buttered paper; place in a moderate oven, and cook for about five minutes. Take up, sprinkle over a little raw chopped green parsley and lobster coral, and cut it into strips of about two and one half to three inches long. Dish up on dish-paper on a hot dish, and serve at once for breakfast or a savory.

TO BROIL FISH.

Any small fish or the steaks of large ones are nice broiled. Prepare as for frying, rub the bars of the gridiron with butter, then place in the fish, skin side down; do not turn until nearly done, and broil slowly; turn up, and lay in a dish, with butter, pepper and salt.

WHITEFISH AU VIN BLANC (WITH WHITE WINE).

Scale, clean and wipe one whitefish; put butter and white wine into a baking-dish; make a deep incision down the back of the fish, so as to lay out flat; put it over the fire, and sprinkle with the dressing two or three times; scatter bread-crumbs over it lightly, then put it into the oven to brown, and serve. Fifteen minutes suffice to cook the whitefish.

Louis Marche, Chef of Burnet House, Cincinnati, Ohio.

SARDINES, SHADINES, TUNNY-FISH AND SALMON.

These are canned goods, all ready for immediate use; are very nice for cold lunches, teas and traveling purposes.

TO COOK CODFISH.

Cut the quantity you want into large pieces and put to soak in cold water; after two or three hours, or over night, it will be softened so it can be readily picked into small pieces with a fork; put it on to cook in tepid water; when it comes to a boil, turn off, and put on other hot water; when done, stir into a thickening made of cream and flour; if only milk can be had, use a piece of butter.

Christie Irving.

LITTLE FISH A LA WADDINGTON.

Petites Poissons à la Waddington.

Butter some little crayfish-molds very lightly, and fill them by means of a forcing-bag and plain pipe with fish farce prepared as below; knock the molds on the table so that the mixture is well pressed to the shapes, and place them in a saute-pan on a piece of paper; cover them with boiling fish stock made from the bones of fish, or water, and bring them to a boil; then put the cover on the pan, draw it to the side of the stove, and let the little fish poach for about fifteen minutes, taking care that they do not continue boiling; when cooked, take up, and when quite cold, turn them out on a clean cloth. Wash the molds, and line them very thinly with aspic jelly, then ornament them with very thin

strips of French chillies, and put little rounds of truffle to represent the eyes; set this garnish with a few drops of aspic jelly, then replace the cooked fish, set these with aspic jelly, and when cold, dip the molds into hot water and turn out the fish; dish them up onto a pile of finely chopped aspic jelly, as in engraving, sprinkle here and there a little lobster coral or red pepper and finely chopped parsley, and at intervals place a little thick tartare sauce; garnish the center with cooked button mushrooms and truffles, if liked. This is a nice and elegant dish for a ball supper, etc.

FARCE FOR LITTLE FISH A LA WADDINGTON.—Take a nice fresh haddock, remove the skin, scrape off the meat, and pound it in the mortar until smooth; then add to it six ounces of panard, one large tablespoonful of thick bechamel sauce and one ounce of butter; pound all together until quite smooth, then add three whole eggs, a dust of red pepper and a pinch of salt, and rub through a fine wire sieve; mix with three tablespoonfuls of cream, and use as directed above.

FISH TOAST.

Pick cold bits of fish to pieces, put into a saucepan, with two tablespoonfuls of flour and butter each; mix well, and add a pint of boiling water. Have ready hot slices of buttered toast, pour the fish over, and serve.

LITTLE CREAMS OF FISH, WITH WHITE WINE SAUCE.

Petites Crèmes de Poisson au Vin Blanc.

Lightly butter some little fish-molds, and sprinkle them alternately with finely chopped truffle and lobster coral; then with a forcing-bag and plain pipe partly fill each with fish farce prepared as below; arrange this around the molds, leaving a little well or hole in the center of each cream; this should be made with the finger, which should be occasionally dipped into hot water; fill the spaces thus formed with about one teaspoonful of cooked lobster and truffles, or button mushrooms cut into small dice; cover this with a little more of the farce, and smooth over the tops with a hot, wet knife; place the molds in a sauté-pan on a piece of paper; cover them with boiling fish stock, place the pan on the stove, and let the liquor reboil; then draw the pan to the edge of the stove, cover

it, and poach the creams for about fifteen minutes; when done, turn them out on a border of the fish farce (see recipe) or potato, and serve with white wine sauce. Serve for a fish entrée for dinner or luncheon while quite hot.

FARCE FOR LITTLE CREAMS OF FISH.—Free from bone and skin ten ounces of scraped fresh haddock, and pound it until smooth; then pound eight ounces of panard; mix these, and season with a little pepper, one salt-spoonful of salt and three whole raw eggs; mix all into a smooth paste, and rub it through a wire sieve; mix with it a large tablespoonful of cream, and use.

CODFISH BALLS.

Take the fish and potatoes that are left from a meal, and a grated piece of bread; mash well together in a pan; season with butter, pepper, a little sage and thyme; then moisten with sweet cream sufficiently to mix it into balls; roll it in flour, and fry in boiling lard until very brown.

Mrs. E. F. Giddings, Grand Rapids, Michigan.

FRIED TROUT.

Brook-trout are generally cooked in this way: Clean, wash and dry the fish, roll lightly in flour, and fry in butter and lard mixed. Let the fat be hot; fry quickly to a delicate brown, and take up the instant they are done. Serve in a hot dish. Use no seasoning except salt.

HERRING LOAF.

One cupful of flaked smoked herring from which all bone and skin have been removed. Have ready two cupfuls of nicely seasoned mashed potatoes. Grease a mold, sprinkle with dried bread-crumbs, put in a layer of potatoes and then of fish, and so on until the mold is filled, having potatoes on the top; place in a pan of hot water in a hot oven. If hot potatoes were used, cook for ten minutes; if cold, for thirty minutes. Turn out on a hot platter, and serve with some nice sauce.

Miss Marion L. Campbell, Friendly Inn Cooking School, Cleveland, Ohio.

LITTLE TIMBALS OF FISH A LA SULTAN.

Petites Timbales de Poisson à la Sultan.

Line some monaco-molds thinly with aspic jelly, and fill them with a purée prepared as below; let the mixture set, then dip the molds into hot water; turn out the timbals, and arrange them on an entree-dish, surround them with a salad of lettuce or endive or small mixed salad, and fill the tops of the timbals with

crayfish bodies (in bottle), or a ragout of any nice cooked fish, such as mussels, oysters, shrimps, pieces of cold salmon, etc., mixed with a little salad-oil, tarragon vinegar, a little finely chopped tarragon, chervil, shallot and mignonette pepper, and use for ball supper or second course.

Purée for Timbal a la Sultan.—Take one fourth pint of picked and finely chopped shrimps, two ounces of raw dried haddock that has been rubbed through a wire sieve, with four washed and boned anchovies; mix these with one tablespoonful of thick mayonnaise sauce, one salt-spoonful of English mustard and the same of French, one dessert-spoonful of tarragon vinegar, two tablespoonfuls of thick cream, one tablespoonful of salad-oil and one ounce of chopped lax; stir together, add one half pint of cool aspic jelly, then pass through the tammy or fine hair-sieve, and use when beginning to set.

EELS.

When eels are good, they have a glossy, bright appearance on the back and a brilliant white underneath. Clean them nicely, take out the entrails, skin, and cut off their heads and tails, cut them up into pieces as long as your finger. For boiling, flour them and cook with parsley until tender, in salt-water. For baking, dip them into bread-crumbs seasoned with butter and herbs.

LITTLE FISH À LA ST. PIERRE.

Petites Poissons à la St. Pierre.

Take one large fish-mold and some small fish-molds, line them thinly with aspic jelly, ornament them with cut truffle to represent the eyes, and gold and silver leaf that is mixed with a little liquid aspic for the bodies, and mask the fins with red-colored jelly; set all with jelly, and then line the molds with mayonnaise aspic, using the part colored red in one fish, and the white in another,

and so on until all the molds are lined; when this is set, place in the centers of the molds any nice pieces of cooked fish, such as salmon, lobster, or any white fish, and a few picked leaves of tarragon and chervil; fill the molds with consomme that has been made to set with a little gelatin, and use when cooling; when the mixture is set, dip the molds into hot water, turn out the fish, and dish them up on a bed of chopped pale-green-colored aspic made by adding a few drops of sap-green to ordinary aspic, and garnish with thick mayonnaise sauce, by means of a bag and a large rose-pipe, and with bunches of French capers, raw cucumber and cooked beet-root, cut into rounds with a pea-cutter, separately mixed with a little salad-oil, tarragon vinegar and a little chopped tarragon; arrange these here and there in little groups, and serve for a cold collation or for a ball supper.

MARINADED HERRING À LA CONNAUGHT.

Harengs Marinés à la Connaught.

Take some hard-boiled eggs, and cut them into slices lengthwise about one fourth of an inch thick, season with a dust of pepper, a little salad-oil, chopped tarragon, chervil and shallot; then place on each slice a stamped-out round of marinaded fillets of herrings, and on the top of the fillets place two pieces of

plainly cooked prawn or prepared crayfish (in bottles); garnish each of the tops with a few French capers, and dish them up on little round slices of raw tomato that have been seasoned similarly to the eggs. If these are to be used as a savory, arrange them on a dish, as in engraving. If for a hors-d'oeuvre, dish them on small plates, allowing one to each person.

FRIED SMELTS.

Wash them, cut off the fins, and dry with a cloth; melt a tablespoonful of butter, and pour it into two well-beaten eggs; salt and flour the smelts, dip into the eggs, roll them in cracker-crumbs or grated bread, and fry in hot lard and butter mixed until they are a rich brown.

FILLETS OF HERRING A LA BRÉMONT.
Filets de Hareng Marinés à la Brémont.

Cut in two some marinaded fillets of herring, in white wine; prepare some croutons, as below, allowing one to each person, place the fillets of herring on them, and garnish each straight down with shreds of French red chillies, French gherkins and white of hard-boiled egg, arranging a line of egg butter (see below) each side by means of a bag and small rose-pipe. For the crouton, cut strips of stale bread two and one half inches long by one wide; make little incisions in the center of each, and fry in boiling fat until a golden brown; drain, and scoop out the center where the incisions were made, and fill the hollow with egg butter, and finish as above.

EGG BUTTER.—Pound together the yolks of three hard-boiled eggs, three ounces of butter, four fillets of Christiania anchovies, a dust of pepper and a salt-spoonful of French mustard, rub it all through a fine hair-sieve, and use.

FILLETS OF BASS À LA CARDINALE.

Bone a bass of about four pounds, skin it well, cut into eight equal pieces lengthwise, trying as much as possible to give them the shape of a cutlet or fillets, put aside; take the trimmings (not the bones), pound well in a mortar, season with salt, pepper and nutmeg, put in one whole egg and one ounce of good, fresh butter. Boil one half cupful of fresh bread-crumbs in one half cupful of milk, stir with a wooden spoon for about five minutes over a hot fire, so as to make a solid paste; remove from the fire and let cool off. When cool enough, mix this paste with the forcemeat in your mortar, and when well mixed, put through a fine sieve. Mask or cover one side of the cutlets with a thin layer of this forcemeat; take what is left over and roll it on a table on which you have sprinkled a little flour. Try to make a ring large enough to fit in the dish on which you intend to serve your fish. If the dish is oval, make the ring oval. Butter a piece of paper, and lay the ring on it, put the whole on a flat pan, flatten the ring all around the top, so as to be able to set the fillets on. This ring is called bordure. Cover with another well-buttered paper and put away in a cool place. (There are special bordure-molds, and if you should have one, put your forcemeat into it, after having well buttered all around and on the bottom.) Put the bones of your bass into a saucepan, season

with salt, pepper, one bay-leaf, a little thyme, one half of an onion, two slices
of carrot, a little parsley, one half of a glassful of dry white wine, two glassfuls
of cold water. Let this boil slowly for twenty-five minutes. Put two ounces of
butter and one tablespoonful of flour into a small saucepan, and cook for ten
minutes, stirring continually with a wooden spoon; add your fish broth after
having strained it, let this sauce cook for twenty minutes, and skim it well.
This sauce must be very smooth. Keep hot without letting boil. Have one half
of a pound of shelled shrimps, and put into a saucepan of cold water, and as
soon as the latter boils, take off the fire, and cool the shrimps off by letting cold
water run over them. When thoroughly cooled off, strain, cut each shrimp into
two or three equal pieces, according to their size, put them into the sauce. Take
the coral of a boiled lobster, chop very fine, sprinkle some of it over your fillets
which have been covered with a layer of forcemeat, so as to 'give a nice red
color. Put these fillets into a flat saucepan, called sauteuse; after having
buttered the bottom of it well, add four tablespoonfuls of your fish broth, if
you have any left; if not, one half a glassful of white wine mixed with a little
water will do; cover with well-buttered paper. Pound the rest of your coral
with one ounce of good butter, pass through a fine sieve; add this to your sauce,
with one tablespoonful of good sherry and one tablespoonful of whipped cream,
so as to make the sauce as light as possible; this sauce should have a pretty
pink color. Twenty minutes before serving, cook your bordure in a mild oven;
ten to fifteen minutes will do; touch the top, and if the forcemeat resists, the
bordure is cooked; keep it warm. Ten minutes before sending the soup to the
table, put your fillets over the fire, and let them simmer about ten or fifteen
minutes. Let the bordure slide on your dish, being careful not to break it; put
your fillets on it, all around the top, wreath-like, and put the sauce in the center
without putting any on the fillets; serve very hot. The fillets of bass a la
cardinale is one of the richest fish dishes gotten up, and has two qualities,
which are to please the eye and palate at the same time.

Paul Resal, Chef of White House (Executive Mansion), Washington, D. C.

FISH SAUCE.

Chop fine six hard-boiled eggs, and stir in two cupfuls of drawn butter. Let
simmer, and add one tablespoonful of pepper-sauce, two of minced parsley, with
a little thyme and salt. Pour over boiled fish.

ESCALLOPS OF SALMON MURILLO.

Remove two escallops from a salmon, pare neatly, and season with pepper
and salt; saute them in butter, adding a little white wine; glide the pan into the
oven, and allow them to cook for five minutes with the cover on; when done,
bread-crumb them, English style and lay the escallops in a little clarified butter
and let them attain a fine golden color, then drain on a cloth. Prepare a good
Colbert sauce, spread it on the bottom of a dish, and place the escallops over;
garnish with small, fresh tomatoes stuffed with prepared crab-meat, also a small
cluster of cooked potatoes, scooped out with a spoon, and two slices of lemon
dipped in chopped parsley; serve very hot.

A. Gallier, President "Societe Culinaire de New York," and Chef of Hotel Brunswick, Fifth Avenue, New York.

SOLE AND SMELTS, FRIED.

Sole et Eperlans Frits.

Remove the skin and fins from a nice fresh sole, wash it well in cold salt-water, dry it in a clean cloth, flour it well, then dip into whole beaten raw egg, and fry in clean boiling fat or lard for ten to twelve minutes, when it should be a nice golden color; take up with a slice and drain on a rack, dish up on a

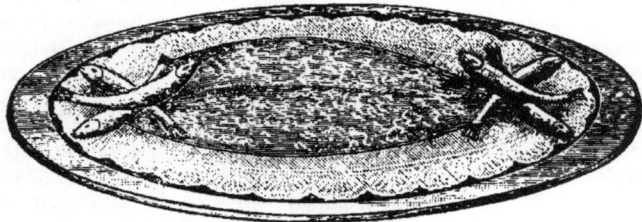

dish-paper, garnish with smelt prepared as below, and serve with any nice sauce for dinner or luncheon. It can be served without sauce as a breakfast dish, or can be eaten cold, if fried in oil.

SMELTS FOR GARNISH.—Remove the fins from some nice fresh smelts, but do not wash them; dry them on a cloth, flour and egg them in the same manner as the sole, and fry them in clean boiling fat for six to eight minutes, until a nice golden color; drain, and use as directed.

FILLETS OF SOLE À LA PYRÉNÉENNE.

Filets de Sole à la Pyrénéenne.

Take the fillets from the sole, and if they are large, cut them in two pieces, bat them out with a wet chopping-knife, and season the skin side with red pepper and salt and a little lemon-juice; cut some raw potatoes in the shape of

corks such as are used in a pint bottle, then roll a fillet around each; cut some strips of foolscap paper, butter them, and in each piece roll a fillet of sole; tie up with a string, and put into a stew-pan, with the juice of one lemon and three fourths of a pint of fish stock, or two wine-glassfuls of white wine, and one half pint of water; put the cover on the pan, and stand it in a moderate oven; cook for fifteen minutes, then take up, and let the fillets cool in the liquor; remove the paper, press out the potato carefully, and by means of a forcing-bag and plain pipe fill up the space formed by it with a ragout prepared as below; when this is set, mask the fillets over the Pyreneenne sauce (see below), and then glaze this over with a little aspic jelly, which should be partly set; dish up the fillets on a border of aspic jelly, and serve with a salad of lettuce or raw cucumber or cooked salsifies in the center; garnish the sides, as in engraving, with croutons which have been prepared as follows: Cut some bread into kite-shapes, and fry them a pale golden color in clean boiling fat; when cool, garnish with little bunches of caviar about the size of a small blackberry, and between each of these sprinkle a little red pepper; arrange little bunches of chopped aspic jelly around the base of the dish, and serve as dressed fish, entree, for second course, or any cold collation.

RAGOUT FOR CENTER OF SOLE A LA PYRENEENNE.—Mix two ounces of chopped cooked lobster or shrimps, three boned and chopped Christiania anchovies, one salt-spoonful of French mustard, the same of mixed English mustard, six or eight drops of lemon-juice, one teaspoonful of chopped tarragon and chervil and one tablespoonful of thick mayonnaise sauce, with one gill of liquid aspic jelly; add a little liquid carmine, to make it a pretty salmon color, stir on ice until set, then put into a forcing-bag with a plain pipe, and use.

PYRENEENNE SAUCE.—Fry together one and one half ounces of butter and the same amount of flour, without discoloring; reduce by boiling the liquor from the sole to one and one half gills; then mix it with the fried butter and flour, stir until it boils, then mix with one half pint of aspic jelly, half a gill of thick cream and a few drops of liquid carmine; reduce to half the quantity, keeping it skimmed while boiling, then tammy, and use when cooling. This sauce is nice for masking any cold fish.

FISH CAKES.

Take cold boiled cod, either fresh or salt; add two thirds as much hot mashed potatoes as fish, a little butter, two or three well-beaten eggs and enough milk to make a smooth paste; season with pepper; make into nice round cakes, and fry brown in sweet beef drippings or very clear, sweet lard.

FLOUNDER DÉ LA CRÈME BLANC.

1 two-pound flounder,	¼ teaspoonful of salt,
½ pint of milk,	1 bay-leaf,
1½ tablespoonfuls of butter,	1 blade of mace,
1 tablespoonful of flour,	A speck of pepper,
1 tablespoonful of cream,	½ teaspoonful of lemon-juice.

Remove the skin from both sides of the flounder, then fillet it carefully; cut the fillets in half lengthwise, roll them up, and fasten with wooden toothpicks or tie them; wash the bones, break them, and put them into a saucepan, with the milk, bay-leaf and mace, and cook gently for one half hour; strain the milk into a clean saucepan, put in the fillets (making them stand up), and simmer gently for ten minutes; take out the fillets carefully, remove the string or toothpicks, arrange them on a hot dish, and keep them hot until required. Make a sauce by melting the butter in a saucepan, adding flour, and the milk the fillets were cooked in, letting it boil a few minutes, stirring all the time, adding salt, pepper and lemon-juice; pour the sauce around the fillets, and garnish with parsley and thin slices of lemon.

Miss Amabel G. E. Hope, Teacher of Cookery, Boston School Kitchen No. 1, Boston.

HALIBUT, SMOKED AND DRIED.

This is a very nice relish for tea in hot weather. It is usually sliced or shredded in long strips, and arranged nicely on a platter; the dried or salt-cured halibut is sometimes heated upon the gridiron, but it is usually eaten uncooked.

FRIED FROGS.

Skin well, and cook for five minutes in salted water, the hind legs only; then throw into cold water to cool, and drain; fry in hot fat, and serve garnished with parsley.

SHRIMPS FOR FLAVORING FISH SOUPS.

Shrimps pounded to a paste and pressed through a sieve may be added to almost all kinds of fish soup, and will greatly improve the flavor. Shrimp butter, to answer the same purpose, may be made of the shells of shrimps.

LITTLE BOMBS OF OYSTERS À LA VERSAILLES.

Petites Bombes d'Huîtres à la Versailles.

Line some little bomb-molds thinly with aspic jelly, and garnish them at the tops with cut truffle; set this with aspic jelly and reline the molds with aspic cream; let this set, then fill up with a puree of oysters prepared as below, and

put the molds aside on ice until the contents are set; dip each mold into hot water, and turn out the bombs onto an entree or flat dish, garnish with a little finely chopped aspic jelly, and serve for an entree for dinner or luncheon, or any cold service.

PUREE OF OYSTERS.—For six to eight molds, take one and one half dozen bearded sauce oysters and pound them until smooth, with four well-washed and boned anchovies; take one and one half gills of the oyster liquor, strain it, and mix with it one fourth of a pint of good-flavored light stock in which one fourth of an ounce of gelatin has been dissolved, one wine-glassful of sherry, the juice of a lemon, a dust of pepper, one teaspoonful of beef extract; mix these, then rub the whole through a clean, slightly warmed tammy-cloth; add one fourth of a pint of stiffly whipped cream, and use.

OYSTER POT-PIE.

Have ready nice, lightly raised biscuit-dough cut into small squares; season the oysters well with butter, pepper and salt, and thicken the liquor with a little flour; place all in a pudding-dish, and cover over the top with a layer of dough; bake half an hour.

OYSTERS À LA DUMAS.

Huîtres à la Dumas.

Take some nice, fresh, raw bearded oysters, and season them with a little cayenne pepper and lemon-juice. Peel, wash, and remove the stalks from some open, fresh mushrooms (which, if large, should be cut into pieces), and then dry them in a clean cloth; season them with pepper, salt and chopped parsley, and put them into a buttered saute-pan, with the liquor from the oysters; place the cover on the pan, and cook them in a moderate oven for about twelve minutes; fry until crisp some thin slices of bacon in a little lard or bacon-fat. Arrange the oysters, mushroooms and bacon alternately on skewers, press the three well together, and then place them in a small piece of pork-caul; sprinkle with fine

flour, dip into well-beaten egg, and fry in clean boiling fat until a pretty golden color; remove each skewer, and dish up on a dish-paper or napkin, as in the engraving, upon a bed of crisply fried parsley. Have the sauce, as below, handed in a sauce-boat. This dish can be served for breakfast, luncheon or for second course, and should always be served very hot.

SAUCE FOR OYSTERS A LA DUMAS.—Take the liquor from the mushrooms and that remaining from the oysters, and mix them with a tablespoonful of brown sauce, a dust of pepper, the strained juice of one lemon and a few drops of carmine; boil up, tammy, and serve hot in a sauce-boat.

SCALLOPED OYSTERS.

Roll fine one quart of crackers. Grease a pan or dish as for a cake, put in a layer of cracker-crumbs; pour off the liquor from the oysters, and add to it fresh milk, twice or three times its quantity; moisten the crumbs with this, and put over them a layer of oysters, season with salt and pepper and bits of butter; alternate the layers of crackers and oysters, with their respective seasonings, and let the top layer be of crumbs with bits of butter over it. Beat up an egg, add to it one half pint of milk, or if any liquid remains, use that, pour this over all; bake from one half to three fourths of an hour; cook with a lid over it for the first half hour, then uncover, and brown to a desired shade.

Mrs. M. A. Townsley, Cedarville, Missouri.

OLIVES À LA BELLE EUGÉNIE.

Olives à la Belle Eugénie.

Line some little fluted timbal-molds about one eighth of an inch thick with aspic jelly that is colored to an olive shade with sap-green, and when this is set, garnish the molds at the bottom in the form of a star, with the white of hard-boiled egg cut into little diamond shapes, garnish the sides of the molds with the same, and set with a little more aspic; take some olives, farced with anchovies or truffle (those kept in bottles do admirably for the purpose), and place one in each of the prepared molds, then fill up with a little more aspic and put them in a cool place until set; take some little fancy square paper cases, and put into each about one dessert-spoonful of the yolk of hard-boiled egg that has been rubbed through a wire sieve; dip the little timbal-molds into hot water, pass a cloth over the bottoms to absorb any moisture, and then turn out, and

place one in the center of each of the paper cases; rub some white of hard-boiled egg through a sieve, and then arrange it and some of the prepared yolk around the olives to form a border; roll some caviar into little balls about the size of half a small Spanish nut, prepare some Montpelier butter and anchovy butter (see below), and put them into separate forcing-bags with small rose-pipes; then arrange these three garnishes alternately on the egg, but leave a little space between each, so that egg can also be seen. Dish up on little glass plates, on each of which is put a fancy dish-paper, and serve to each person for a hors-d'œuvre or for a savory. If for the latter, arrange all on one dish. These timbals are also very pretty for a ball supper, etc.

ANCHOVY BUTTER.—Take three ounces of fresh butter, two yolks of hard-boiled eggs and six boned Christiania anchovies; pound together, then rub through a sieve, and add a few drops of liquid carmine, the juice of half of a large or one small lemon; mix all, and use.

OYSTER PIE.

1 quart of oysters, including the liquor,	1 tablespoonful of butter,
1 cupful of milk, or	½ teaspoonful of salt,
¼ cupful of sweet cream,	½ teaspoonful of pepper.

Put into a deep pan or pudding-dish, and cover with a crust made of

1 quart of flour,	A pinch of salt,
1 tablespoonful of lard,	Water or milk enough to make a
1 teaspoonful of baking-powder,	batter to roll.

Bake twenty minutes with a hot fire.

Mrs. F. A. K., Dayton, Ohio.

FRIED OYSTERS.

Select oysters,	A little salt, a dash of red pepper,
6 yolks of eggs,	Flour, cracker-dust,
2 tablespoonfuls of sweet-oil,	Sifted, crushed bread-crumbs.

Have three soup-plates ready, one containing flour, one cracker-dust and one with the sifted bread-crumbs (chapelure); the fourth contains the yolks, the oil and seasoning, as indicated, well mixed. Dry the oysters on a clean towel, pass one by one through the flour, then through the egg mixture, then the cracker-dust; return it again to the egg mixture, and pass through the bread-crumbs, pressing the oysters lightly. If convenient, do not fry the oysters at once, but let them remain for an hour or so; then fry them in clear, hot lard until straw yellow. This will appear a little complicated to a private house cook, but one trial will convince the cook that it is time and patience well rewarded. It requires a little extra trouble to produce this excellent dish, but it pays well.

Eugene Stuyvesant Howard, of Universal Cookery and Food Association.

DEVILED CLAMS.

Chop fifty clams very fine; take two tomatoes, one onion chopped equally fine, a little parsley, thyme and sweet marjoram, a little salt, pepper and bread-crumbs, adding the juice of the clams until the mixture is of the consistency of sausage; put it into the shells, with a lump of butter on each, cover with bread-crumbs, and bake half an hour.

CLAM CHOWDER.

25 clams, chopped fine,	The clam-juice,
6 potatoes, chopped fine,	1 pint of milk,
2 small onions, chopped fine,	1 pint of water,
A piece of salt pork, also chopped.	6 crackers, rolled,
Butter about the size of an egg,	1 nutmeg, grated,
Salt and pepper to taste,	1 teaspoonful of celery-seed.

Boil these slowly for at least four hours, adding water if it should become too thick; half an hour before the time of serving, add to it a coffee-cupful of tomato catchup and two tablespoonfuls of Worcestershire sauce; when ready for the table, cut a lemon into slices, and serve with it.

CLAM CHOWDER (CONEY ISLAND STYLE).

Put into a saucepan four good-sized raw potatoes, cut into small squares, cover them with one gallon of white broth, add one small ham-bone and one finely chopped onion; let it simmer until the potatoes are fully done, remove the ham-bone, add one tin of tomatoes and the juice of two tins of clams; chop the clams, put into a pot, add one teaspoonful of thyme, and salt and pepper; serve with a handful of broken crackers and a little finely hashed parsley.

Eugene Stuyvesant Howard, member of the Universal Cookery and Food Association, London, England, and Chef de Cuisine, Louisville Hotel, Louisville, Kentucky.

LOBSTER À LA CANNES.

Homard à la Cannes.

Take some cold, heart-shaped croutons, and with a forcing-bag and rose-pipe mask them over with lobster puree (see below), and ornament, as shown in the engraving, with little balls of caviar and thinly cut slices of scalloped cucumber; take one fourth of a pound of fresh butter, and work it in a basin with a wooden

spoon until quite smooth; then make it into a border, using for the purpose a large bag with a large rose-pipe, and sprinkle over it some crisp, finely shredded lettuce; dish up the croutons on the border, and serve for a savory or second-course dish or for a cold collation.

PUREE FOR LOBSTER À LA CANNES.—Take the meat from a freshly cooked hen lobster, pound it until quite smooth, then mix with it a teaspoonful of French mustard, half a teaspoonful of mixed English mustard, a dust of red pepper, a teaspoonful of essence of anchovy and a teaspoonful of tarragon vinegar, color with a few drops of carmine, add two ounces of fresh butter; mix all in the mortar, then rub through a fine hair-sieve, and use.

SALAD OF LOBSTER À LA RUSSE.

Salade de Homard à la Russe.

Line some little fancy jelly-molds thinly with strong aspic jelly, and ornament the top of each with a little mayonnaise aspic, using a forcing-bag and pipe for

the purpose; arrange around this some French capers and little picked leaves of chervil, and fill up the molds with cooked lobster that is cut into little dice shapes, a little cut French gherkin and aspic jelly; leave until set, then dip each mold into hot water; pass a clean cloth over the bottoms to absorb any moisture, and turn out. Prepare a border of aspic jelly, and when set, turn it out in the same manner as the small molds, and dish up the little molds on it; place a wax figure in the center, and fill up all around this with a nice mayonnaise of lettuce, any nice pieces of lobster, seasoned with salad-oil and tarragon vinegar, arranging the mayonnaise on the top by means of a forcing-bag and rose-pipe; sprinkle over this a little yolk of hard boiled egg that has been rubbed through a sieve, lobster coral and quarters of plovers; eggs when in season, or prepared crayfish bodies. Serve for a second-course, ball supper or luncheon dish.

LOBSTER À LA ST. CLOUD.

Homard à la St. Cloud.

Line a mold about one eighth of an inch thick with aspic jelly, and when this is set, garnish it alternately with little bunches of green, red and white garnish, as below; set these garnishes with a little more aspic jelly, and then arrange slices of cooked lobster all over it, setting them with aspic jelly; fill up the inside of the mold with the ragout, as below, and leave it until set; then dip

the mold into hot water, pass a clean cloth over the bottom of it to absorb any moisture, and turn the contents out onto the dish on which it is to be served. If a mold with a pipe has been used, fill up the inside with any nice pieces of cold fish that may have been left from the previous dinner, mixed with a little crisp and well-washed lettuce, a few capers, and turned olives which may or may not be farced with anchovies; season these all together with a little salad-oil, tarragon and chilli vinegar and a little picked tarragon and chervil, and then cover the top with a good, thick mayonnaise sauce to a good height, as in the engraving; sprinkle the mayonnaise over with a little coral and chopped tarragon and chervil; stick here and there a sprig of green tarragon and chervil, and garnish around the dish, as a border, with finely chopped aspic jelly.

RAGOUT FOR LOBSTER A LA ST. CLOUD.—Take two ounces of cooked lobster, two ounces of any cooked fish, three yolks of hard-boiled eggs, three large Christiania anchovies that have been boned, two or three French gherkins; cut all into small dice shapes, and add about twelve very thinly cut slices of raw cucumber and one tablespoonful of raw, small picked leaves of tarragon and chervil; put them into a basin, and mix with a gill of thick mayonnaise sauce, half a tablespoonful of tarragon vinegar and two and one half gills of aspic jelly; stir these all together on ice (if you have it) until the mixture begins to set; pour into molds, and leave until cool.

GREEN GARNISH FOR MOLD.—Take a little mixed parsley, tarragon and chervil, and put them into a stew-pan, with enough cold water to cover them, a tiny bit of soda and a pinch of salt; bring to a boil, then strain, and press quite dry, rub through a sieve, and mix with it about three tablespoonfuls of aspic jelly and a few drops of sap-green, and stir until cold; then put it into a forcing-bag with a plain pipe, and force it out about the size of peas into the mold.

RED GARNISH.—Mix a little coral from the lobster in a stew-pan, with enough aspic jelly to make it moist; stir as for the green mixture until set, then put it into a forcing-bag, and use in the same manner as the green.

WHITE GARNISH.— Chop fine the white of a hard-boiled egg, then mix with it one teaspoonful of thick cream and one half a gill of aspic jelly; stir until set, put into a forcing-bag, and use in the same manner as the green.

SALAD OF LOBSTER À LA TURQUE.

Salade de Homard à la Turque.

Line a piccolo border-mold about one fourth of an inch thick with aspic jelly, and fill up the center with lobster purée, then set aside in a cool place until firm; line some little egg-molds similarly to the border-mold, and place them

in a basin containing crushed ice; when the aspic jelly is set, line them again about one eighth of an inch thick with lobster purée, and when in season, place a bantam's or plover's egg, boiled, in the center; when these are not obtainable, use the yolk of a hard-boiled egg; fill up the molds with a little cool aspic jelly, close the two parts of the mold together, and put them aside on ice until firm; when ready to serve, dip the border-mold into hot water, pass a clean cloth over the bottom to absorb any moisture, then turn out onto the dish on which it has to be sent to the table; turn out the little eggs similarly, and arrange one in each of the spaces of the border-mold, and set this with a little finely chopped aspic jelly by means of forcing-bag with a small, plain pipe; fill up the center of the border with a nice lettuce salad, and on this arrange some cooked lobster prepared as below, and also one of the little eggs; garnish around the dish with a thick mayonnaise sauce, made by mixing with half a pint of mayonnaise a fourth of a pint of liquid aspic, and stirring on ice until beginning to set; then use by means of a forcing-bag and large rose-pipe, and sprinkle here and there with a little lobster coral and chopped parsley, and garnish with some cooked prawns and little sprigs of tarragon and chervil, as in engraving. Serve for a dressed fish, for a second-course dish, for a ball supper, etc.

PUREE FOR LOBSTER A LA TURQUE.—Pound all together until smooth, one half pound of cooked lobster, six washed and boned anchovies, two yolks of hard-boiled eggs, a dessert-spoonful of anchovy essence, a dust of red pepper, a few drops of liquid carmine, two tablespoonfuls of thick cream and one tablespoonful of salad-oil; when pounded, mix in three fourths of a pint of aspic jelly, rub through a tammy-cloth or fine hair-sieve, and use when cooling.

GARNISHING FOR LOBSTER A LA TURQUE.—Take the body from a cooked lobster, free it from bones, and cut it into slices about one fourth of an inch thick; place the pieces on a dish or tin, and mask them over with a little aspic jelly, sprinkle with a little lobster coral and finely chopped parsley, and leave them until set, then trim the edges, and use.

LITTLE BOMBS OF LOBSTER À LA BERLIN.

Petites Bombes de Homard à la Berlin.

Take some little bomb-molds and thinly line them with aspic jelly, ornament them at the tops with cut truffle to form a star, and around the middle of the molds arrange a row of little round pieces of truffle, and form a border of cut

truffle and sprigs of chervil at the bottom of the mold; mask the garnish all over with more aspic jelly, fill the molds with lobster puree, as below, put them away to set, and when cold, dip each mold into hot water; turn out the bombs, and dish up on a border of aspic jelly; the mold for the border may be ornamented with truffle and chervil to correspond with the garnish of the little molds. Take a wax figure for the center, and garnish around the figure with a nice mayonnaise of cooked artichoke bottoms or other vegetables that are cut into little square pieces, or cooked salsifies, using when cold, and seasoning with oil and lemon-juice instead of butter; also place little sprigs of chervil and tarragon around the top near the figure, and chopped aspic jelly around the dish.

PUREE OF LOBSTER FOR LITTLE BOMBS A LA BERLIN.—Take six ounces of freshly cooked lobster, four anchovies, one salt-spoonful of carmine, one tea-spoonful of anchovy essence, a dust of red pepper and one good tablespoonful of salad-oil; pound all together, and rub through a fine hair-sieve or tammy, and mix with the puree two and one half gills of whipped aspic jelly and a gill of stiffly whipped cream; put into the molds with a bag and plain pipe, and set aside until firm.

LOBSTER À LA BOULEVARD.

Homard à la Boulevard.

Line some small walnut-molds very thinly with aspic jelly, and when this is set, mask it over with a little brown chaudfroid sauce (see below); let this set, then fill up the molds with a puree of lobster (see below), close the molds, and set them aside on ice until cold, then dip each one separately into hot water, and turn out. Have some well-washed, crisp celery that is very finely shredded and seasoned with a little salad-oil, and a little finely chopped shallot, a little salt and tarragon vinegar; partly fill some little paper cases with this, place one of the little walnut shapes in each case, and arrange here and there in each some little bunches of small salad; dish up on a paper on a dish, if they are to be served for a savory, or if for a hors-d'oeuvre, arrange each case on a small plate on a paper. These are also very nice served for a ball supper or for any collation.

PUREE FOR LOBSTER A LA BOULEVARD.—Pound until smooth one fourth of a pound of cooked lobster, a few drops of liquid carmine, a teaspoonful of anchovy essence, a dust of red pepper, one teaspoonful of French and the same of English mustard, two yolks of hard-boiled eggs, one teaspoonful of tarragon vinegar and four olives; mix with one gill of aspic jelly, rub all through a fine hair-sieve, and use for filling the molds when beginning to set, enough for eight to ten molds.

BROWN CHAUDFROID SAUCE FOR LOBSTER A LA BOULEVARD.—Take two table-spoonfuls of brown sauce, one half ounce of gelatin, one and one half gills of aspic jelly and one half ounce of glaze; reduce one fourth, tammy, and use when cooling.

LOBSTER À LA BORDELAISE.

Cut the raw lobster into medium-sized pieces; remove with care the pouch and intestines. Put some butter and oil into a stew-pan; heat it, and put the lobster in; parboil over a very hot fire; season well with fine salt, pepper and grated nutmeg; when it has taken on some color, pour over a little brandy, let stew. Take a small quantity of chopped, washed shallot, moisten with half a bottle of white wine, and let cook for fifteen minutes; sprinkle over it a little cayenne and a pinch of chopped parsley; add a little fine butter and juice of a citron. Pour it over the lobster, and serve.

Louis Marche, Chef of Burnet House, Cincinnati, Ohio.

LOBSTER À LA NEWBURG.

Cut the meat of a freshly boiled lobster into large dice; melt in a saucepan a good-sized piece of butter; when very hot, add the lobster, let it fry for about five minutes, pour in a glassful of sherry wine, or, if handy, a glassful of Madeira; cover the saucepan, and let it boil two minutes. In a tumblerful of good, fresh cream mix two yolks of eggs, a pinch of cayenne pepper, a pinch of nutmeg, one half teaspoonful of corn-starch and a little salt; beat this mixture with a fork, and pour it into the saucepan, toss it until the sauce gets thick, add another glassful of sherry or Madeira wine, and serve. This dish can be made on a chafing-dish on the table; if so, omit the corn-starch and add the yolks of two more eggs.

A. J. Pillauet, Chef West Hotel, Minneapolis, Minnesota.

DRESSED CRAB.

Crabe Dressé.

Put a fresh crab into a stew-pan, and boil it in slightly salted water for thirty or forty minutes, according to the size of the fish; when cooked, take it up, and set aside until cold, then remove the large and small claws, crack the large claw-shells, remove all the bone, and with a fork carefully remove all the inside,

making it quite crumby, and separating all the pieces carefully; put aside about two tablespoonfuls of this to use later on; join all the little claws together, and reserve them for twisting around the crab when it is dished up; this forms a pretty garnish. Take all the creamy part from the body of the crab, throw away the bag, which will be found inside the case near the head, chop up all the creamy part, and then put it into a basin with that from the claws, and add for seasoning one dessert-spoonful of anchovy essence, one tablespoonful of French tarragon vinegar and the same of chilli, one tablespoonful of salad-oil, one teaspoonful of mixed English and the same of French mustard, a dust of cayenne pepper, a pinch of salt, two tablespoonfuls of stiffly whipped cream, the strained juice of one lemon, a pinch of castor-sugar, a little fresh-chopped tarragon and chervil; stir all together with a wooden spoon, and with it fill up the body case of the crab that has been well washed and dried, piling up well in the center; take that set aside from the large claws, and slightly sprinkle it over this creamy part; place the case thus filled on a dish on a paper, arrange the little claws around it, and here and there garnish it with sprigs of raw green parsley, and serve for breakfast, luncheon, second course, ball suppers, etc.

TIMBAL OF CRAB À LA ROSETTE.
Timbale de Crabe à la Rosette.

Take a plain timbal-mold, put it on ice in a basin, and line it about one eighth of an inch thick with aspic jelly, ornament the bottom of the mold one inch deep, as in engraving, with plainly cooked vegetables, carrots, turnips, cucumber and French beans, cut in lengths about one half inch long and about the thickness of a thick straw; place around the edge of these a ring of cucumber peas or green peas, set this garnish with a little aspic jelly, then pour into the mold a layer of crab puree, prawn or lobster (see below) to about the same depth as the vegetables; let this partly set, then arrange on the side of the mold another layer of the vegetables of the same depth as the preceding layers, in a slanting direction from left to right, pour on a little aspic to set it, then add another layer in a contrary direction (see engraving), set with aspic, fill up the mold with crab puree, and put aside until the contents are set; when ready to

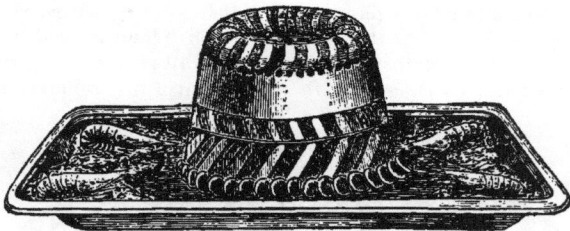

dish up, dip the molds into hot water, pass a clean cloth over the bottom to absorb any moisture, turn out in the center of a cold entree-dish; place little rounds of aspic jelly all around the base, garnish each corner of the dish with the cooked vegetables, mixed with a thick mayonnaise sauce, place on the top of each of these bunches some plainly cooked prawns, and serve for an entree or second-course dish, or for a cold collation.

CRAB PUREE.—Remove the bones from a small, freshly cooked crab, and with a fork take all the meat out of it; put this into a basin, and mix with it a dust of red pepper, a salt-spoonful of salt, a teaspoonful of French and English mustard, a dessert-spoonful of anchovy essence and a tablespoonful of tarragon vinegar; pound all together until quite smooth, add a few drops of liquid carmine, one half gill of cream and two and one half gills of liquid aspic jelly; rub all together through a fine hair-sieve, and use as described above.

EEL IN JELLY À LA DIEPPE.
Anguille en Gelée à la Dieppe.

Skin and bone a good-sized eel, lay it open on a dish, and farce it by means of a forcing-bag and pipe, with the prepared farce; to do this, spread out the farce in a long strip, then place in the center of it any nice pieces of cold cooked fish, such as lobster, sole, oysters, and also some farced olives; roll the eel up with the farce inside, sew up the fish so that the farce cannot escape, truss it with tape in a round form, put it into a piece of buttered muslin, and place it in a pan with sufficient boiling fish stock to cover it, add a few vegetables, such as carrot, onion, celery and herbs, and boil for twenty-five to thirty minutes, according to the size of the eel; then take up, and when cold, remove the tape, etc.; mask it over with mayonnaise aspic, and when cold, ornament it straight down the back

with truffles, French gherkin, French red chillies and the white of hard-boiled egg; set this with a little aspic jelly, then dish up the eel, as in engraving, on aspic that is colored an olive shade with sap-green, and garnish the center with any nice salad or mixed vegetables, olives, anchovies and chopped jelly; arrange around the base of the dish two rows of little blocks of aspic jelly, forcing between each a little chopped aspic jelly; place in the eel at regular intervals some skewers, and serve for dinner, luncheon or for a cold collation. Glass eyes can be used to garnish the fish, if they are obtainable.

FARCE FOR EEL À LA DIEPPE.—Pound four ounces of any white fish, with four ounces of panard and three raw yolks of eggs, until smooth, season with salt and a little red pepper, and rub through a sieve; then mix with a few drops of liquid carmine, a salt-spoonful of anchovy essence and chopped parsley, and use.

ANCHOVIES À LA COLMAR.

Anchois à la Colmar.

Take some of the prepared Christiania anchovies, curl each one up, and place it on a little round crouton of fried bread, garnished with the white and yolk of

hard-boiled egg that have been rubbed through a wire sieve; garnish around each crouton with anchovy cream (see recipe), using a forcing-bag and small rose-pipe for the purpose; dish up on paper, and serve one to each person. These can also be served as a savory or for any cold collation.

VARIED HORS-D'ŒUVRES.

Hors-d'œuvres Variés.

Take some farced olives, small square pieces of prepared lax, French capers, Christiania anchovies, cleansed crisp radishes, crayfish bodies, and raw cucumber that has been finely cut and seasoned with a little red pepper, salt and salad-oil. Form a border with the cucumber, and arrange the other delicacies according to the size of the plate on which they are to be served. If small plates are used, the contents may be varied, the fish being sprinkled, just

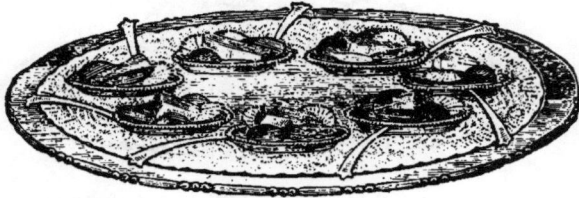

before serving, with a little salad-oil. The above can be used as a savory, in which case a flat or entree dish would be used. If serving as hors-d'œuvres, a single plate can, if convenient, be placed before each guest; or several can be placed at intervals about the table, or they may be handed with spoon and fork, to allow the guests to help themselves.

BROILED OYSTERS.

Drain select oysters in a colander; dip them, one by one, into melted butter to prevent them sticking to the broiler; broil quickly over a bed of live coals; when nicely browned on both sides, season with salt and pepper and plenty of butter, and lay them on hot, buttered toast; wet with a little hot milk, and serve very hot or they will not be nice. Oysters cooked in this way and served on broiled beefsteak are nice.

CHAPTER VI.

Chickens, turkeys, geese and ducks are better killed the day before using, and during the winter two or three days' keeping will be no injury. Also avoid feeding them for twenty-four hours before killing.

The best way is to tie the feet together, hang from a horizontal pole, tie the wings together over the back with a strip of soft cotton cloth, let them hang five minutes, then make an incision in the throat or cut off the head, and allow them to hang until the blood has ceased to drip. Chickens only should be scalded; other fowls and game should be picked dry until all the feathers are removed except the very soft down, then pour on hot water; this will swell the fowl, and the down can be easily rubbed off with the palm of the hand. Wipe dry, and singe over burning paper to remove the hair.

If it is an old fowl, feed a teaspoonful of vinegar half an hour before killing, which is said to make it tender. Also, in boiling a fowl, a very little soda or a tablespoonful of vinegar added to the water will make it quite tender.

To cut up a chicken, lay upon a board, cut off the feet at the first joint, cut a slit in the neck, take out the windpipe and crop, cut off the wings and legs at the joints which unite them to the body, separate the first joint of the leg from the second, cut off the oil-bag, make a slit horizontally under the tail, cut the end of the entrails loose, extend the slit on each side of the joint where the legs were cut off; then with the left hand hold the breast of the chicken, and with the right bend back the rump until the joint in the back separates, cut it clear, and place in water; take out the entrails, using a sharp knife to separate the

75

eggs and all other particles to be removed from the back, being careful in removing the heart and liver not to break the gall-bag (a small sack of blue-green color, about an inch long, attached to the liver), separate the back and breast; commence at the high point of the breast and cut downward toward the head, taking off the breast with the wishbone; cut the neck from that part of the back to which the ribs are attached, turn the skin off the neck, and take out all lumps and stringy substances; very carefully remove the gall-bag from the liver, and clean the gizzard by making an incision through the thick part and first lining, peeling off the fleshy part, leaving the inside whole and ball-shaped; if the lining breaks, open the gizzard, pour out the contents, peel off the inner lining and wash thoroughly. After washing in the second water the chicken is ready to be cooked.

When young chickens are to be baked, with a sharp knife cut open the back at the side of the backbone, press apart, and clean as above directed, and place in a dripping-pan, skin side up.

Keeping a panful of water in the oven will keep fowls from scorching.

Wild game should be fried in butter before boiling, as it improves the flavor.

If the fishy taste in wild game is objectionable, it can be removed by putting a small onion, cut fine, into the water in which it is cooked, or carrots, if onions are not liked.

POULTRY-KNIFE.

Game can be kept two days in warm weather by cleaning thoroughly, rubbing the insides and necks with pepper, placing inside several pieces of charcoal, covering with a cloth, and hanging in a dark, cool place.

If, from the odor, you feel they are at all stale, soaking a few hours in charcoal-water or soda-water will sweeten your game when apparently spoiled.

There is nothing so repulsive as underdone game or poultry. Be sure it is well done in cooking.

To select poultry, try if the wing will spring easily, or the breast-bone bend readily under the pressure of the thumb. The skin that attaches the wing to the body should break.

A steamer for cooking turkeys can be improvised by placing some pieces of kindling in the bottom of a wash-boiler; upon these place the turkey; put in only enough hot water to cover the kindling, put on the boiler-lid, and set over the fire. If the water boils away, replenish with hot water. Keep closely covered, to prevent the escape of steam. One hour will be sufficient time to steam it before baking.

The breasts of many of our wild game birds, when properly taken off, make beautiful ornaments, and are useful in trimming hats, muffs, etc. To properly remove them, it is necessary to skin the birds. To do this, with a sharp knife cut the skin on the back from the neck to the tail in a straight line; then skin each side by cutting the connecting tissue. When removed, rub with water in which salt and saltpeter have been dissolved in the proportion of one part of saltpeter to four of salt, and tack up on the side of the house or barn, where the sun can dry the skin thoroughly.

Garnish means to add a trimming to meat, poultry or salads. In dishing up roast meat, lay a spoonful of jelly of gooseberries just on the slice to be served to one person. Trim the edges of dishes upon which poultry is served. Celery and parsley leaves, hard-boiled eggs, water-cresses, lettuce and jellies are the principal articles used.

CHICKEN AND LITTLE TONGUES À LA VIENNOISE.

Take a nice white fowl, picked, singed and boned, with the exception of the bottom part of the back and legs and wings, turn the bird inside out, season with chopped parsley, salt and pepper, then turn it back into its natural form, and farce it from the neck-end with the farce prepared as below; sew up the opening, take off the feet, skin them, and return to the bird, having trimmed and shortened them at the bone; rub the bird well all over with butter, wrap it in a well-greased paper, place it on a baking-tin, and roast it in front of the fire for forty to fifty minutes, according to the size of the fowl; keep it well basted while cooking, and when a nice golden color, take up and set aside until cold; then mask it over with brown and white chaudfroid sauce (as in engraving), garnish with aspic cream that is cut with a fancy cutter, and sprigs of chervil and French red chilli, setting the garnish with a little more aspic jelly; dish up on a bed of chopped aspic, garnish around with the little prepared tongues, arrange here and there some financiere on hatelet skewers, arrange

between these some blocks of aspic and any nice vegetables, seasoned with salad-oil, tarragon vinegar, chopped shallot, salt and pepper, and serve for a ball supper or for any cold collation.

FARCE FOR CHICKEN A LA VIENNOISE.—Pass one pound of veal, rabbit or chicken and one pound of lean raw pork or bacon through a sausage-machine, then rub it through a coarse wire sieve, and mix in a basin with two wine-glassfuls of cooking sherry, twelve raw bearded sauce oysters cut into dice shapes, one salt-spoonful of pepper, one chopped shallot, two ounces of lean cooked ham or tongue, a little salt, two whole raw eggs and one teaspoonful of finely chopped parsley; mix, and use.

TONGUES FOR CHICKEN A LA VIENNOISE.—Line some little tongue-molds with liquid aspic jelly, garnish with tiny sprigs of chervil, set with aspic, fill each with the puree prepared as below; leave them in a cool place until set, then dip them into warm water, turn out onto a cloth, and use. For the puree take six ounces of lean cooked ham or tongue, one tablespoonful of tomato sauce, one yolk of hard-boiled egg, a dust of pepper and a few drops of carmine; pound together until smooth, then mix with it one fourth of a pint of oyster liquor, the same quantity of strong, well-flavored stock that has been mixed with one fourth of an ounce of gelatin and one half wine-glassful of sherry; rub through a fine hair-sieve before setting, then slightly dissolve, and mix with one tablespoonful of thick cream, and use when beginning to set.

CHICKEN À LA BECHAMEL.

Take a nice fat fowl, pick, singe and draw it, and truss it either with skewers or strings for boiling; rub it all over well with lemon-juice, and then place it in a buttered cloth, with two or three slices of fat bacon on the breast; tie it up in a cloth, put it into a stew-pan, and let it simmer gently on the side of the stove for about one hour; then remove the stew-pan from the stove, and let the bird remain in the liquor until cold; take it up, and remove the trussing strings or skewers, and mask it over about one fourth of an inch thick with white chaudfroid sauce, and afterward mask it over with a little liquid aspic jelly;

dish up, and garnish it straight down the breast with little rounds of cooked ox-tongue or lean ham about one eighth of an inch thick and one and one half inches in diameter, stamped out with a plain round cutter; mask these over with a little aspic jelly that is colored with a few drops of liquid carmine, using this when it is cooling, and placing the pieces on a baking-tin or flat dish while masking them; and after the jelly is quite set, cut the rounds out and arrange them as directed above, overlapping each other. Have some finely chopped aspic jelly, and by means of a forcing-bag with a small, plain pipe, garnish the rounds as shown in the engraving; have some prawns or crayfish, with whole truffles, arranged on hatelet skewers, and pierce these through the breast and through the wings of the bird, garnishing the latter with one of the rounds of tongue or ham; around the poularde place as a border some good-sized, prettily cut blocks of aspic, and also here and there some chopped aspic between, and little sprigs of fresh tarragon and chervil. This forms a nice dish for any cold collation.

CHICKEN CHEESE.

Cook a chicken until it is very tender. Cook the gravy or liquor of the chicken all down to a jell; take out all the bones, and chop the meat; season with salt and pepper, and a little sage if desirable, and put it into a mold; turn out and slice.

Olive A. Buckman, Randolph, Ohio.

LITTLE TONGUES AND CHICKENS À LA D'ORLÉANS.

Make some little tongues, as in recipe for "Little Tongues in Chaudfroid," and chickens, as below, in the respective molds; have some aspic cream, with which mask the little chickens when they are turned from the shapes, and garnish with truffles and French red chillies, as shown in the engraving; then mask over with a little cool aspic jelly to set; take some aspic colored red with a little carmine, and when cooling, mask the tongues with it; chop some of the jelly fine, put it into a forcing-bag with a plain pipe, and force the jelly between the little tongues and the little chickens, and on the top round the hatelet skewer,

the little tongues and the little chickens, and on the top round the hatelet skewer, handsome dish for ball suppers, wedding breakfasts, etc. The tongues or the chickens will make a very pretty entree.

THE LITTLE CHICKENS A LA D'ORLEANS.—Take a pound of cooked chicken, pheasant, rabbit or partridge, two tablespoonfuls of thick bechamel sauce, one tablespoonful of salad-oil, one dessert-spoonful of tarragon vinegar, one fourth of a pint of thick cream and a pinch of salt and white pepper; pound the meat, mix in the other ingredients, add three fourths of a pint of liquid aspic jelly, pass the whole through the tammy or through a fine hair-sieve, and put into the prepared molds; thinly line the little chicken-molds with aspic jelly, and ornament them with little finely cut shreds of red chilli and tarragon and little leaves of chervil; set these with a little more aspic, and fill the molds with the above mixture; leave till cold. When required, just dip them into hot water, and turn them out onto a clean cloth to absorb any moisture; dish them around the lower border of rice as directed.

STEWED CHICKEN (BUCKEYE STYLE).

Cut two young chickens into eight pieces each. Put over a brisk fire a large frying-pan, with three spoonfuls of good oil, and let it get very hot; put the chicken into it, and fry to a light-brown color on both sides; add two medium-sized, finely chopped onions, one half pound of bacon cut into very small dice, let fry a few minutes longer, and sprinkle over it one tablespoonful of flour; add a large tumblerful of good white wine, one half pint of beef broth, one bay-leaf, a little thyme and a fagot of parsley, cover the pan, and let boil until cooked. Cut six potatoes into large dice, boil them for one minute, then fry them in butter until brown, but not cooked; take them from the butter, and put them on the pan containing the chicken, and boil for ten minutes longer; season to taste, and serve on a platter, with a piece of toast fried in butter.

A. J. Pillauet, Chef West Hotel, Minneapolis, Minnesota.

CHICKEN AU GROS SEL.

Clean and singe the chicken, scald the legs, and cut off the claws; make an incision at the upper extremity of the thigh, and put the legs inside; put back the rump, and truss the chicken so as to give it a nice shape; take half a citron, and rub the chicken, mainly on the fillet; apply a bard of pork-fat on the fillet, and tie so as to keep in position. Furnish a stew-pan with two carrots, two or three onions cut into slices, and a bouquet of garnished parsley; place the chicken into the stew-pan on its back, salt lightly, and season with some grains of pepper; moisten with bouillon (meat jelly), half skimmed, not quite covering the chicken; put on top a leaf of buttered paper; cover the stew-pan, and leave to cook for one half hour over a slow fire. At the end of this time, satisfy yourself whether the chicken is sufficiently cooked; turn the whole into another saucepan, and skim it; add a tumblerful of meat sauce to give it body; reduce one half, and add a fillet of aromatic vinegar; clarify the juice with the white of an egg, and pass through a strainer, or through the corner of a napkin; dress the chicken on a serving-dish; remove the bard of pork-fat and untie; put on the edge of the dish two pinches of coarse salt and two quarters of a citron; serve the gravy in a sauce-cup.

Louis Marche, Chef of Burnet House, Cincinnati, Ohio.

DRESSING FOR POULTRY.

1 loaf of bread,	1 quart of milk,
5 eggs,	3 onions,
1 teaspoonful of sweet marjoram,	

Pepper, salt and a little thyme, two ounces of butter and hashed parsley; soak the bread, after having removed all the crust, in cold milk; when soft, press out the milk, add the eggs, salt and pepper to suit the taste, also marjoram, thyme, butter, parsley and the onions, grated, then the dressing will be ready for use.

N. B.—Hot water, or warm water or milk must never be used for dressing, as it makes it sonky.

Eugene Stuyvesant Howard, Member of the Universal Cookery and Food Association, London, England, and Chef de Cuisine, Louisville Hotel.

BOILED CHICKEN, WITH CAPER SAUCE.

Select a chicken of good size, stuff and truss, dredge it thickly with flour, put it into a pot, with just enough water to cover, and add one fourth of a cupful of rice; cover the pot closely, and set it over the fire to simmer until the chicken is tender; serve with caper sauce.

BROILED SPRING CHICKEN.

Split, sprinkle with salt and pepper, and rub all over with butter; pinion the legs to the side, place on a gridiron over a hot fire, with the inside of the chicken down; turn often; when a nice brown, dish, pour over it melted butter, and sprinkle with pounded crackers; serve with broiled tomatoes.

CHICKEN AU RÉVEIL.

Take a nice cleansed chicken, truss it for boiling, rub it well with lemon-juice and sprinkle it with salt, place a strip of fat bacon on the breast, and tie the bird up in a piece of buttered muslin, then put it into a stew-pan, with two or three sliced onions, one carrot, one turnip and a strip or two of celery; cover with light stock or water that is seasoned with lemon-juice and salt; bring this

to a boil, and simmer gently for one hour; then take up the bird, remove the muslin and bacon, and dish up the chicken on a puree of potato; cover with cheese-cream sauce, arrange some little tongues, as below, around the chicken, as shown in the engraving, and garnish each end of the dish with cooked artichoke bottoms and braised onions; ornament the top of the bird with two hatelet skewers, and serve hot for a remove for dinner or luncheon. Turkey or pheasant can be served in the same way.

TONGUES FOR CHICKEN AU RÉVEIL.—Butter some little tongue-molds, sprinkle them with a little raw chopped parsley, and fill them with the farce, as below, using a forcing-bag and small, plain pipe for the purpose; stand the molds in a tin on a fold of foolscap paper, surround them with boiling water to three parts their depth, watch the water reboil, then draw the pan to the side of the stove, and let the contents poach for fifteen minutes; then turn out the tongues, and use as directed above. For the farce take one half pound of lean cooked ham or tongue, and pound it until smooth, then six ounces of panard, with one large tablespoonful of thick bechamel sauce, one ounce of butter, a dust of cayenne, a few drops of carmine and one large tablespoonful of sherry; mix in three raw eggs, rub through a wire sieve, and use.

CHICKEN AU RIZ, WITH RICE.

Take about four ounces of rice to each chicken; clean the rice, and let it boil for forty-five minutes in some consomme (meat jelly), with a little butter; prepare the chicken, and let it boil; cook the rice as dry as possible, moisten it with part of the chicken dressing, and thicken with one yolk of egg and a little butter; place the rice on a round dish, and put the chicken, cut into pieces, above it; pour over the rice a little hot gravy, and serve.

Louis Marche, Chef of Burnet House, Cincinnati, Ohio.

CHICKENS À LA CHANCELIERE.

Take two good fat chickens, bone them, free the feet from the top skin, and clip the nails off, and press them into the leg where the bone has been taken from; fill the chickens with farce (see "Chicken a la Viennoise"), and truss them for boiling, making them as nice shape as possible; place a piece of fat bacon on the breast of each, and tie them up in a well-buttered cloth; put into a stew-pan the bones from the birds, the liquor and beards from the oysters used in the preparation of the farce, some vegetables, such as carrots, onions, celery,

leek, thyme, parsley and bay-leaf, two blades of mace, a little salt and one tea-spoonful of peppercorns; place the poulardes on this, and cover with light stock or water; put the pan on the stove, just bring the contents to a boil, skim it, and let it simmer very slowly for from one and one fourth to one and one half hours; take up, put away until cold, then remove the cloths and bacon, and mask one side of each poularde with tongue puree (see recipe), and the other side with aspic cream; take some prettily cut shapes of truffle, and ornament the breasts of the birds with them, using a little liquid aspic jelly to keep the garnish in its place; then coat over the truffle with a little more of the jelly, to give it a glazed appearance. Place in the center of the dish in which the poulardes are to be served a block of boiled rice and some finely chopped aspic jelly; arrange the poulardes as shown in the engraving; place a hatelet skewer in the center of the rice, garnish the back and front of the rice block with financiere garnish, and arrange around the base of the dish some tomatoes and little timbals of pate de foie gras, and serve for a ball supper or luncheon dish. The stock left from the braising of the poulardes will make excellent soup.

CHICKEN SAUTÉ, WITH TOMATOES.

Cut one chicken into small pieces; put into a stew-pan a morsel of butter, and let it become hot; put in the chicken, the side with skin undermost, season, and cook over a hot fire, turning the pieces of chicken from time to time; cut some nice tomatoes into halves, removing the juice and pips, mince, and put them into warm oil; after they have been dried, add them to the chicken, with a little pinch of chopped garlic; moisten the whole with one glassful of white wine, cover the stew-pan, and cook for thirty minutes; add a little meat jelly, and sprinkle with chopped parsley; let it boil a few minutes; season and dress, heaping to a point upon a round serving-dish, and serve.

Louis Marche, Chef of Burnet House, Cincinnati, Ohio.

SALMIS OF CHICKEN À LA RÉGENCE.

Take any nice pieces of cold cooked fowl (that left from a previous meal could be used for the purpose), cut them into neat shapes, removing the skin and any untidy pieces, then put them into a good salmis sauce colored with a few drops of carmine; make them quite hot in the bain-marie, dish them on a border, as

below, and garnish with little croustades; pour some of the sauce prepared for the salmis around the base of the dish. Serve at once for an entree for a dinner party.

CROUSTADES FOR SALMIS OF CHICKEN À LA RÉGENCE.—Take one fourth of a pound of fine flour, two ounces of butter, and rub together until smooth, season with salt and pepper; mix with one whole egg and a little cold water into a smooth paste; then roll it out thinly and line some little molds with it; then line the paste with buttered paper, and fill up with raw rice, and bake for fifteen to twenty minutes; stamp out some small rings from the same paste to garnish, and bake until a pale golden color, then remove the croustades from the molds, and fill them up with red and white garnishing quenelles and pieces of cut truffles and cooked button mushrooms and financiere that have all been mixed with a little thin creamy veloute sauce; place four of the rings on each, and use.

BORDER FOR SALMIS OF CHICKEN À LA RÉGENCE.—Butter a Breton border-mold, and garnish it with rings of boiled Naples macaroni (see "Sweetbread a l'Impératrice"), then with a forcing-bag and plain pipe fill up the mold with a farce of chicken, knock the mold on the table so that the mixture sinks well into the shape, then put it into a stew-pan on a fold of paper; cover it with boiling water, watch the water reboil, then draw the pan aside, and poach for fifteen minutes; turn out, and use.

LITTLE CHICKEN CREAMS À LA FRANCILLON.

Take one half pound of raw chicken, and pound it until smooth; then pound two ounces of panard with two tablespoonfuls of thick bechamel sauce and one ounce of butter, add a pinch of salt and white pepper, then mix into the pounded chicken until quite smooth; work in two whole eggs; pass through a fine wire sieve or coarse hair-sieve, and add one large tablespoonful of thick cream. Butter the egg-molds all over both parts, and ornament them with cucumber (cut into pea-shapes) or peas, fill up the molds with the mixture, using a forcing-bag and plain pipe for the purpose; make a well in the center by dipping the finger into a little hot water, and working it around until the space is formed; fill this up with cooked asparagus peas (see recipe) and a little thick creamy veloute sauce; join up the two parts of the molds, and poach them for about fifteen minutes in a stew-pan containing boiling water, resting each egg-mold

in a dariol to keep it upright; turn out the molds, dish them on a border of potato or farce prepared in a piccolo-mold, pour veloute sauce around them, and garnish with cooked peas, cucumber or asparagus points.

CHICKEN IN ASPIC.

Boil a three-pound chicken carefully until tender; remove the meat, crack the bones, and return them to the water in which the chicken was cooked; add one onion, four cloves, a blade of mace, a bay-leaf; simmer gently for two hours, strain, and turn out to cool; when cool, remove all fat from the surface, turn out the jelly, and remove the sediment from the bottom. If the jelly is not sufficiently thick, add one fourth of an ounce of gelatin to it, and reheat; color with a teaspoonful of caramel, season with salt and red pepper; cut the chicken into blocks half an inch square, the same as for salad; put a layer of gelatin in the bottom of the mold; when hard, put in the chicken, layer of celery, and seasoning of salt and pepper, then another layer of gelatin, which must be cool, but not thick; so continue until you have used all the chicken; cover the whole with the liquid jelly, and stand away until perfectly cold; when ready to serve, turn this mold out on a bed of water-cress or lettuce, or both; garnish it with finely chopped, hard-boiled eggs, first a row of whites, and then a row of yolks, and then serve it with a bowl of mayonnaise dressing. Stoned olives and radishes may also be used as a garnish. This makes a much handsomer dish than plain salad, and is a very nice dish for evening parties and card parties.

Mrs. S. T. Rorer, author of "Mrs. Rorer's Cook Book," and Principal of Philadelphia Cooking School, Philadelphia, Pennsylvania.

CURRIED CHICKEN À LA MARIE.

Cut up a small picked and cleansed chicken into neat joints, using only the best parts. Take four or five large peeled onions, cut them into very fine slices, and put them into a stew-pan, with two ounces of butter, a sprig of thyme and bay-leaf, and fry on the stove until a pale golden color; then add one table-spoonful of curry-powder, a pinch of salt, one ounce of good glaze, one and one half ounces of fine flour; mix with these one and one half pints of new milk, add the joints of chicken, then put on the stove and stir until boiling, and simmer gently for about one hour, during which time stir the curry frequently to prevent it burning; when cooked, take up the joints and set aside until cold; then add to the contents of the pan the strained juice of one lemon, one fourth of a pint of thick cream, and dissolve in it one fourth of an ounce of gelatin; reboil, and rub through a tammy or very fine hair-sieve, getting as much of the puree through as possible, then stir on ice until beginning to set, and with it mask the pieces of the bird that have been freed from skin; set the pieces on a baking-tin that is standing on crushed ice, and mask over with a little cool aspic jelly, dish up in a pile, and garnish here and there with finely chopped aspic jelly, and form a border around the chicken with some plainly boiled cold curry-rice and farced olives, sprinkling the rice at intervals with a little lobster coral or coralline pepper and finely chopped raw parsley. Serve for a cold entree, ball supper, etc. The remains of the chicken can be used up for stock, etc.

STEWED CHICKEN (VIRGINIA STYLE).

Disjoint one chicken, put into a saucepan, cover with water or white stock, add one teaspoonful of whole white pepper, four cloves, one blade of mace and two small onions all tied up in a cloth; let simmer slowly for one hour, then remove the spices; put into another saucepan two ounces each of butter and flour, stir well, and add the broth of the chicken, stirring lively; when thick, add the chicken, season to taste, add corn dumplings made as below, and serve.

Corn Drop Dumplings for Stewed Chicken (Virginia Style).—Take one tin of corn, chop it very fine or run it through a meat-cutter, add three eggs, a little flour, and salt and pepper to suit the taste; drop this paste from a teaspoon into a pot of boiling water, and boil for ten minutes, then lift the dumplings out of the water, and serve with the stewed chicken. When fresh corn is in the market, it may be grated and used instead of the tinned article.

Eugene Stuyvesant Howard, member of the Universal Cookery and Food Association, London, England, and Chef de Cuisine, Louisville Hotel.

BOILED CHICKEN, WITH EGG SAUCE.

Stuff a large, plump chicken with bread-crumbs seasoned with pepper, salt and thyme, tie a buttered paper around it, put it into a kettle of warm water, and cover closely; when done, take up the chicken, and make a sauce of one cupful of the chicken liquor, thicken with one tablespoonful of butter rolled in flour, poured over two beaten eggs; boil for one minute, with one tablespoonful of chopped parsley, season, and pour over the yolks of ten hard-boiled eggs which have been pounded and placed in the bottom of the bowl; stir, and serve with the chicken.

ROAST CHICKEN.

Procure a nice, plump chicken weighing about two and one half pounds, singe, draw, and wash it in cold water, wipe with a dry towel, cut off the feet from the joint of the leg, make an incision just under the thigh, and insert the legs inside; detach the skin as much as possible from the breast, and put a layer of forcemeat over the breast under the loosened skin, and fill the body with the same forcemeat; sew the chicken up, truss it nicely, rub over it one even tablespoonful of salt, spread over it one even tablespoonful of butter, and lay a few thin slices of larding-pork over the breast; place it in a roasting-pan, add one cupful of boiling water; place it in a hot oven, baste frequently, and roast until done, which will take about one hour if the chicken is young. Place the feet, giblets and neck in a saucepan, cover with cold water, add one onion, one even teaspoonful of salt, and boil until tender. Fifteen minutes before serving, remove the boiled liver and rub it fine. Transfer the chicken to a hot dish, take out the threads, and place the chicken in a warm place. Remove the fat from the gravy, mix one half tablespoonful of corn-starch with one half cupful of cold water, add it to the gravy, let it cook for a few minutes, and add sufficient giblet broth to make a creamy sauce; strain it through a sieve, add the fine rubbed liver, and serve in a sauciere with the chicken.

Mrs. Gesine Lemcke, Principal German-American Cooking College, Brooklyn, N. Y.

CREAM OF CHICKEN À L'OEUF.

Take one pound of raw chicken, free it from skin and bone, and pound it until smooth; mix with it four tablespoonfuls of bechamel sauce, and take from the mortar. Then pound one half pound of panard with one and one half ounces

of butter, a salt-spoonful of salt and a tiny dust of white pepper, and add it to the meat; mix into it four whole raw eggs and three tablespoonfuls of cream, and rub all together through a coarse hair or fine wire sieve, and put the mixture into a well-buttered egg-mold that is ornamented with cut truffle; tie up the mold with tape or string, put it into a stew-pan on a fold of paper, cover with boiling water; watch the water reboil, then draw the pan to the side of the stove, and let the contents poach for three fourths of an hour; then take up, remove the tape, turn out the cream, and dish up on a square crouton of bread that is masked with supreme sauce, garnish with skewers with large truffles and cockscombs on them, and serve with supreme sauce around the base for an entree for dinner or luncheon. The above-given quantities will be found sufficient for ten to twelve people.

CHICKEN PIE.

Mix a crust with sweet milk, and shorten with butter; line the sides (not the bottom) of a milk-pan; have a young chicken cut up, and one quart of potatoes peeled, sliced and about an inch thick; place a layer each of chicken, potatoes and dough cut into small strips; add pepper, salt, butter and some small bits of pickled pork; continue these layers until the pan is full; to this add one pint of cold water; put on the upper crust, with a hole cut in it; after cooking awhile, add two pints of hot water; cook for one hour in a moderate oven.

Mrs. James Gladden, Stockwell, Indiana.

TURBAN OF CHICKEN À LA VÉNITIENNE.

Butter a turban-mold well, and fill it with savory farce, as below, and let it steam for about twenty minutes, then turn it out onto a cake-bottom that is masked over lightly with white farce, as below; mask the savory farce all over with a thin layer of the white farce, and arrange all around this the breast fillets of a raw chicken (that have been sliced and larded), fastening these fillets onto the turban with a little of the white meat farce, using a forcing-bag and pipe for the purpose; then garnish with little rounds of cut tongue and truffle,

sticking these with farce; place a buttered paper around the turban, and put it into the oven to cook for about twenty minutes, with a paper on the top, and a few very thin slices of fat bacon to keep the fillets moist; dish up, remove the paper band, and serve with velouté sauce, round and braised olives in the center, with cockscombs that have been warmed in their own liquor. This will be enough for twelve persons. The cockscombs are kept in bottles ready for use.

SAVORY FARCE FOR TURBAN OF CHICKEN A LA VÉNITIENNE.—Pound one half pound of raw white meat, and rub it through a sieve, then mix with it two ounces of chopped cooked tongue or ham and two or three cooked chicken livers that have also been passed through a sieve; add a salt-spoonful of mignonette pepper and salt, a dust of pepper, one half of a finely chopped shallot, one tea-spoonful of chopped olives, the same of button mushrooms, one tablespoonful of thick bechamel sauce, and two raw yolks of eggs; mix all, and put into the buttered mold by means of a forcing-bag and pipe.

WHITE FARCE FOR MASKING TURBAN OF CHICKEN A LA VÉNITIENNE.—Pound six ounces of chicken, rabbit or veal until smooth, then pound six ounces of panard, and mix; add two and one half small or two large eggs, a pinch of salt and white pepper and one ounce of butter; then pass through the sieve.

PRESSED CHICKEN.

Cut up the fowls, and put into a kettle with a tight cover, so as to retain the steam; put about two teacupfuls of water and plenty of salt and pepper over the chicken, then let it cook until the meat cleaves easily from the bones; cut or chop all the meat (freed from skin, bone and gristle) about as for chicken salad; season well, put into a dish, and pour over it the remnant of the juice in which it was cooked; this will jelly when cold, and can be sliced or set on the table in shape. Nice for tea or lunch. The knack of making this simple dish is in not having too much water; it will not jelly if too weak, or if the water is allowed to boil away entirely while cooking.

CHICKEN CUTLETS A LA REINE.

Butter some cutlet-molds, and arrange in them alternate layers of cooked breast of chicken and tongue (or ham), stamping out the pieces with a cutter the same shape and size as the mold; fill up the molds with a cream of chicken, as below; place them on a baking-tin, surround them with enough water to cover the bottoms, place a buttered paper on the top, and cook in a moderate oven for fifteen minutes; then turn out the cutlets on a border of potato, and mask them with supreme sauce; then garnish each cutlet with a piece of

stamped-out truffle in any pretty design; serve peas in the center, and with a puree of cooked lean ham or tongue form a little rose on the top of each cutlet, using a forcing-bag with a small rose-pipe for it; pour supreme or veloute sauce around the dish, and use as a dinner party entree.

Chicken Cream for Chicken Cutlets a la Reine.—Take the meat from the legs of a fowl, remove the skin and bone, and pound until smooth, then mix with it one large tablespoonful of thick bechamel sauce and raw whites of three eggs, season with salt and pepper and one tablespoonful of cream; rub through a fine wire sieve, add a wine-glassful of sherry, and use.

Chicken for Chicken Cutlets a la Reine.—Remove the breast fillets from a fowl, freeing it from skin, place them on a buttered baking-tin, sprinkle with lemon-juice and salt; put a buttered paper on the top, and cook in a moderate oven for ten to twelve minutes; put into press until cold, and then cut into very thin slices, and stamp out as above.

Tongue Puree for Cutlets a la Reine.—Pound one fourth of a pound of cooked tongue or ham until smooth, with one tablespoonful of thick bechamel sauce, a dust of pepper, two yolks of hard-boiled eggs; then rub through a sieve, and use.

CHICKEN LIVERS, WITH MADEIRA.

12 chicken livers,	¼ cupful of Madeira,
1 tablespoonful of flour,	24 stoned olives,
1 tablespoonful of butter,	¾ cupful of brown stock.

Wash and wipe dry the livers, cut them into quarters, put into a chafing-dish, add the butter, cover, and cook for five minutes; add the flour, and stir until well blended, add the stock, and stir until smooth and thick; if not dark enough, add a little caramel; add the Madeira, and season with salt and cayenne. If the seasoning is added before the wine, very little must be used, as wine intensifies the flavor of salt. Turn in the olives, slip a hot-water pan underneath, cover, and simmer for ten minutes.

Miss Cornelia Campbell Bedford, Superintendent New York Cooking School, New York.

CHICKEN À LA RUBANÉE.

Take a roast fowl, cut it into neat pieces, remove the skin from it, then put it into a saute-pan; cover it over with rubanee sauce, and simmer for about fifteen minutes; then dish up in a pile, pour the remaining sauce over, and

garnish here and there with prettily cut croutons. Serve for an entree for dinner or luncheon. Pheasant or partridge can be used in the same way, and any cold bird can be used up similarly.

SCALLOPED CHICKEN.

Boil a chicken whole in salted water until very tender; when cold, pull off the skin, cut the best meat, light and dark, into small bits, making one pint.

1 pint of fresh bread-crumbs,	1 heaping tablespoonful of butter,
1 cupful of rich cream,	1 tablespoonful of corn-starch,
1 cupful of milk,	1 teaspoonful of salt,
½ canful of sliced mushrooms,	¼ teaspoonful of white pepper.

Melt the butter in a saucepan, add the corn-starch, stirring constantly to prevent burning, add the milk gradually, and cook five minutes, then add the cream, salt and pepper. Butter a baking-dish, pour in a layer of the sauce, then a layer of bread-crumbs, then chicken, then mushrooms, so on until all are used, the sauce last. Reserve one half cupful of the bread-crumbs, add melted butter until very moist; cover the top with these, and bake in a hot oven until a rich brown—about twenty minutes. If desired, a little pepper may be sprinkled on the top crumbs.

Miss Emily E. Squire, Author of "Woronoco Women's Wisdom," Westfield, Mass.

SMOTHERED CHICKEN.

Take two nice, well-dressed chickens, cut them open at the back, place them in a deep pan, and season well with salt and pepper, then sift on flour enough to almost cover them; slice one tomato, lay it upon the chickens, spread on them one cupful of mixed butter and lard, and pour over them two or three pints of boiling water; set in the oven, and with a deep pan cover them closely to keep in all the steam; when tender, remove the cover, and let them brown slightly, then they are ready for the table.

Mrs. J. T., Dublin Depot, Virginia.

CHICKEN DORMERS.

Take some hard-boiled fresh eggs, remove the shells, and dry the eggs in a clean soft cloth, then cut each into halves lengthwise, using a hot, wet knife for the purpose; take out the entire yolk and some of the white, so as to form little cases; fill up these spaces by means of a forcing-bag and plain pipe with a ragout, as below; smooth over the top with a hot, wet knife, and set them aside until cold; then flour them and dip into whole raw beaten-up egg, and into freshly made white bread-crumbs twice; place in a frying-basket, and plunge

them into clean boiling fat, and fry until a nice golden color; then dish up on a flat dish, as shown, for ball supper, etc.

RAGOUT FOR CHICKEN DORMERS.—Put into a stew-pan two ounces of butter and two ounces of fine flour, and fry together without browning; then mix with it one half pint of light, good-flavored stock or new milk; stir until boiling, season with a little salt and pepper, and mix with it two raw yolks of eggs; stir again over the fire until the sauce thickens, but do not let it boil, and wring it through a clean tammy-cloth; mix with it four tablespoonfuls of finely minced chicken or other white meat, four yolks of hard-boiled eggs that have been rubbed through a sieve, one tablespoonful of lean cooked ham or tongue, one teaspoonful of finely chopped raw green parsley, one finely chopped shallot and the strained juice of a lemon; mix all, and use as directed. Sufficient for fourteen to sixteen dormers.

PEPITORIA.

Cut into pieces some boiled chicken, mix with spices, garlic, hops, onions and parsley, add a little of the chicken stock, let it come to a boil; make the sauce with this stock, that is, thicken it with butter and flour, add one or more slices of hard-boiled egg, and serve.

Gustave Berand, Chef of Calumet Club, Chicago, Illinois, formerly Chef of William Astor, New York.

LITTLE CHICKENS À L'IMPÉRIALE.

Lightly butter some small chicken-molds, and by means of a forcing-bag with a large, plain pipe fill them with farce, make a well in the center of each, and nearly fill these spaces with a puree of chicken, as below, then cover this over with a little more of the farce that was used for lining the molds, and smooth over the tops with a hot, wet knife; put a fold of paper into a saute-pan, place the molds on this, cover them completely with boiling water; place the pan on the stove, watch the water reboil, place a buttered paper over the molds, put the cover on the pan, and let the contents steam for about fifteen minutes; when cooked, turn the molds onto a clean cloth. Arrange a fried crouton of bread in the center of a border of potatoes on an entree-dish, stand the chickens upright on this, resting them against the crouton, mask them carefully with a

good creamy supreme sauce, and by means of a forcing-bag with a large rose-pipe force a little puree of green peas between each chicken; arrange at the top little stamped-out rounds of ox-tongue about one eighth of an inch thick and one half of an inch in diameter that have been warmed in a little sherry between two plates; arrange some financiere on a hatelet skewer, and stick this in the center of the croutons; serve supreme sauce around the base and over the chickens; place a round of cooked tongue on the top between each chicken, and serve.

PUREE FOR LITTLE CHICKENS A L'IMPERIALE.—Take, for eight to ten molds, six ounces of raw chicken, free it from skin and bone, and pound it until smooth, rub through a fine sieve, then mix with two tablespoonfuls of thick cream, a pinch of salt, a dust of pepper; mix well, put into a forcing-bag with a small, plain pipe, and use.

FRIED CHICKEN.

Clean and wash it well, and with a sharp knife cut it open in the back; dredge with flour, pepper and salt. Put equal quantities of butter and lard into a hot frying-pan, then put in the chicken, and keep it well covered until brown on both sides. The secret of a nice fricassee is in having plenty of hot lard or butter.

L. H. B., Postville, Iowa.

LITTLE CHICKENS À LA RENAISSANCE.

Line some little chicken-molds very thinly with aspic jelly, and garnish them with truffle in little diamond shapes shraight down the breast; line them again thinly with white chaudfroid sauce, and again with a puree of chicken prepared as below, and inside this puree put one teaspoonful of the ragout of lobster, as below; smooth this with a wet knife, and then cover it with the puree of chicken; put aside on ice until set, then dip the molds into hot water, and turn out the little chickens; dish them on a border of rice or aspic jelly, place a wax figure in the center of the border, fill up the spaces between each chicken with aspic jelly, as in engraving, and garnish the dish with lobster butter, and olives prepared as below; place a chicken and four olives on the wax cup on top of the figure; place some olive-colored aspic around the base of the dish, and garnish with little sprigs of tarragon and chervil.

PUREE OF CHICKEN FOR CHICKENS A LA RENAISSANCE.—Pound three fourths of a pound of cooked chicken or white meat, and mix it with one half pint of aspic

jelly, one fourth of a pint of thick cream, one wine-glassful of sherry and a pinch of salt; when smooth, pass through a tammy or fine sieve, and use.

RAGOUT FOR CHICKENS A LA RENAISSANCE.—Mix one fourth of a pint of aspic jelly, two tablespoonfuls of chopped lobster, three boned anchovies cut into diamond shapes, three chopped, turned olives, one teaspoonful of chopped capers, a pinch of chopped tarragon and chervil, one tablespoonful of mayonnaise sauce, a few drops of liquid carmine and a dust of pepper, then use.

OLIVES FOR CHICKEN A LA RENAISSANCE.—Turn some olives, and fill them (by means of a forcing-bag and pipe) with the mixture used for the little chickens; line some fluted dariols with olive-colored aspic, place an olive in each, set with aspic, and when turned out, garnish the dish as described above.

STEAMED CHICKEN.

Rub with salt and pepper, place in a steamer, and steam one and one half hours; when done, keep hot. Prepare a sauce of one pint of gravy, one pint of cream, six spoonfuls of flour, one tablespoonful of butter, pepper, salt and a few drops of extract of celery.

CHICKEN SAUTÉ.

Disjoint a tender chicken after singeing and removing the pin-feathers, season with salt and pepper, roll in flour, brown in salt-pork fat, and put into a stew-pan; brown two tablespoonfuls of butter, add one tablespoonful of chopped onion, and fry for five minutes, then add two tablespoonfuls of flour, and brown; add slowly one pint of milk and one half pint of white stock, and season with salt, pepper and a speck of cayenne; pour this sauce over the chicken, and cook until tender; add one can of mushrooms, cook for ten minutes, and serve.

Mrs. Althea Somes, Teacher of Cookery, Manual Training School, Boston, Mass.

CHICKEN SAUTED MASCOT.

Divide a fine chicken into pieces, and season each one with salt and pepper. Have a stew-pan, and in it put four spoonfuls of clarified butter; when very hot, place the pieces of chicken in, one by one, beginning with the legs, and when well browned on one side, turn them over, then put the pan, uncovered, into the oven for ten minutes. Peel six fine, fresh tomatoes, suppress the watery matter and soft insides until only the thick part remains; fry them in butter, seasoning well. Have also two green peppers cut into small strips, boil them for ten minutes in salted water, drain well, and then stew in the butter the same as the tomatoes; mix, and let stand until the chicken is dressed. The pieces of chicken being cooked, drain off all the butter and substitute a glassful of brandy and a large one of white wine, to detach the glaze from the bottom of the sauce-pan; let boil a few minutes; dress the chicken into a dish, pour the tomatoes and peppers over the chicken, gravy over all. On each end of the dish arrange a cluster of lozenge-shaped potatoes fried in clarified butter.

A. Gallier, President "Societe Culinaire de New York," and Chef of Hotel Brunswick, Fifth Avenue, New York.

TURKEY SCALLOP.

Pick the meat from the bones of a cold cooked turkey, and chop it fine; put a layer of bread-crumbs on the bottom of a buttered pudding-dish, moisten them with a little milk; then put in a layer of turkey with some of the cold dressing, and cut small pieces of butter over the top; sprinkle with pepper and salt, then another layer of bread-crumbs, and so on until the dish is nearly full; add a little hot water to the gravy left from the turkey, and pour over it; then take two eggs, two tablespoonfuls of milk, one tablespoonful of melted butter, a little salt, and cracker-crumbs enough to spread thick, with a knife, over the top of it all; put on some small bits of butter, and cover it over with a plate; bake three fourths of an hour. About ten minutes before serving, remove the plate, and let it brown.

ROAST TURKEY, WITH OYSTERS.

Clean a turkey, and lay it in a dripping-pan; prepare a dressing of stale bread, composed of one quart of bread-crumbs and one cupful of butter, and water enough to moisten; add to this two dozen oysters and pepper and salt to suit the taste; mix all, and stuff the turkey with it; put butter over the outside, put some water into the dripping-pan, set it in the oven, and bake until done, basting quite often. Never parboil a young turkey.

Mrs. Wm. Thurston, Monroe, Nebraska.

COLD TURKEY À LA GRANDE DUCHESSE.

Pick, singe and cleanse the turkey, and draw the sinews from the legs; cut off its head, and open it at the back of the neck and remove the backbone and breast-bone as far as the leg-joint, removing the entrails with the carcass; then stuff it, sew it up, and truss it for boiling. The feet should be just dipped into boiling water, and then the outer skin removed, the sinews cut off, and the toes cut short, and the lower part of the leg with the foot replaced; tie the turkey up in a well-buttered cloth, and put it to boil for one and one half to two hours, according to the size of the bird, in good stock, with vegetables, such as carrot, onion, celery and herbs (basil, marjoram, bay-leaf, thyme and parsley), a few black and white peppercorns, six or eight cloves and a blade or two of mace; let the stock come to a boil, then draw the pan to the side of the oven and let it simmer gently until cooked. Take up the turkey, remove the cloth, and let it get cold; it is best to boil the turkey the day before it is to be dished up. When cold, remove the strings, and mask the bird over with white chaudfroid sauce,

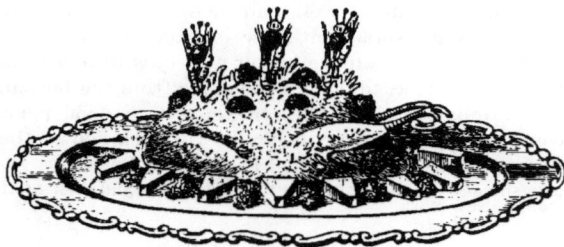

putting on two or three coatings of the sauce until it is well masked; when the sauce is somewhat set, lightly mask that over with aspic jelly which is not quite set, so as to give the surface a polish, and at once sprinkle over it some finely shredded blanched pistachio-nuts; when the aspic is set, dish up the turkey and garnish it around with ornamentally cut pieces of aspic; take three hatelet skewers, and on them place some of the prepared crayfish or cooked prawns and truffle or financiere garnish and pate de foie gras, and arrange them on the breast of the turkey, as in the engraving, also garnish the breast with truffles. This dish can be served for any cold collation, ball supper, etc. Chickens may be prepared in a similar manner.

STUFFING FOR TURKEY.

Take some bread-crumbs, and turn on just enough hot water to soften them; put in a piece of butter, not melted, the size of a hen's egg and one spoonful of pulverized sage, one teaspoonful of ground pepper and one teaspoonful of salt; then mix thoroughly, and stuff your turkey.

PLAIN STUFFING.

Take stale bread, cut off all the crust, grate very fine, and pour over it as much melted butter as will make it crumble in your hands; season with salt and pepper to suit the taste.

ROAST DUCK.

Prepare your duck for roasting, and use the following stuffing:
Chop fine and throw into cold water

3 good-sized onions. Take   A little salt and pepper.
1 large spoonful of sage,   A piece of butter the size of a walnut.
2 tablespoonfuls of bread-crumbs, Add the onions, drained.

Mix well, and stuff the duck; if an ordinary-sized duck, bake one hour.

DUCK À LA PROVENÇALE.

Take a picked, singed and boned duck, turn it inside out, and season it with salt, pepper, lemon-juice, finely chopped shallot, chopped Spanish olive, chopped parsley, thyme, bay-leaf, and lean cooked tongue or ham. Prepare a farce, as below, and fill up the inside of the duck; then roll it up in the form of a gelatin, tie on it a piece of fat raw bacon, slitted here and there, and tie it up in a strong cloth, so as to keep the shape as nice as possible; put into a stew-pan two or three sliced onions, a few slices of carrot, turnip, celery, fresh mushroom, a good bunch of herbs, one pint of cooking white wine, the juice of two lemons, one teaspoonful of black and white peppercorns, six or eight cloves, two blades of mace, a few bacon-bones, and enough good light stock to cover;

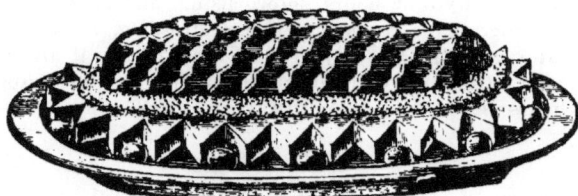

simmer gently for about one hour, then take up and retie the bird, and leave it in press in the stock until cold; then take up, remove the cloth, etc., and mask over with brown chaudfroid; garnish with hard-boiled white of egg, French chillies and gherkins; set this garnish with a little more aspic jelly, then dish up the bird, garnishing with blocks of aspic cream and aspic jelly and Spanish olives; serve for dinner or luncheon with iced orange sauce in a boat.

FARCE FOR DUCK A LA PROVENÇALE.—Take one half pound of cooked chicken, one half pound of cooked pheasant or other game, and pound both together, with six ounces of cooked tongue or ham and four yolks of hard-boiled eggs; rub through a wire sieve, then add one wine-glassful of sherry, mix with six ounces of freshly made white bread-crumbs, a good pinch of salt and pepper, two finely chopped shallots, one teaspoonful of chopped truffle, the same of tongue and three whole raw eggs; mix well, then use.

APPLE STUFFING.

Take one pint of tart apple sauce, and mix with it one small cupful of bread-crumbs, a little powdered sage, one small onion sliced fine, and season with cayenne pepper. This is used for roast goose, duck and game.

WILD DUCKS.

Nearly all wild ducks are liable to have a fishy flavor, and when handled by inexperienced cooks, are sometimes uneatable from this cause. Before roasting them, guard against this by parboiling them with a small peeled carrot put within each. This will absorb the unpleasant taste. An onion will have the same effect; but unless you mean to use onion in the stuffing, the carrot is preferable. In my own kitchen, I usually put in the onion, considering a suspicion of garlic a desideratum in roast duck, whether wild or tame.

ROAST WILD DUCK.

Parboil according to directions for preparing wild duck; throw away the carrot or onion, lay in fresh water half an hour; stuff with bread-crumbs seasoned with pepper, salt, sage and onion, and roast until brown and tender, basting for half the time with butter and water, then with the drippings; add to the gravy, when you have taken up the ducks, a teaspoonful of currant jelly and a pinch of cayenne; thicken with browned flour, and serve in a tureen.

ROAST GOOSE.

Dress the fowl twenty-four hours before using, and soak in salt-water two hours before cooking; make a mashed-potato dressing, seasoned with onion, butter, pepper and salt; fill the body of the goose, grease it all over well with butter, and dredge with flour; place in a pan, with a pint of water; baste well, and cook two hours; serve with onion gravy and apple sauce.

BOILED GOOSE.

Soak over night in sweet milk; in the morning, wash, and allow it to stand in cold water one hour; fill the body with well-seasoned bread-dressing, using salt, pepper, onions and sage. Tie up in a thin cheese-cloth; boil two hours; serve with giblet sauce and gooseberry jam.

PIGEON PIE.

Clean and truss three or four pigeons, rub the outsides and insides with a mixture of pepper and salt; rub the insides with a bit of butter, and fill them with a bread-and-butter stuffing or mashed potatoes; sew up the slit, butter the sides of a tin basin or pudding-dish, and line (the sides only) with pie paste rolled to one fourth of an inch in thickness; lay the birds in; for three large tame pigeons, cut one fourth of a pound of sweet butter, and put it over them; strew over a large teaspoonful of salt and a small teaspoonful of pepper, with a bunch of finely cut parsley, if liked; dredge one large tablespoonful of wheat flour over, put in water to nearly fill the pie; lay skewers across the top, cover with a puff-paste crust; cut a slit in the middle, ornament the edge with leaves, braids or shells of paste, and put it in a moderately hot or quick oven for one hour; when nearly done, brush the top over with the yolk of an egg beaten with a little milk, and finish. The pigeons for this pie may be cut in two or more pieces, if preferred. Any small birds may be done in this manner.

ROAST PIGEON.

When clean and ready for roasting, fill the bird with a stuffing of bread-crumbs, one spoonful of butter, a little salt and nutmeg, and three oysters to each bird (some prefer chopped apple). They must be well basted with melted butter, and require thirty minutes' careful cooking.

CUTLETS OF PIGEON À LA PIÉMONTAISE.

Pick and singe the pigeons, and bone them with the exception of the leg, and cut each bird in two, so that the meat attached to each leg will form a cutlet; scald the feet, cut off the nails, peel off the outer skin; season the cutlets with black pepper and salt, a little chopped shallot, parsley and lean cooked ham or tongue, and put them into a buttered saute-pan, with the skin side uppermost; saute them for about two minutes, then place them in the oven for four or five minutes; remove them, and put them to press, and when the cutlets are cold, trim them neatly and mask them over lightly with veal or beef farce; smooth the farce over with a hot, wet knife, so that each leg takes a nice cutlet

shape; dip them into well-beaten whole egg, and then into freshly made bread-crumbs; bat the crumbs with a knife until they are all smooth; place the cutlets in a saute-pan, with about two ounces of clarified butter, and fry until a nice golden color. Dish up on a border of potato, and serve with a puree of mush-rooms in the center, and espagnol sauce, in which the bones of the bird have been used for flavor, around the base. A cutlet frill, if liked, may be placed on each foot, and the cutlets can be fried in lard or oil if more convenient. Serve as an entree for dinner or luncheon while quite hot. Other birds can be used in the same way.

CHESTNUT DRESSING.

Shell the nuts first, then pour on boiling water to scald them a few moments; then remove the brown skin, or covering, which is called blanching, and put them to boil in lukewarm water; let them cook until soft, and mash them; mix with a little sweet cream, bread-crumbs, pepper and salt. This is used for turkeys.

POTATO STUFFING.

Take one third of bread-crumbs, two thirds of mashed potatoes, butter the size of an egg, salt and pepper, one egg and one half teaspoonful of ground sage; mix thoroughly, and fill the fowl.

4

BROILED QUAIL.

Remove the feathers without scalding, and dress the quails carefully; then soak a short time in salt-water, split down the back, dry with a cloth, and rub them over with butter, and place on the gridiron over a clear fire; turn frequently, and put bits of butter over them; when taken up, season with salt. Prepare a slice of thin toast, nicely buttered and laid on a hot dish, for each bird, and lay a bird, breast upward, on each slice; garnish with currant jelly.

QUAILS À LA TOSCA.

Pick, singe and bone some quails, leaving half the leg-bone in the bottom part of the leg with the foot on; season them with finely chopped fresh mushrooms, shallots, parsley and a little salt and coralline pepper; put them into a buttered saute-pan, saute them for two or three minutes, and put them to press until cold; then mask them over with the sauce prepared as below, sprinkle with fine flour, dip them into whole beaten egg and freshly made white bread-

crumbs; repeat this twice, batting them with a palette-knife to keep them quite smooth, then fry in clean boiling fat until a pretty golden color; when cooked, dish up on a border of potato, in the center of which place a crouton of fried bread that is scooped out and filled with a puree of fresh mushrooms; garnish with prepared financiere, as in engraving, fixing it with a hatelet skewer, which will give a pretty finish to the dish, and serve with champagne sauce.

SAUCE FOR MASKING QUAILS A LA TOSCA.—Take half a pint of hot, thick bechamel sauce and mix with it three raw yolks of eggs; stir this over the fire until it thickens, then tammy, and add one tablespoonful of finely chopped cooked ham or tongue, two yolks of hard-boiled eggs that have been rubbed through a wire sieve and one dessert-spoonful of finely chopped parsley; mix all, and use as described above.

ROAST QUAIL.

Pluck and draw the birds, rub a little butter over them, tie a strip of bacon over the breasts, and set them in the oven for twenty or twenty-five minutes.

QUAILS À LA LESSEPS.

Cailles à la Lesseps.

Take some boned quails with the feet left on, and place inside of each bird one peeled, dried, raw potato, cut about two and one half inches long by one and one half inches wide, and form into cylinder shapes; dry these with a cloth, and rub them well with butter; fasten up the birds in little bands of buttered paper, place them in a buttered saute-pan, with one half wine-glassful of sherry, and put into the oven for about fifteen minutes; when done, take up, and set aside until cold, then remove the papers and the potatoes, and by means of a forcing-bag and a plain pipe fill the birds with a ragout, as below; put them in a cool place until the ragout is perfectly set, then cut the birds into halves with a wet, warm knife, and mask each with brown chaudfroid sauce; when well coated, mask lightly with a little liquid aspic jelly, and dish up around a timbal of clear ice prepared as below. Arrange between each half bird a little finely

chopped aspic, and garnish the top of the birds with a little pate de foie gras that has been passed through a wire sieve, using a forcing-bag and a large rose-pipe for the purpose; garnish the dish here and there with little sprigs of picked chervil and tarragon, and when about to serve, put a lighted night-light in the center of the ice timbal, and serve at once.

RAGOUT FOR FILLING THE QUAILS À LA LESSEPS.—To four quails take one half breast of a cooked chicken cut into small pieces, six button mushrooms, two or three truffles and two ounces of foie gras; mix these with the sauce prepared as below; leave until nearly set, then use.

SAUCE FOR RAGOUT FOR QUAILS À LA LESSEPS.—Put a dessert-spoonful of extract of beef into a stew-pan, with one fourth pint of tomato sauce, one wine-glassful of sherry and one half pint of aspic jelly; reduce to one half the quantity, keep skimming while boiling, then tammy, and use.

ICE TIMBAL FOR QUAILS À LA LESSEPS.—Set a plain timbal-mold that is filled with cold water in the charged ice-cave for two and one half to three hours; when frozen, dip into cold water, turn out the ice, and put it in the center of the dish on which the quails are to be served, first placing between the timbal and the dish a little wadding.

POTTED QUAIL.

Singe, draw and wash quickly six fine, fat quails, season them with one scant even tablespoonful of salt, evenly distributed. Fry in a saucepan one half cupful of finely cut larding-pork light brown, add two ounces of butter and the quail; let them cook until they have obtained a light brown color all over, then add one cupful of boiling water; continue cooking until done, which will take about an hour. Place the giblets in a saucepan, cover with cold water, add a little salt, one onion, boil until tender, then chop them fine. Shortly before serving, toast six pieces of baker's bread, then butter them, lay on a hot dish, place one quail on each piece of toast. Mix one half tablespoonful of corn-starch with one fourth cupful of cold water, stir it in the gravy, cook two minutes on top of the stove, add some of the giblet-water to make a creamy sauce; strain the gravy, add the giblets, pour a little over each one, and serve the rest separately. Decorate the dish with water-cress.

Mrs. Gesine Lemcke, Principal German-American Cooking College, Brooklyn, N. Y.

SALMIS OF QUAILS À L'EMPRESS.

Salmis de Cailles à l'Empress.

Take some roast or braised quails, cut them into halves, dust over with sifted fine flour, and place them in a saute-pan, cover them with sauce prepared as below, and boil them in it for ten to fifteen minutes; then dish them up on

a border of potato, garnish the center of the dish with potato puree, braised olives and French red chillies; pour the sauce around the dish, and serve at once for an entree for dinner or luncheon while quite hot.

SAUCE FOR SALMIS OF QUAILS A L'EMPRESS.—Take two washed fresh mushrooms, one ounce of cut-up lean bacon, two large sliced onions, a bunch of herbs, one ounce of butter and two fresh tomatoes; fry these for twenty minutes; then add to the pan one ounce of good glaze, a wine-glassful of sherry, the juice of a lemon, a few drops of carmine, one and one half pints of brown sauce, a dust of pepper and two chopped French gherkins; boil with any bird-bones, such as pheasant, etc., for twenty to thirty minutes, keeping well skimmed while cooking; then rub through the tammy, reboil, and use.

PEAFOWLS.

Many farmers have these in plenty, and use them the same as turkeys. Any recipe for turkeys will do for these, and they are very delicious,

ROAST PARTRIDGE.

Choose young birds, with dark-colored bills and yellowish legs, and let them hang a few days, or there will be no flavor to the flesh, nor will it be tender. The time they should be kept depends entirely on the taste of those for whom they are intended, as what some persons would consider delicious would be to others disgusting and offensive. They may be trussed with or without the head, the latter mode being now considered the most fashionable. Pluck, draw and wipe the partridge carefully inside and out; cut off the head, leaving sufficient skin on the neck to skewer back; bring the legs close to the breast, between it and the side bones, and pass a skewer through the pinions and thick part of the thighs. When the head is left on, it should be brought around and fixed onto the point of the skewer. When the bird is firmly and plumply trussed, roast it before a nice, bright fire; keep it well basted, and a few minutes before serving, flour and froth it well, dish it, and serve with gravy and bread sauce, and send to the table hot, and quickly; a little of the gravy should be poured over the bird.

SUPRÊME OF PHEASANT À LA ST. HUBERT.

Suprême de Faisan à la St. Hubert.

Take a nice cleansed pheasant, remove the breast fillets from it, and cut them into as many nice long pieces as possible, not quite one fourth of an inch thick; bat them out with a cold, wet knife, and season with a little pepper and

salt, finely chopped parsley and shallot and two tablespoonfuls of good game stock; place them in a buttered saute-pan, with a buttered paper over, and cook in a moderate oven for about eight minutes. Mask the supremes over with a little tomato puree; dish up on a border of farce or potato, and between each piece of the meat place a little quenelle that is prepared of pheasant and poached in small quenelle-tins. Serve with a compote of French plums in the center, and Hubert sauce (see recipe) around the dish, and use for an entree for dinner or luncheon.

QUENELLES FOR SUPRÊME OF PHEASANT A LA ST. HUBERT.—Take five ounces of raw pheasant, pound it until smooth, then pound four ounces of panard, one half ounce of butter, two whole raw eggs, a little salt and pepper; mix all, and then rub through a fine wire sieve; mix with one dessert-spoonful of cream a few drops of carmine, and put into quenelle-molds slightly buttered and masked with chopped truffle, poach for twelve to fifteen minutes, then turn out on a cloth, and use.

BEIGNETS OF PHEASANT À LA DOMINIQUE.

Beignets de Faisan à la Dominique.

Prepare a purée of pheasant, and form it into ball shapes about the size of a walnut, rolling each with a little flour to prevent it sticking; make a little well inside the ball by pressing the finger inside it, and place inside the well a little piece of good set glaze about the size of a small Spanish nut, and a piece of truffle or cooked button mushroom about the same size as the glaze; roll up again into balls, and by means of a forcing-bag and small, plain pipe cover the balls over with profite-role paste (omitting the cheese), and after covering them with the paste, roll them again with a little flour and drop them into clean hot fat, and fry them over a quick fire for eight or ten minutes, during which time keep them constantly turned over and over; they should be a pretty golden color when cooked. Then take up on a pastry-rack and drain them; brush them over very lightly with raw white of egg that has been just mixed up with a fork, and sprinkle on the top of each beignet alternately a little finely chopped lean cooked

ham or tongue and a little finely chopped truffle or parsley. Dish up in a pile on a hot dish on a dish-paper, and serve for an entree for dinner or luncheon.

Purée for Beignets of Pheasant a la Dominique.—For twelve beignets take three fourths of a pound of cold cooked pheasant, pound it until quite smooth, and mix with it two large tablespoonfuls of thick bechamel sauce, one ounce of good butter, a pinch of salt and a slight dust of cayenne pepper; when mixed into a perfectly smooth paste, rub it all through a fine wire sieve, and use as directed.

PHEASANT PIE À LA FRANCAISE.

Take a square fleur-mold, butter it inside, and place it on a baking-tin on a double fold of foolscap paper that is buttered; then line the mold about one fourth of an inch thick with short paste, pressing the paste well into the shape of the tin. Take a picked, singed, cleaned and boned pheasant, cut it up into neat joints, lay these open and season them with a little mignonette pepper, a very little salt, and washed and chopped fresh mushroom, a little shallot, thyme, bay-leaf, parsley and the livers of the pheasants finely chopped; place a little piece of pate de foie gras about the size of a Spanish nut in each piece of pheasant, and then roll up the pieces in cylinder shapes, and place these pieces one on the other in the pie until it is full; wet the edges of the paste, and roll out some

more paste about half the thickness of that used for the lining of the mold, cover
the pie over, and trim the edges; roll out the remainder of the paste perfectly
thin like a wafer, and stamp it out in rounds about one and one half inches in
diameter, and by means of a knife work out the rounds of paste in the form of
small shells. Wet the top of the pie paste over with a little cold water, using a
paste-brush for the purpose, and then place the little shells on the top until it
• is quite covered; make a little hole in the center of the top, so as to be able to
fill the pie with gravy when cold; place a band of buttered paper around, so as
to stand about three inches above the pie, and put it into a moderate oven, and
bake for one and one half to two hours; during the baking keep the top of the
pie covered over with a wetted paper to prevent the paste getting browned, as
it should be a pretty fawn color when cooked. Put it away until cold, then fill
up with gravy made from the bones, as below, and then remove the tin from it;
place the pie on a dish-paper, and garnish it around with nice blocks of cut aspic
jelly, and serve for any cold collation, such as for supper, luncheon, race
meetings, etc.

GRAVY FOR FILLING UP PHEASANT PIE.—Take the bones of the birds, chop
them up finely, and put them into a stew-pan, with one ounce of butter, a sliced
lemon, two bay-leaves, a sprig of thyme and parsley, a sprig of marjoram and
a pinch of mignonette pepper; put the cover on the pan, and fry the contents for
about fifteen minutes, giving the pan an occasional shake while frying; then
add about one quart of good stock, and let it simmer gently on the side of the
stove for about three fourths of an hour; strain, and remove the fat, and dissolve
in the liquor one fourth of an ounce of gelatin, and use when cooling, and when
about the consistency of cream.

LARKS À LA SOTTERVILLE.

Mauriettes à la Sotterville.

Take some singed and cleaned larks, bone them, but leave the feet and bottom part of the legs on; then by means of a forcing-bag and plain pipe farce
each bird with a puree prepared as below; form them into neat shapes, wrap
each bird in a band of buttered foolscap paper, tie them up with thin string, put
them into a tin, with a little warm butter, and bake for about fifteen minutes,
during which time keep them well basted; set them aside until cold, then mask
with fawn-colored chaudfroid sauce (see recipe), and when this is set, mask all

over with aspic jelly; when quite cold, trim them, and dish up on a border of aspic cream, as below, standing them against a crouton of fried bread; then by means of a forcing-bag and pipe garnish between the larks with finely chopped aspic cream; arrange here and there some financiere garnish that has been masked with aspic jelly, and also some finely shredded cut truffles. Arrange just above the larks the heads of the birds prepared as follows: Cleanse the heads, roll them up in buttered paper, and cook them in a moderate oven for five minutes; set aside until cold, and brush each over with warm glaze or cool aspic jelly; cut out with a pea-cutter some little rounds of hard-boiled white of egg to fit the birds' eyes, place these in the spaces, and in the center of these put a smaller round of red chilli, then mask with aspic jelly.

FARCE FOR LARKS À LA SOTTERVILLE.—To twelve birds take six ounces of cooked pheasant or chicken, six raw bearded oysters and their liquor, two ounces of pate de foie gras, two tablespoonfuls of good brown sauce, one teaspoonful of warm glaze, two ounces of panard and two raw yolks of eggs; pound

until smooth, season with a dust of pepper and a little salt, rub through a wire sieve, mix with two or three French red chillies that have been freed from seeds, and cut into little square pieces, put into a forcing-bag with a plain pipe, and use.

ASPIC CREAM FOR BORDER FOR LARKS À LA SOTTERVILLE.—Take one quart of aspic jelly, one pint of thick cream and one half ounce of gelatin; dissolve, tammy, and when cooling, fill a border-mold with it; let it remain until set, then dip into hot water, and turn out; set any of the remains of the cream aside until quite cold, for chopping up.

LARKS À LA REYNIÈRE.
Mauviettes à la Reynière.

Take some boned larks, and farce them with a little pate de foie gras, then put each into a small band of buttered paper, and tie them up; butter a stewpan, and put into it one or two slices each of carrot, onion, turnip, leek and celery, a bunch of herbs, such as thyme, parsley and bay-leaf, and a few peppercorns; place the larks upon these vegetables, put a buttered paper over them, and fry for about five minutes; add one fourth of a pint of stock, place the pan in the oven for ten minutes, then take up the larks, and remove the paper;

butter some little molds, sprinkle them with chopped truffle, then line them with beef farce, using a forcing-bag and pipe for the purpose; make a well in the center of each with the finger, which should be dipped into hot water occasionally, place a lark in the space thus formed, and cover with more farce; place

a piece of paper in the bottom of a stew-pan, upon which set the molds; pour in boiling water until it reaches three fourths the depth of the molds, watch it reboil, then draw the pan to the side of the stove, and poach for about fifteen minutes; turn out of the molds onto a border of farce, pour the sauce over them, place the prepared heads and feet of the larks on the top of the portions, as in engraving, and serve as an entree for dinner. To cook the heads and feet of birds, cleanse them, put into a buttered paper, and bake in the oven for ten to twelve minutes; just before serving, brush over with a little warm glaze.

LARKS IN BASKETS.

Farce some boned larks with beef farce prepared as in recipe "Little Creams of Beef;" make a well inside each with the finger, occasionally dipping the latter into hot water; place inside the spaces thus formed a little slice of blanched beef-marrow that is masked over with a little finely chopped parsley,

close the farce well over this, and place the larks in little bands of buttered paper, and put them into a saute-pan between two pieces of fat bacon to cook for about fifteen minutes; then remove the paper, and place the larks in little short paste-cases (see recipe "Little Croustades of Calf's Brains"), and add a little sauce sufficient to reach to the top of the breast; then with a forcing-bag and pipe cover the bird entirely with some of the beef farce, smooth it over with a wet, warm knife, and ornament the edges of the basket with a little white farce in the shape of peas, using a bag and small pipe for the purpose; place the cases in a moderate oven, with a buttered paper over, and cook for about fifteen minutes. Have the heads and feet cleansed and cooked as for "Larks à la Reyniere," and put on top of the farce, and garnish with handles of paste made with the remains of the paste used for the baskets; then dish up on a paper, one to each person, and serve. These can also be served cold.

SAUCE FOR LARKS IN BASKETS.—Put into a stew-pan the bones from the birds, one half pint of good brown sauce, with one half ounce of glaze, one wine-glassful of sherry, one fourth of a pint of tomato sauce and a pinch of castor-sugar; boil down for about fifteen minutes; keep skimmed while boiling, then tammy, and use.

CROUSTADE OF GAME À LA NORMANDE.

Croustade de Gibier à la Normande.

Prepare one half pound of short paste, and line a buttered mold with it about one eighth of an inch thick; trim the edges of the paste neatly, then line it with

buttered paper, and fill the inside with raw rice or any other dry grain, put into a moderate oven for twenty-five to thirty minutes; remove the paper and rice, return the croustade to the oven, and let it dry well on the inside; when ready to serve, remove the pegs which fasten the mold, take the latter off the croustade, dish up, and fill the center with a ragout made from any kind of cold game (or poultry can be used if liked), adding to one half pound of game one or two truffles, if you have them, cut into slices, four or five cooked button mushrooms, and a little financiere may be used; mix these ingredients into a good, thick salmis sauce, make hot in the bain-marie, and then fill the croustade; garnish the edge of this with a puree of game or poultry livers and little fancy rings of of paste, then arrange some savory custard (see recipe) on the top in the form of an inner ring, and serve hot, with a little of the sauce around the base of the dish, and a little of the liver puree, with a few of the paste-rings at each end.

LITTLE CROUSTADES OF GAME À LA BRISTOL.

Petites Croustades de Gibier à la Bristol.

Line some little fluted molds very thinly with short paste about one eighth of an inch thick, pressing it well into the shape of the molds, trim off the edges neatly, and line the insides with buttered paper; fill the papers with raw rice, and bake in a moderate oven for about forty minutes; when done, remove the rice and the paper from the paste-cases, and put the latter back into the oven to dry, and when ready to use, brush over the outsides very lightly with raw white of egg that has been mixed with a fork, using as little as possible; then sprinkle the cases with finely chopped parsley, fill them with a ragout of game, and arrange on the top of the ragout by means of a forcing-bag and rose-pipe a little liver farce, then place around the edges of the croustades little rings made from the short paste and masked in the same way as the cases; place the cases upon a hot dish on a dish-paper, and serve. Use as an entree for dinner or luncheon.

RAGOUT FOR CROUSTADES A LA BRISTOL.—Take about one half pound of any remains of cold cooked game or poultry, remove the bones and skin, and cut the meat into dice; mix it with two or three cooked button mushrooms, and then mix these into reduced salmis sauce; make hot in the bain-marie, and use.

COLD GAME PIE À LA CLEVELAND.

Take one pound of raw veal, put into two parts; cut one part of it into small slices about three inches long and one half inch thick. Take a pound of fresh loin of pork, proceed the same as you did before; cut half of it into thin slices; put both veal and pork which you cut up into a bowl. Take a thin slice of cooked lamb, cut into five or six equal parts lengthwise. Take one partridge, bone it, and take all the nerves out of it; put ham and partridge into the bowl with the rest. Cook one half glassful of dry white wine in a small saucepan, with a chopped shallot, one bay-leaf, a little thyme, a few slices of onion, one half handful of whole black pepper. After having let this boil for a few minutes, strain through a sieve on your meats in the bowl, put a little salt over it. Take half a pound of fat larding-pork, take off the skin, add to the other half of your veal and pork, pass twice through a chopping-machine. This will make the forcemeat to put into your pie.

PASTE FOR PIE.—Soak one pound of flour with one fourth pound of butter, one and one half glassfuls of cold water; mix everything well. This paste must be hard, but not stringy; let it rest for two hours.

The mold used for this pie is oval, and opens on the sides with hinges; it has no bottom. Put this mold on a roast or pastry pan which you have well buttered. Have a piece of paste to fit in your mold about one fourth of an inch thick; that means to have the bottom and the sides all garnished with the paste; fill the bottom with a thin layer of forcemeat you have ready; cut four truffles into thick slices; put your partridge meat on top of those; cover all this again with forcemeat, and continue putting your veal, pork and forcemeat in until the mold is filled; over all this put a few large slices of larding-pork, to prevent the pie from drying up; put again over the latter a thin cover of paste. To make this cover stick to the rim of the other paste, which must surpass the mold a little, you must wet the edge of the cover. Make a sort of bordure around the pie, and decorate the top with a few leaves, which you cut out of paste; make a hole in the center of the pie, and put a kind of chimney made of thick paper in that hole; when you see the juice boil out of that chimney, the pie is cooked. A six-pound pie takes two and one half hours to cook; to prevent burning, put a few sheets of paper, which you have soaked in butter, all around on top of the pie before putting it into the oven; when cooked, take out of the oven and let it cool off; when cold, fill the hole in the center with good melted meat jelly. These pies are choice cold dishes. They can be made with every kind of game, such as grouse, ducks, etc. They are generally served after entrees, always before the roast; are equal to foie gras, and are served with great advantage at receptions, dinners and suppers.

Paul Resal, Chef of White House (Executive Mansion), Washington, D. C.

FOIE GRAS À LA CHATEAU DORÉ.

Take an opened tin of foie gras, and stand it in the bain-marie until the contents are quite hot; then, when ready to serve, turn it out onto a plate, and

cut it into portions, and dish it up, as in engraving, on a border of chicken or rabbit farce, with a small round of fried bread in the center; garnish the foie gras with financiere that has been warmed in the bain-marie, and with hatelet skewers; pour good espagnol sauce around the dish, then place some cooked button mushrooms at each end of the dish, and serve hot as an entree for a dinner party.

RABBIT STEW.

Take a couple of rabbits, and divide them into quarters, flour them, and fry in butter; then put them into a stew-pan, with some good gravy; season with pepper, salt and a sprig of sweet herbs; cover them close, and let them stew until tender; then take the rabbit out in a deep dish, thicken the gravy with flour and butter, pour over the rabbit.

CREAM OF RABBIT A LA DUXELLE.

Crème de Lapereau à la Duxelle.

Take a rabbit-mold, lay it open, and place it upon crushed ice in a basin; line both sides with aspic jelly about one eighth of an inch thick, and when this is set, line them again with fawn-colored chaudfroid sauce (see recipe); let this set, then fill the two parts of the mold with a puree of rabbit, as below, keeping the mold in motion while adding this, so that the mixture becomes well embedded. Take the contents of a small jar of pate de foie gras, and with a hot, wet knife cut it through into two pieces; place one piece in the center of the puree in each side, then partly close the mold, and pour into it the remaining part of the

rabbit puree, which must be in a semi-liquid state, so as to join all the contents together; close the mold firmly with the pegs, put it into some ice, and leave it for about thirty minutes, when it will be set; when ready to serve, dip the mold into hot water, and turn out the rabbit, put in two glass eyes, dish it on a bed of finely chopped aspic jelly, and garnish it, as in engraving, with little timbals, as below, cooked halves of artichoke bottoms that are seasoned with a little salad-oil, tarragon vinegar, chervil and tarragon, and serve for an entree or any cold collation.

PUREE FOR CREAM OF RABBIT A LA DUXELLE.—Pound until smooth one pound of cooked rabbit, two tablespoonfuls of good veloute sauce, one ounce of fresh butter, two tablespoonfuls of thick cream, one wine-glassful of sherry, one tablespoonful of brown sauce, a dust of pepper and a little salt; then mix with one pint of good-flavored stock in which one ounce of gelatin has been dissolved; rub the puree through a tammy or fine hair-sieve; use when it is becoming set.

TIMBALS FOR GARNISH FOR CREAM OF RABBIT A LA DUXELLE.—Line some fluted dariol-molds with plain aspic jelly, and when this is set, fill them with raw, ripe tomato that has been freed from seeds and skin and cut into tiny dice, then mix with a little cut tarragon and chervil, and set with a little red-colored aspic prepared by adding a little carmine to ordinary aspic.

BLIND HARE.

3 pounds of veal, minced fine,
1 pound of ham, with lightly beaten eggs,
2 pounds of minced beef,
1 pint of stale bread-crumbs,

1 tablespoonful of cinnamon,
2 grated nutmegs,
1 teaspoonful of salt,
½ teaspoonful of pepper.

Mix all, form it into an oval-shaped loaf, sprinkle with grated bread-crumbs, put it into the oven, and bake three hours.

FILLETS OF HARE (LARDED) AND ROAST LARKS.

Remove the back fillets from the hare, free them from the fine skin, lard them with lardons of fat bacon, trim the lardons evenly with a pair of scissors, steep the fillets in warm butter, put them on a well-buttered tin, and bake them in a quick oven for about fifteen minutes, keeping them well basted while cooking; then take up, cut them into nice escallops somewhat slanting, but keep them in their natural form as nearly as possible, brush them over with a little warm glaze; dish up on croutons of fried bread on a hot dish; garnish around with roast larks (allowing one to each person) that have been cooked in the same manner as the hare, each arranged on a crouton and brushed over with a

little warm glaze; garnish the dish with water-cress that has been picked, well washed and dried, seasoned with tarragon and chilli vinegar, a little salad-oil, finely chopped shallot, a little mignonette pepper and a little salt; serve with browned bread-crumbs and courte sauce in sauce-boats for second course or luncheon. In serving this dish, one fillet of hare and one lark and a portion of the cress should be helped to each guest.

RABBIT FRICASSEE.

Skin and clean carefully; open down the breast, let it lie a couple of hours in a pan of cold water; wipe dry, and place in a meat-pan; season well with salt and pepper, a generous lump of butter and a dredge of flour; pour in enough hot water to keep from burning; bake half an hour, and baste occasionally.

BROILED SQUIRREL.

Skin your squirrels, and lay them in salt-water to remove the blood; remove the head and feet and broil whole; season with salt, pepper and butter; serve with currant jam or grape jelly.

Meats.

CHAPTER VII.

Meat, when used for soup, should be put on to cook in cold water; also any salted meat, like ham or corned beef; but where it is intended to be used as boiled meat, it should be put on in boiling-hot water, so as to harden the fibrine and confine the juices of the meat. The meat should in all cases be kept under the water. Turn it frequently, so it may cook on all sides. It should boil only gently. A pod of red pepper added to the pot will keep the odor of boiling from filling the house. Remove all scum as it rises; allow twenty minutes to a pound.

In roasting meat in the oven, it should be frequently basted; this is done by dipping the water or juices in the roasting-pan over the meat with a large spoon.

The fire should not be allowed to get low before replenishing, as it checks the heat; try to keep the fire at a steady heat.

In broiling meat, the gridiron should be very hot before putting on the meat; as soon as it sears or scorches, turn over.

Do not salt your meat until nearly done, as it extracts the juices.

To thaw out frozen meats, lay them in cold water, which should be done only shortly before using.

After slicing from a ham, rub the cut side with corn-meal, as this prevents the ham from becoming rancid, and rubs off easily when needed again.

In cooking tough meat or an old fowl, add a pinch of soda to the water to make it tender.

If you have not tripods to lay in your roasting-pan to keep the meat up out of the juices, lay across the pan some clean pieces of wood.

Veal, mutton and pork will keep perfectly fresh and good for weeks without salt or ice, in warm weather, by keeping it submerged in sour milk, changing the milk when mold appears; rinse in cold water when wanted for use.

111

For curing hams, trim nice and smooth when thoroughly cold after killing; pack in salt and let them remain for five or six weeks, then take them up and dip them into boiling brine; then rub the flesh side with pulverized black pepper as long as it will stick; hang in a dry place.

To keep hams that have been smoked, rub the flesh part with molasses, then sprinkle with as much black pepper as will stick to the molasses; hang them up and keep dry.

To prevent meats from scorching, keep a panful of water sitting in the oven; the steam arising also tends to make the meat tender.

Always save all drippings from roasted or fried meats to use for frying potatoes; also allow the water from boiling meat to stand until the next day, and remove the fat from the top to your dripping-jar; never allow any burned grease of any kind to be put into this jar.

In broiling meat over coals, never allow them to smoke the least; after the coals have burnt down somewhat, throw on a handful of salt to deaden the blue flame that arises. If the dripping from your meat takes fire, remove from the stove to cool for a few moments; don't try to blow it out, as there is danger of burning the face.

Have a tin cover made at your tinner's to fit into your dripping-pan to cover over your meats and poultry while cooking, as they are so much nicer cooked in this way. It should be high, and just the shape of the pan it is to cover.

Nice lard can be made from leaf-lard, and many housekeepers prefer it; procure it at the butcher's, and fry it out yourself; a teacupful of water added will keep it from burning.

To preserve sausages, cut and roll them in small, thin cakes, and fry them until well done; pack closely in jars, and cover with melted lard one inch thick; set away in a cool place, and you will have nice, sweet sausage all spring and summer.

To sweeten salt pork, cut as many slices as you will require for breakfast, and soak till morning in sweet milk and water, then rinse until the water is clear, and fry.

A beefsteak can be well cooked in hot suet, and after taking out the steak, stir a spoonful of flour in the pan, pour in hot water and let it boil, and you have a nice gravy.

Rub flour and butter together, and brown in a skillet; then put the meat gravy with it, and you have a nice gravy.

TENDERLOIN OF BEEF (WEST HOTEL STYLE).

Cut out of a good tenderloin of beef six steaks one inch thick, and season with pepper and salt; broil them on a good charcoal fire for six minutes (three minutes on each side). Broil six large, fresh mushrooms, seasoned with salt, pepper, ground thyme and ground sage. Cut out of three large tomatoes six slices as thick as possible, fry them in butter. Make a good bearnaise sauce; put the bearnaise sauce on a hot platter, put the fried tomatoes on top of the sauce, and the tenderloin on top of the tomatoes, then the mushrooms on top of the tenderloin; pour over the mushrooms a good brown gravy; finish with a glassful of champagne, and add a tablespoonful of chopped parsley.

A. J. Pillauet, Chef West Hotel, Minneapolis, Minnesota.

HAMBURGH STEAK.

Chop one pound of beef with a little garlic and one onion, season with salt and pepper, form into small cakes in the shape of codfish balls, flour them and fry them medium done; serve with brown sauce.

Eugene Stuyvesant Howard, Member of the Universal Cookery and Food Association, London, England, and Chef de Cuisine, Louisville Hotel.

RAW HAMBURGH STEAK, OR STEAK À LA TARTARE.

Chop one pound of lean beef, season with salt and pepper, make into small cakes with a cavity in the center, into which put a yolk of one egg without breaking it; serve with chopped onions on one side of the dish and capers on the other.

Eugene Stuyvesant Howard, Chef de Cuisine, Louisville Hotel.

SIRLOIN OF BEEF À LA POMPADOUR.

Aloyau de Boeuf à la Pompadour.

Take a piece of well-hung sirloin of beef, trim it neatly, remove all the unnecessary fat, and skin the top side half the depth of the meat, then lard the skinned part with lardons of fat bacon in four or five rows, according to the size

of the sirloin, tie it up to keep it in a nice form, put into a well-buttered braising-pan, and braise with vegetables, thus: Season the beef with pepper and salt, put into the stew-pan two ounces of butter, one large sliced carrot, two or three sliced onions, a few slices of turnip and celery, herbs, such as thyme, bay-leaf, parsley, marjoram, basil, four or five cloves, one blade of mace, six black peppercorns; put the meat on top. When cooked, take up, and brush over with a little warm glaze, remove the string, and place the beef on a hot dish; garnish around with turnip cups (see recipe) and bunches of cooked carrots and turnips; pour the sauce around the dish, and serve for a remove for dinner or luncheon.

SAUCE FOR SIRLOIN OF BEEF A LA POMPADOUR.—Take the gravy from the braise, remove all the fat, and mix with the gravy two ounces of tomato pulp that has been mixed with two ounces of butter and one and one half ounces of arrow-root; stir all together until it boils, color with a few drops of carmine, flavor with a wine-glassful of sherry and a pinch of pepper.

CARROTS AND TURNIPS FOR SIRLOIN OF BEEF A LA POMPADOUR.—Take some peeled and cleansed carrots and turnips, and cut them out with a plain round vegetable-scoop; put them separately into cold water, bring to a boil, then strain and rinse them, and braise them in stock until tender.

FILLET OF BEEF À LA GODARD (ORNAMENTAL).

This remove is one of the most elegant which can be served at a sumptuous dinner or can be presented to the guest. Two good, small fillets of beef, but not too fat, are neatly trimmed, larded and braised in a good stock. When done, glazed and of a nice color, they are carved into slices; that is to say, this carving stops some distance from the extremities and penetrates no further than three parts of the meat. The carved pieces are put back in their places. These fillets are dished up on a fond of cooked rice, cut into long shape, and on an inclined plane on both sides. Between the two fillets are dished three quenelles, with pieces of truffles large enough to fill the empty space under these quenelles. At the bottom of the dish is arranged a beautiful ring of slices of sweetbreads, partly crumbed with bread and partly with truffles; they are done in clarified butter. Between the quenelles and the chain formed by the sweetbreads are distributed groups of mushrooms. At both ends of the dish some fine whole truffles surround the top of the fillets; this garnish is similarly repeated on the other side of the dish. Between the two fillets, and in the center of the dish, a pretty garnish-cup is fixed on the foundation. This cup may be of metal, masked with English or Nouilles paste, and ornamented; it may also be made with bread, or even cut out of large turnips, which in the north of Europe become very large, white, and with little skill some elegant cups can be made out of these turnips, to use with so rich and elegant a remove. A good, light espagnole sauce must be served; that is, not too thick, but juicy, beaten well and thinned with good stock and some Madeira, as well as with the liquor of the truffles. This same is sent up separately.

Louis C. Zerega, Chef Hotel Ponce de Leon, St. Augustine, Florida.

SMOTHERED BEEF, WITH SAVORY RICE BORDER.

Cut two pounds of round of beef into one-inch cubes, put into a bean-pot, with a slice of onion, and cook (closely covered) in the oven two hours; cook slowly at first; pick over and wash one cupful of rice; put one can of tomatoes on to boil with four cloves, simmer ten minutes, strain; cook the rice with the strained tomatoes in a double boiler until tender, add one heaping tablespoonful of butter, one teaspoonful of salt and a dash of pepper, and a pinch of curry if liked; put the meat in the center of a platter and arrange the rice as a border. This is an inexpensive and savory dish.

Mrs. Althea Somes, Teacher of Cookery, Manual Training School, Boston, Mass.

BEEF LOAF.

Grind on a sausage-grinder, or let the butcher chop for you, three pounds of lean beef and one fourth of a pound of salt pork. Add to it

1 teacupful of cracker-crumbs,	2 teaspoonfuls of salt,
3 well-beaten eggs,	1 teaspoonful of pepper,

Sage to taste, mix well, and pack tightly in a small bread-pan which has been well greased, sprinkle crumbs over the top, bake two and one half hours; baste while baking with one tablespoonful of butter dissolved in one cupful of boiling water; slice when cold. Another way to bake it is to mold into a loaf and put it under press for an hour, then place in the meat-pan and cover the loaf entirely with hot water, and bake until the water has all cooked away.

FILLET OF BEEF À LA JUSSIENNE.

Filet de Boeuf à la Jussienne.

Remove all the unnecessary fat from a fillet of beef, and lard the top with lardons of fat bacon; trim these evenly with a pair of scissors, and tie the fillet up with pieces of thin string. Put into a stew-pan the vegetables—one sliced carrot, two or three sliced onions, turnips, a little marjoram, basil, four or five cloves, mace, peppercorns, celery and some herbs; cover over with a buttered paper, put the lid on the pan, and stand it on the stove for fifteen to twenty minutes, then add one fourth pint of sherry and one fourth pint of good stock, and cook in a moderate oven, allowing twenty minutes for each pound of meat after the gravy has boiled; during cooking, keep it well basted, and add more stock as that in the pan reduces. When cooked, put the fillets on a baking-tin, brush it over with a little warm glaze, return it to the oven for about ten minutes; then remove the strings, put two or three hatelet skewers into the fillet, and dish up, and garnish with slices of cooked tomatoes, button mushrooms, small braised button onions, and serve with sauce prepared as below, in a sauce-boat.

SAUCE FOR FILLET OF BEEF A LA JUSSIENNE.—Take the gravy from the braised fillet, removing all the fat, and put it into a stew-pan, with the pulp of three tomatoes (made by passing them through a sieve), one ounce of glaze, one half pint of brown sauce and one fourth pint of sherry; boil this down to one fourth part, tammy, and mix with two or three fresh mushrooms that have been washed and chopped fine, and a few drops of carmine; reboil for ten minutes, then tammy, and use.

MINIONS OF TENDERLOIN PELISSIER.

Cut from a tenderloin two small, well-pared, round-shaped steaks; season with salt and pepper, and marinate them for one hour in a dish with a little olive-oil to soften them. Saute (stew) them on both sides in butter, and when cooked, drain, and roll them in a good half glaze placed in another stew-pan. Cover the bottom of the dish with bearnaise sauce, and dress the minions on top: on each of these lay a small portion of puree (soup) of artichoke bottoms, and at each side of the dish place two stuffed and baked French mushrooms; pour the stock from the sautense (stew) over the meat.

A. Gallier, President "Societe Culinaire de New York," and Chef of Hotel Brunswick, Fifth Avenue, New York.

POT-BAKED BEEF.

Take a piece of meat—crossed-rib is best—put a slice of bacon or some lard into the bottom of the pot, then the meat, and fill up with water till the meat is covered; then take two onions, some peppercorns, cloves, bay-leaves, one carrot and a crust of brown bread, salt and some vinegar; throw all of this in over the beef; keep the pot well covered; fill up with more hot water if it boils down, and let it boil three hours; then brown a tablespoonful of flour, with some butter, thin the gravy, and let it boil up once more with the meat; then put the beef into a deep dish, and strain the gravy over it; add more vinegar to taste.

FILLETS OF BEEF À LA RIGA.
Filets de Boeuf à la Riga.

Take, for six to eight persons, one pound of fillet of beef, and cut it into thin slices; bat these out with a wet chopping-knife, season them with a little pepper and salt, and place a thin slice of fat bacon (cut to the same shape as the fillets) on each; thinly mask this bacon with beef farce, using a forcing-bag and plain pipe for it, and on the farce place a thin slice or two of button mushrooms or truffles, and roll up the fillets in cylinder shapes, with farce, etc., inside; place in little bands of buttered paper, and tie them up with thin string to keep them in proper form. Put about one ounce of butter into a stew-pan,

with two or three slices of carrot and turnip, a little celery, a bunch of herbs (thyme, parsley and bay-leaf), one or two sliced onions and six or eight peppercorns; place the fillets on the vegetables, and fry all together for about fifteen minutes with the lid on the pan, then add one fourth of a pint of good stock, and put the pan into the oven; braise the fillets for one hour, occasionally basting them while cooking, then take up and remove the papers, brush the fillets over with a little warm glaze, and place them on a baking-tin in the oven for another four or five minutes to get crisp; dish up as in engraving, and garnish with slices of cooked tomatoes (see recipe) around the top and between the fillets at the bottom; place peas in the center, and pour espagnol sauce around the base.

CORNED OR SMOKED BEEF TONGUE.

Soak the tongue twenty-four hours before boiling, which requires from three to four hours, according to size. The skin should always be removed as soon as it is taken from the pot. An economical method is to lay the tongue, as soon as the skin is removed, in a jar, coiled up, with the tip outside the root, and a weight upon it. When it is cold, loosen the sides with a knife, and turn it out. The slices being cut horizontally all around, the fat and lean will go together.

STEAK ROAST.

Take a round of steak, pound, pepper and salt it well. Make a dressing of dry bread-crumbs and spread over the top of the steak; roll it up, and tie with a string, put into a pan, and roast for forty minutes.

Mrs. D. R. Connell, North Lewisburgh, Ohio.

BAKED BEEFSTEAK.

Score the steak well. If a small one, put into a pie-pan; if not very fat, add bits of butter to it; season with salt and pepper, and grate bread-crumbs over it; put a little water into the pan to keep it from sticking. Bake about twenty minutes, unless preferred very well done.

Miss Mollie K., Springfield, Ohio.

POTTED BEEF.

The beef should be well boiled, and all the fat taken off. Chop it very fine; season with salt, pepper, allspice and a little sage. Melt butter enough to knead it well together. Pack it closely in bowls (to turn it out nicely), and pour melted butter over it, and it will keep a week in cool weather.

CORNED BEEF.

100 pounds of meat,	4 pounds of sugar,
4 quarts of coarse salt,	4 ounces of saltpeter, pulverized.

Mix the sugar, salt and saltpeter well, and spread it between the layers of meat.

Miss E. C., Hoosick, New York.

BOILED CORNED BEEF.

Wash it well, put it into a pot, and if very salty, cover well with cold water; if only slightly corned, use boiling water; skim often while boiling, and allow at least one half hour for every pound of meat. If it is to be eaten cold, do not remove as soon as done, but allow it to remain in the liquor until nearly cold; then lay it in shape in an earthen dish, with a piece of board upon it, and press with a stone or a couple of flat-irons.

STUFFED CORNED BEEF.

Take a piece of well-corned rump or round, nine to ten pounds; make several deep cuts in it; fill with a stuffing of a handful of soaked bread, squeezed dry, a little fat or butter, a good pinch of cloves, allspice, pepper, a little finely chopped onion and a little marjoram or thyme; then tie up tightly in a cloth and saturate it with vinegar; boil about three hours.

JELLIED MEAT.

Boil a shank of meat five or six hours, separate the bone and fat from the meat and gristle, tear the meat into shreds, and cut up the gristle. When the liquor is cold, skim off the fat, and add enough of it to the meat to make the consistency that of soft hash. Add salt, pepper, mace and allspice to taste, and cook fifteen minutes, stirring constantly. Veal can be used in the same way.

E. A. Mordy, Newton Lower Falls, Massachusetts.

MEAT BRUNSWICK STEW.

Put half a gallon of water into your dinner-pot. Add

A small quantity of red pepper,	3 tomatoes, pared,
½ teaspoonful of black pepper,	2 slices of lean or shoulder meat,
1 tablespoonful of salt,	1 pint of Irish potatoes, pared,
1 onion, cut up fine.	

Boil about one half hour; then sift about one and one half pints of flour, add a little salt, dip in some of the boiling water, and make the dough rather stiff. Let it cool a little, and then work it with the hands until smooth; roll out very thin, cut into small dumplings with a knife, put them into your stew, and boil five or ten minutes longer.

S. Webster, Oak Forest, Virginia.

LITTLE CREAMS OF BEEF.

Petites Pains de Boeuf.

Butter some little bomb-molds, and sprinkle them all over with finely chopped button mushrooms and chopped raw green parsley from which all the moisture has been pressed; then fill them with beef farce prepared as below, and put them into a stew-pan; place a piece of paper between them and the stew-pan; pour in boiling water to about three fourths of the depth of the molds; watch the water

reboil; then draw the pan to the edge of the stove, place on the cover, and let the little creams steam for about fifteen minutes. When poached, turn out of the mold, and dish on a potato border, and with a forcing-bag and rose-pipe garnish the top of each cream, as in engraving, with a purée of potato; pour white mushroom sauce (see recipe) around the base of the dish, and serve for an entrée.

BEEF FARCE FOR LITTLE CREAMS OF BEEF.—Pound ten ounces of lean beef until quite smooth; then pound four ounces of panard, and mix both; add two tablespoonfuls of thick reduced espagnol sauce, a few drops of carmine, a dust of pepper, a pinch of salt, one ounce of good butter and two and one half eggs; work into a smooth paste, rub through a wire sieve, then mix in two tablespoonfuls of cream, and use by means of a forcing-bag and plain pipe.

DRIED BEEF FRIZZLED IN CREAM.

Chip the beef as thin as paper with a very sharp knife. Melt in a frying-pan butter the size of an egg, stir the beef about in it for two or three minutes, dust in a little flour, add one half teacupful of rich cream, boil, and serve in a covered dish.

FRESH BEEF OR SHEEP'S TONGUES.

Procure four or five small tongues at the butcher's, wash thoroughly, put on with cold water to cover and a little salt, and boil until very tender; take out and remove the skin, then put into a stone jar and cover with hot spiced vinegar. These are nice to have on hand for teas. Will keep well three or four weeks.

Christie Irving.

BOILED OX-TONGUE À LA DORNA.

Langue de Boeuf Bouillie à la Dorna.

Take a pickled ox-tongue that has been in soak for twelve hours, put it into a stew-pan with sufficient cold water to cover it, add two or three cleansed carrots, also onions, a bunch of herbs (thyme, parsley, bay-leaf, basil, marjoram), a stick of celery, two leeks, twenty-four peppercorns (black and white), three blades of mace and twelve cloves, all tied together in a piece of muslin; bring to a boil, remove the scum, and let it simmer for two and one half to three hours; then take up, press into shape, place a large skewer through the root and one through the tip of the tongue, and put it aside in the larder until next day.

Then take up, and with a sharp-pointed knife trim off all the outside fat part, put it again into a large stew-pan, pour over it a little cooking sherry and about one pint of good, rich clear gravy, and simmer it for one hour; then take up the tongue onto a hot dish, brush it all over with good bright glaze, place a frill around the root, and serve for a remove, with the prepared ragout arranged on the dish, for dinner or for luncheon or in the second course, using while quite hot.

RAGOUT FOR OX-TONGUE A LA DORNA.—Put the gravy in which the tongue was braised into a stew-pan, with one pint of thick espagnol sauce, one teaspoonful or arrow-root that is mixed with a little gravy, add the contents of a large bottle of financiere that has been warmed in the bain-marie, a bottle of truffles and the contents of a small tin of button mushrooms; stir all together until boiling, and serve with the tongue.

RAGOUT OF VEAL À LA BOURLIER.

[Emille Bourlier is the acknowledged *gourmet* of Louisville, Kentucky.]

Take one pound of veal, and slice it very thin, add one veal kidney, also sliced very fine; put into a saucepan, with two ounces of butter and one chopped onion, and fry until nearly done; flour it, stir, and add enough broth to cover it; let it simmer for one half hour, then add two medium-sized potatoes cut into small dice (potatoes cooked), boil it up, and serve with a little hashed parsley on top.

Eugene Stuyvesant Howard, Chef de Cuisine, Louisville Hotel.

VEAL LOAF.

Have the butcher chop three pounds of veal and one half pound of salt pork very fine, and add to it

3 eggs,	6 small crushed crackers,
2 tablespoonfuls of milk,	1 tablespoonful of salt,
1 tablespoonful of pepper,	Butter the size of a hickory-nut.

Mix it all well; make it into long rolls, put bits of butter over them, and bake two hours, basting often with the gravy of water and butter slightly seasoned; when cold, slice.

Mrs. M. A. Townsley, Cedarville, Ohio.

VEAL CUTLETS PIQUÉS.

Trim five or six cutlets, lard them on one side with thin slices of bacon, arrange them in a stew-pan, the bottom of which you have covered with minced carrots and onions; salt, and sprinkle with a little melted butter, moisten with clear broth, allowing the jelly to fall on the meat; moisten again with the same quantity, and let it boil down in the same way; moisten a little more, and finish cooking the cutlets at the mouth of the oven at moderate heat. By sprinkling them often with their juice, they ought to acquire a fine color. Dress them with their juice, strained and skimmed. Serve separately a garnishing of puree or tomato sauce.

Louis Marche, Chef of Burnet House, Cincinnati, Ohio.

BREAST OF VEAL (VIENNA STYLE).

Bone a breast of veal, refill with the dressing given in the recipe for dressing for fowl, and sew it up; braise it in a very slow oven, basting it as often as convenient. Chop the bones, and roast the same with two sliced onions, a little garlic, one carrot, a little celery, two bay-leaves and one teaspoonful of whole black pepper until brown. Cover with white broth, and let this simmer for about an hour, then strain it over the veal, and let it simmer for one half hour in a covered vessel; then serve.

Eugene Stuyvesant Howard, Member of the Universal Cookery and Food Association, London, England, and Chef de Cuisine, Louisville Hotel.

VEAL RESSOLES, WITH TOMATO SAUCE.

Chop cold veal very fine, add one half the quantity of cracker-crumbs, season with salt, pepper, sage and onion-juice; moisten with beaten egg, and shape into round balls; put on a baking-tin, with a bit of butter on top, and brown in a hot oven.

Mrs. Althea Somes, Teacher of Cookery, Manual Training School, Boston, Mass.

VEAL CROQUETTES.

2 pounds of chopped broiled veal,	½ cupful of cream,
1 tablespoonful of butter,	2 eggs,
1 slice of grated brown bread,	The juice of one lemon,
Salt and pepper to taste.	

Make this into balls, and fry.

Mrs. Samuel Hart, Marietta, Ohio.

VEAL AND HAM PIE.

Trim the veal and ham into escallops, and season with pepper and salt in moderation; next chop a handful of mushrooms and some parsley very fine, and put them into a small stew-pan, with a small pat of butter and one shallot, also chopped fine; fry these lightly over the fire, then add nearly one pint of veloute sauce or good stock; boil the whole for five minutes, and pour it into the pie; place six yolks of hard-boiled eggs in the cavities, cover with puff paste; bake the pie for one and one half hours, and serve.

Louis C. Zerega, Chef Hotel Ponce de Leon, St. Augustine, Florida.

LITTLE TONGUES IN CHAUDFROID.

Petites Langues en Chaudfroid.

Take one pound of raw rabbit, veal or chicken, one half pound of fresh fat and lean pork or ham, one fourth of a pound of panard and one tablespoonful of thick bechamel sauce; pound these and rub through a fine wire sieve, then mix in a basin with four raw yolks of eggs and a pinch of salt and pepper; add to it two ounces of chopped lean ham or tongue, two chopped truffles, four

button mushrooms and two tablespoonfuls of liver farce. Butter some little tongue-molds, and by means of a forcing-bag and a large, plain pipe fill up the molds with the mixture, then place them in a saute-pan, sprinkle over them a little sherry, and cook in a moderate oven for about fifteen minutes, with a well-buttered paper over; keep them well basted with sherry while cooking, then take up and set them aside until cold; turn out, mask them with brown chaudfroid sauce, after which glaze them over with a little liquid aspic jelly; arrange them on a dish on a border of rice and a centerpiece of the same to rest them against, garnish with chopped aspic jelly and a hatelet skewer, and serve for a cold entree or cold collation.

BROILED VEAL CUTLETS.

Trim evenly; sprinkle salt and pepper on both sides; dip into melted butter, and place upon the gridiron over a clear fire; baste while broiling with melted butter, turning over three or four times. Serve with melted-butter sauce or tomato sauce.

ROAST VEAL.

A shoulder of veal weighing five or six pounds will require two hours for cooking. Make a dressing the same as for a turkey, and pile it in one corner of the dripping-pan; sprinkle a little flour, pepper and salt over the meat, and cover it with another pan. Keep a little warm water in the pan, and one half hour before serving, remove the upper pan, to allow the meat to brown nicely. Serve with mint sauce.

EGGED VEAL HASH.

Chop fine remnants of cold roast veal; moisten with the gravy or water; when hot, break into it three or four eggs, according to the quantity of veal; if to your taste, shake in a little parsley. Should you lack quantity, one half cupful of fine stale bread-crumbs is no disadvantage.

CALF'S LIVER AND BACON.

2 or 3 pounds of liver,	A small piece of butter,
Bacon,	Flour,
Pepper and salt to taste,	2 tablespoonfuls of lemon-juice,
¼ pint of water.	

Cut the liver into thin slices, and cut as many slices of bacon as there are of liver; fry the bacon first, and put that on a hot dish before the fire. Fry the liver in the fat which comes from the bacon, after seasoning it with pepper and salt, and dredging over it a very little flour; turn the liver occasionally to prevent its burning, and when done, lay it around the dish with a piece of bacon between each; pour away the bacon-fat, put in a small piece of butter, dredge in a little flour, add the lemon-juice and water, give one boil, and pour in the middle of the dish.

BRAISED CALF'S LIVER.

Take a calf's liver, wash and lard; cut one onion, one stalk of celery, one carrot and one turnip into slices, put them into a braising-pan or a deep baking-pan; lay the liver on the vegetables, pour over one pint of soup stock or hot water, cover the pan, and bake in a moderate oven for two hours. Take up the liver and lay on a hot dish; put one ounce of butter into a frying-pan and let brown, then stir in one tablespoonful of flour, mix well, strain the gravy into the pan in which the liver was cooked, and pour into the frying-pan; stir until it boils, season with one tablespoonful of Worcestershire sauce, a little minced parsley, salt and pepper to taste; pour over the liver, and serve.

BRAISED LIVER.

Wash the liver; cut into slices one onion, one stalk of celery, several bunches of parsley, one carrot and one turnip; put them in the bottom of a braising-pan, lay the liver on top, add one pint of soup stock, cover the pan, and bake in a moderate oven for two hours. When done, take up the liver, put one tablespoonful of butter into a frying-pan, stir it over the fire until brown, add one tablespoonful of flour; strain the gravy from the braising-pan into the butter, and stir until it boils; then flavor with a tablespoonful of mushroom and walnut catchup each; pour over the liver, and serve.

COOKED BRAINS.

Put the calf's or sheep's brains in strong salt-water for an hour, skin them, put them into a saucepan, with a piece of salt and enough cold water to cover them, one tablespoonful of vinegar, three or four black and white peppercorns, a sprig of thyme, parsley and bay-leaf and one sliced onion, and let them come to a boil. The brains cooked thus will keep well, and can be used in many ways, either for breakfast, luncheon or dinner, served with some nice sauce.

LITTLE CROUSTADES OF CALF'S BRAINS.

Petites Croustades de Cervelles de Veau.

Take some little molds and line them with short paste about one eighth of an inch thick, pressing the paste well to the bottom of the molds to get them into a nice shape; prick the bottoms well with a fork to prevent it blistering; trim the edges evenly, and line the paste with a buttered paper, putting the buttered side next the paste; fill up the inside quite full with raw rice or flour, place the

molds on a baking-tin, and cook the paste in a moderate oven for twenty to thirty minutes, when it should be a pretty fawn color and perfectly crisp; then take out the papers and rice, remove the cases from the molds, and return them to the oven for a few minutes to dry; when ready to serve, fill them with a ragout prepared as below; cover over each croustade with a lid of puff, and bake a light fawn color, and dish up on a paper as shown in the engraving. Serve for an entree.

RAGOUT FOR CROUSTADES OF CALF'S BRAINS.—Take a set of calf's brains and prepare them as in recipe "Cooked Brains," above; then cut them into neat pieces about the size of a nickel piece; mix them into a good hot, thick, creamy veloute sauce, add a little chopped parsley, and use as directed above.

STEWED RABBIT, LARDED.

Take a rabbit, a few strips of bacon, rather more than one pint of good broth or stock, a bunch of savory herbs, salt and pepper to taste, and a thickening of butter and flour. Well wash the rabbit, cut it into quarters, larding them with strips of bacon, and fry them; then put them into a stew-pan, with the broth, herbs and a seasoning of pepper and salt; simmer very gently until the rabbit becomes tender, then strain the gravy, thicken with butter and flour, give it one boil, pour it over the rabbit; garnish with slices of cut lemon, and it is then ready to serve.

FRIED CALF'S BRAINS.

Remove the fibrous membranes, and throw into cold water, in which mix one half teaspoonful of salt and one teaspoonful of vinegar; boil five minutes, take up and plunge into cold water; cut into slices, season with pepper and salt, dip into beaten egg, and then into grated bread-crumbs, and fry in hot butter.

TIMBAL OF SWEETBREAD À LA CZARINA.
Timbale de Ris de Veau à la Czarina.

Prepare a pair of calf's sweetbreads, and when cool, cut one of them into slices, and stamp out in rounds a little larger than a dime piece; also cut out similar-sized rounds of button mushrooms and truffles. Well butter and line with a buttered paper a mold, and arrange these rounds alternately all over; then cover the garnish with a layer of veal farce about one and one half inches thick, using a forcing-bag and plain pipe for it; smooth this over with a wet, hot spoon, and fill up the center of the mold with a ragout, as below, and cover the top over with a layer of farce about one inch thick; then place the mold in a

stew-pan containing boiling water, which should come about half way up the mold. Watch it reboil, and steam for one hour, turn out, and garnish with hot button mushrooms and truffles, pour espagnol sauce around the base, and serve for a hot entree.

RAGOUT FOR TIMBAL OF SWEETBREAD A LA CZARINA.—Cut up the trimmings from the sweetbread, truffle and mushroom into little square pieces, and put them into a sauce prepared as follows: Put into a stew-pan four tablespoonfuls of very thick tomato sauce, one half wine-glassful of sherry, one ounce of glaze and one shallot chopped fine; boil down to half the quantity, keeping it skimmed while boiling, add the trimmings, and put away on ice until cold and set, then use.

FRIED LIVER, WITH BROWN SAUCE.

Cut the liver into slices, cover with boiling water, and let stand five minutes; take out of the water and wipe dry; dredge with flour, salt and pepper. Put two slices of fat bacon into a frying-pan, put in the liver, fry brown on one side, and then on the other. Place on a hot dish with the bacon, cut into small pieces. To the grease in the pan add one tablespoonful of flour, and stir until brown; pour in one half pint of soup stock, one tablespoonful of Worcestershire sauce and mushroom catchup each, with salt to taste; pour over the liver, and serve,

SWEETBREAD À L'IMPÉRATRICE.

Ris de Veau à l'Impératrice.

Take a large sweetbread or two moderate-sized ones, put them into cold water, with a little salt, bring to a boil, then rinse, and put to press until cold. Take some larding bacon, and lard the top, trim the lardons with a pair of scissors, place the sweetbread in a buttered paper, and tie it up; put it into a buttered stew-pan, with one sliced onion, one carrot, a few slices of turnip, a bunch of herbs (bay-leaf, thyme and parsley) and about one dozen peppercorns; fry for fifteen minutes with the pan covered; then add about one fourth of a pint of good stock, place in a moderate oven, and braise for about one hour, during which time keep basted, frequently adding more stock as that in the pan reduces. When cooked, take up, remove the paper, place the sweetbreads on a baking-tin, and brush it over the top with a little warm glaze; put it into the oven again for about ten to fifteen minutes; then take up, and brush over again with a little thin glaze, and arrange on a border prepared as below, and shown in picture, and serve a good supreme sauce around the dish, and macaroni

prepared as below, in the center space of the border and at each corner of the dish. Serve hot for an entree for a dinner party.

MACARONI FOR SWEETBREAD A L'IMPERATRICE.—Put some macaroni to cook in boiling water, seasoned with a little salt, for one half hour, then strain it, and cut it into lengths of about one half inch, sprinkle with a little grated Parmesan cheese, and moisten with a little thick cream, season with a dust of pepper made hot in the bain-marie, and use.

BORDER FOR SWEETBREAD A L'IMPERATRICE.—Take a Breton border-mold, butter it, and then line it entirely with rings of plainly boiled macaroni, made by cutting it crosswise about one eighth of an inch thick, then by means of a forcing-bag and large, plain pipe fill it up with the farce; knock the mold down on the table to allow the farce to sink well into the mold, place it in a stew-pan on a fold of paper, cover it with boiling water, place it over the fire, watch the contents come to a boil; then draw aside, and poach for fifteen minutes; then turn out, and use.

FARCE FOR BORDER.—Pound one half pound of cooked lean ham until smooth; then pound six ounces of panard, with one large tablespoonful of brown sauce, a dust of cayenne pepper, one ounce of butter and one ounce of grated Parmesan cheese; add the ham, mix with three whole eggs and a tablespoonful of thick cream, rub through a fine-wire sieve, and use.

SWEETBREAD.

Egg and bread-crumbs,	3 slices of toast,
3 sweetbreads,	Oiled butter,
Brown gravy.	

Choose large, white sweetbreads; put them into warm water to draw out the blood, and to improve their color; let them remain for rather more than one hour; then put them into boiling water, and allow them to simmer for about ten minutes, which renders them firm. Take them up, drain them, brush over the egg, sprinkle with bread-crumbs; dip them into egg again, and then into more bread-crumbs; drop on them a little oiled butter, and put the sweetbreads into a moderately heated oven, and let them bake for nearly three fourths of an hour. Make three pieces of toast; place the sweetbreads on the toast, and pour around, but not completely over them, a good brown gravy.

SWEETBREAD À LA FINANCIÈRE.

Ris de Veau à la Financière.

Blanch some fresh sweetbreads, and when cold, lard them with lardons of fat bacon; braise them over as in above-named recipe, and when cooked, brush the sweetbreads over lightly with warm glaze, and replace in the oven to crisp the bacon. Dish up on croutons of fried bread, as shown in the design, and garnish

with prepared financiere (that has been made hot by standing the bottle in the bain-marie), and arrange on hatelet skewers; serve with a good financiere sauce (see recipe) around the base, and use for a dinner-party entree.

SWEETBREADS, WITH MUSHROOMS.

Parboil sweetbreads, allowing eight medium-sized ones to a can of mushrooms; cut the sweetbreads about one half inch square; stew until tender; slice mushrooms, and stew in the liquor for one hour; then add to the sweetbreads one coffee-cupful of cream, pepper and salt, and one tablespoonful of butter. Sweetbreads boiled and served with green peas make a very nice dish.

LARDED AND STUFFED SWEETBREADS.

Parboil half a dozen large sweetbreads; prepare a dressing of grated bread-crumbs, lemon-peel, butter, cayenne pepper and nutmeg; mix with well-beaten yolks of eggs. Cut open the sweetbreads, and stuff them with the mixture; then sew up. Have ready some slips of fat bacon and lemon-peel, as thick as small straws; lard the sweetbreads in alternate rows of bacon and lemon; then put the sweetbreads into a pan, set in the stove and bake brown. Serve with veal gravy thickened with the beaten yolk of one egg, and flavored with lemon-juice.

ESCALLOPS OF SWEETBREAD À LA MUNICH.

Escalopes de Ris de Veau à la Munich.

Blanch a nice white throat-sweetbread by putting it into enough cold water to cover it, with a pinch of salt, let it come to a boil, then strain it, and wash it in cold water, and put it to press between two plates; when it is cold, cut it into escallops about one half of an inch thick, and lard each alternately with fat bacon and truffle; trim the lardons evenly, then wrap each escallop in a little square piece of buttered paper. Put into a stew-pan two ounces of butter and a few slices of carrot, onion and turnip, a little celery, four or five peppercorns, a small bunch of herbs (parsley, thyme and bay-leaf), place the escallops on the vegetables, put the cover on the pan, and fry for fifteen to twenty minutes; then add one fourth of a pint of stock, and let the escallops braise for three quarters of an hour, basting them occasionally while cooking; take them up, remove the papers, glaze them over lightly, and sprinkle them with a very little finely chopped raw green parsley; dish them up on a border of potatoes, with a

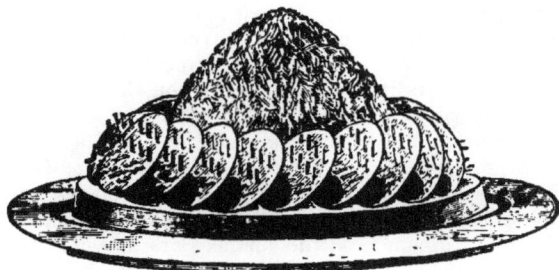

slice of tomato between each (see recipe "Tomato for Garnishing"), or a round of nice black truffle. Garnish the center with a pile of grated cocoanut or boiled rice that has a little warm butter poured over it, and a little pepper, and serve cocoanut sauce around the base.

COCOANUT SAUCE FOR ESCALLOPS OF SWEETBREAD A LA MUNICH.—Fry lightly together in a stew-pan two ounces of fine flour and two ounces of butter, then mix in three fourths of a pint of veal, rabbit or chicken stock, stir until it boils; add one fourth of a good-sized grated cocoanut and one gill of cream; boil together for about ten minutes, add a pinch of salt, the strained juice of a lemon, tammy, and use while hot.

MUTTON STEW AND GREEN PEAS.

Select a breast of mutton, not too fat, cut it into small, square pieces; dredge it with flour, and fry it a nice brown in lard and butter, and salt and pepper; cover it with water, and set it over a slow fire to stew until the meat is tender; take out the meat, skim off the fat from the gravy, and just before serving, add one quart of green peas previously boiled with the strained gravy, and let it boil gently until the peas are well done.

BUCKEYE CROQUETTES.

Provide one calf's head; have it split to remove the brains, lay the brains in an earthen dish, cover with cold water, add one teaspoonful of salt. Put the head into a pot, with enough water to fairly cover it; boil slowly until the meat will drop from the bones, skim the impurities off, then remove the pot from the stove, and allow it to stand until cool enough to handle the meat; put the meat into a chopping-bowl, chop finely; season as follows:

2 eggs,   1 salt-spoonful of salt,
1 dozen leaves of finely rubbed sage,   1 quill of garlic,
Pepper to taste.

Whip the seasoning into the eggs, then stir it into the meat; add the brains, and dredge enough flour into the mixture to make it stiff, so as to work it into small cakes; brown in a quick oven. Serve with fricasseed potatoes.

Mrs. Jos. A. Sanders, Columbus, Ohio.

DOUBLE HAUNCH MUTTON (ORNAMENTAL).

This is a rich and luxurious remove— rich in its simplicity, luxurious in its bold preparations and fine form. For such a remove it is necessary to select one of those good, fat, young, tender sheep, the juicy and succulent flesh of which is so agreeable to the taste and so light on the stomach. Before being cooked, the piece must be neatly trussed, for if not, the cooking will put it out of shape; both legs must be run through with an iron skewer, then wrapped around, as well as the saddle, with thick paper; it must be roasted on the spit or baked in the oven, according to its weight and the thickness of its flesh, a consideration which should not be lost sight of; from one to one and one half hours will be required for the cooking. When the piece is placed on the dish, a ruffle is put on each leg-bone, and the surfaces are glazed with a paste-brush. Some rich gravy is sent up separately, also a garnish of varied or plain vegetables, but always accompanied by potatoes. Such a piece must be carved in the dining-room; the meat is served on hot plates, with the light gravy running from it on the bottom of the dish.

Louis C. Zerega, Chef Hotel Ponce de Leon, St. Augustine, Fla.

LAMB CHOPS À LA TRIANON.

Broil twelve lamb chops (well seasoned with salt and pepper) on one side only. Put them on a pan, and put another pan over them, with a flat-iron or something to keep them on press. Keep them in a cool place. Mix one piece of butter and two spoonfuls of flour, add one pint of cream, a little nutmeg, one pinch of cayenne pepper, one pinch of salt; let boil until very thick; then put in the white meat of a chicken, twelve cooked fresh mushrooms, one spoonful of chopped parsley, four yolks of eggs; mix well, let boil two minutes longer; take from the fire, and put this mixture on a plate, keep it in a cool place until of the consistency of chicken croquette; garnish the chops on the cooked side with a spoonful of the mixture; dip a knife into hot water and smooth the mixture all over the chops, sprinkle bread-crumbs over, and a little melted butter, put into a buttered pan, and bake in a hot oven for seven minutes to brown lightly. Dress on a platter, put a frill on the chop handle, and serve with a garnish of French peas and a nice brown sauce. Finish with a glassful of sherry wine.

A. J. Pillauet, Chef West Hotel, Minneapolis, Minnesota.

BAKED LEG OF MUTTON.

Take a six-pound leg of mutton, cut down the under side, and remove the bone. Fill it with a dressing made of

4 ounces of suet,	1 very small onion,
2 ounces of chopped ham,	A very little thyme and parsley and
6 ounces of stale bread,	sweet marjoram,
2 eggs,	Nutmeg, salt and pepper.

Sew up, lay in a pan, and place in a hot oven; baste with butter, and cook three hours.

CUTLETS OF LAMB À LA CHATELAINE.

Côtelettes d'Agneau à la Châtelaine.

Take a neck of lamb, and cut as many cutlets from it as possible, bat them out with a cold, wet chopping-knife, and remove any unnecessary fat and skin, then season with pepper and salt and put them into a buttered saute-pan, and saute them on one side for two or three minutes; then put them to press until

cold. Prepare a white farce thus: Pound until smooth eight ounces of meat, either veal, rabbit or chicken, which has been cut up small; then pound four ounces of panard, and mix with the pounded meat; add one half ounce of butter and two tablespoonfuls of thick soubise sauce or white onion sauce; season with a little white pepper and salt, mix until quite smooth with three raw yolks of eggs, then pass through a wire sieve. When the cutlets are cold, trim them, if necessary, and then mask the unsauted side with the farce; smooth this over with a wet, hot knife, and put them, with the farced side uppermost, into a buttered saute-pan; place a buttered paper over, and put into the oven for twelve to fifteen minutes. When the farce is set, remove from the oven, and put the cutlets aside to get cool; then mask them with white chaudfroid sauce, and ornament with truffle, as in engraving, setting this with a little aspic jelly. Dish the cutlets on a border of aspic jelly or rice; place a wax figure or fried crouton of bread in the center to rest the cutlets against, and garnish with chopped aspic jelly and a cold compote of French plums.

5

FRIED LAMB STEAKS.

Dip each piece into well-beaten egg, and roll it in bread-crumbs or corn-meal, and fry in butter and lard. After taking up the meat, add one tablespoonful of flour, a lump of butter the size of a walnut and one pint of hot water, with one half a teaspoonful of lemon-juice, and pour it hot over the steaks.

SPICED LAMB.

Boil a leg of mutton weighing five pounds, for two hours, and while boiling, add one tablespoonful of whole cloves and a stick of cinnamon, broken. Slice cold, and serve with sweet pickle peaches.

CUTLETS OF LAMB À LA RATISBON.

Côtelettes d'Agneau à la Ratisbon.

Trim a neck of lamb neatly for braising, and tie it up with string; put into a stew-pan that is well buttered at the bottom, with a few slices of cleansed carrot, onion, celery and turnip, bay-leaf, thyme, parsley and a few peppercorns,

placing the meat on top of these. Cover the meat over with a piece of buttered paper, and put the cover on the pan, and fry for about fifteen minutes; then add one fourth of a pint of good stock, and place the stew-pan in the oven for about one hour, keeping it braising gently, and basting it frequently, and adding a little more stock occasionally as that in the pan reduces. When cooked, take it up, and put it to press between two plates, and when cold, cut it into neat cutlets, and mask each over with brown chaudfroid sauce, then ornament each cutlet with three or four very finely cut strips of white of hard-boiled egg, cut into lengths of about two and one half inches; arrange these like little branches on the cutlets, and attach to the egg a few little sprigs of picked chervil; make little dots here and there on the chervil with lobster-coral garnish, and put a little aspic over each cutlet to set the garnish; trim the cutlets around neatly, and dish them up on a border of rice about one inch deep, and in the center of the border place a roll of rice, prepared in the same way, to stand the cutlets against. Put some very finely chopped aspic jelly into a forcing-bag with a small, plain pipe, and between each cutlet force out a little of the jelly, which will give a very pretty finish to the dish, and also keep the cutlets from falling; arrange some chopped aspic jelly on the top, garnish it with some nice sprigs of tarragon and chervil, place little blocks of jelly around the edge of the rice border, and through the center of the rice block stick a long hatelet skewer on which five or six cooked artichoke bottoms have been arranged that have been seasoned with a little salad-oil and tarragon vinegar, also any nice cold cooked vegetables that are seasoned with a little oil and tarragon vinegar. Serve for an entree or any cold collation.

LAMB CUTLETS À L'ANGÉLIQUE.

Côtelettes d'Agneau à l'Angélique.

Take the best end of a neck of lamb, trim off all unnecessary fat, and cut it into neat cutlets; bat them out with a cold, wet chopping-knife, season with pepper and salt, steep them in warm butter or salad-oil, and grill the cutlets in front of a brisk fire, turning them only once during the cooking; when suffic- iently cooked, they should be a nice brown color. Take them up, put the cut- lets into a saute-pan containing some of the sauce as below, and just bring to a

boil. Take a puree of peas or other vegetables, and by means of a forcing-bag with a rose-pipe arrange it lengthwise on the dish on which the cutlets are to be served; dish up the cutlets straight down on this, arrange on the top of each one teaspoonful of cooked cucumber that is cut into shreds, pour angelic sauce around the base of the dish, and serve very hot for an entree for dinner, etc. Frills may or may not be used, as liked.

SAUCE FOR CUTLETS À L'ANGÉLIQUE.—Put into a stew-pan two wine-glassfuls of sherry, one teaspoonful of beef extract, two finely chopped washed mush- rooms and the essence from a bottle of truffles; boil to half the quantity, tammy, rewarm in the bain-marie, and use.

STEWED HONEYCOMB TRIPE (BOSTON STYLE).

Cut one pound of freshly cooked honeycomb tripe into strips two inches long and one half inch wide, put butter the size of an egg into a large frying-pan, and put the pan on a quick fire. As soon as the butter melts, put the tripe into it, and toss continually until all the water is removed from the tripe. In another frying-pan fry three onions, sliced very thin; when brown, put them on the pan with the tripe, add three fresh tomatoes, peeled and sliced, a pinch of cayenne pepper, two soup-spoonfuls of vinegar and salt to taste; boil the whole quickly for three minutes, and serve on a hot dish. If you have no fresh tomatoes, canned ones may be used.

A. J. Pillauet, Chef West Hotel, Minneapolis, Minnesota.

LAMB CUTLETS À L'ESPAGNE.

Côtelettes d'Agneau à l'Espagne.

Trim the best end of a neck of lamb, and braise for one hour; when cooked, take up the lamb, and put it into press, and when cold, cut it into neat cutlets, and mask these with chaudfroid sauce, as below; then ornament each cutlet with little rings of green and white mayonnaise aspic (see recipe), as shown in engraving, and dish up the cutlets on a border of rice, resting them against a crouton, which should be stood upright in the center of the border. Place in the center some cooked cut-up artichoke bottoms and raw ripe tomatoes cut into little dice shapes, or other salad may be used; garnish with chopped aspic jelly, place frills on each of the bones, if liked, and serve for an entree or for ball supper.

CHAUDFROID FOR CUTLETS A L'ESPAGNE.—Take three fourths of a pint of aspic jelly, one wine-glassful of sherry, one ounce of glaze and two tablespoonfuls of tomato sauce; boil these together until reduced one fourth, keeping well skimmed; then tammy, add one teaspoonful of tarragon vinegar, mix, and use.

BROILED TRIPE.

Prepare tripe as for frying; lay it on a gridiron over a clear fire of coals, let it broil gently; when one side is a fine brown, turn the other side (it must be nearly done through before turning); take it up on a hot dish, butter it, and if liked, add a little catchup or vinegar to the gravy.

FRIED TRIPE.

Procure your tripe at the butcher's. Scrape and wipe out the liquor, and dry it between a towel. Dip into a thin batter, put into a skillet, with hot butter and lard mixed. Fry a nice brown, and serve hot. Do not season with anything, as it is prepared when you get it.

CRACKNELS.

These can be had at the butcher's at a very low price. They are what is left from frying out lard. Put them into a pan, with a little warm water, and some bread-crumbs or cold corn-bread broken fine; season with pepper and salt, fry until a nice brown, and serve hot. Very relishing in cold weather.

Mrs. W. B. R., Jackson, Michigan.

LITTLE CROUSTADES À LA NASSAU.

Petites Croustades à la Nassau.

Line some little fluted cups with a short paste and press it well into the mold, so as to get a good impression; cut out some little rounds of paper, and butter them on one side, then place inside the paste; cook for about twenty minutes in a moderate oven; remove the paper, have some blanched calf's or sheep's brains

cut into neat slices about one fourth of an inch thick, put them in the cases, and cover over with a good thick veloute sauce; then bake one half pound of lean veal or rabbit and three ounces of fat and lean bacon (raw meat would be best), and pound and pass through a sieve; then mix it with two raw yolks of eggs, one salt-spoonful of salt, a pinch of mignonette pepper, and a peeled and chopped shallot. When mixed, mask the little cases over with it by means of a hot, wet knife (which will smooth the puree). Ornament around the edges of the cases with a little of the farce, using a forcing-bag with a small, plain pipe for the purpose; sprinkle each croustade with a little chopped lean ham or tongue, and on the center place two strips of truffle across. Cook in the oven with a buttered paper over for about fifteen minutes. Dish on a napkin or paper, and serve hot for a dinner or luncheon entree.

LAMB CUTLETS IN CHAUDFROID.

Côtelettes d'Agneau en Chaudfroid.

Roast a neck of lamb or mutton, and put it away until cold, then cut up into neat cutlets, and mask them over with brown and white chaudfroid; leave until set, then pour over them a little liquid aspic jelly, set aside until quite cold, and

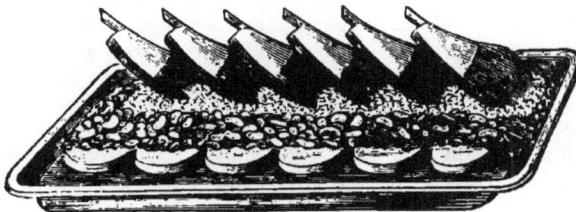

then dish on a bed of chopped aspic, and garnish at intervals with cooked artichoke bottoms, raw tomatoes and any other nice cooked vegetable; place a cutlet frill on the top of each cutlet, if liked, and serve as a cold entree or for a cold collation.

NECK OF MUTTON À LA CLARENCE.

Carre de Mouton à la Clarence.

Trim off all the unnecessary fat and skin from a small neck of mutton, skewer it, and wrap it up in a well-greased paper, put it to roast in a moderate oven for about one hour, during which time keep it well basted, and when cooked, take it up, remove the paper, and set aside until cold; then mask it with brown and white chaudfroid sauce, and also garnish with a little liquid aspic; when this is set, place it on a dish, and garnish with little timbals, as below, that are arranged on cooked artichoke bottoms, and on which is placed a slice of raw seasoned tomato, allowing one to each person; garnish with chopped aspic and little blocks of aspic jelly, and serve for a luncheon or any cold collation, or for a remove for dinner.

TIMBAL FOR NECK OF MUTTON A LA CLARENCE.—Line some little fluted timbal-molds with aspic jelly, and ornament the top of each with white of hard-boiled egg that is cut into any pretty design; set this with a little more jelly, then fill up the molds with a cooked macedoine of vegetables and aspic jelly, leave until set; then dip into hot water, and dip out.

ARTICHOKE BOTTOMS FOR NECK OF MUTTON A LA CLARENCE.—Take some cooked artichoke bottoms, season them with salad-oil, a little chopped tarragon and chervil, a few drops of tarragon vinegar and chopped shallot, and use.

TENDERLOIN À LA JARDINIERE.

Wash, trim and lard three nice pork tenderloins, season with one half table-spoonful of salt and one half teaspoonful of pepper, and place them in a roast-ing-pan. Pour over each one tablespoonful of butter, and lay a few slices of carrot and onion in the bottom of the pan, and set them in the oven to roast. As soon as light brown, add a little boiling water, and baste frequently until done. In the meantime cut one good-sized, well-cleaned carrot into fine slices, lay several slices over one another, and cut into fine strips, place them in a saucepan, cover with boiling water, add one half tablespoonful of sugar, and boil until tender. Drain one can of peas in a sieve, rinse off with cold water, place them in a saucepan, cover with boiling water, add one teaspoonful of sugar, and cook fifteen minutes. Mix one tablespoonful of corn-starch with one half table-spoonful of butter, add it to the peas with one half teaspoonful of salt; cook two minutes, add one teaspoonful of finely chopped parsley. Finish the carrots the same way. Lay the tenderloins on a hot dish, and lay the peas and carrots around them; then lay small parisienne potatoes in clusters around it.

Mrs. Gesine Lemcke, Principal of German-American Cooking College, Brooklyn, N. Y.

FRIED HAM.

Lay the ham in a skillet, and pour boiling water over it to freshen it; let it boil about ten minutes, then pour the water off, and fry in its own fat.

TO BROIL HAM.

Cut the slices thin then pound like beefsteak; cook on a griddle over hot coals (it need not be cooked much); save the gravy, and butter the meat when done.

Mrs. Thomas Trundle, Adamstown, Maryland.

BAKED HAM.

Most persons boil ham. It is much better baked, if baked right. Soak it for an hour in clean water, and wipe it dry. Next spread it all over with thin batter, and then put it into a deep dish, with sticks under it to keep it out of the gravy. When it is fully done, take off the skin and batter crusted upon the flesh side, and set away to cool. It should bake from six to eight hours. After removing the skin, sprinkle over with two tablespoonfuls of sugar, some black pepper and powdered crackers. Put into a pan, and return to the oven to brown; then take up and stick cloves through the fat, and dust with powdered cinnamon.

HAM-AND-EGG LUNCH LOAF.

Chop remnants of cold boiled ham, corned beef or salt pork; add crushed crackers and from three to six eggs, according to the amount of your meat. Bake in a round baking-powder box or empty spice-box, and when cold, it can be sliced for the table.

Mrs. Alice Farwell, Hubbardstown, Massachusetts.

HAM PATTIES.

One pint of ham which has previously been cooked, mix with two parts of bread-crumbs, wet with milk. Put the batter into gem-pans, break one egg over each, sprinkle the top thickly with cracker-crumbs, and bake until browned over. A nice breakfast dish.

BOILED HAM.

Pour boiling water over it, and when cool enough, scrape and wash clean. Put into a boiler, and cover it with cold water; bring to the boiling-point, then place on the back of the stove to boil gently for three or four hours, or until tender, so as to stick a fork into it. Turn the ham once or twice in the water. When done, take up and put into a baking-pan to skin. Dip the hands in cold water; take the skin between the fingers, and peel as you would an orange. Set in a moderate oven, and bake one hour, as this draws out the superfluous fat, leaving the meat more delicate, and in warm weather it will keep in a cool place a long time. Any tendency to mold may be removed by setting it in the oven awhile. To glaze a boiled ham, sprinkle with sugar and pass a hot knife over it, or brush it over with the well-beaten yolk of an egg, sprinkle well with grated crackers or bread-crumbs, and cover it with sweet cream; then put it into the oven to brown. The nicest portion of a boiled ham serve in slices, and the ragged parts, odds and ends, are chopped fine for sandwiches, or by adding three eggs to one pint of chopped ham a delicious omelet may be made.

HAM MOUSSE À LA L. P. MORTON.

Pound one half pound of very lean ham in a mortar for about a quarter of an hour. When thoroughly pounded, remove from the mortar and put aside. Take the nerves out of the breast part of a young roasting chicken, pound the same as the ham, and mix them both; add the whites of two eggs, two tablespoonfuls of thick cream, one tablespoonful of sherry, a wee bit of cayenne pepper, a little grated nutmeg; mix this well in the mortar. (This is called forcemeat). Pass through a very fine sieve, put into a bowl on ice to let it rest, so as to get it very firm. Cut four medium-sized truffles into small dice, mix them with the forcemeat, add also to it one pint of the best cream (whipped into froth). When you add the cream, proceed slowly, and mix with a wooden spoon. Butter well the bottom and sides of a plain mold, called charlotte-mold, fill it with forcemeat, and keep on ice. One hour before serving, put this mold into a saucepan half full of boiling water, and put a cover on it (be careful not to let the water go over your mold); put this on the edge of the stove, but be careful not to let the water boil. You will be able to tell if your mousse is cooked by pressing lightly with your hand flat on the top. If you feel the mousse resists the pressure, it is done. When ready to unmold, take a sharp knife, and cut a very thin slice off the top, which, of course, will be the bottom, once unmolded. This will make your mousse stand even on the dish. Serve a sauce supreme separate.

SAUCE SUPREME.—Take the legs and bones of the chicken from which you have already cut the breast, put into a saucepan, with one small carrot, one small onion, one bay-leaf, two whole black peppers, one clove, a little thyme, a little celery, a little parsley, four glassfuls of cold water and a teaspoonful of salt. Put two ounces of good butter into a saucepan, one tablespoonful of flour; let this cook together for ten minutes, stirring all the time, on the edge of the stove, without letting it get brown. Strain your broth into it, and let it cook for about twenty minutes; skim it well and take off the fire, but keep it warm. When ready to serve, add to it one half glassful of good double cream, but before adding the latter, let the sauce boil, and add the cream gradually, stirring the sauce with a wooden spoon continually. Also add one teaspoonful of good sherry and two chopped truffles. Serve very hot. According to the taste and practice of the person who makes it, the mousse can be decorated with truffles. As you will have seen in this recipe, there is no salt mentioned in the preparation of the ham mousse, the ham itself being salty enough.

N. B.—The mousse is a delicate and light dish, agreeable to the taste and easy to digest, and the most esteemed by the best epicures.

Paul Resal, Chef of White House (Executive Mansion), Washington, D. C.

TO BOIL BACON-HAM.

After cleaning the ham well, place it in a large boiler, and fill it with cold water. Let it boil slowly five or six hours, then take it out and put it into a dish to drain. While it is still hot, or when it is cool, remove the skin and place it into the oven to brown. Mix one teacupful of vinegar, one tablespoonful of black pepper, a little ground mustard, two or three tablespoonfuls of sugar, and baste the ham with it while it is roasting.

Mrs. J. T., Dublin Depot, Virginia.

BOAR'S HEAD.

Tête de Sanglier.

Take a boar's head (or a pig's head, which is often used instead, and forms a nice dish), bone it, and put it in pickle three weeks or a month before using thus: Rub it well two or three times a week with the following ingredients pounded together until smooth: Two pounds of salt, one fourth of a pound of moist sugar, one fourth of a pint of strained lemon-juice, one half teaspoonful of cocoa, two sprigs of sage, two teaspoonfuls of French mustard, one teaspoonful each of ground ginger, ground nutmeg, ground allspice, ground cloves, ground mace, about thirty pounded peppercorns, black and white, one half ounce of pepper, the peel of one lemon, one tablespoonful of tamarinds, one tablespoonful of powdered cumin-seed and twelve pounded almonds. Then rinse it well, and lay it out flat, and stuff the inside with a well-seasoned farce made of two and one half pounds of veal and two and one half pounds of fresh pork; then place

about six yolks of hard-boiled eggs that are masked with a little chopped parsley in the farce and six or eight turned olives and mushrooms, six filleted Christiania anchovies, one and one half pounds of strips of tongue, one half pound of bacon, thirty-six pistachio-nuts and six or more large truffles, and fasten up the head in the cloth and boil for five or six hours in stock or fresh water, with a good plateful of vegetables—carrot, onion, six bay-leaves, six or eight sprigs of thyme, one teaspoonful of black and white peppercorns, six or eight cloves, six blades of mace and one head of celery. Let it cook gently, and when done, take up, and tighten the cloth, and put it away until the next day; then put it on a silver dish, put the eyes and tusks in, mask it with glaze, and garnish it with butter and cut aspic jelly, truffles, cockscombs, mushrooms and paper cap, as shown in the engraving. The eyes and tusks are kept ready for use.

DEVILED HAM.

Take lean boiled ham, and chop it very fine, season it well with black and red pepper and dry mustard; press it solid, and slice thin. Boiled beef's tongue may be served in the same manner.

Mrs. R. W. Mills, Webster Grove, Missouri.

HAM AND EGGS.

Cut the ham into pieces the size of a fried egg; fry it in its own fat, and when done, break the number of eggs required in the ham fat, and fry them. When done, lay each egg on a piece of the ham, and serve.

HAM TOAST.

Chop the lean cooked ham into small pieces, put it into a pan, with a little pepper, a lump of butter and two well-beaten eggs. When warmed through, spread it on hot, buttered toast.

M. L. Hann, Wellington, Kansas.

SCRAPLE.

Take a hog's jowl, a part of the liver and heart, and the feet, cleanse thoroughly, put on to boil in cold water, cook until all the bones can be easily removed; then take out in a chopping-bowl and chop fine; season with sage, salt and pepper, return it to the liquor (which you must strain) on the stove; then thicken with corn-meal and one teacupful of buckwheat flour until the consistency of mush; dip out into deep dishes, and when cool, slice, and fry a rich brown, as you would mush. It is very nice for a cold morning breakfast. If you make more than you can use at once, run hot lard over the rest, and you can keep it all through the winter.

PIG'S FEET.

Wash in hot water, and scrape thoroughly with a sharp knife. Lay them in salt-water all night, to remove the blood. Put on to cook with enough cold water to cover, slightly salted. Cook for three to five hours, until the bones loosen. Take out the meat in a chopping-bowl, chop medium fine. Strain the liquor in the pot in which they were boiled, and season with vinegar and pepper to taste; take out the meat into bowls or small crocks, and cover it with the juice, to which you have added more hot water, as it will bear diluting. When cold, if not wanted for immediate use, pour melted lard over the top. If used right away, turn out of the bowls, and cut down into slices one half inch thick.

Christie Irving.

PORK CHOPS AND FRIED APPLES.

Season the chops with salt and pepper and a little powdered sage and sweet marjoram; dip them into a well-beaten egg, then into grated bread-crumbs. Fry for twenty minutes, then put them on a hot dish. Have some sour apples cut into slices around the apple, so the core will be in the middle of each piece, about three fourths of an inch thick; lay them into the skillet the chops were taken from, and fry a nice brown. Turn them carefully, so as not to break them, and serve on the chops or in a separate dish.

HAM AND CHICKEN À LA DOUGLAS.

Jambon et Poulet à la Douglas.

Put a nice York ham into cold water to soak for a day or two, during which time change the water occasionally, then trim off all the unnecessary underskin, and saw off the tip-end of the knuckle-bone; tie up the ham in a clean cloth, and put it into a saucepan with good-flavored cold stock; bring this to a boil, then skim; cover over with the stew-pan, and let the ham simmer gently for two and one half to three hours. When cooked, set the ham aside in the stock until perfectly cold, then take up the ham, remove the cloth, peel off the top skin very carefully to within four or five inches of the knuckle, and then with a very sharp knife trim the fat quite evenly, but remove as little as possible; wipe it over carefully with a clean, soft cloth, then brush it over with a little liquid aspic jelly, using the jelly while it is of the consistency of single cream. Dish up the ham on a flat silver dish, place a frill on the knuckle, garnish the top with fancy

hatelet skewers, place around the dish a bed of finely chopped aspic jelly, and surround it with little creams of chicken, as below. This dish can be served for a ball supper or for any cold collation.

LITTLE CREAMS OF CHICKEN FOR GARNISHING HAM A LA DOUGLAS.—Take some little ham-molds, line the top parts with aspic cream and the lower parts with red-colored aspic, using a little ice for the purpose of setting them. When this is set, fill up the inside with a puree of chicken prepared as follows: Take the meat from a boiled or roasted chicken, free it from bone and skin, and pound it until smooth, with one wine-glassful of sherry, one half pint of thick cream, a pinch of salt, three or four drops of lemon-juice and a pinch of pepper; mix with one pint of good-flavored chicken gravy in which one ounce of glaze is dissolved, with one half ounce of gelatin, rub it through a tammy, and use.

BARBECUED PORK.

Put a loin of pork into a hot oven without water, sprinkle with flour, pepper and salt, baste with butter, cook two or three hours, or until very brown. Pour into the gravy one half teacupful of walnut catchup. Serve with fried apples.

ROAST SPARERIB.

Trim off the rough ends, neatly crack the ribs across the middle, rub with salt and sprinkle with pepper, fold over, stuff with bread-dressing, sew up tightly, place in a dripping-pan, with a pint of water, baste frequently, turning over once so as to bake both sides equally until a rich brown.

SAUSAGE.

20 pounds of chopped meat,   2 ounces of pepper,
8 ounces of salt,   1 ounce of powdered sage.
1 tablespoonful of ginger.

When cool, pack in pans, and first cover it thick with lard, then with paper. When cutting for use, loosen a portion of the paper, and press it back again. Keep in a cool, dry place.

Mrs. R. C. B., Sandusky, New York.

BOLOGNA SAUSAGE.

10 pounds of beef,   ¼ ounce of powdered mace,
2½ pounds of pork,   ¼ ounce of powdered cloves,
Chopped fine,   2½ ounces of powdered black pepper,
Salt to taste.

Mix well, and let it stand twelve hours. Stuff in muslin bags ten inches long and four inches wide. Lay them in ham pickle five days, and smoke them eight days. Hang them up in a dark place.

Julia A. P., Georgetown, New Jersey.

HEADCHEESE.

Take the heads, tongues and feet of young, fresh pork, or any other pieces that are convenient. Having removed the skin, boil them until all the meat is quite tender, and can be easily stripped from the bones; then chop it very fine, and season it with salt and pepper, and ground cloves, if you choose, or sage-leaves rubbed to a powder; mix it all well with your hand; put it into deep pans with straight sides, and press it down hard and firm with a plate that will fit the pan, putting the under side of the plate next to the meat, and placing a heavy weight on it. In two or three days turn it out of the pan, and cut it into thin slices. Use mustard and vinegar over it. This is desirable for a supper or breakfast dish.

SALMAGUNDI.

A salmagundi is a sort of vegetable mosaic made with pickled herring, cold dressed chicken, salt beef, radishes, olives, etc., all arranged with regard to contrast in color, as well as flavor, and served with oil, vinegar, pepper and salt. The following is a good recipe for a salmagundi:

Take cold fowl or turkey or veal, or all together; chop the meat very small, separating the white from the brown, and putting among the latter the brown part of the veal, if it is roasted. By the brown meat is understood the legs and backs of the poultry. Chop likewise the lean of some cold ham, a few boned and washed anchovies, a handful of picked parsley, half a dozen shallots, some pickled gherkins, the yolks and whites, separate, of six hard-boiled eggs, and some roasted beet-root after it has become cold. Now butter a basin, and place it with the bottom upward upon a dish. Lay around this basin a ring of chopped white meat one and one half inches wide and about one inch high; then lay upon this

1 ring of ham, then	1 of meat,
1 ring of brown meat,	1 of the yolk of an egg,
1 of the white of an egg,	1 of parsley,
1 of anchovies.	

Keep on until the whole of the materials are consumed and the basin is covered, crowning the whole with a root of beet-root, garnished with a few pickled mushrooms. The sauce must be served in a sauce-tureen. It is thus made: Rub up a couple of good teaspoonfuls of strong mustard from the mustard-pot, with three tablespoonfuls of salad-oil, some salt and a little cayenne pepper. When it has become a stiff paste, add, gradually,

1 tablespoonful of white-wine vinegar,	3 or 4 lemons, the juice of,
1 dessert-spoonful of mushroom catchup,	2 tablespoonfuls of raw capers,
1 tablespoonful of soy.	

Should the sauce not be sufficiently thin, add more lemon-juice or vinegar.

KIDNEYS À LA LOUISVILLE.

Rognons à la Louisville.

Remove the skin and core from some mutton kidneys; split them open, and season them with a little salt and pepper and finely chopped shallot; steep them

in warm butter, then dip each into freshly made white bread-crumbs, and grill or broil them for eight to ten minutes, turning only once while cooking. When cooked, take up and arrange each kidney on a slice of tomato (see recipe "Tomatoes for Garnishing"); place a raw bearded oyster in the center of the kidney; cover this by means of a bag and plain pipe with a purée of mushrooms, sprinkle a few drops of glaze over, and serve for a breakfast or luncheon dish, or as an entrée for dinner, using while quite hot.

PURÉE OF MUSHROOMS FOR KIDNEYS À LA LOUISVILLE.—Take for six kidneys five or six well-washed fresh mushrooms pressed from the water, chop them fine, and put into a stew-pan, with one ounce of butter, a little salt and pepper and one small chopped shallot; put on the stove, and draw down gently until into a pulp; then add one ounce of fresh white bread-crumbs, the strained liquor from the oysters, and one ounce of cooked lean ham or tongue; stir until reboiling, then add a little finely chopped raw green parsley, and use.

Chapter VIII.

Early peas will boil in one half to three quarters of an hour; they are best put on with cold water; add salt when nearly done.

String-beans require two hours or more; the first water should always be poured off.

Lima beans will cook in three quarters of an hour; put on to cook in hot water.

Asparagus will boil in three quarters of an hour; use cold water.

Spinach will boil in fifteen minutes; use hot water.

Summer beets will boil in one hour; use hot water.

Winter beets will require three hours; use hot water.

Corn will boil in twenty minutes; use hot water.

Onions will boil in one and one half hours; use hot water.

New potatoes will boil in one half hour.

Dried corn must be soaked over night; allow it to cook one hour.

Summer squash is better steamed, as putting it into water makes it too watery; cook three quarters of an hour.

Turnips require a long time to cook; if cut thin, they will cook in one and one quarter hours; but if only cut into halves, it will require two and one half hours.

Winter or navy beans will take from two and one half to three and one half hours to cook. They may be hurried a little by the addition of a pinch of soda; plenty of water must be kept on them.

Cauliflower should be tied up in a net or a piece of white mosquito-netting when boiling, and served with rich drawn butter. Boil twenty minutes. Look carefully through this vegetable for worms—just the color of the stalk.

112

All vegetables are better to be seasoned when they are ready for the table. Never let them stand after coming off the fire. Put them instantly into a colander, over a pot of boiling water, if you have to keep them back for dinner.

Saratoga potatoes can be purchased at any large grocery in pound packages; also dried peas, corn, beans and canned asparagus, baked beans, etc.

In the spring, when potatoes begin to sprout, take such a quantity as you wish, place in a tub, and pour boiling water over them. Let them stand long enough to kill the sprouts, and then remove the water, and they will keep all summer, and are better than new ones. Steam them if you would have them very white when mashed.

To prevent onions bringing tears to your eyes when peeling them, hold them under water while handling and slicing them.

OLIVE POTATOES.

Pommes de Terre Olives.

Cut some raw peeled potatoes into quarters, and form them into olive shapes, as shown in the engraving, and put them into cold water, with a little salt; bring to a boil, then strain, and rinse the potatoes with warm water, and dry them in a clean cloth; put into a tin or saute pan some boiling clarified butter,

place the potatoes in it, put into the oven, and let it remain there until the potatoes are a nice golden color; then drain, and sprinkle with a little finely chopped raw green parsley, and serve with steak, fillets of beef, salmon, etc., or as a separate vegetable for luncheon or dinner.

MASHED IRISH POTATOES.

Peel and wash well the number required for the meal, and put them into a kettle to cook; cover them with boiling water, and let them boil until well done; then drain off the water and mash them very fine; pour in one cupful of good cream, a little at a time, put in a piece of butter the size of a walnut, and salt to suit the taste; beat them with a large spoon until very light and white.

Mrs. J. T., Dublin Depot, Virginia.

SARATOGA POTATOES.

Peel and slice on a slaw-cutter into cold water, wash thoroughly and drain; spread between the folds of a clean cloth, and pat them dry. Fry a few at a time in boiling lard, as you do fried cakes or crulls. Salt them as soon as they are taken out of the lard. They are used for garnishing game and steaks. They are often eaten cold, and consequently are nice for lunches, picnics, etc.

BROWNED POTATOES.

Let them boil nearly done, and three quarters of an hour before taking out a roast of meat, put the potatoes into the dripping-pan, and baste them frequently with the gravy of the meat; when they are a delicate brown, drain on a sieve, and serve immediately.

STEWED POTATOES.

If large ones are used, cut into halves or quarters, and let them soak in cold water one hour. Put on to cook with cold water enough to cover them. When nearly done, drain off all the water but half a pint, add one pint of milk and a pinch of salt; when this boils, stir in one tablespoonful of butter and one teaspoonful of flour rubbed smooth in a little cold milk. A handful of chopped parsley adds to the flavor.

Potatoes left over from any meal may be cooked in this manner for the next meal, as desired.

Mrs. L. A. Ashley, Springfield, Ohio.

POTATO CAKES.

Take cold mashed potatoes that have been seasoned; cut them, and mold into little cakes; fry them in hot butter a light brown color.

H. M., Elkton, Indiana.

CUPPED POTATOES.

Boil and mash potatoes, and season the same as for the table. Wet a teacup, and press some of this into the cup. Turn out on a tin as many as you wish for dinner. Beat one egg, and rub over each cake; then set them in a hot oven until nicely browned.

Mrs. R. C. B., Sandusky, New York.

FRIED POTATOES.

Slice cold boiled potatoes thin, season with pepper and salt; put on in an iron skillet one tablespoonful of lard, and let it get very hot before putting in the potatoes. Cover them, and stir occasionally; when a light brown appears through them, dish up in a hot, deep dish.

If raw potatoes are used, have the lard cold when you put them in, and take your sliced potatoes out of the water right into the cold lard. Keep well covered, and turn over often.

CREAMED POTATOES.

Cut into dice cold Irish potatoes; have them not too well done. Put into a skillet a large lump of butter, one tablespoonful of flour; let them cream together, not fry, then gently stir in one pint of milk; when it is hot, put in your potatoes, and season with salt and pepper. Shake the pan so they will not brown; keep covered. When the potatoes are heated through, dish up.

QUIRLED POTATOES.

Prepare the potatoes the same as to boil; let them cook thoroughly, then mash and season well, and press them through the colander into the dish you wish to serve them in; set them into the oven to brown.

SCALLOPED IRISH POTATOES.

Peel and slice thin; then into a tin basin put a layer of potatoes, sprinkle with pepper, salt and a little flour, a small piece of butter, then another layer of potatoes, then seasoning, until you have your basin filled; then pour over sweet milk to half the depth of potatoes, and bake one half hour.

Mrs. J. Willis, Springfield, Ohio.

POTATO SOUFFLÉ.

Boil four good-sized potatoes, and rub them through a sieve. Take one cupful of sweet milk and one cupful of butter; let them come to a boil in a saucepan; add the potatoes, a pinch of salt, a little white pepper, and beat to a cream; then put in, one at a time, the yolks of four eggs, beating it well. Drop a pinch of salt into the whites, and beat to a stiff froth; add this to the mixture, stir in lightly, and pour into a well-buttered dish; bake twenty minutes. Eat with meats that have gravies.

Mrs. M. A. E., New London, New Hampshire.

POTATOES À L'ALBERT.

Pommes de Terre à l'Albert.

Take some new potatoes, cleanse, and peel them into olive shapes, using a garnishing-knife for the purpose; put them into cold water, with a pinch of salt, bring them to a boil, and let them simmer until cooked without breaking; dish

them up in a pile on a hot dish, and pour over them some tomato puree, sprinkle with a little chopped raw green parsley, and serve for dinner or luncheon as a dressed vegetable.

POTATOES À LA DUMANOIR.

Peel, wash and drain eight sound potatoes, cut them into Julienne-shaped pieces, and wash and drain them again; season with a pinch of salt and one half pinch of pepper. Butter lightly eight tartlet-molds with clarified butter, cover the bottoms with Parmesan cheese; arrange a layer of potatoes on top, sprinkle more cheese over them, and continue until all are filled, finishing by sprinkling cheese over the surface and dropping a little clarified butter over all. Set them on a very hot stove for twenty-five minutes; unmold, and place them in a hot dish with a folded napkin, and serve.

Gustave Beraud, Chef of Calumet Club, Chicago, Formerly Chef of William Astor, New York.

FRIED SWEET POTATOES.

Peel, and slice them as you would bread; fry them in as little lard as possible to keep them from burning.

Mrs. W. B. R., Jackson, Michigan.

BAKED SWEET POTATOES.

Pare and cook like Irish potatoes, then mash, and season with butter, pepper and salt. Pile upon a pie-pan, and set in the oven to brown. Slip off on a platter as whole as possible.

MOCK SWEET POTATO.

Take a ripe squash, cut into good-sized pieces, part nicely, and boil until tender in enough water to prevent burning; then take out, put into a buttered pan, and bake a nice brown. Eaten hot or cold.

Mrs. M. A. Park, Jacksonville, Illinois.

TOMATOES.

Scald and peel some ripe tomatoes; put into a skillet, with some butter, sugar, salt and pepper; let them boil fifteen or twenty minutes. Take one pint of sweet cream or rich milk, stir in two tablespoonfuls of flour, and then add to the tomatoes; let them come to a boil, and then serve.

Lillie Ball, Franklin, Ohio.

INDIAN STEW OF TOMATOES.

Boil six smooth tomatoes, cut them into halves, and press out the seeds; put them into a saucepan, add

½ green pepper, chopped fine,	½ teaspoonful of pepper.
1 teaspoonful of salt,	¼ teaspoonful of ginger.
1 teaspoonful of turmeric dissolved in a little cold water,	

Cover the tomatoes with stock. If you have chicken-bones, they may be added, and you may then use water. Cook slowly for one half hour; see that the tomatoes are not robbed of their shape; when done, remove the bones, if you have used them, add one tablespoonful of lemon-juice, one tablespoonful of butter, and one tablespoonful of flour moistened in a little cold water; bring to the boiling-point, and serve. This is one of the daintiest ways of serving this vegetable.

Mrs. S. T. Rorer, Principal Philadelphia Cooking School.

STUFFED TOMATOES.

Select some large tomatoes of even size, and scoop out a small place in the top, and fill with a stuffing made as follows: Fry a small onion, chopped fine, in one tablespoonful of butter; when nearly done, add some bread-crumbs moistened with a little milk or water, and season with pepper and salt; put a little bit of butter on each, and then bake.

Another dressing is made as follows: Chop very fine, cold meat or fowl of any kind, with a very small piece of bacon added; fry one finely chopped onion in one tablespoonful of butter, and when nearly done, add the meat, some bread-crumbs, pepper and salt; cook one minute; mix well, add the yolk of an egg, and fill the tomatoes; place in a baking-dish; sprinkle bread-crumbs over them, with some small bits of butter, and bake. Use either as a garnish or as a dish by itself.

TOMATO OYSTERS.

Pare four large tomatoes, and cook them well; season with one half teaspoonful of butter, pepper and salt to taste. Pour one quart of boiling milk over a dish of crackers, then add the cooked tomatoes, with one half teaspoonful of soda dissolved in a little cold milk.

Mrs. S. R. Dixon, East Liverpool, Ohio.

TOMATO CUSTARD.

1 pint of tomatoes, stewed and strained,	1 teacupful of sugar,
4 eggs,	2 pints of milk.

Bake in small cups, quickly. This is a good dish for invalids.

Mrs. J. E. Butler, Folsom, California.

BAKED TOMATOES.

Cover the bottom of an earthen dish with ripe tomatoes, sliced; then a layer of bread-crumbs, seasoned with pepper, salt and butter; then another layer of tomatoes, and so continue until the dish is filled, letting the topmost layer be of the bread-crumbs. Bake fifteen minutes.

L. E. C., Sherman, New York.

TOMATO TOAST.

Cook four common-sized tomatoes and two small onions, pared, and sliced fine, for three quarters of an hour; drain off the water, add salt and pepper to suit the taste, two thirds of a cupful of sweet milk or cream, a piece of butter the size of a hen's egg. Have ready some pieces of toasted bread, and pour the tomatoes over them.

Hattie M. H., Cattaraugus, New York.

TOMATO FRITTERS.

Scald and peel the tomatoes in the usual way; then put them into a tray, and chop them fine (the tomato goes nearly half to water); season with pepper and salt to suit the taste, and stir in flour to make a thin batter, with one half teaspoonful of soda in it. Fry over a quick fire in butter or lard, and serve hot.

Mrs. I. W. Pritchett, Fayetteville, Alabama.

FRIED GREEN CORN.

Cut the corn from the cob, and put it into a skillet that has hot butter and lard mixed; season with pepper and salt. Stir it often to keep from burning, and cook it with a cover over it. Corn cooked on the cob, if any is left from the meal, may be cooked in this way or put into the oven and browned.

BAKED CORN.

One dozen ears of corn. With a sharp knife split the kernels down through the middle, and scrape the corn from the cob into a baking-dish; season with pepper and salt, one tablespoonful of sugar, butter the size of an egg, and put enough milk over it to just barely cover it. Bake in a hot oven twenty-five minutes.

DRIED SWEET CORN AND BEANS.

Pour one quart of water over one pint of dried sweet corn; let it cook until nearly done. Cook one pint of soup-beans in the same manner; then pour them together, and cook until well done; season with butter and salt; set in a hot oven, and bake one half hour.

Mrs. A. C. Tinkey, Lexington, Ohio.

GREEN CORN ON THE COB.

Take off the outside husks and the silk, letting the innermost husks remain on until after the corn is boiled, as it makes the corn much sweeter. Boil one half hour in plenty of water; drain, and after taking off the husks, serve hot.

CORN CUSTARD.

Cut corn from the cob; mix it—not too thinly—with milk, add two or three beaten eggs, pepper and salt to taste. Bake half an hour. To be served as a vegetable.

Mrs. B. F. Anthony, Providence, Rhode Island.

HULLED CORN.

Fill a large pot half full of wood ashes; then nearly fill with water, and boil ten minutes. After draining off the lye, throw out the ashes, and put the lye back into the kettle; pour in four quarts of shelled corn, and boil until the hull will rub off; then put all into a tub, and pour on a pailful of cold water. Take an old broom and scrub the corn. As the water thickens, pour off and add clean cold water. Put through four waters, and then take out in a pan, and rub between the hands; pick out all hulls, and put it on to cook in cold water; when half boiled, pour off, and renew with cold water. Do not salt it until it is tender, and do not let it burn. Put into jars, and eat with milk.

Mrs. W. Chamberlain, Dubuque, Iowa.

TO HULL CORN.

One large mixing-spoonful of soda to one quart of corn; add water enough to cover it; let it soak over night, and boil in the same water until the hulls will rub off.

H. W. J., North Charleston, New Hampshire.

CORN FRITTERS.

Scrape the corn from six good-sized ears, mix with it one large cupful of bread-crumbs, season with pepper, salt and one teaspoonful of sugar. Drop one tablespoonful of the mixture into hot lard, not too deep, turn over like griddle-cakes.

Leffie Maize, Ashland, Ohio.

CANNED CORN.

Take one and one fourth ounces of tartaric acid, and dissolve in one half pint of water. Of this solution, take one tablespoonful to each pint of corn, after first bringing the corn to the boiling-point. When opened for use, put in one teaspoonful of soda for each three pints of corn.

Edith R. Martin, Remsboro, West Virginia.

CORN OYSTERS.

Grate one dozen ears of corn into a pan; add a pinch of salt and a little pepper. Drop in spoonfuls into a well-greased skillet. As soon as brown, turn over like griddle-cakes. They should be the size of large oysters. Excellent breakfast dish.

SUCCOTASH.

Use double the quantity of corn that you do of beans. Cook the beans three or four hours. Put in the corn, that has been cooking in another kettle, an hour before serving. Let them cook well, being careful not to let it stick to the kettle. Season with salt and pepper and a lump of butter.

STRING-BEANS.

Take off the point and butt of the bean, wash, and break as small as you can, and lay in cold water until ready to use. Put on to cook in cold water; when this boils, pour it off, and add other boiling water and a piece of salt pork; cook one hour. Season, and send to the table hot.

LIMA BEANS.

Shell, wash, and put them into boiling water, with a little salt; when boiled tender, drain off the water. Serve with a cupful of sweet cream or milk, with a lump of butter in it the size of an egg. Salt and pepper, and let them simmer a few moments.

CREAMED CABBAGE.

One pint of cold cooked cabbage chopped fine and placed in a baking-dish; heat one pint of milk; melt in a saucepan one tablespoonful of butter, add two tablespoonfuls of flour, and then the hot milk, stirring until smooth after each addition; add one teaspoonful of salt and a little pepper; pour the milk mixture over the chopped cabbage; melt two tablespoonfuls of butter, add eight tablespoonfuls of rolled cracker-crumbs; sprinkle this over the top of the moistened cabbage. Bake until hot and a delicate brown.

Miss Marion L. Campbell, Friendly Inn Cooking School, Cleveland, Ohio.

FRIED CABBAGE.

1 head of cabbage, chopped fine,	1 teaspoonful of soda,
1 cupful of good bacon-grease,	2 teaspoonfuls of sugar,
1 or ½ pint of boiling water,	½ pod of red pepper,
Salt to suit the taste.	

Fry in a skillet, stirring occasionally, until brown.

Mrs. J. T., Dublin Depot, Virginia.

BOILED CABBAGE.

Take off the outer leaves, cut the head into quarters, and boil in a large quantity of water until done; drain, and press out the water, chop fine, and season. Boil three quarters of an hour, or until tender. The water can be drained off when they are half done, and fresh water added, if desired.

SMOTHERED CABBAGE.

After the meat is fried, cut fine a small head of cabbage, and put it into the dish where the meat was fried; pour on a very little water, and season with pepper and salt. Cover it tightly, and let it stand fifteen or twenty minutes.

Mrs. E. Smith, Moore's Hill, Indiana.

TO BOIL ONIONS.

Boil for one half hour, then pour off the water. Take one pint of milk, butter the size of an egg; put in the onions and stew until done.

Mrs. B. F. A., Providence, Rhode Island.

ONION STEW.

Peel the onions, slice, and let them stand in cold water one half hour; put them on to boil in fresh, cold water for three minutes, then pour off the water, add more, let it boil the same as before, and repeat this three times. In the fourth water let them cook until tender; strain, and put in milk, a piece of butter, pepper and salt to taste. Thicken with flour.

A. K. D., New Waterford, Ohio.

STUFFED ONIONS.

Have some large onions, cut into halves, hollow the center; make a forcemeat of either game or poultry, fill the cavities, cook in stock, and serve.

Gustave Berand, Chef of Calumet Club, Chicago, Illinois, Formerly Chef of William Astor, New York.

DECORATIVE VEGETABLES.

Cut slices of white potato, carrots or turnips into fancy shapes; cook until

a pin can be stuck into them, then drain on a sieve. Use to garnish meats, salads or boiled ham.

CARROTS.

Wash and scrape as new potatoes, cut into thin slices as you would cucumbers. Put on in cold water, with a little salt, and boil until tender. Pour off most of the water, and add a lump of butter dipped into flour.

CARROTS, STEWED.

Cut the carrots lengthwise, and boil until tender; then slice very thin, and put into a saucepan, with two tablespoonfuls of butter and a cupful of cream or milk; season, and stew a quarter of an hour.

TURNIPS.

Peel and wash them; cut into thin slices, and pour boiling water over them. Cook them one half to three quarters of an hour. Mash them smooth, and season with butter, pepper and salt.

BOILED SALSIFY.

"I do not know," says M. Soyer, "why this vegetable, which is held in such high esteem in Europe, should be so little esteemed by us. I will here supply their manner of cooking it, and perhaps you will give it a fair trial. Take twelve middling-sized ones, scrape them well until quite white, rub each with a lemon, and put it into cold water. Put into a stew-pan one fourth of a pound of beef or mutton suet cut into small dice, one onion, a bit of thyme, a bay-leaf, one tablespoonful of salt and four cloves; put on the fire, and stir for five minutes; add two tablespoonfuls of flour, and stir well; then add three pints of water. When just boiling, put in your salsify, and simmer until tender. They will take nearly one hour. Dish on toast; sauce over with Dutch, maitre d'hotel or onion sauce, or a very good demi-glaze or Italian sauce. Should any remain, they may be made into fritters, thus: Put them into a basin, add a little salt, pepper, two spoonfuls of vinegar, one half chopped shallot and one spoonful of oil; place in the salsify, and let it remain for some hours. When ready to serve, make a small quantity of batter, dip each piece into it, and fry for five minutes in lard or fat; dish up with fried parsley over."

FRIED SALSIFY, OR SALSIFY FRITTERS.

Boil the salsify until tender, or, if preferred, take the remains of dressed salsify. Drain and dry the roots by pressing them in a soft cloth. Make a little frying-batter, dip each root separately into this, throw them into hot fat, and fry them until they are lightly browned. Take them up, drain them on a sieve, and serve very hot, piled high on a dish and garnished with fried parsley. No sauce will be needed for them when dressed in this way. Sometimes the salsify is dipped into egg and bread-crumbs, instead of batter, before frying. When batter is used, it may be made as follows: Put three tablespoonfuls of flour into a bowl, with one salt-spoonful of salt and one ounce of fresh butter; add as much lukewarm water as will melt the butter, and beat the whole to a smooth batter. Put it into a cold place, and ten minutes before it is wanted add the well-whisked white of an egg. The salsify is occasionally soaked in vinegar, with a little pepper and salt, before it is fried, but this is not necessary. When it has been done, the roots should be thoroughly drained afterward. Time, one hour to boil the salsify; to be fried until crisp.

SALSIFY, OR VEGETABLE OYSTERS.

Scrape vegetable oysters, and throw them into cold water to prevent discoloring. When you have sufficient, cut them into pieces one half inch long, and boil in just enough water to cover until tender. Drain off the water, add one quart of milk, butter the size of an egg, and a little salt. Thicken with one tablespoonful of flour made smooth in a little cold milk. Have ready a pan of nice biscuits; split them open on a platter, turn the oysters over, and serve.

Mrs. F. C. K., Douglas, Michigan.

SALSIFY CROQUETTES.

Wash and scrape the salsify, and boil until perfectly tender, rub it through a colander or mash it, and mix with the puree a little butter, cream, salt, cayenne and lemon-juice; beat it until the ingredients are thoroughly mixed and constitute a stiff, smooth paste. Place this on ice, and when it is quite cold, shape it into the form of corks. Dip these into clarified butter, or, if preferred, into beaten egg and grated bread-crumbs, and fry them in hot fat until they are crisp and brown. Lift them up, drain, and serve.

EGG-PLANT.

Cut the egg-plant through the center; dig out of the shell the contents, and put them into a chopping-bowl. Chop fine; season with salt, butter and pepper; mix one cupful of bread-crumbs in the mess, and return it to the shells, pouring in some hot water. Put into a pan, and bake in the oven. Dish up in their own shells.

BAKED EGG-PLANT.

Boil until soft, and scoop out all the inside; mash fine, and to every cupful add one tablespoonful of cracker-crumbs, one teaspoonful of butter, and pepper and salt to taste; put into a dish for the table, beat an egg very light, and spread a part over the top of the dish, then sprinkle with rolled cracker, and lastly spread with the remainder of the egg. Set into the oven to brown.

FRIED EGG-PLANT.

Cut the egg-plant into slices one half inch thick; pare the pieces, and lay them in a weak salt and water brine, and keep them well under the brine for an hour or more; then wipe each slice, and dip it into a beaten egg, and roll it in bread-crumbs or grated crackers. Fry it in hot lard until soft and a nice brown color.

Bettie Ferguson, Stockton, Alabama.

SCALLOPED VEGETABLE OYSTERS.

Scrape the roots, and cut them into small pieces; boil them until tender; then take bread or cracker crumbs, and put a layer of each into a pudding-dish. Season each layer with pepper and salt, butter and parsley; when the dish is full, pour one quart of sweet milk over it, and bake one and one half hours.

Mrs. Louisa Ash, Mount Vernon, Ohio.

STEWED MUSHROOMS.

If fresh, let them lie in salt and water about one hour, then put them into the stew-pan, cover with water, and let them cook gently for two hours; dress them with cream, butter and flour as oysters, and season to taste.

BAKED MUSHROOMS.

Place some large, flat ones, nicely cleaned and trimmed, on thin slices of well-buttered toast, putting a little nudgel of butter in each, as also a snuff of pepper and salt; lay them on a baking-tray, and cover them carefully; heap the hot ashes upon them, and let them bake on the hearth for fifteen or twenty minutes.

BROILED MUSHROOMS.

Gather them fresh; pare and cut off the stems; dip them into melted butter. Season very little with salt and pepper, and broil them on both sides over a clear fire. Serve on toast.

PARSNIPS.

Boil until tender; then slice them, and dip the slices into a batter such as you would make for pancakes. Fry in hot lard until brown. Add pepper and salt to suit the taste.

Mrs. Lou Russel, St. Mary's, Kentucky.

TO COOK PARSNIPS.

Scrape nicely and split lengthwise: wash in cold water, and put on to cook in a steamer over boiling water. When done enough to insert a fork, put into a meat-pan; season with salt and pepper; turn over them a bowl of gravy. Put them into the oven, and bake brown. Serve on a platter.

ASPARAGUS.

Scrape the stems lightly to within two inches of the points, throw them into cold water for a few minutes; tie in bunches of equal size, cut the large, white ends off, that they may be all of the same length; then throw into boiling water, a little salted, and boil rapidly for twenty or twenty-five minutes, or until quite tender. Have prepared a round of bread nicely toasted, which dip quickly into the boiling asparagus-water; then dish the asparagus upon it with the points meeting in the center. Send to the table with rich melted butter.

ASPARAGUS UPON TOAST.

Tie the bunch of asparagus up with soft string, when you have cut away the wood, and cook about twenty-five minutes in salted, boiling water. Have ready some slices of crustless toast; dip each into the asparagus liquor; butter well while hot, and lay upon a heated dish. Drain the asparagus, and arrange upon the toast. Pepper, salt and butter generously.

TO COOK SUMMER SQUASHES.

Peel, and remove the seeds, place over the fire, with a little water and salt; when tender, mash, and season with one tablespoonful of sugar, one tablespoonful of butter and two tablespoonfuls of cream. This will make a dish for a common-sized family.

Emma C. Holler, Vannatl, Ohio.

BAKED HUBBARD SQUASH.

Chop the squash open with a hatchet, in small pieces four or five inches square; take out all the seeds, but do not peel off the skin; lay the pieces in a small dripping-pan, and pour in a pint of warm water; set it into the oven to bake, keeping a little water in the pan while they cook. They require one half to three quarters of an hour to cook. Serve in their own shells.

Mrs. W. B. Reid, Jackson, Michigan.

BAKED SQUASH.

Pare the squash, remove the seeds, steam until tender; then strain through a colander, and for every pint of squash add one half pint of bread or cracker crumbs, one tablespoonful of butter, one half cupful of sweet milk and pepper and salt to taste; bake for one hour.

F. H. C., College Hill, Ohio.

DRIED SQUASH FOR PIES.

Cut into thin slices, and dry over the stove or outdoors. When wanted for use, soak in water over night, drain off before cooking, and add fresh milk.

Mrs. M. A. Park, Jacksonville, Illinois.

SQUASH FRITTERS.

Take three medium-sized squashes, cook until tender, mash, and drain them well; season with pepper and salt; add one cupful of milk or cream, the yolks of two eggs, flour to make a stiff batter, and stir in the well-beaten whites of the eggs; have a skillet of hot lard, and fry brown. Serve immediately.

E. H. McG., Binghamton, New York.

VEGETABLE-DISH.

TIMBAL OF MACARONI À LA MILANAISE.

Timbal-case should be left in the mold to be made hot in the oven, and when just on the point of sending to the table, garnish with macaroni dressed with cheese, some bechamel sauce, scallops of fowl, truffles, tongues and mushrooms; turn the timbal out on the dish, glaze it, pour some bechamel sauce around the base, and serve.

Louis C. Zerega, Chef Hotel Ponce de Leon, St. Augustine, Florida.

STEWED MACARONI.

Boil two ounces of macaroni in water until tender; drain well. Put into a saucepan one tablespoonful of butter, mixed with four tablespoonfuls of veal or beef stock and one tablespoonful of flour, one fourth pint of cream; season with salt and white pepper, put in the macaroni, let it boil up, and serve while hot.

MACARONI, WITH CHEESE.

Throw into boiling water some macaroni, with salt according to quantity used; let it boil a quarter of an hour, drain off the water; place the macaroni in a saucepan, with enough milk to cover, boil until done. Butter a pudding-dish, sprinkle the bottom with plenty of grated cheese, put in the macaroni, a little white pepper, plenty of butter, and sprinkle on more cheese, then another layer of macaroni, seasoned, then cheese. Cover the last layer of cheese with bread-crumbs. Some add a very little dry mustard flour on every layer of the macaroni to improve the flavor. Set in a quick oven to brown.

FRIED CUCUMBERS.

Peel large, well-grown cucumbers, and cut them into thin slices; sprinkle with salt and pepper, dip into beaten egg, then into grated cracker, and fry brown in boiling lard.

CUCUMBERS FRIED IN BATTER.

Pare three or four good-sized cucumbers, cut them into very thin slices, sprinkle with pepper and salt, and let stand twenty minutes. Beat one egg, mix with

1 pint of sifted flour,	1 teaspoonful of baking-powder,
1 teaspoonful of butter,	A pinch of salt, and sweet milk to make batter.

Beat until very smooth; dip the slices of cucumber into this batter, and fry in boiling lard; take up, drain on brown paper, and serve hot.

STEWED CUCUMBERS.

Peel, cut them into quarters, take out the seeds, and soak them in cold water for one half hour; put into a saucepan, cover with boiling water, add one tea-spoonful of salt, and boil tender; when done, drain, turn into a vegetable-dish, pour over cream sauce, and serve.

SAUER-KRAUT.

Buy your cabbage the last of September, by the hundred. Remove the outer leaves and cores of cabbage, and cut fine on a slaw-cutter; put down in a keg or large jar, put a very little sprinkle of salt between each layer, and pound each layer with a wooden masher or mallet; when your vessel is full, place some large cabbage-leaves on top, and a double cloth wrung out of cold water, then a cover with a very heavy weight on it—a large stone is best. Let it set for six weeks before using, being careful to remove the scum that rises every day, by washing out the cloth, the cover and the weight in cold water. After six weeks, pour off the liquid, and fill over it with clear, cold water. This makes it very nice and white.
    Christie Irving.

TO COOK SAUER-KRAUT.

Pour over boiling water enough to cover the quantity you wish to use. Let it boil for three hours, well covered. Some prefer a piece of salt or pickled pork cooked with it. Again, others boil it down, and add enough butter to fry it.

STEWED CELERY.

Clean the heads thoroughly; take off the coarse green outer leaves; cut into small pieces, and stew in a little broth; when tender, add one cupful of sweet cream, one teaspoonful of flour and a piece of butter the size of a hickory-nut; season with pepper and salt, and a little nutmeg if agreeable.

A YANKEE BOILED DINNER.

Put the kettle on the stove with two and one half pints of water in it. Get a medium-sized cabbage-head, wash, and cut in two. Take out the heart (or stalk) lay the halves together, and put them into a kettle. Prepare as much pork as you want for dinner, and put in your cabbage. Next a good-sized, white, sweet beet (red will do, but it is not quite so nice); wash, peel and cut lengthwise into four pieces. If desired, put in turnips with the beets, cut crosswise. Boil slowly for two hours, and then put in your potatoes and slices of squash. If the pork is not salty enough, season with a pinch of salt. A red-pepper pod is an improvement, also. Boil until the potatoes are done.

Jane M. Revenaugh, Eagle Lake, Minnesota.

CAULIFLOWER.

Choose those that are compact and of good color. Strip off the outside leaves, wash them thoroughly, and lay them head downward in a panful of cold water and salt, which will draw out all the insects. Boil them in plenty of boiling water, with a little salt, and when the stalks are tender they are ready; then take a pint of boiling water, stir into it a batter made of a little flour, a little milk and the yolk of an egg; let it boil a few minutes until as thick as cream; then put in a piece of butter, a little pepper and salt and some nutmeg. Serve with the cauliflower while hot.

Emma C. Butz, Newcastle, Pennsylvania.

SPINACH.

Wash free from dirt and grit, and boil twenty minutes in salted water; drain, and chop very fine; add butter, salt, pepper and nutmeg to taste. Garnish with hard-boiled eggs cut into slices.

GUMBO, OR OKRA.

Slice the young, tender pods in rings one eighth of an inch thick; boil in salt-water twenty minutes; drain, and season with pepper and butter; or the pods may be boiled whole in salt-water, and put on buttered toast.

Mrs. M. Wilda Mills, Webster Groves, Missouri.

STEWED ARTICHOKE BOTTOMS.

Dried artichoke bottoms should be soaked for two or three hours in warm water, then boiled in salt and water, and served with white sauce poured over them; or stewed in gravy flavored with catchup, salt and pepper, and thickened with flour. Time to boil, three quarters of an hour.

Chapter IX.

Good bread makes the plainest fare appetizing, while the most luxurious table lacks something without it. Great care and attention must be taken with bread, from the time the sponge is set until it is safely out of the oven. For it must not be allowed to rise too long, and when all ready for the oven in beautiful loaves, it may be spoiled by being poorly baked. The sponge is the first process, and in different ways of making bread must be of different consistency; also, whether it is new or old wheat. But one must be an accomplished cook to be able to detect all these contingencies.

However, in all localities there are good brands of flour to be had, and it is well to stick to the one with which you are most successful. Some succeed with a brand that another person cannot handle at all. The sponge should always be kept warm and at an even temperature, not being allowed to stand in a draft. In winter it may be helped very much by setting it in another vessel containing hot water, and keeping it hot by filling in from the tea-kettle. A stone crock is the best thing to set bread in, as it retains the heat so much better than tin, and they come now in shallow forms like the wooden bowls, and are very nice for bread-making.

In molding it the first time, all the flour to be used should be put in at this stage, and it is best to knead it the longest at this point. In the summer-time,

157

sponge setting over night is apt to turn sour just a little; this can be remedied by just a pinch of soda dissolved in hot water.

In all these recipes a cupful of yeast means wet yeast, and in using dry yeast enough water must be put over it to make the required quantity.

Bread should be kneaded very little at the second molding. And when set to rise, do not let it rise to its fullest capacity before putting it in the oven. It is best to grease over the tops of the loaves with butter when setting it to rise the last time. This keeps the crust tender when baking.

When putting the bread in the oven, it should be hot enough to hold the hand in and count twenty rather quickly. Care must be taken with the fire, to keep the heat steady, allowing it to gradually die away toward the last of the baking; and this is the best time to set in your rolls, as a more moderate fire is necessary for them.

Flour should be kept in a cool, dry place. If possible, have some kind of a close receptacle for it, and do not provide too large a quantity, as it sometimes spoils by keeping too long. It should be watched to see that it is kept free from mites, as these are more destructive than mice.

Always sift all flour before using it. For convenience, a quantity may be sifted apart in a closely covered pail, so as to be ready in cases of emergency.

In buying Graham flour, never get but small quantities at a time. The coarser kinds make a good quality of Graham bread, used for dyspeptics; screened a little finer, it is called cannell flour or middlings, and is nice for gems and batter-cakes. Brown bread is not made stiff enough to knead, but just a stiff batter that can be poured into the pans.

In mixing bread, use a short-handled wooden spoon as long as you can; use enough flour always to keep the loaf from sticking to the board or your hands, but care must be taken not to get in too much flour. Expert handling can only come by experience, and you must not be discouraged if at first it sticks to everything it touches. Try to get your loaves into the pans for the last rising rather soft. If you can get pans with high sides you will find them nicer, as they keep the bread from spreading apart or running over the sides.

To insure good baking-powder biscuit, care must be taken to keep the dough very soft; so soft, in fact, that you are only just able to get them up and into the pan. They must be baked quickly in a very hot oven. Never roll your dough thinner than an inch.

When bread or biscuit becomes stale, you can freshen it by pouring a little hot water over the loaf, and draining it off quickly; then set in the oven to heat through, and it will be as good as new.

When crackers become soft from long standing, put them into a pan, and bake them over. They will be as crisp as fresh ones.

A PRACTICAL LESSON IN BREAD-MAKING.

One of the most interesting and instructive lectures before the Women's Economic Congress during the congresses of women was one on bread-making, by Mrs. Emma P. Ewing, of the Chautauqua School of Domestic Science.

She came before an audience of some fifteen hundred people, followed by a boy who bore a good-sized basket and a brand-new bread or molding board. The board was placed on a small table, and out of the basket Mrs. Ewing produced a two or three quart bowl heaped with sifted flour. She had besides this another bowl, a half pint measure and a small package, which she said was a cake of compressed yeast. In a glass she crumbled up the yeast cake, and added about four tablespoonfuls of water. Then while she stirred this very thoroughly until it looked like thin milk, she told us that this yeast was prepared by a chemically scientific process, and that the small cake she used could be absolutely depended upon to raise all the dough that could be mixed with one pint of water, in exactly three hours. She now measured two half pints of water into the bowl, and said that if she was in her own kitchen, one of the half pints should be milk, and that the whole should be milk-warm. Into this water Mrs. Ewing stirred the dissolved yeast, and then added one level teaspoonful of salt. She now began to stir in the sifted flour with a spoon-shaped wooden fork, which process she continued until the dough was of such consistency that it no longer stuck to the bowl. This, she said, was the rule for the amount of flour to be used, and it varied with the different brands of flour. Her selection always was the best patent process flour she could obtain. Mrs. Ewing now sprinkled a little flour on her molding-board, and rolled the dough upon it. Then she began kneading it, using for this purpose the heavy part of the palm of her hand, so that the dough was thoroughly welded and stretched. She showed by holding up a portion of the dough and stretching it out into a thin cake how glutinous it was, and explained that this was the quality which it was most necessary to preserve in order to retain the most nutritious portion of the flour. She explained that too long fermentation, or what is generally known as "rising," destroyed this glutinous quality. Having worked her dough into a beautiful round bunch, kneading it for five minutes, she proceeded to slightly grease her bowl, and then placed the dough in it. This dough, she said, should be placed where the temperature was seventy-five degrees, when it would rise to just the right lightness—scientifically determined in just three hours.

Here some one asked her how about people who had no thermometers. Mrs. Ewing said everybody should have one, but as seventy degrees was mild summer heat, that seventy-five degrees meant a temperature a little warmer than this, which nearly any one could determine. She especially cautioned about keeping the dough too warm. Another person asked her the question, "If one were going to make six or ten loaves, would the same proportional amount of yeast be needed?" Mrs. Ewing replied very emphatically, "Yes," and said that this was really the rock on which bread-makers were lost. She said that less yeast in a larger baking would raise the dough, but not in three hours, and the longer fermentation required caused it to turn sour. She especially deprecated the habit of setting bread to rise over night, and laid great stress on the fact that one cake of yeast would raise this amount of dough to the right fermentation in just three hours. Mrs. Ewing now produced from her basket another bowl, which, as all the audience could see, was filled with a beautifully light dough. Mrs. Ewing turned this lightly out on the bread-board, on which she had sprinkled flour, and began to knead it. She said she had set this dough just three hours before in the house of a friend, and here it was ready for the second kneading. Into this dough Mrs. Ewing kneaded flour until it would no longer stick to the bread-board, which she again said was the test of the required amount of flour. She now cut the dough into two parts, kneaded each part into a long, slender loaf, which she placed in pans about ten by four inches in size.

These loaves, she said, should rise just one hour, and should then bake in what housekeepers knew as a rather quick oven for just twenty minutes. The result would be perfect, sweet, delicious bread. The exact temperature of the oven should be 375 degrees, provided one could test it with a thermometer.

Out of her basket Mrs. Ewing now produced two loaves of beautifully browned bread. These, she said, represented this process perfected, as she had baked this bread two days before. The audience wanted to taste it, and it was broken into bits, and distributed to all who cared to try it. It was sweet, moist, delicious bread, although two days old.

WHITE BREAD.

Three pints of good bread-flour; stand in a warm place over night, where it will get dry and light. In the morning, make a sponge of one half cupful of flour, one fourth of a cupful of milk, in which dissolve the yeast; let this rise until ready to fall, then add one and one half pints of new warm milk (or scalded skimmed milk is used), one even tablespoonful of granulated sugar, one even tablespoonful of fresh lard or butter, one even teaspoonful of salt; knead ten minutes; let it rise until one half as large again as when mixed, taking care always that it does not get hot in rising; knead five minutes more in the bowl; let it rise until twice as large, then form into one large double loaf or two small ones. No extra flour should be used when shaping the loaves. Let it rise about thirty minutes in a warm place, then set it in the ice-box or in a cool place five minutes to chill the surface. Bake one hour if large, three quarters of an hour if small; bake rather slowly, not hot enough to scorch it. If the sponge is made at seven o'clock, the bread should be ready for the oven by eleven o'clock. There is no danger of having sour bread with this recipe. One secret in having deliciously light bread is drying the flour before using.

Miss Emily E. Squire, Author of " Woronoco Women's Wisdom," Westfield, Mass.

POTATO BREAD.

Pare and boil six good-sized potatoes, drain off the water, mash fine, and pour over them about three pints of lukewarm water, and run through a colander; add flour until this is a thin batter, then put into it a coffee-cupful of yeast from the jug; let stand until it rises, then stir in the flour, as much as you can with a spoon, and let rise again; work in enough more flour to knead rather stiff, and let rise the third time; when light this time, work out into loaves, and let rise. All the flour must be sifted.

BUTTERMILK BREAD.

One pint of buttermilk, one and one half teaspoonfuls of soda, one half cupful of lard, flour enough to make a medium stiff dough, and a little salt; bake quickly.

Sallie Cochran, Ennell's Springs, Indiana.

GRAHAM BREAD.

Two thirds of a cupful of molasses, one pint of sweet milk, one teaspoonful of soda, a pinch of salt, one quart of Graham flour.

Miss F. Crandell, Hoosick, New York.

SALT-RISING BREAD.

Pour half a pint of boiling water on two tablespoonfuls of corn-meal and a pinch of salt; let it stand ten minutes, then stir in two tablespoonfuls of flour, and set it in a warm place to rise over night. In the morning, add half a pint of fresh sweet milk or warm water, and flour enough to make the yeast smooth, then put it into a kettle of water hot enough to bear your hand in, and be careful to keep it the same temperature; when this rises, pour it in the batter made of two quarts of scalded morning's milk, when cooled, and flour enough to make a batter. Be careful not to scald the flour by mixing when the milk is too warm. Beat this well, and set it to rise again in a warm place, which it will do in twenty-five or thirty minutes if managed right. Be careful that the place is not too hot. Now stir in flour to make a stiff batter that cannot be stirred with a spoon, then pour it out on a molding-board which has been well covered with sifted flour, and add a piece of lard the size of a large apple, and mix it well with the dough; work it well, and after dividing it up into small loaves, put into well-greased pans, and set in a warm place to rise again; when risen sufficiently, bake as quickly as possible, and the bread will be whiter and nicer; when done, have a small brush or cloth to dip into butter to wash over the top crust; it prevents it from hardening. This bread is considered the best kind for invalids.

Mrs. J. T., Dublin Depot, Virginia.

MILK-SPONGE BREAD.

Put a pint of boiling water into a pitcher, with a teaspoonful of sugar, one fourth of a teaspoonful of salt and the same of soda; let it stand until you can bear your finger in it; then add flour to make a thick batter; beat it hard for two minutes. Now place the pitcher in a kettle of hot water—not hot enough to scald the mixture; keep the water at the same temperature until the emptyings are light. If set early in the morning, and watched carefully, they will be ready at eleven o'clock to make a sponge the same as for other bread, with a quart of very warm milk. Let this sponge get very light, then make into loaves, and set to rise again, taking care they do not get too light this time before putting in the oven, or the bread will be dry and tasteless.

WHEY BREAD.

Set a panful of sour milk on the stove, and cook until the whey rises well; pour this off, and use a quart of it for your bread. Scald first a cupful of sifted flour with the hot whey, beat it smooth, and allow it to cool; then put in one pint more of flour, one tablespoonful of salt and one tablespoonful of white sugar; turn in enough cool whey to cool it, and stir it to a thick batter; add a cupful of yeast, and set to rise; then make out as other bread.

HOMINY BREAD.

Two cupfuls of boiled grits; while hot, mix with one tablespoonful of lard or butter, add one pint of sweet milk, one cupful of corn-meal, four well-beaten eggs, then salt. The batter should be as thin as boiled custard; if it is not, thin it. Bake with the heat at the bottom. It makes an elegant bread.

Mrs. A. E. Kirtland, Author of "Mrs. Kirtland's Cook Book," Montgomery, Alabama.

SOFT-EGG BREAD.

Two beaten eggs, one level teaspoonful of soda, two cupfuls of sour milk, one cupful of sweet milk, four tablespoonfuls of meal, two teaspoonfuls of lard and salt. Bake in a pan, dip with a spoon.

Mrs. A. E. Kirtland, Author of "Mrs. Kirtland's Cook Book," Montgomery, Alabama.

BROWN BREAD.

Two pints of corn-meal, one cupful of molasses, one pint of rye flour, one teaspoonful of saleratus, sour milk enough to make a batter not too thick. Bake three or four hours.

Mrs. Ophelia M. Smith, Hadley, Massachusetts.

RYE BREAD.

Make a sponge of one quart of warm water, one teacupful of wet yeast, thickened with enough rye flour to make a batter, and put it in a warm place to rise over night; in the morning, scald a pint of corn-meal; when cool, add it to the sponge; stir in enough rye flour to make the dough thick enough to knead, knead but little, let it rise, mold into loaves, put them into deep pie-tins, and let them rise and bake.

BOSTON BROWN BREAD.

Two cupfuls of corn-meal, one cupful of rye-meal, three cupfuls of sour milk, one half cupful of molasses, one tablespoonful of soda, a pinch of salt; steam four hours, and bake twenty minutes.

Mrs. S. H., Marietta, Ohio.

BREAD FOR DYSPEPTICS.

Mix Graham flour, water and a little salt until stiff enough to handle; then make it into rolls about the size of a bologna sausage, and bake in a hot oven. Oatmeal may be used in the same way with a little flour, and let the mixture stand a few hours before baking.

M. E. D.

LIGHT BISCUIT.

One pint of warmed sweet milk, one half pint of melted lard, one teacupful of white sugar, butter the size of an egg, one teaspoonful of salt, one half pint of yeast. Stir in enough flour to make a rather stiff batter. Mix this up early in the morning, and let it rise until ten or half-past ten, and add enough more flour to knead smooth; then let it stand to rise until late in the afternoon, and mold into small tea-biscuits, and bake in time for supper; serve hot. This quantity makes about fifty biscuits one and one half inches in diameter.

Mrs. A. Winger, Springfield, Ohio.

BISCUIT WITHOUT SHORTENING.

One quart of flour, a pinch of salt, two and one half heaping teaspoonfuls of baking-powder, enough milk or milk and water to make a soft dough; roll out, and cut as other biscuits. Bake in a quick oven.

SODA-BISCUIT.

One pint of sour cream, one teaspoonful of soda, flour to mix as soft as possible, and cut rather thin.

Miss A. M. Taft, Fountain, Dakota.

PARKER HOUSE ROLLS.

Take two tablespoonfuls of white sugar, one teaspoonful of salt, three fourths of a teacupful of good yeast, one cupful of shortening, one quart of warm milk, and four quarts of flour before sifting; put on the milk to scald, add the butter while hot; then let this cool, and mix in enough flour to make a smooth batter; then add the sugar, salt and yeast, and set it to rise; when light, add the rest of the flour, and knead in a loaf, let rise again, then cut out, and put into a greased pan, and let them rise again; when light, bake in a moderately hot oven. If wanted for breakfast, mix them at night, but if for tea, mix them in the morning.

Mrs. Ophelia M. Smith, Hadley, Massachusetts.

TEA-ROLLS.

Scald one pint of milk, add one tablespoonful of sugar, one half cupful of yeast, and flour to make a batter; let this rise over night. In the morning, add one half cupful of butter, one teaspoonful of salt, well-beaten whites of two eggs; mix this stiff, knead it well, and let it rise; then knead again, and roll it three fourths of an inch thick; cut with a biscuit-cutter, and butter one half, and roll the other half over it; let it rise until very light, then bake.

A. M. S., Windsor, New York.

SPICED ROLLS FOR LUNCHEONS.

Take a piece from your bread-dough, and roll it out half an inch thick, brush the top with melted butter, and cover thick with cinnamon and fine white sugar; commence at one side, and roll up as jelly-cake; then cut it an inch thick, and lay in a pan as biscuit, close together, and let them rise, and bake twenty minutes.

RUSKS.

Two eggs, two and one half cupfuls of sugar, one tablespoonful of lard, one tablespoonful of butter, one quart of sweet milk, one half nutmeg, one cupful of yeast, flour enough to make a stiff batter; set to rise; when light, knead it moderately stiff, and let it rise again; after it is light, mold it into rolls, put them into a baking-pan, and let them stand again until light, then bake half an hour.

A. M. H., Henry Clay, Delaware.

DRIED RUSKS.

1 pint of warm milk,	¼ cupful of butter,
2 eggs,	½ cupful of yeast,
1 teaspoonful of salt.	

Set a sponge with these ingredients, leaving out the eggs, and stirring in enough flour until you have a thick batter. Early next morning add the eggs, well beaten, and flour enough to roll out; let this rise in the bread-bowl two hours; roll out into a sheet nearly an inch thick, cut into round cakes, and arrange in your baking-pan two layers, one upon the other, carefully; let these stand for another half hour, and bake; when they are done, lift them apart, leaving one side soft; pile loosely in a pan, and when the fire is declining for the night, set them in the oven and leave them until morning; then take them out, and put into a clean muslin bag, and hang up to dry in the kitchen. Use the third day. Put as many as you need into a deep dish, and pour over them iced milk, or water if you cannot procure the milk; take out when soaked soft, drain them, and eat with butter. They will keep for weeks and grow better every day.

MUFFINS.

One egg, one half cupful of butter and lard, mixed, melted and poured into one pint of sweet milk, three teaspoonfuls of baking-powder. Sift the baking-powder with enough flour to make a stiff batter; beat it hard, and bake in gem-pans. These are excellent made of Graham flour.

Mrs. R. W. Thorne, Tiblow, Kansas.

BUTTERMILK MUFFINS.

2 eggs,   1 teaspoonful of salt,
1 teaspoonful of soda dissolved in 1 quart of buttermilk,
1 tablespoonful of hot water,   Flour enough to make a good batter.

Beat the eggs well, add them to the buttermilk, then the flour, salt and soda; pour into the muffin-pans, and bake in a quick oven.

Mrs. Bettie Ferguson, Stockton, Alabama.

CREAM MUFFINS.

1 pint of sweet cream,   1 tablespoonful of butter,
3 eggs—the yolks well beaten,   Whites of eggs, beaten to a froth,
½ teaspoonful of salt,   Flour enough to make a stiff batter.

Fill the hot, well-greased muffin-rings half full with the batter, and bake quickly.

Mrs. D. D. H., Marion, Virginia.

PARK HOUSE GRAHAM MUFFINS.

4 eggs,   A pinch of salt,
1 teacupful of brown sugar,   ½ teacupful of good yeast,
2 tablespoonfuls of melted butter or lard, 2 quarts of Graham flour.

Milk enough to make a stiff batter; mix, and let it rise over night. In the morning, fill the muffin-rings half full, and bake in a quick oven.

Mrs. Julia F. Fisher, Circleville, Indiana.

WHOLE-WHEAT FLOUR MUFFINS.

Dissolve half a cake of compressed yeast in half a pint of milk, and add sufficient quantity of rich milk to make a pint; stir into it three cupfuls of whole-wheat flour, and set in a warm place to rise; when light, stir in two well-beaten eggs, and turn into gem-irons, half filling them; let them rise until very light, and bake in a quick oven.

ST. CHARLES CORN MUFFINS.

2 teacupfuls of white corn-meal,
1 cupful of boiling water,
1 cupful of milk,
1 heaping tablespoonful of butter.
2 eggs,
½ teaspoonful of salt,
1 teaspoonful of baking-powder,

Pour the boiling water over the meal, and stir, that all may be wet and scalded; add the melted butter, salt and milk, then the beaten eggs. Put the iron gem-pans into the oven to heat, putting into each mold a small piece of butter or lard; add the baking-powder to the batter, and beat up thoroughly; then pour into the hot mold. Bake carefully about twenty or twenty-five minutes. This batter, when ready, will be very thin.

WHOLE-WHEAT GEMS.

One cupful of sour milk, one fourth of a cupful of sweet milk, one half teaspoonful of soda, two tablespoonfuls of sugar, one egg, one and three fourths cupfuls of whole-wheat flour. Bake in hot gem-pans well greased with butter.

GRAHAM GEMS.

Three eggs, three tablespoonfuls of sugar, one pint of sweet milk. Graham flour enough to thicken it. Drop into the gem-pans and cook quickly. A little soda or baking-powder may be added if desired.

S. E. R., Chesterfield, Virginia.

"POOR MAN'S" CORN GEMS.

1 pint of corn-meal,
1 pint of flour,
1-3 of a pint each of milk and water.
1 teaspoonful of salt,
2 teaspoonfuls of baking-powder,

Sift the corn-meal, flour, salt and powder together; add the milk and water, mix into a firm batter; two thirds fill well-greased, cold gem-pans. Bake in a well-heated oven fifteen minutes.

CORN-MEAL GEMS.

Pour boiling water over one pint of meal to make a stiff dough; when cool, add one egg, a pinch of salt, and sweet milk enough to drop from the spoon. Fry in as little lard as possible, and when nicely browned, take them up, and serve.

Mrs. W. B. R., Jackson, Michigan.

SODA-CRACKERS.

One quart of flour, one tablespoonful of butter, one half teaspoonful of salt. Make a stiff paste with buttermilk, beat until very light; roll thin, cut into squares, stick with a fork, and bake quickly.

FRENCH CRACKERS.

One and one half pounds of flour, one half pound of sugar, one fourth of a pound of butter, whites of five eggs. Mix stiff, roll thin, and prick with a fork. Bake in a very hot oven.

CRACKERS.

The white of one egg, one tablespoonful of butter, one teacupful of sweet milk, one half teaspoonful of soda, one teaspoonful of cream of tartar. Mix very stiff, beat well, roll thin, and bake.

Julia C. Melton, Opelika, Alabama.

EGG CRACKNELS (CREAM CRACKERS).

1 quart of flour,	1 teaspoonful of baking-powder,
1 large pinch of salt,	4 tablespoonfuls of butter,
5 tablespoonfuls of sugar,	4 eggs.

Sift together flour, sugar, salt and powder; rub in the butter, cold, add the eggs, beaten, and mix into a firm, smooth dough. Flour the board, turn out the dough, and give it a few minutes' rapid kneading; cover with a damp towel fifteen minutes, then roll it out to the thickness of one eighth of an inch, cut out with a biscuit-cutter; when all are cut out, have a large potful of boiling and a large tin pan of cold water. Drop them, a few at a time, into the boiling water; when they appear at the surface and curl at the edges, take them up with a skimmer, and drop them into the cold water; when all are thus served, lay them on greased baking-tins, and bake in a fairly hot oven for fifteen minutes.

WATER-CRACKERS.

1 pound of flour,	1 teaspoonful of salt,
1 tablespoonful of lard,	½ teaspoonful of soda.

Mix with water, beat well, roll thin, stick with a fork, and bake in a hot oven.

CORN-BREAD.

2 heaping cupfuls of corn-meal,	1 large tablespoonful of butter, melted, but not hot,
1 heaping cupful of flour,	
3 eggs, beaten separately,	1 large tablespoonful of white sugar,
2½ cupfuls of milk,	1 teaspoonful of baking-powder,
1 teaspoonful of salt.	

Bake steadily, but not too fast, in a well-buttered mold; turn out upon a plate when done, and eat at once, cutting it into slices as you would cake. In cutting corn-bread, do not forget to hold the knife perpendicularly, and cut toward you.

Marion Harland.

NEW ORLEANS CORN-BREAD.

1½ pints of corn-meal,	2 heaping teaspoonfuls of baking-powder,
½ pint of flour,	1 tablespoonful of lard,
1 tablespoonful of sugar,	1¼ pints of milk,
1 teaspoonful of salt,	2 eggs.

Sift together corn-meal, flour, sugar, salt and powder; rub in the lard, cold, add the eggs, beaten, and the milk; mix into a moderately stiff batter; pour from bowl into a shallow cake-pan. Bake in a rather hot oven for thirty minutes.

DELICATE CORN-BREAD.

1 pint of sour or sweet milk,
1 teaspoonful of soda or baking-powder.
1 tablespoonful of lard,
A pinch of salt.

Stir in white meal enough to make a batter the consistency of sponge-cake. Bake half an hour or twenty minutes by a quick fire.

Mrs. W. B. R., Jackson, Michigan.

RAISED GRIDDLE-CAKES.

1 cupful of white corn-meal,
2 cupfuls of flour,
2 cupfuls of milk,
1 pint of boiling water,
¼ teaspoonful of baking-powder.
2 tablespoonfuls of yeast,
1 tablespoonful of brown sugar,
2 eggs,
1 teaspoonful of salt,

Scald the meal at night with boiling water, beat well; while warm, stir in the flour, sugar, milk and yeast; let it rise all night. In the morning, add the eggs, baking-powder and salt, and if too thin, add corn-meal to make the batter the right consistency. Leave a cupful for the next morning's rising.

Mrs. Albert.

CORN-MEAL GRIDDLE-CAKES.

1 pint of corn-meal,
1 heaping teaspoonful of butter,
1 salt-spoonful of salt,
1 teaspoonful of sugar.

Pour boiling water slowly upon the mixture, stirring until all is moistened, and leave it for thirty minutes; then break into the mixture three unbeaten eggs, which must be well beaten into the dough; add five teaspoonfuls of cold milk, one spoonful at a time, until it is all smooth, and then bake on both sides a nice brown. Serve hot, one griddleful at a time, as they are baked.

SOUTHERN HOE-CAKE.

One quart of good, sweet meal, sifted, one teaspoonful of salt, and turn on boiling water, stirring all the time to make a stiff batter. Wet the hands in cold water, and form the meal into oval cakes, then spread on a board (hard wood), set before the fire to bake; when baked on one side, turn and bake the other; when done, split it open, butter well, and serve very hot. The hoe-cake, for most of us, must be baked as a thick griddle-cake, for we have no open fires.

SARATOGA JOHNNY-CAKE.

One cupful of sour milk, one cupful of sweet milk, one egg, two tablespoonfuls of sugar, two tablespoonfuls of butter, one half teaspoonful of soda, one and one half cupfuls of corn-meal. Bake one half hour.

SWEET JOHNNY-CAKE.

One cupful of coarse chopped suet, one cupful of sour milk, one cupful of sugar, one teaspoonful of soda, a pinch of salt, corn-meal enough to make a thin batter. Bake in a long pan for half an hour.

Mrs. T. K. M. B., Chelsea, Vermont.

SOUTHERN ASH-CAKE.

1 quart of scalded corn-meal,	1 tablespoonful of melted lard,
1 teaspoonful of salt,	Cold water to make a soft dough.

Mold with the hands into oblong cakes. A clean spot is swept upon the hot hearth, the bread put down and covered with hot wood ashes, and it must be washed and wiped dry or carefully brushed before it is eaten. A much neater way is to lay a cabbage-leaf above and below the cake. The bread is thus steamed before it is baked, and is made ready for eating by stripping off the leaves. The hoe-cake was a mixture of corn-meal, water and salt, shaped into cakes by the hands, and baked upon a board before the fire, or, in earlier times, upon a hoe, from which it was named.

BREAKFAST COFFEE-CAKE.

Take a piece of bread-dough, and add one half cupful of sugar and one table-spoonful of melted butter, then roll out an inch thick, and put on a greased pie-pan, brush the top with melted butter, and cover thickly with cinnamon and sugar; let it rise, and bake quickly. Cut into long, narrow strips to serve. Eat hot or cold. It is nicely made Saturday with other baking, to use Sunday morning for breakfast.

CORN-MEAL SCONES.

1 quart of corn-meal,	2 teaspoonfuls of baking-powder,
1 teaspoonful of sugar,	1 large teaspoonful of lard,
$\frac{1}{2}$ teaspoonful of salt,	2 eggs,
Nearly one pint of milk.	

Sift together flour, sugar, salt and powder; rub in the lard, cold, add beaten eggs and milk; mix into dough, smooth and just consistent enough to handle. Flour the board, turn out the dough, give it one or two quick kneadings to complete its smoothness; roll it out with a rolling-pin to an eighth of an inch in thickness, cut with a sharp knife into squares larger than soda-crackers, fold each in half to form three-cornered pieces. Bake on a hot griddle eight or ten minutes; brown on both sides.

CORN-MEAL FLAPJACKS.

1 quart of boiling milk scald	1 tablespoonful of butter,
2 cupfuls of corn-meal, and add	1 teaspoonful of sugar.

Cover, and set away over night. In the morning, add

2 yolks of eggs,	1 teaspoonful of baking-powder, which should
1 scant cupful of flour,	be well stirred in.
1 teaspoonful of salt,	

Just before baking on a griddle, add the beaten whites of two eggs, mixed in lightly.

CORN-PONE.

Two quarts of sweet milk, eight teacupfuls of corn-meal, four teacupfuls of flour, one teaspoonful of salt, one teacupful of molasses. Mix, and bake three hours in a very slow oven.

Mrs. Robert Beckett, Fair Haven.

WAFFLES.

Three eggs (whites and yolks beaten separately), one tablespoonful of butter, or a piece the size of a hen's egg, one half teaspoonful of soda, or a teaspoonful of baking-powder, a pinch of salt, one quart of flour. Mix with sour cream enough to make a batter; cook in waffle-irons over the coals of fire until of a light brown color.

Mrs. Carrie Bell, Eminence, Kentucky.

CORN-MEAL AND RICE WAFFLES.

½ cupful of corn-meal,
½ cupful of flour,
1 cupful of cold boiled rice,
2 well-beaten eggs,
1 tablespoonful of melted butter,
½ teaspoonful of baking-powder,
1 teaspoonful of salt,
1 pint of milk.

Beat the mixture well before baking. Care must be taken to have the irons well greased, as with rice they are more liable to stick.

FLOUR AND INDIAN WAFFLES.

2½ cupfuls of sifted flour,
½ cupful of sifted Indian meal,
1 teaspoonful of baking-powder,
2 cupfuls of rich milk,
1 teaspoonful of salt,
1 heaping tablespoonful of butter,
2 eggs, beaten very light,

Mix salt, baking-powder, flour and meal, and melt the butter; make a hollow in the flour, and pour in butter, eggs and milk, stirring as you pour, that all may be a smooth batter. Heat the waffle-irons; oil them well with fresh lard, and fill three quarters full. Bake over a clear fire. Turn the waffle-iron often, that the waffles may not burn.

FRIED MUSH.

The mush made as in the preceding recipe may be poured into a dish to the depth of one and one half inches, and when cold, cut into slices from one half to three fourths of an inch thick, and fried brown on both sides in dripping lard or butter. This is a good dish for breakfast. The best way to make mush for frying is to mix

1 pint of corn-meal,
2 teaspoonfuls of salt.
1 quart of cold milk, free from lumps,

Then stir the mixture very gradually, so as not to reduce the water below the boiling-point, into two quarts of boiling water; let it boil half an hour, stirring continually to prevent scorching, as it will more readily scorch by reason of the milk, pour it into a dish to the depth of about one or one and one half inches, and when thoroughly cold, slice, and fry as previously directed.

MUSH CROQUETTES.

One quart of mush, butter the size of an English walnut stirred in while the mush is hot, then set away to cool; when about lukewarm, stir into it two well-beaten eggs and one salt-spoonful of salt, form into croquettes about three inches long, and set aside; drop them into smoking-hot, deep lard; when a golden brown, lay out on soft paper to absorb the superfluous grease. Serve hot.

CORN-MEAL MUSH.

One cupful of white corn-meal, two quarts of boiling water, with one tablespoonful of salt. To prevent the meal from lumping, mix it with enough cold water or milk to make a thin batter, then gradually pour in the batter, so as not to reduce the water below the boiling-point, stirring it with a wooden spoon or rounded stick, cover closely, and let it cook gently (simmer) from one to two hours, stirring frequently to prevent scorching. It should be of a consistency to readily heap upon a spoon, but not too thick. To be served hot, and eaten with milk, butter or syrups.

FRIED MUSH (HOTEL STYLE).

Cut the mush into pieces one inch thick and three inches long, dip into well-beaten egg, roll in sifted cracker-crumbs, and fry as doughnuts in boiling lard.

CORN-MEAL FRITTERS.

3 cupfuls of milk,	½ teaspoonful of baking-powder,
2 cupfuls of best Indian meal,	1 tablespoonful of sugar,
½ cupful of flour,	1 tablespoonful of melted butter,
4 eggs, beaten separately,	1 teaspoonful of salt.

Beat the yolks of the eggs very light, and add to all the ingredients (except the flour and baking-powder, which should be added last); when these are well mixed, add the whites of the eggs, next the flour mixture. Drop into boiling lard by the spoonful; when done, lay in the draining-pan, with brown paper in the bottom of the pan to absorb the fat. Eat with a sauce made of butter and sugar, seasoning with cinnamon and a surprise of ginger.

SAUCE FOR FRITTERS.

Take one heaping tablespoonful of butter and two heaping tablespoonfuls of flour rubbed together, one and one half cupfuls of boiling water, and cook five minutes; add one and one half cupfuls of brown sugar, one salt-spoonful of ginger, one even teaspoonful of cinnamon (or if preferred, juice of one half lemon), one half nutmeg; stir until the sugar is all melted. Serve hot.

OATMEAL CRISP.

Scald the oatmeal with boiling water, stirring with a spoon, and making a pretty stiff dough; knead well together, dust the molding-board with a little Graham flour, and roll thin, cut into small cakes, and bake in an oven fifteen or twenty minutes, or until they are dry and hard, but only slightly browned.

GERMAN PUFFS.

Four eggs, one pint of sweet milk, five tablespoonfuls of sifted flour, one teaspoonful of salt. Beat the eggs separately until very light; then add a little flour and a little milk to the yolks; taking care that there are no lumps; add the whites last. Bake, and serve immediately with butter sauce or very rich liquid sauce.

Mrs. Lizzie Bailey, Monticello, Arkansas.

CORN-MEAL PUFFS.

1 quart of boiling milk,
2 small cupfuls of white corn-meal,
½ cupful of flour,
1 small cupful of powdered sugar,
1 salt-spoonful of salt,
4 eggs, beaten separately,
1 tablespoonful of butter,

½ teaspoonful of soda, dissolved in hot water,
1 teaspoonful of cream of tartar, sifted into the flour,
¼ teaspoonful of mixed cinnamon and nutmeg.

Boil the milk, and stir in the corn-meal and flour; boil ten or fifteen minutes, stirring carefully to prevent scorching, then add the butter; remove from the fire, and beat hard; when cold, add eggs, sugar, spices and soda, and beat hard; bake in greased cups or deep gem-irons. To be eaten with the following sauce:

½ cupful of butter, beaten very light,
1 cupful of powdered sugar.

1 cupful of cream,

Set the dish in a basin of hot water, and stir until it is all like cream; it will take but a short time.

PUFFETS FOR TEA.

Three eggs, one cupful of sugar, two thirds of a cupful of butter, one pint of sweet milk, three pints of flour, three teaspoonfuls of baking-powder. Bake in muffin-rings, and serve warm.

M. A. L., Central City, Nebraska.

YEAST WITHOUT HOPS.

12 large potatoes, boiled, mashed and pressed through a sieve; add
3 quarts of lukewarm water,

1 cupful of yeast,
1 cupful of sugar,
1 cupful of salt.

Mix thoroughly, and set in a warm place four or five hours. When bubbles rise it is ready for use. One teacupful of this yeast will make three quart loaves, and no sponge is necessary. Keep in half-gallon jars, corked tightly, and in a cool place. It will be good for weeks.

Mrs. C. I. Kemper, Bethany, West Virginia.

JUG YEAST.

Wash and peel six potatoes the size of a large egg, cut into quarters, and put on the stove to boil in a quart of water; as it boils away, fill up from the tea-kettle to the quantity; when your potatoes are nearly done, put a handful of hops to steep in a pint of water; take out the potatoes when well done, put into a crock, and mash fine; on these put a pint of flour, and scald this with the hot potato-water and hop-water; beat until perfectly smooth and free from lumps; into this put a cupful of granulated or other good white sugar and not quite half a cupful of salt. It should be quite thin; if not thin enough at this stage, add a little cold water; when cool enough, stir into this a pint of good yeast, or two good-sized yeast cakes dissolved in warm water, let it stand twenty-four hours, stirring very frequently; then put it away in a stone jug, corked tightly, and keep in a cool place, but not where it will freeze. This recipe makes a pint over a gallon.

YEAST CAKES.

Boil six potatoes in one quart of strong hop tea. When soft, mash them fine, and to this, when lukewarm, add

1 cupful of flour,	1 tablespoonful of ginger,
½ cupful of sugar,	1 cupful of yeast.

Set this sponge in a warm place to rise; when light, stir in enough corn-meal to make it quite thick; let it rise over night; then mold it, and cut into small cakes, and lay them out to dry in the shade.

E. J. Burroughs, Bridgeport, Connecticut.

WET YEAST.

Pour one pint of boiling water over one large handful of hops; cook this for fifteen minutes, and pour it over one pint of flour; when cool, add one teaspoonful of sugar, one teaspoonful of salt, one teaspoonful of ginger and one half cupful of yeast. After standing two or three days it will be ready for use.

Mrs. Louisa Ash, Mount Vernon, Ohio.

DRIED YEAST.

Put a pint of good strong hops into half a gallon of water, and let it boil half an hour. Have one quart of flour in a jar, and strain the boiling hop-water on the flour, and stir it well; set it in a cool place, and when cool enough to bear your finger in it, pour in one teacupful of good yeast to start it, and put it in a warm place until it rises; then stir it down, and continue this until fermentation ceases, which will be in about two days. Now have a pan with a quart of sifted corn-meal, pour your yeast into it, adding enough more meal to knead well, then roll out and cut into cakes; spread the cakes on a cloth over an old table or board, where the wind will blow over it, and turn it often during the day until it is thoroughly dried. If used two months after making, it will be as good as when first made.

Mrs. Julia C. Richardson, North Grove, Indiana.

BAKING-POWDER.

9 ounces of bicarbonate of soda,	4 ounces of tartaric acid,
4 ounces of cream of tartar,	10 ounces of wheat flour.

Cover over closely after thoroughly sifting it several times. Put away in air-tight boxes or wide-mouthed bottles, labeled.

Mrs. R. P. Crouse, Attica, New York.

Eggs, Omelets Breakfast and Tea Dishes.

CHAPTER X.

During the season when eggs are plentiful and cheap, many persons pack them, small end down, in a box well covered with coarse salt, never allowing the eggs to touch each other. Have small holes bored in the bottom to drain off the moisture. Some use oats in which to pack.

To one half peck of unslaked lime add three pailfuls of water; when cold, add one ounce of cream of tartar and one half pound of salt. This will keep eggs for a long time.

Duck and goose eggs are very strong as a food, though some do use them.

To boil eggs, three minutes will boil them very soft, five minutes will cook hard all but the yolk, and eight minutes will cook them hard all through.

In breaking eggs, break them separately over a cup to be sure they are perfect.

In poaching eggs, add a little vinegar to the hot water to set the whites; the water should be salted, also.

It is best to save all egg-shells to settle coffee.

To tell good eggs, put them into water; if the large ends turn up, they are not fresh. This is an infallible rule to distinguish a good egg from a bad one.

If possible, have double kettles to cook all grains. The price of one can be saved in a short time by the saving of what usually sticks to the kettle when cooked in the ordinary way.

Wheat, oatmeal and barley are best to be soaked over night.

Rice and hominy are much nicer when preserved in the whole grain; this can be done by steaming them. Hominy will take three or four hours, and rice from one and one half to two hours.

Oatmeal and cracked wheat are better for being cooked in a double boiler, which any lady can have by setting one vessel into another, and keeping the under one well supplied with hot water. Add salt to make a strong brine, which will generate a greater heat. It is also very nice steamed from three to four hours.

In making buckwheat cakes, it is best to save a little of the batter, and not cook it all. That which is saved is the yeast for another mess, and it can be kept perfectly sweet by filling the vessel with cold water and letting it stand until night in a cool place. When ready to use, pour off the water, which absorbs the acidity, and mix with tepid water. In the morning, stir in half a teaspoonful of soda dissolved in hot water.

Hominy grits, cerealine and prepared wheat are all nice for breakfast use, and if soaked over night, need very little cooking. Eat with sugar and milk or molasses, as preferred.

These grain foods should be used more than they are, as they contain so much more nutrition than many things that are used; and for growing children there is nothing better.

Persons living in the country who do not find it convenient to purchase wheat already cracked, can use their coffee-mill for cracking it. Although not done so evenly, it is much sweeter than that you buy.

EGGS AND GRAVY.

Put a young, well-fed fowl into a stew-pan, with four ounces of butter, some spice, a faggot of herbs and half a dozen small onions, let it brown slightly and equally; add half a pint of stock, close the lid tightly, and finish the cooking over a very slow fire. Parboil the liver of the fowl in some good gravy, remove it, and poach half a dozen eggs in the same liquor. Rub down the liver to a paste, and use it to thicken the gravy in which the fowl has been stewed. Place the fowl on a hot dish, with balls of spinach around it; lay a poached egg on each ball, flattening it with the back of the slice; pour gravy over the fowl, and serve hot. Time, one hour to stew the fowl.

PICKLED EGGS.

Remove the shells from three or four dozen hard-boiled eggs; do not break them, but arrange carefully in large-mouthed jars. Boil one pint of vinegar, with allspice, ginger and a couple of cloves of garlic. When the flavor of the spice is extracted, add another pint of vinegar, bring it to a boil, and pour scalding hot over the eggs; when cold, seal up the jars for a month. This will be found a cheap pickle when eggs are plentiful, and for its piquancy is much liked.

POACHED EGGS.

Place on the fire a shallow stew-pan, with water, salt and a tablespoonful of vinegar; when it boils, add the eggs, one at a time; permit them to boil two minutes; take them up carefully with a strainer, and serve on delicately toasted slices of bread cut into the shape of diamonds or hearts; garnish with parsley.

FRIED EGGS.

The frying-pan should be scrupulously clean, or the white part of the egg will be spoiled. Dripping, butter or cotton-seed oil may be used. Break the eggs first into a cup, and slip each one into the pan as soon as it is hot. As the eggs fry, raise their edges with a slice, give them a slight shake, and ladle a little of the butter over the yolk. In two or three minutes they will be done; take them out with the slice, pare off the rough edges, and drain from the greasy moisture. Serve on slices of bacon, or lay them in the middle of the dish with bacon or ham as a garnish. Allow two eggs for one person.

EGGS À LA CARACAS.

¼ pound of smoked beef,	1 cupful of canned tomatoes,
4 hard-boiled eggs,	1 teaspoonful of onion-juice,
4 raw eggs,	1-8 teaspoonful of cinnamon,
2 heaping tablespoonfuls of grated cheese,	¼ teaspoonful of paprika or a dash of cayenne,
2 tablespoonfuls of butter.	½ cupful of mayonnaise.

Free the beef from fat and rind, and chop fine; add the tomatoes, onion-juice and paprika, and cook slowly until the tomatoes are tender; add the cheese, butter and cinnamon, and simmer five minutes; stir in the raw eggs, well beaten, stirring until as thick as scrambled eggs. Turn into a hot dish, and garnish with the hard-boiled eggs, sliced and dipped into mayonnaise.

Miss Cornelia Campbell Bedford, Superintendent New York Cooking School.

EGGS FOR LUNCH.

Boil the eggs hard; when cold, take off the shells, and divide the eggs lengthwise into halves; take out the yolks, crumble them in a bowl, adding salt, pepper, mustard and a little melted butter; when all are well mixed, fill up the hollows of the whites with this mixture, and serve.

Aunt Lena, Canaan Four Corners, New York.

SCRAMBLED EGGS.

Pour one cupful of cream into a frying-pan; when hot, pour in one dozen eggs previously broken in a dish; cook slowly, stirring constantly, so that the eggs will be evenly done; season with pepper and salt, and serve hot.

Miss Maggie Tichenor, Waupun, Wisconsin.

FRICASSEED EGGS.

Boil three eggs hard, and lay them in cold water. Melt a slice of butter in a stew-pan, and throw in a finely chopped small onion; fry until soft. Mix a dessert-spoonful of flour with the butter to a smooth paste, add two tablespoonfuls of gravy, and stir until thick. Cut the eggs into quarters, and lay them gently in the gravy. Shake the pan around, then throw in a small cupful of cream, shake the pan again, but do not break the eggs. When the sauce is thick and fine, put the eggs on the dish, and serve with the sauce thrown over, and a garnish of lemon around the dish. Time, ten minutes to boil the eggs and ten minutes to prepare the fricassee.

FROTHED EGGS.

Mix the juice of a lemon with one tablespoonful of water, and beat up with it the yolks of eight eggs and the whites of four, sweeten to taste, and add a pinch of salt; put the mixture into an omelet-pan, and fry carefully. Have ready four whites of eggs whipped with a pound of fine sugar to a high froth, and flavored with vanilla or lemon. Place the omelet on a dish, and heap the frothed egg over it. Brown it lightly in an oven or before the fire. Time to fry, about four minutes. Sufficient for four persons.

POTTED EGGS.

Pound the yolks of twelve hard-boiled eggs, with anchovy sauce; mix them to a paste with two ounces of good fresh butter, and season with two teaspoonfuls of salt and one of white pepper. Have ready some small pots, and chop the whites of the eggs very small. As the pots are being filled with the paste, strew in the chopped whites, and cover over the tops with clarified butter. These eggs will not keep long.

STUFFED EGGS.

Six hard-boiled eggs cut in two, take out the yolks, and mash fine; then add two teaspoonfuls of butter, one of cream, two or three drops of onion-juice, salt and pepper to taste; mix all thoroughly, and fill the eggs with this mixture; put them together. Then there will be a little of the filling left, to which add one well-beaten egg, cover the eggs with this mixture, then roll in cracker-crumbs, and fry a light brown in boiling fat. Plain baked eggs make a quite pretty breakfast dish. Take a round whiteware dish thick enough to stand the heat of the oven, put into it sufficient fresh butter, and break as many eggs into it as are desirable, putting a few bits of butter on the top, and set in a rather slow oven until they are cooked. Have a dish of nicely made, buttered toast arranged symmetrically on a plate, and garnish it and the dish of eggs with small pieces of curled parsley.

EGGS À LA SUISSE.

Spread the bottom of a dish with two ounces of fresh butter; cover this with grated cheese; break eight whole eggs upon the cheese without breaking the yolks; season with red pepper, and salt if necessary; pour a little cream on the surface, strew about two ounces of grated cheese on the top, and set the eggs in a moderate oven for about a quarter of an hour. Pass a hot salamander over the top to brown it.

EGGS POACHED À LA MORNAY.

Poach two eggs very soft in slightly salted sweet cream, adding four drops of tobasco sauce; lay the eggs on toast. Make a well-buttered, rich bechamel sauce, and add to it some fine cooked spaghetti cut into lengths of one third of an inch, and a little grated Parmesan cheese; stir all well together, and cover the surface of the eggs with this preparation; bestrew with a little more of the cheese and bread-raspings; pour a little melted butter over, and bake in a very hot oven to a fine color.

A. Gallier, President "Societe Culinaire de New York," and Chef of Hotel Brunswick, Fifth Avenue, New York.'

EGGS BROUILLE.

6 eggs,	1 teaspoonful of salt,
½ cupful of milk or cream,	A little pepper,
2 mushrooms,	3 tablespoonfuls of butter.
A slight grating of nutmeg.	

Cut the mushrooms into dice, and fry them for one minute in one tablespoon-ful of the butter. Beat the eggs, salt, pepper and cream together, and put them into a saucepan. Add the butter and mushrooms to these ingredients; stir over a moderate heat until the mixture begins to thicken. Take from the fire, and beat rapidly until the eggs become quite thick and creamy. Have slices of toast on a hot dish; heap the mixture on these, and garnish with points of toast. Serve immediately.

CREAMY OMELET.

Have ready a heavy iron spider about seven inches in diameter; heat it, grease it with one half tablespoonful of butter by running the butter on a broad knife around the top edge of the hot spider and letting it run down the side over the bottom of the pan. Beat three eggs slightly with a spoon, add three tablespoonfuls of hot water; pour the mixture into the greased spider, cook slowly for six or eight minutes; when of a creamy consistency, sprinkle with salt and pepper, and roll like jelly roll; serve at once on a hot platter.

Miss Marion L. Campbell, Friendly Inn Cooking School, Cleveland, Ohio.

APPLE OMELET.

Stew eight large apples very soft, mash them fine, and season with one cup-ful of sugar, one tablespoonful of butter, and nutmeg or cinnamon to suit the taste; when the apples are cold, add four well-beaten eggs. Bake slowly for twenty minutes, and eat while warm.

PUFF OMELET.

Have the pan ready hot and greased. Separate the whites and yolks of three eggs, add one fourth of a teaspoonful of salt to the whites, beat them stiff; beat the yolks until creamy; beat in three tablespoonfuls of hot water; put in the beaten whites, pour into the greased pan, cook for a moment on top of the stove, then place in the oven; when well puffed and dry, fold and serve on a hot platter. Three tablespoonfuls of chopped meat may be beaten into the yolks when the omelet is being made. An omelet is ready when a knife run gently into the center of it will not show dampness when withdrawn.

Miss Marion L. Campbell, Friendly Inn Cooking School, Cleveland, Ohio.

FRENCH OMELET.

6 eggs.	1 cupful of boiling milk,
1 tablespoonful of melted butter,	1 cupful of bread-crumbs.
Salt and pepper to taste.	

This is sufficient for two cakes. Fry them in suet drippings, and when nearly done, turn each one together in the shape of a half moon.

Miss Sarah G. Crandell, Hoosick, New York.

MEAT OMELET.

Made like the creamy omelet, but just before rolling it, sprinkle it with three tablespoonfuls of chopped meat.

PLAIN OMELET.

Break three eggs into a bowl, add a little salt and white pepper and one table-spoonful of cream; whip well. Put one teaspoonful of butter into a frying-pan, let it get hot, put the egg mixture into it; when the mixture commences to get hard, fold it up on the opposite side of the handle, and keep on the fire for a minute, elevating the handle, giving the omelet the shape; then with a short move of the hand turn the pan over the center of the dish, and serve at once.

N. B.—The omelet should never be allowed to brown, as an "Omelet, nice and brown," an order given so often by ignorant people, is a culinary monstrosity.

Eugene Stuyvesant Howard, Member of the Universal Cookery and Food Association, London, England, and Chef de Cuisine, Louisville Hotel.

BAKED OMELET.

Stir five tablespoonfuls of sifted flour into three pints of milk; strain it through a sieve; add the yolks of eight well-beaten eggs, and just as it goes into the oven, spread on the whites beaten stiff. Bake quickly.

HAM OMELET.

Three eggs, two gills (one half pint) of milk, two tablespoonfuls of flour, one gill of grated ham (cold boiled ham will do). Beat the eggs, milk and flour well, then add the grated ham, and fry in nice lard or the drippings of roasted ham.

Mrs. E. C. W., Mount Vernon, Ohio.

GREEN-CORN OMELET.

Boil a dozen ears of sweet corn, cut it off the cob, season it with salt and pepper, and stir into it five well-beaten eggs; take a tablespoonful of it and roll it in bread-crumbs, then fry brown.

OMELET, WITH HAM.

Make a plain omelet, and just before turning one half over the other, sprinkle over it some finely chopped ham. Garnish with small slices of ham.

Jelly or marmalade may be used in the same way.

BUCKWHEAT CAKES.

1 quart of lukewarm water,   ½ cupful of wet yeast,
1 cupful of flour.

To this add enough buckwheat flour to make a thin batter. Let them stand over night to raise, and in the morning dissolve one half spoonful of soda in one half cupful of lukewarm water, and stir this into the batter, then cook quickly.

Ella Finch, Otwell, Indiana.

SELF-RAISED BUCKWHEAT CAKES.

One quart of lukewarm water, two tablespoonfuls of molasses. Into this stir enough of the self-rising or prepared buckwheat flour to make a thin batter. The molasses is put in to give them a nice brown color in cooking, and not to sweeten them, as some might suppose. The advantage of this prepared flour is that it is not necessary to set them over night, as they are ready to bake as soon as mixed. This flour can be obtained at any grocery; also wheat flour for wheat pancakes, which comes prepared in the same way.

FLANNEL-CAKES.

3 eggs,
½ cupful of butter and lard, mixed,
2 quarts of sifted meal.

1 teaspoonful of salt,
1 teacupful of flour,

Mix with sweet milk or water until very thin. Fry quickly on a hot, well-greased griddle.

Mrs. J. T., Dublin Depot, Virginia.

PANCAKES.

2 eggs,
2 quarts of sour milk.
Enough flour to make a stiff batter.

2 large teaspoonfuls of soda,
A pinch of salt,

Cook on a hot griddle. This makes a large quantity of batter.

Agnes Blair, West Liberty, Ohio.

CORN-MEAL PANCAKES.

Take two cupfuls of Indian meal and one teaspoonful of salt; pour over it boiling water to make a batter; stand until cool, and then add the yolks of three beaten eggs, flour to make the proper consistency, one and one half teaspoonfuls of baking-powder; just before baking, add the stiffly beaten whites.

FRENCH PANCAKES.

2 eggs,
2 ounces of butter,
½ pint of new milk.

2 ounces of sifted sugar,
2 ounces of flour,

Beat the eggs thoroughly, and put them into the basin with the butter, which should be beaten to a cream; stir in the sugar and flour, and when these ingredients are well mixed, add the milk; keep stirring and beating the mixture for a few minutes; put it on buttered plates, and bake in a quick oven for twenty minutes. Serve with a cut lemon and sifted sugar, or pile the pancakes high on a dish, with a layer of preserves or marmalade between each.

BREAD PANCAKES.

3 well-beaten eggs,
1 tablespoonful of melted butter,
1 good handful of flour,
½ teaspoonful of soda.
Mrs. R. H. H., Columbus, Nebraska.

1 quart of sour milk,
2 cupfuls of bread-crumbs,
1 teaspoonful of salt,

BREAD PANCAKES.

Soak the bread, and drain; to two cupfuls of bread add one of flour, milk enough to make a thin batter, two teaspoonfuls of baking-powder and one egg, beaten light.

CORN-MEAL CAKES.

Scald one teacupful of corn-meal; to this add another teacupful of meal and one teacupful of sifted flour; add one pint of cold water, and put in one half teacupful of wet yeast and one half teaspoonful of salt. If the batter is too thick to pour well, add more water. Set in a warm place to rise over night. In the morning they will be very light and ready to fry, without stirring them, as soon as the griddle is hot.

WAFFLES.

Two beaten eggs, one quart of light flour, one iron tablespoonful of melted lard, one level teaspoonful of soda, sour milk enough to make a batter as thick as cream. Don't fill irons too full; the irons must be hot, and well greased.

Mrs. A. E. Kirtland, Author of " Mrs. Kirtland's Cook Book," Montgomery, Alabama.

RICE WAFFLES.

1½ pints of boiled rice,
1½ pints of flour,
1 teacupful of sour milk,
A pinch of salt.

3 eggs,
1 teaspoonful of soda,
1 tablespoonful of butter,

Mix all, and bake immediately in well-greased waffle-irons.

RICE GRIDDLE-CAKES.

1 egg,
2-3 of a cupful of cooked rice,
1-3 of a cupful of flour,

1 teaspoonful of soda,
2 teaspoonfuls of cream of tartar, or
3 teaspoonfuls of baking-powder,

Sweet milk enough to make a batter thin enough to fry.

Any cooked grains, hominy, wheat, oatmeal, or grits of any kind, can be used in the same way.

BREAKFAST GRIDDLE-CAKES.

To one and one half pints of corn-meal stir in boiling water until it is a stiff mush, and set away to cool; add one egg, one and one half pints of flour, one teaspoonful of soda, buttermilk enough to make a batter, not too thin, and bake like buckwheat cakes on a griddle. If sour milk is used, add another egg. If sweet milk or water is used, add two tablespoonfuls of cream of tartar.

A. B. V. D., Hammonton, New Jersey.

RYE BREAKFAST CAKES.

2 cupfuls of rye-meal,
½ cupful of molasses,
A little salt.

1¼ cupfuls of sweet milk,
1 teaspoonful of soda,

Mix very soft, and bake at once in a roll-pan or muffin-rings.

Mrs. Mary A. Dodge, Newcastle, Maine.

RICE CAKES.

Boil some rice, and let it cool; then add a little water or milk. making it about the consistency of buckwheat cakes; add a little salt and a handful of flour; beat in one egg. Bake on a griddle.

Mrs. Solon H. Ayres, Charleston, Nebraska.

FRIED BREAD.

One egg, one half teaspoonful of salt, one half pint of cold water or milk; beat well, and dip into it slices of bread; fry them in butter. Serve hot.

Miss A. E. M., Wilmot Flat, New Hampshire.

STEAMED BREAD.

Slice up the stale bread, and lay the slices carelessly on a plate; set the plate in a steamer, with something to tip it a little, to allow the steam free circulation; set it over a kettle of boiling water, and cover it tightly. Serve with butter the same as toast.

MILK TOAST.

Toast the quantity of bread you will want for the meal. To prepare for the toast, boil one quart of milk; when nearly boiled, stir in a tablespoonful of corn-starch, wet up to a thin paste with milk, a lump of butter and one half teaspoonful of salt. Arrange the bread in a dish, a piece at a time, and pour some of the milk over each piece. Do not dip your bread into the milk.

Christie Irving.

SAVORY TOAST.

Fry one half tablespoonful of finely chopped onion in one tablespoonful of drippings, add one cupful of cold cooked meat, chopped, cover with roast-meat gravy, soup stock or hot water, add one fourth cupful of stewed tomatoes, one fourth teaspoonful of salt and a little pepper; pour over eight little circles of toast, and garnish with parsley and toast points.

Miss Marion L. Campbell, Friendly Inn Cooking School, Cleveland, Ohio.

HAM TOAST.

Slices of toasted bread, with the crusts cut off, two eggs, two tablespoonfuls of butter, some cold grated ham or tongue. Put the yolks and whites, well beaten, into a stew-pan, with the butter; stir them two minutes over the fire, spread them over the toast, and lay over them a sufficient quantity of cold ham or tongue, grated or chopped fine, to cover the eggs. Serve it up very hot.

Clara Maxwell, Fort Scott, Missouri.

CREAM TOAST.

Toast thin slices of bread to a delicate brown, lay in a covered dish, and pour boiling water over; pour off the water, and let drain. Put one pint of rich, sweet cream on the stove in a quart cup, add three tablespoonfuls of butter, two beaten eggs and one tablespoonful of corn-starch, let boil up once, and pour over the toast.

COFFEE-ROLLS.

Work into a quart of bread-dough a rounded tablespoonful of butter and half a teacupful of white sugar; add some dried currants (well washed and dried in the oven), sift some flour and sugar over them, work into the dough thoroughly, make into small, long rolls, dip them into melted butter, place in the pan; let it rise a short time, and bake.

SALLY-LUNN.

5 eggs,
1½ cupfuls of sugar,
1 cupful of wet yeast.

1½ cupfuls of butter,
3 cupfuls of warm sweet milk,

Flour enough to make a rather stiff batter, and when it is light, stir in two tablespoonfuls more of flour; pour into jelly-cake pans, let it rise again, then bake; when done, butter each cake, and pile them one above the other as a jelly-cake. Serve hot. Half the above quantity is sufficient for a small family.

HOMINY.

Thoroughly wash two cupfuls of hominy, and put it into a well-greased kettle, pouring over two quarts of cold water; salt the water a little; let it cook slowly all day, pouring on hot water as it dries down. Never stir it while cooking, if you would have the grains whole when done. Eaten hot or cold, with milk or butter.

Mrs. W. B. Reid, Jackson, Michigan.

STEAMED HOMINY.

Soak one cupful of hominy in three cupfuls of water and salt to suit the taste, over night. In the morning, turn it into a quart pail, then put the pail into a kettle of boiling water, cover tightly, and steam one hour; add one teacupful of sweet milk, and cook half an hour longer.

FRIED HOMINY.

Have a frying-pan with hot butter in it, and put in as much hominy as required for the meal; pour over it a very little water or milk to keep it from burning on, salt to suit the taste. Do not stir it while cooking, but leave the kernels whole.

CRACKED WHEAT.

The water must be cold when the wheat is put in. Use one third of wheat to two thirds of soft water; cover closely, and cook slowly, without stirring, for three hours.

TO COOK OATMEAL.

Two teacupfuls of oatmeal, one tablespoonful of salt; put them into a quart tin pail, and fill it three fourths full of water, cover closely, and set in a kettle one third full of water, and boil it for three hours; stir it two or three times when it first commences to boil.

E. E. D., La Crosse, Wisconsin.

BREAKFAST DISH.

Take a quarter of a pound of fresh cheese, cut into thin slices, put into a frying-pan, and turn a cupful of sweet milk over it, add one fourth of a teaspoonful of dry mustard, a pinch of salt and pepper and a piece of butter the size of an egg. Roll three Boston crackers very fine, and sprinkle in gradually; then turn at once into a warm dish, and serve immediately.

Lottie E. Klump, Felton, Delaware.

BREAKFAST STEW.

Chop fine whatever cold meats remain on hand; add one pint or more of good soup stock; season with salt, pepper and a small pinch of ground cloves, thicken with browned flour, and pour boiling hot over little squares of nicely toasted bread. Garnish with slices of lemon, and serve at once.

WELSH RAREBIT.

Three ounces of mild cheese, one wine-glassful of ale or beer, a pinch of red pepper. Grate the cheese, add the beer or ale and pepper, put on a moderate fire, stirring it constantly until it forms a smooth paste. Serve it on a hot piece of toast on a very hot dish. The rarebit must boil yet in the dish to be perfect.

WELSH RAREBIT.

To one quart of warm milk, grate or slice thin one fourth of a pound of cheese. Let this come to a boil, and pour it over sliced toasted bread. This is an excellent breakfast dish.

POTATO AND BEEF HASH.

Mince some cold beef, a little fat with the lean, put to it as much cold boiled potatoes, chopped, as you like (same quantity as of meat, or twice as much), season with pepper and salt; add as much gravy or hot water as will make it moist, then put into a stew-pan over a gentle fire; dredge in a small quantity of wheat flour; stir it about with a spoon, cover the stew-pan, and let it simmer for half an hour, taking care that it does not burn. Dish it with or without a slice of toast under it for breakfast. This hash may be made without potatoes; if water is used instead of gravy, a bit of butter may be added, more or less, according to the proportion of fat with the lean meat.

DRIED BEEF.

The most common way of serving dried or smoked beef is to shave it into thin slices or chips, raw; but a more savory relish may be made of it with little trouble. Put the slices of uncooked beef into a frying-pan, with just enough boiling water to cover them; set them over the fire for ten minutes, drain off all the water, and with a knife and fork cut the meat into small bits; return to the pan, which should be hot, with a tablespoonful of butter and a little pepper. Have ready some well-beaten eggs, allowing four to half a pound of beef; stir them into the pan with the minced meat, and toss and stir the mixture for about two minutes. Send to the table in a covered dish.

MEAT AND POTATOES.

Mince beef or mutton, with onions, pepper and salt; add a little gravy, put into scallop-shells or small cups, filling them three fourths, and fill them up with potatoes mashed with a little cream, put a bit of butter on the top, and brown them in an oven.

HASHED COLD MEAT.

Take your bones, and stew them in a little water, with an onion, some salt and pepper, and if you like, a little savory herbs; when the goodness is all out of the bones, and it tastes nice, thicken the gravy with a teaspoonful of corn-starch, and if it is not very strong, put in a bit of butter, then place your stew-pan on the hot hearth, and put in your slices of meat, warm, but do not boil. Serve with toasted bread.

CHICKEN CUTLETS.

Season pieces of cold chicken or turkey with salt and pepper, dip into melted butter; let this cool on the meat, and dip into beaten egg and in fine bread-crumbs; fry in butter until a delicate brown; serve on slices of hot toast, with either a white or curry sauce poured around. Pieces of cold veal make a nice dish, if prepared in this manner.

JELLIED VEAL.

Boil the veal until tender, pick it fine, put into a mold, add the water it was boiled in, and set it in a cold place; season with salt and pepper to taste; a layer of hard-boiled eggs improves it.

RICE AND MEAT CROQUETTES.

One cupful of boiled rice, one cupful of finely chopped cooked meat—any kind—one teaspoonful of salt, a little pepper, two tablespoonfuls of butter, one half cupful of milk, one egg. Put the milk on to boil and add the meat, rice and seasoning; when this boils, add the egg, well beaten; stir one minute; after cooling, shape, dip into egg and crumbs, and fry as before directed.

HAM CROQUETTES.

One cupful of finely chopped cooked ham, one of bread-crumbs, two of hot mashed potatoes, one large tablespoonful of butter, three eggs, a speck of cayenne. Beat the ham, cayenne, butter and two of the eggs into the potato; let the mixture cool slightly, and shape it like croquettes; roll in the bread-crumbs, dip into beaten egg and again into crumbs, put into the frying-basket, and plunge into boiling fat; cook two minutes; drain, and serve.

BEEF PATTIES.

Chop fine some cold beef; beat two eggs, and mix with the meat, and add a little milk, melted butter and salt and pepper; make into rolls, and fry.

BREADED SAUSAGES.

Wipe the sausages dry, dip them into beaten egg and bread-crumbs, put them into the frying-basket, and plunge into boiling fat; cook ten minutes. Serve with a garnish of toasted bread and parsley.

MUSHROOMS.

Wash your mushrooms, and cut them up; put on to cook with cold water and a very little salt, as too much destroys the flavor; cook half an hour, then stir into the liquid a piece of butter dipped into flour, add a little pepper. Serve on toasted bread.

FONDUE.

Butter the size of an egg,   ½ pound of cheese,
1 cupful of bread-crumbs,   1 cupful of milk,
3 eggs.

Cut the butter and cheese into small pieces, and place them in a large bowl with the bread; on this pour scalding milk, after which add the yolks, well beaten, and a little salt; mix well, cover, and set on the back of the stove, stirring occasionally until dissolved, when add the whites, beaten to a stiff froth; place in a buttered pie-plate, and bake in a quick oven for about twenty minutes. Serve immediately. Many eat mustard with it.

Christie Irving.

CHICKEN IN JELLY.

A little cold chicken (about one pint), one cupful of water or stock, one fifth of a box of gelatin, one half teaspoonful of curry-powder, salt, pepper. Cut the meat from the bones of a chicken left from dinner. Put the bones on with water to cover, and boil down to one cupful. Put the gelatin to soak in one fourth of a cupful of cold water. When the stock is reduced as much as is necessary, strain, and season, add the curry and chicken, season, and simmer ten minutes; then add the gelatin, and stir on the table until it is dissolved, turn all into a mold, and set away to harden. This makes a nice relish for tea or lunch. If you have mushrooms, omit the curry, and cut four of them into dice; stir into the mixture while cooking. This dish can be varied by using the whites of hard-boiled eggs or bits of boiled ham. To serve, dip the mold into warm water, and then turn out on the dish. Garnish with parsley.

BOSTON BAKED BEANS.

Pick over one quart of pea-beans, wash, and soak over night in cold water; in the morning, heat to a simmering-point. Mix one level teaspoonful of salt, one level teaspoonful of mustard, six level teaspoonfuls of sugar and a speck of cayenne pepper. Mix well with the beans, and put into an earthen bean-pot. Score the rind of a piece of fat salt pork (with a thin layer of lean) weighing from one half to one pound, and put on top of the beans; fill up the pot with hot water, cover tightly, and bake from twelve to twenty-four hours, according to the color liked, in a hot oven; add hot water frequently to keep the beans well moistened.

Miss Angeline M. Weaver, Instructor Hyde School Kitchen, Boston, Massachusetts.

MUSH BISCUIT.

Two quarts of cold mush, one half cupful of butter or lard. Mix enough flour with this to turn out on the molding-board; roll out an inch thick, cut out with a biscuit-cutter, and bake in a hot oven fifteen or twenty minutes, or until they are a rich brown color.

HONEY.

This is a charming addition to the breakfast-table. To keep it, put the honeycomb into a large sheet of good writing-paper, paste the edges up so as to form a bag, and hang it up in a dry place. Honeycomb may be kept fresh and good for a year by putting it into a tureen or covered dish, with a cloth below the lid to make it tight, and setting it in a cool place. Several combs may be placed one above another. Keep them as whole as possible.

BIRDS' NESTS.

Chop very fine one ounce of beef suet or cold meat, half a cupful of bread-crumbs, season with chopped parsley, powdered thyme and marjoram, a little grated rind of a lemon and half its juice, and one well-beaten egg to bind the mixture. While you are preparing this mixture, have four eggs on the stove to boil hard; ten minutes will be sufficient. Warm half a pint of gravy. When the eggs are boiled hard, take them from the shells, and cover them thickly with the mixture. Put a little butter into a stew-pan, fry them a light brown, dish them up, cut them into halves (first cut off the top of the white, that they might stand), and serve them hot with the hot gravy poured over them.

YORKSHIRE BUCK.

Same as a rarebit, with the addition of two strips of crisp bacon and one poached egg on top.

Eugene Stuyvesant Howard, Member of the Universal Cookery and Food Association, London, England, and Chef de Cuisine, Louisville Hotel.

BREAKFAST VANITIES.

Mix and sift together one pint of pastry-flour, one half teaspoonful of salt, one teaspoonful of baking-powder; mix this to a stiff dough with milk or water, roll out thin, cut into small squares, drop into boiling fat.

Miss Ida M. Foster, City Hospital, Wilkesbarre, Pennsylvania.

Relishes

CHAPTER XI.

There are certain articles usually called side-dishes, or relishes, which some may not know how to prepare, although having the material at hand. These are nice used for teas as the accompaniment of cold meats. Some one of them should always appear upon the table.

ONION RELISH.

Peel four Bermuda onions, slice thinly crosswise, and put to stand for two hours in one cupful of cold water to which has been added one cupful of vinegar. Drain off the water a few minutes before serving, arrange in a dish, and sprinkle heavily with granulated sugar. To be eaten with beans.

Miss Angeline M. Weaver, Instructor Hyde School Kitchen, Boston, Massachusetts.

DEVONSHIRE RELISH.

One medium-sized head of cauliflower, scalded in salt and water; three green peppers, sliced, scalded and well drained; one quart of small-sized green tomatoes, sliced thin and scalded in salt and water; drain the above well, put into a jar, and pour hot vinegar over them, letting it remain three days; then drain them, and make a dressing of one quarter of a pound of ground mustard, one and one half cupfuls of sugar and one half cupful of flour; mix the flour and mustard smooth with cold vinegar, pour into boiling vinegar, and cover the pickles with it, but just before covering add three heads of celery (cut into small pieces and scalded until tender) and one teacupful of grated horse-radish. This is an excellent relish, and a decided change from the ordinary mustard pickles containing turmeric and oil.

187

MUSTARD RELISH.

Beat the yolks of two eggs, and stir into this

3 tablespoonfuls of mustard,	1 teaspoonful of salt,
1 tablespoonful of black pepper,	1 teaspoonful of sugar,
½ teaspoonful of cayenne pepper,	½ cupful of sharp vinegar.

Cook until the thickness of cream. If too thick, add vinegar.

Mrs. Mary J. Humphrey, Le Roy, New York.

CRANBERRY SAUCE.

Wash, and pick over the cranberries; put on with enough cold water to cover them; add a pinch of soda. This will bring a great deal of stuff to the surface, which can be skimmed off. Let them cook until they burst, mash them all with a wooden spoon, then add the sugar—two pounds to three quarts of fruit; boil slowly one and one half hours. Always cook in porcelain or an earthen crock, never in tin. Some strain them when done, and put into a jelly-mold.

ASPARAGUS SUÉDOISE SAUCE.

Asperges Sauce Suédoise.

Open a tin of asparagus, and place it on some pounded ice until perfectly cold. Take a timbal-mold (specially made for the purpose), and fill it with plain cold water; place it in the charged ice-cave, and let it remain for two and one

half to three hours, occasionally turning the mold from side to side in the cave, so as to get the water thoroughly frozen; then dip the mold into tepid water, pass a clean cloth over the bottom to absorb any moisture, and turn out the ice onto the dish on which it is to be served on a dish-paper or on a folded napkin. Drain the asparagus on a clean cloth, cut off the hard part from the bottom of the stems, and then arrange it in a group, as shown in the engraving, in the center of the timbal of ice; garnish around the top of the timbal with little sprigs of nice green fresh chervil, and serve for second course or luncheon or for any cold collation, with iced suédoise sauce in a sauce-boat.

ONION SAUCE.

Boil half a dozen small white onions in a little salt-water. Melt a tablespoonful of butter in a saucepan, add one tablespoonful of sifted flour, mix, pour in one half pint of white stock, and let it boil; season with salt and pepper; press the onions through a sieve, add to the sauce, let boil up once, and take up.

CELERY.

When brought home, if not wanted immediately, it should be wrapped in a wet cloth. An hour before dinner put into cold water, then clean, and arrange on a celery-dish. A more ornamental way is to cut the stalks into pieces four inches long, split these four or five times with a sharp knife, lay in water until they curl; remove to a glass dish; eat with vinegar, pepper and salt.

RHUBARB.

Wash your stalks, and cut them up into inch pieces, not removing the skin, as the chief richness of this vegetable is in the skin; add a great deal of sugar, but no water. Cook until tender; serve hot or cold. It is best to cook it in a crock.

PREPARED MUSTARD.

Put one pint of vinegar on the stove to boil. Stir with a little cold vinegar one tablespoonful of flour, two tablespoonfuls of ground mustard, one teaspoonful of salt and two of sugar and about one third of a teaspoonful of cayenne pepper; stir all together and add to the boiling vinegar. It may be too thin or too thick, but one or two trials will enable any one to tell when they have sufficient flour; but if too thick, add a little cold vinegar.

TO PREPARE HORSE-RADISH FOR WINTER.

In the fall, mix the quantity wanted in the following proportions: One coffee-cupful of grated horse-radish, two tablespoonfuls of white sugar, one half teaspoonful of salt, one and one half pints of cold vinegar. Bottle, and seal.

To make horse-radish sauce, take two tablespoonfuls of the above, add one dessert-spoonful of olive-oil (or melted butter or cream) and one of prepared mustard.

WATER-CRESS.

Water-cress possesses valuable medicinal properties of a stimulating nature, and is said to be particularly useful in strengthening the nerves. The expressed juice, which contains the peculiar pungency and taste of the herb, is used in medicine. External impurities in water-cress may be removed by washing, but not the impurities which are absorbed within. If the full virtues of this herb are to be experienced, it should be eaten frequently and freely. It is mostly used with bread and salt, as an accompaniment to cheese. It is also used to garnish dishes; it is excellent served as a salad; and it is good boiled as spinach. Water-cresses are good from autumn until early summer unless when cut off by frost. Bronze-leaved specimens are the most highly esteemed.

FRIED APPLES.

Quarter and core apples without paring. Prepare a frying-pan by heating and putting in beef drippings, or lard and butter mixed, lay the apples in the pan, skin side down, sprinkle with a very little sugar, and brown thoroughly. Cover while cooking.

GLACÉ BAKED APPLES.

Select rosy-cheeked Baldwin apples with long stems; wipe carefully, and make a cut one half inch deep around each, half way between the stem and blossom ends; put into an earthen dish, with two cupfuls of water to six apples; sprinkle lightly with sugar, bake in a hot oven until the pulp puffs out from the crack; put into a glass dish, and pour over them the water which has been cooked with sugar until syrupy. Put away to cool, so that the liquid will candy on them.

Miss Angeline M. Weaver, Instructor Hyde-School Kitchen, Boston, Massachusetts.

CUCUMBERS.

It does not seem to be generally known that the cucumber is one of the most useful vegetables we have, and can be dressed in a greater variety of palatable ways than any other except the tomato. It is better than squash, and more delicate than the egg-plant, prepared in the same manner; can be stewed, fried or stuffed, and, above all, can be parboiled, mashed up in a batter and fried as fritters—more pleasant and easily prepared than any other vegetable or fruit. When a cucumber just becomes too old to be used raw or for pickling, it is then at its best for cooking, and may be used for that purpose even until the seeds become hard. A raw cucumber is, for most persons, an indigestible abomination, however much they may admire its flavor and odor.

FONDUE.

Slice a stale penny roll; pour over it three gills of boiling milk; when soaked, beat it well, and mix with it half a pound of finely grated cheese, with the yolks of four eggs well whisked. All this may be prepared when most convenient; immediately before it is wanted, beat the whites of four eggs into a solid froth, and add them; pour the whole into the paper forms, and bake them to your taste.

FONDUE À L'ITALIENNE.

Grate half a pound of Parmesan, Gruyere or any good, dry cheese, and stir over the fire half a pint of cream, with enough flour to thicken it; when of the consistency of melted butter, add the cheese and a little salt; mix until the heat has gone off, then blend with the above ingredients four well-beaten yolks of eggs, and, last of all, five whites whipped to a fine froth; bake in a papered tin and in a hot oven, filling the tin to only half its depth. The fondue should rise very high, and be served immediately, or it will fall, and the appearance be spoiled. Time to bake, twenty minutes. Sufficient for five or six persons.

CHEESE FONDUE.

Put to boil one pint of new milk with a tablespoonful of butter in it; dissolve two tablespoonfuls of flour in a little cold milk, and stir in the boiling milk; set off to cool, season with salt and pepper to taste; add five ounces of grated cheese to the mixture, and four eggs beaten separately until very light; mix all, and pour in a buttered dish; bake twenty minutes. Serve at once, as it falls.

Mrs. A. E. Kirtland, Author of "Mrs. Kirtland's Cook Book," Montgomery, Alabama.

FONDUE À L'ITALIENNE.

Mix half a pint of cream with a little flour and a little salt; keep stirring it over the fire until it is as thick as melted butter; then add about half a pound of finely grated cheese; mix it all well until it is half cold. Then take four eggs, separate the yolks from the whites, put the former to the cheese, and beat it well together. Then beat the whites to a solid froth, and add them to the rest; pour the mixture into an ornamented mold or deep dish lined with paper cut in a fringe at the top, and only half fill, as it will rise very high. The oven must be very hot, in order to cause the rising, and the dish must be served immediately, or it will fall; to prevent which, let the cover be of metal, strongly heated; twenty minutes ought to bake it.

FONDUE IN CASES.

This fondue may be made in any form desired—small paper cases, molds or tart-tins. Pound in a mortar, with egg to moisten, equal quantities of Swiss, Parmesan and cream cheese (a quarter of a pound of each); moisten with five eggs; mix the egg gradually while pounding; bake in a hot oven, allowing time to give the fondue a rich color. Serve quickly. Time, about ten minutes to bake.

PARMESAN RINGS.
Ronds au Parmesan.

Put into a stew-pan one fourth of a pint of single cream, one fourth of a pint of new milk, one teaspoonful of salt, a dust of red pepper and three ounces of butter; bring this to a boil, then add five and one half ounces of fine flour that has been sifted; stir well together, and cook on the stove for five or six minutes; then remove from the fire and mix into it four raw, well-beaten eggs and one fourth of a pound of grated Parmesan cheese; mix well, then put some of the

mixture into a forcing-bag with a plain pipe, and force it out onto a frying-strainer in the form of rings; brush these over with whole beaten raw egg, and then put them into hot, clean fat, and fry for eight to ten minutes, when they should be a nice golden color. Take them up, dust them over with grated Parmesan cheese, and serve hot on a dish-paper for a savory. These are also nice as a cold dish, and can be used for ball suppers, etc.

RAMEKINS.

2 eggs,	2 ounces of melted butter,
2 spoonfuls of flour,	2 ounces of grated cheese.

Mix all well, and bake it in molds or tart-pans for a quarter of an hour.

RAMEKINS À LA PARISIENNE.

Boil half a pint of milk and half the quantity of cream; melt one ounce of butter and a little salt; mix in one spoonful of flour, and stir it over the fire for five minutes; pour in the milk and cream by degrees, and work it smooth, taking care that it is thoroughly cooked; then take it off, and add half a pound of grated cheese, some coarsely ground pepper and an atom of nutmeg, with a very little powdered sugar, the yolks of eight eggs and the whites of two, well beaten; when perfectly mixed, add the whites of six eggs beaten to a froth. The batter should be as thick as cream. Make little paper trays, fill them three parts full, and bake them in a very slow oven eighteen minutes.

FRIED RAMEKINS.

Grate half a pound of cheese, and melt two ounces of butter; when the latter is getting cool, mix it with the cheese and the well-beaten whites of three eggs. Lay buttered papers on a frying-pan, put slices of bread upon it, and lay the cheese on the top; set it over the fire for about five minutes, then take it off, and brown it with a salamander.

EGGS AND CHEESE.

These are mixed in various ways by French cooks, under the names of fondues or foudeaux, ramekins and other titles, for the purpose of preparing entremets, or side-dishes, for elegant tables. Gruyere and Parmesan are the most proper sorts to be used, but any dry cheese of good flavor may be employed.

POTTED CHEESE.

Scrape and pound cheese, with a piece of butter, cayenne pepper, a few grains of pounded mace, one teaspoonful of sifted sugar, one glassful of vinegar and a little salt; press it into your potting-jar for shape.

COTTAGE (DUTCH) CHEESE.

Take a crockful of clabbered milk, and set it on the stove to heat a little; when the whey and clabber separate, pour it into a jelly-bag, and hang it up where it will drain until dry; season with salt, a piece of butter or rich cream; use pepper if desired; mix with the hand, and make into small balls, or if much cream is used, serve in a dish.

Mrs. N. A. McDonald, Sago, Ohio.

CHEESE STRAWS.

Take a pint of flour and half a pint of grated cheese; mix them, and make a paste with lard as you would for pies; roll out in a thick sheet, cut into strips one half inch broad and five or six inches long; bake a light brown. Place a white napkin on a plate, and pile the "straws" in log-cabin shape upon it. This is a delicate dish, to be eaten with salads.

Mrs. C. S. K., Springfield, Ohio.

CHEESE FLEUR IN SURPRISE.

Fleur au Fromage en Surprise.

Lightly butter a fleur-ring, and place it on a buttered paper on a buttered baking-tin, line it entirely with cheese paste (see below) about one fourth of an inch thick, trim off the edges neatly, and prick it well at the bottom; fit a buttered paper to the inside of the fleur, and fill up the center with raw rice;

bake in a moderate oven for about twenty minutes, and when cooked, take up, remove the paper and rice, and fill up the case with cheese purée (see recipe); then by means of a forcing-bag with a large rose-pipe cover over quickly with the whites of four eggs that have been whipped stiff with a pinch of salt and a dust of red pepper; sprinkle with grated Parmesan cheese and a few browned bread-crumbs, put into a quick oven for about ten minutes; then place on a hot dish, and serve hot for a second-course or a savory dish.

CHEESE PASTE.—Take one fourth of a pound of fine flour, two ounces of butter, one ounce of grated Parmesan cheese, a little salt and pepper and one whole raw egg; mix into a stiff paste with cold water, then roll out, and use.

PINEAPPLE CHEESE.

The preparation of the curd does not differ materially from that for the best factory and other styles of long-keeping cheese. But greater care and skill are needed, for a slight defect which would not much affect the value of factory

cheese is fatal to the pineapple. The rind must be perfect, else invisible cracks will open during curing, and the least admission of air is followed by internal molding. In the mold the cheese stands with the point downward. A neck three and one half inches in diameter extends upward from the bottom of the cheese,

7

and receives the pressure. These necks are cut off, broken up, and mixed with the next day's curd. To perfect the rind, the bottom is seared with a hot iron. The mold is constructed from four blocks of four-inch scantling. The carving, which can be done by any pattern-maker or skilful carpenter, is done mainly upon these quarters. They are then attached to one another in pairs by iron bolts. Two halves are then fitted to one another by dowels, and held together by a strong framework or gripe with its wedges. The mold, when complete, is a block fifteen inches high and eight by eight inches in size. A bag of strong drilling is thrust downward through the neck, and the mold is then ready to receive the curd. The pressure is applied either by screw or lever, the latter being preferable. This is the simplest method and crudest for pressing. But there is a great saving of time and labor by the crowders and gang-presses now used in factories. These gang-presses are somewhat ingenious and elaborate, and press fifty cheeses each. The cheeses come from the press with a smooth surface, and the impression upon them is made by the net and the process of netting. Nets are made of the best linen twine, are made by hand, and with great care. After being drawn over the cheese, and accurately secured, the cheese is hung in a bath of hot water, the temperature of which is regulated by the conditions of the curd and of the weather. They are then withdrawn, one by one, and subjected to a machine, which at the same time stretches and twists so as to give an even impression of the net over the entire surface of the cheese. It is very easy to net cheese if there is no attempt made to make them handsome. But the whole question of profit turns upon their beauty, and only a skilled hand can do the work with success. After setting, they pass to the curing-room, and are hung in the nets for several weeks, or until the nets are required for use upon fresh cheese.

SANDWICHES À LA VICTORIA.

Cut some white bread into thin slices and butter them well, then mask some with a chicken puree prepared as below; place a slice of plain bread and butter

on the top of this, and press well together; when all the slices have been thus prepared, mask over the top of each with a thin layer of the same chicken puree, and with a plain round cutter stamp out in rounds about two and one half inches in diameter, and then cut them into half-moon shapes. Mask each sandwich over with a white chaudfroid sauce, resting them on a broad palette-knife during the process; then garnish each of them across in three divisions alternately with chopped and pressed parsley, chopped tongue, and yolk of hard-boiled egg that has been passed through a wire sieve; set this garnish by sprinkling a few drops of aspic jelly over it; then dish up on a dish-paper, as in the engraving, placing in the center some well-washed small salad, and garnishing around the outside of the sandwiches with little blocks of aspic jelly, and place around the jelly at regular intervals some little bunches of the yolk of hard-boiled egg and a little chopped parsley, and serve for a luncheon or second course dish, tea or for evening parties or ball supper.

PUREE OF CHICKEN FOR SANDWICHES A LA VICTORIA.—Pound together into a paste one half pound of cooked chicken, with two ounces of butter, a little salt and white pepper, a dust of pepper, one tablespoonful of thick cream, one and one half tablespoonfuls of bechamel sauce, one dessert-spoonful of tarragon and the same of chilli vinegar, and rub through a wire sieve.

HAM SANDWICHES.

Cut thin slices from a well-boiled ham, trim off all the fat, cut into strips. Butter thin slices of stale bread, lay the ham on them, spread with a little mustard, cover with upper slices of bread, and press together.

TURKEY SANDWICH.

Cut slices of cold turkey as thin as possible, dip into plain salad dressing, place between slices of stale bread, press together, and serve.

SANDWICHES À LA LOUISE.

Take some thin slices of stale bread, butter them, then spread them over with egg puree, as below, and on the egg place a layer of washed and boned anchovies, and then a sprinkling of small salad; close this over with another

slice of buttered bread, pressing well together, and with a plain round cutter stamp out into rounds about two inches in diameter. Mask over with sauce, as below, taking care the sauce is used when cooling, and sprinkle each with a little lobster coral or coralline pepper and chopped Spanish olive. Dish on a paper on a plate, and garnish around with little bunches of picked fresh salad and little blocks of aspic jelly, and in the center arrange layers of yolk and white of hard-boiled egg that have passed through a wire sieve, and some chopped cooked beet-root.

EGG PUREE FOR SANDWICHES A LA LOUISE.—Take four yolks of hard-boiled eggs, two ounces of good butter, one tablespoonful of bechamel sauce, a dust of pepper, six raw bearded oysters; pound until smooth, then rub through a fine hair-sieve, and use,

SARDINE SANDWICH.

Remove the skin of half a dozen sardines, split, and take out the bones. Spread slices of bread very thinly with butter, place on each two halves of the fish, squeeze a little lemon-juice over them, add a crisp leaf of lettuce to each, and put a slice of buttered bread on top.

EGG SANDWICH.

Boil half a dozen eggs hard; when cold, remove the shells, and cut into thin slices; season with salt and pepper; butter slices of bread; put four slices of egg into each sandwich.

SANDWICHES À LA FIANE.

Take some little sandwich-molds, line them thinly with aspic jelly, ornament them with shreds of red French chilli, white of egg and picked leaves of chervil, setting these with a little more aspic; fill the molds with some thinly cut slices of pate de foie gras. Line some more molds with a plain aspic, and fill these up with a puree of chicken or any white meat, let this partly set, then pour

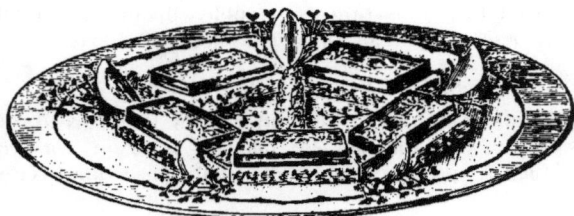

a little liquid aspic into the molds containing the foie gras, and place those containing the chicken to those with the foie gras; then leave until set and firm, and when cold, turn out the contents of each pair of molds by dipping them into hot water, and place each on a fried crouton about the same size as the molds. Dish up on a cold dish on a paper, and garnish here and there with bunches of well-washed cress, and when in season, quarters of boiled plovers' eggs that are sprinkled with a little pepper. Serve as a cold entree for dinner, luncheon, tea or ball supper.

CHICKEN PUREE FOR SANDWICHES A LA FIANE.—Take for six to eight molds, four ounces of cooked chicken, one half gill of strong chicken stock, one ounce of butter, two tablespoonfuls of cream, a pinch of salt and white pepper and one dessert-spoonful of bechamel sauce; pound until smooth, then mix with one and one half gills of cool aspic jelly, tammy or rub through a fine hair-sieve, and use when beginning to set, so as to allow the two mixtures to join together.

CHEESE SANDWICH.

Butter slices of thinly cut bread, sprinkle over a few sprigs of chopped parsley. Cut the cheese into thin slices, put between the bread, and serve. Cheese mixed with butter and spread on bread, or grated over slices of buttered bread, makes excellent sandwiches.

TONGUE SANDWICH.

Cut up half a pound of cold boiled beef tongue, put it into a mortar, with the yolks of two hard-boiled eggs, one tablespoonful of mustard, salt and a little cayenne pepper, pound to a paste; moisten with a very little cream; spread the paste on slices of bread, press together, cut in two, and serve. Tongue may also be sliced thin, spread with French mustard, and laid between slices of buttered bread.

BALLETTES OF FOIE GRAS À L'IMPÉRIALE.
Ballettes de Foie Gras à l'Impériale.

Line some little molds thinly with aspic jelly, and garnish them with egg mixtures in red and white, stamped out into tiny rings the size of a five-cent piece (see recipe "Egg Garnishes for Soups and Molds"); set this garnish with a little aspic jelly, and then fill up the centers with a nice piece of pate de foie gras; set this with a little more liquid aspic jelly, close up the molds, and leave

them until the contents are firm; then dip each mold into hot water, and turn out onto a bed of finely chopped aspic jelly; garnish with sprigs of tarragon and chervil and halves of cooked artichoke bottoms that are filled with flageolets mixed with a little salad-oil, tarragon and chilli vinegar, and serve for an entree for dinner or luncheon or any cold service.

SOUFFLÉ OF FOIE GRAS À LA MONTRÉAL.
Soufflé de Foie Gras à la Montréal.

Place a double band of paper around the outside of a silver or paper souffle case so that it stands about four inches above the case, fix it with a little sealing-wax, and then line it with a mock foie gras or liver farce prepared as below by means of a forcing-bag with a plain pipe, forcing out the mixture to the thickness and length of finger-biscuits; smooth this over with a wet, warm knife, then fill up the insides of the case with the cream mixture, as below, and put the souffle into the ice-box for about one hour; then remove the paper band, and garnish the top of the souffle, as in the engraving, with cooked artichoke bottoms that have been sliced, and seasoned with a little salad oil, tarragon vinegar, chopped tarragon and a little finely chopped aspic jelly. Serve on a napkin or dish-paper for an entree or second-course dish or for a cold collation.

CREAM MIXTURE FOR SOUFFLE OF FOIE GRAS A LA MONTREAL.- Whip one pint of double cream until perfectly stiff, then whip half a pint of consomme or good chicken stock of the consistency of jelly, with half a pint of aspic until spongy, add this to the cream, with a dust of pepper and a pinch of salt; cut up the contents of a small tin of pate de foie gras into tiny dice shapes with a wet, warm knife, and mix with the other ingredients, add two or three chopped truffles, and put all into a forcing-bag with a plain pipe, and use as directed above.

MOCK FOIE GRAS OR LIVER FARCE FOR SOUFFLE A LA MONTREAL.—Cut into square pieces one pound of calf's liver, one half pound of raw bacon and one onion, add a pinch of salt and pepper, and fry over a quick fire in two ounces of

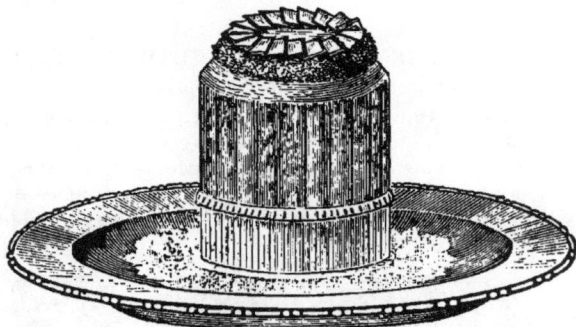

butter for two or three minutes; remove from the pan, and pound, and pass through a wire sieve while hot; then add two or three shredded truffles, mix with half a pint of liquid aspic jelly, and stir on ice until the mixture is getting set, then put into a bag with a large, plain pipe, and use as instructed.

MOUSSE OF FOIE GRAS À LA ROSSINI.

Mousse de Foie Gras à la Rossini.

Line a plain round charlotte-mold thinly with liquid aspic jelly, ornament it with truffles, gherkins, red chillies and white of hard-boiled egg that are cut into slices, then stamped out in any pretty designs, setting them to the mold with a little more aspic to keep them in their places. Take the contents of a jar of pate de foie gras, and rub it through a clean, fine wire sieve, and mix it with two wine-glassfuls of sherry. Take half a pint of good-flavored light

stock, mix it with a little more than one fourth of an ounce of gelatin, and when dissolved, strain, and leave until somewhat cool; whip it in a whipping-tin until quite spongy, add this to the foie gras, and pour it into the prepared mold; leave it on ice until cold and firm; then dip it into hot water, pass a clean cloth over the bottom to absorb any moisture, turn out the mousse onto a bed of plainly boiled cold rice, garnish it with little blocks of cut aspic jelly, and serve for a cold entree or for second course or any cold collation.

LITTLE BOUCHÉES OF FOIE GRAS À LA RUSSE.
Petites Bouchées de Foie Gras à la Russe.

Thinly line some little molds with aspic jelly, garnish them with little thinly cut strips of hard-boiled white of egg, and place here and there around the mold some little beads of the prepared red garnish, using a forcing-bag with a small, plain pipe for the purpose, and at the bottom of the mold form a little border all around with finely shredded lettuce, setting it with a little more liquid aspic jelly. Place a little piece of pate de foie gras in the center of each mold, then fill them up entirely with liquid aspic jelly, and put aside until set. Take some little square paper cases, nearly filling them with the prepared salad, turn out the little bouchees by dipping them into hot water, and draining them on a clean cloth, and place one in each case on top of the green salad, and by means of a forcing-bag with a medium-sized pipe form a little border of finely chopped aspic jelly all around the edge of the case; place a tiny sprig of raw green chervil or a small cleansed radish at the four corners of the case, dish up on a dish-paper on

entree or flat dish, and serve for cold entree, second-course dish or for any cold collation.

RED GARNISH FOR LITTLE BOUCHEES OF FOIE GRAS A LA RUSSE.—Take about two ounces of finely chopped lean cooked ham or tongue, mix it with sufficient liquid aspic jelly to cover it, season with a little pepper and a few drops of carmine, stir until beginning to set, then put into the forcing-bag, and use as directed.

SALAD FOR LITTLE BOUCHEES OF FOIE GRAS A LA RUSSE.—Take the heart of a nice, well-washed, crisp lettuce, dry it well, cut it into shreds, mix with it a little freshly chopped tarragon and chervil, season with a little salad-oil and salt; mix, and use.

TIMBALS OF FOIE GRAS À LA BÉATRICE.
Timbales de Foie Gras à la Béatrice.

Line the little egg-molds very thinly with strong aspic jelly, then ornament them with finely shredded raw, crisp green lettuce, green French gherkins cut into shreds, and a little tarragon and red chilli; set these with a little aspic jelly, then fill up the centers with pieces of pate de foie gras and truffle cut into strips, add a little aspic jelly to set this, and put on ice to get cold. Line a border-mold with aspic jelly, ornament it around the edge similarly to the eggs, then fill up with aspic, and put aside to get cold; when ready to serve, dip the molds into warm water, and turn out; arrange an egg shape in each of the spaces of the piccolo, put some chopped aspic into the center by means of a forcing-bag and pipe, and dish another egg on the top of this, as in the engraving; garnish around this with chopped aspic jelly and quarters of plovers' or chickens' eggs that are sprinkled with chopped truffle and shreds of red chilli, and then masked with aspic jelly, and here and there some nice vegetable, to a pint of which one table-spoonful of salad-oil, one tablespoonful of tarragon vinegar, a few drops of chilli vinegar and a pinch of mignonette pepper have been added. Place in each

corner of the dish, as in the engraving, a little round of thick mayonnaise, using a forcing-bag and pipe for the purpose, with some of the vegetables, and serve for a cold entree or for any cold collation.

TIMBAL À LA JARDINIÈRE.
Timbale à la Jardinière.

Line a fancy border-mold, as shown in the design, with aspic jelly about an inch thick, then garnish it with little fresh sprigs of raw chervil and tarragon, and here and there place in the mold some quarters of hard-boiled egg that are garnished with strips of French red chilli, and then set in the mold with a little aspic jelly, and fill up the inside of the mold between the egg with cooked veg-etables; set this with cool aspic jelly, and place on ice until quite firm, then dip

the mold into hot water, and turn out on a flat cold dish, and fill up the center of the timbal with any nice cooked meat, such as chicken or other bird that is cut into thin slices and seasoned with vinaigrette sauce; then by means of a large forcing-bag and rose-pipe cover over with a good thick mayonnaise sauce. Serve for a second-course dish or for luncheon, etc.

LITTLE TIMBALS À LA BELLE EUGÉNIE.

Petites Timbales à la Belle Eugénie.

Take some little fluted dariol-molds, and line them about one eighth of an inch thick with strong aspic jelly; then arrange alternately around the molds from top to bottom, strips of cooked filleted sole that are cut about two inches long by one fourth of an inch thick, and boned Christiania anchovies, with raw peeled tomatoes that are also cut into strips; set this garnish to the sides of the molds with a little aspic, and fill up the centers with about one teaspoonful of picked shrimps or two or three of the prepared crayfish; cover this with aspic, and put aside until set; when ready to serve, plunge each mold into hot water, and turn out the timbals; dish them up on a border of aspic jelly, place a wax figure with a top in the center, and garnish it around with a ragout of cold pieces of cooked sole, anchovies, turned olives and tomatoes that are cut up into little square pieces, and seasoned with a little finely chopped tarragon and chervil,

salad-oil and tarragon vinegar; arrange some chopped aspic jelly around the base of the border, cut some strips of aspic jelly, and place one between each little timbal, as shown in the engraving. Fill the center of the cup at the top of the wax figure with the same mixture that was used for garnishing the base; arrange some chopped aspic jelly around this as a border, and garnish with strips of fresh tarragon; then place on the top of each timbal by means of a forcing-bag and pipe a little stiff mayonnaise sauce. Serve for an entree or ball-supper dish or for a cold collation.

TIMBAL A LA WINDSOR.

Timbale à la Windsor.

Take a bomb-mold, line it thinly with aspic jelly, and then arrange all over it sticks of cooked asparagus that have been ornamented with strips of French chilli and little sprigs of chervil set on the asparagus with a little liquid aspic jelly; set the asparagus with a little more aspic to keep it in place; then fill up the inside of the mold with a puree of white meat, as below, and put it away to get set; then dip the mold into hot water, and turn it out on an entree-dish; garnish around with little blocks of aspic jelly and cooked artichoke bottoms that are sliced, also sliced raw tomatoes, seasoned with a little mignonette pepper, salad-oil and tarragon vinegar. Serve for an entree, second-course or luncheon dish.

PUREE FOR TIMBAL A LA WINDSOR.—Take a pound of either cooked chicken or rabbit; pound it until smooth, then mix it with one tablespoonful of tarragon vinegar, one half ounce of good butter, one tablespoonful of mayonnaise sauce,

a dust of pepper, two tablespoonfuls of thick bechamel sauce, and mix with this three fourths of a pint of liquid aspic jelly; rub through a tammy or fine hair-sieve, then add two tablespoonfuls of stiffly whipped cream, and use when beginning to set.

PLOVERS' EGGS IN ASPIC À LA VICTORIA.

Œufs de Pluviers en Aspic à la Victoria.

Line both parts of the little egg-molds with aspic jelly. Cut some small diamond shapes from white of hard-boiled egg, and little rings from sliced truffle; arrange these in star shapes in the tops of the egg-molds, set these with a little aspic jelly, and garnish the molds all over with little picked leaves of chervil (shreds of lettuce and tarragon may also be used); set this garnish with a little more aspic, place a plainly boiled plover's egg in the top of each mold, fix the two parts of the mold together, and carefully fill up with aspic jelly; put them aside on ice until set, then turn out. Prepare a border-mold in the same manner

by lining it with aspic jelly, and garnish it with stars and chervil, etc., similar to the little molds, and fill up with aspic; when it is set, turn out, and place one of the prepared eggs in each hollow of the piccolo-border and one in the center, and garnish the center round the eggs, and dish with chopped aspic by means of a forcing-bag and pipe, and blocks of foie gras at the corners of the piccolo shape, as in the engraving. Little green tarragon and chervil leaves may be placed here and there on the garnish.

EGG À LA MILLAIS.

(Œuf à la Millais.

Take a large egg-mold, and line both halves about one eighth of an inch thick with strong aspic jelly. Then take four or five newly laid eggs, and boil them for eight minutes, and when cold, shell and cut them into slices about one fourth of an inch thick, and place them on a baking-tin or dish, and mask them lightly over with liquid aspic jelly to prevent them from breaking when being arranged in the mold; then ornament the mold with these slices, arranging them to over-lap straight down, commencing in the middle of the mold and garnishing around each by means of a forcing-bag and a small, plain pipe with chopped truffle and ox-tongue (see below). Set each layer of egg garnish with a little aspic jelly to keep it in place; when both halves of the mold are covered with the garnish, fill up the inside of each part with a chicken cream, as below, and when about to close up the mold, put into each part about two tablespoonfuls of liquid aspic to join the parts firmly together, and tie the mold over with a piece of broad tape to keep it closed. When cold, arrange some finely chopped aspic jelly on the dish on which the egg is to be served, then dip the mold into hot water, and turn the egg on the chopped jelly; garnish around the edge with halves of cooked artichoke bottoms seasoned with salad-oil and tarragon vinegar, and on

these arrange a mayonnaise of cooked potatoes (see recipe), and here and there around the dish place little blocks of cut aspic jelly. Serve this dish for a cold entrée or for any cold collation. Enough for six to eight persons.

TRUFFLE FOR EGG A LA MILLAIS.—Chop one or two truffles up finely, and mix them with enough liquid aspic jelly to cover them; then mix on ice until set, put into the forcing-bag with a plain pipe, and use.

TONGUE FOR EGG A LA MILLAIS.—Chop up one ounce of lean cooked tongue or ham, put it into a little stew-pan, with enough aspic jelly to cover it, and dis-solve; add a few drops of carmine to give it a brighter color; stir until set, and then use.

CHICKEN CREAM FOR EGG A LA MILLAIS.—Take one fourth of a pound of cooked chicken or pheasant, etc., pound it until smooth, and then mix it with one fourth of a pint of good-flavored velouté sauce in which one fourth of an ounce of gelatin is dissolved; rub it through a hair-sieve, and then mix it with two tablespoonfuls of cooked cucumber that has been cut up into tiny dice shapes, and one fourth of a pint of stiffly whipped cream, two chopped French gherkins and one ounce of chopped lean ham or tongue, and stir on ice until it begins to set, then use.

EGGS IN CHAUDFROID À LA BRESSOIRE.

Œufs en Chaudfroid à la Bressoire.

Take some little copper egg-molds, and thinly line them with liquid aspic jelly, garnish the top of each mold with a little round of truffle, and arrange little diamond shapes of the same all around it; place a sprig or two of chervil toward the bottom of the mold, and set the garnish with a little aspic; then line

the molds again with aspic cream, and fill them up with the ragout; leave them until set, then dip each mold into hot water, turn out the eggs, and dish them up on a border of aspic jelly made in a piccolo-mold; place in the center of the border a lettuce salad (see recipe) and a little chopped aspic jelly; arrange another egg on top of this, and serve for a luncheon or second-course dish or for any cold collation.

RAGOUT FOR EGGS IN CHAUDFROID A LA BRESSOIRE.—Take one half pint of good-flavored chicken stock or clear soup that is quite in a jelly in strength equal to aspic, mix with it one half pint of stiffly whipped double cream, a dust of pepper and a little salt, one ounce of grated Parmesan cheese, three ounces of finely minced cooked chicken, two ounces of lean cooked ham, minced, three yolks of hard-boiled eggs cut into tiny dice shapes, and two ounces of pate de foie gras that have been rubbed through a sieve; mix well, stir on ice until it begins to set, then use.

LITTLE SWANS À LA PHRYGIENNE.

Petits Cygnets à la Phrygienne.

Line some swan-molds thinly with aspic, and for the bills put little strips of truffle, also tiny rounds for the eyes; set these with a little aspic, then line with

aspic cream, and fill up the inside of the molds with a puree as follows: For eight or ten molds, take the contents of a small jar of pate de foie gras freed from fat, and six ounces of cooked chicken that has been pounded until quite smooth and rubbed through a fine sieve; mix these well in the mortar and add one half pint of strong good-flavored warm chicken or any light stock that would set into a stiff jelly when cold, and use when setting. Pour in a little liquid aspic to set, and then close up the molds, and leave them on ice until set; dip each mold into hot water, turn out the swans on a clean cloth, and dish them up on a border of finely chopped aspic jelly that is lightly colored with a little sap-green; garnish the dish with little timbals of tomatoes and olives prepared as below, and serve for any cold collation.

TIMBALS FOR LITTLE SWANS.—Take some fluted molds, and line half of them with liquid aspic jelly that is colored with a little carmine; line the other half with liquid aspic that has been colored with sap-green. Fill those with the red jelly with raw tomato that has been skinned and freed from pips, seasoned with a little finely chopped shallot, tarragon and chervil, and set with more of the red jelly. Those with the green fill up with Spanish olives that are farced with ham butter, using a forcing-bag and pipe for the purpose, setting this with more of the green jelly; leave all until set, then turn out, and use as directed.

NEW CARROTS À LA FRANCAISE.

Carrottes Nouvelles à la Francaise.

Take some young carrots, wash, peel, and cut them into small olive shapes; turn them with a garnishing-knife, and put them into cold water, with a little salt; bring to a boil, then strain, and dry the carrots in a clean cloth, and fry them in a stew-pan with a pat of fresh butter over a steady fire for fifteen to

twenty minutes; then add one wine-glassful of sherry and one fourth of a pint of good-flavored stock; bring this to a boil, and cook the carrots for about one hour, occasionally adding a little more stock as that in the pan reduces; when the carrots should present a glazed appearance, add to them a tiny dust of sugar and a few cooked shredded button mushrooms. Put them into paste cases, as below, ornament around the tops of the cases with little rings of the same paste; dish on a paper on a hot dish, and serve.

PASTE CASES FOR CARROTS A LA FRANCAISE.—Rub one fourth of a pound of fine flour with two ounces of butter, a little salt and cayenne until smooth, then mix in one whole raw egg and a little cream, making it into a stiff, dry paste; roll this out thinly, and with it line some little tins; prick the paste well at the bottom to prevent it blistering; line them with a buttered kitchen paper, and fill up with raw rice; bake them in a moderate oven until a pretty golden color and quite crisp; then remove the rice and papers, and use as directed above. Stamp out some tiny rings of the same paste with a fluted cutter, bake them; then brush each over with a very little raw white of egg, sprinkle them with a little chopped raw green parsley, and use for ornamenting the tops of the cases when prepared.

ÉCLAIRS À LA PALMERSTON.

Éclairs à la Palmerston.

Put into a stew-pan one half pint of water, four ounces of butter, a dust of pepper and a good pinch of salt; let this boil, then mix in five ounces of fine flour, and cook on the side of the stove for ten minutes, stirring it occasionally; remove it from the stove, and let the mixture cool a little, then add by degrees three whole raw eggs, working the paste quickly with a wooden spoon. When it is quite smooth, add two large tablespoonfuls of grated Parmesan cheese, mix up well, put the paste into a forcing-bag with a plain pipe, and force it out onto a greased baking-tin in lengths of about three inches by one inch, as shown

in the design; brush them over with whole beaten-up egg, and bake in a moderate oven for about twenty-three minutes; then remove, and cut them longways, and fill them up by means of a forcing-bag and pipe with whipped cream; dish them up in a pile on a dish-paper or napkin. Serve hot or cold for luncheon or dinner savory.

SOUFFLÉ À LA MARGUERITE.

Soufflé à la Marguerite.

Take a large paper case about six inches in diameter, and surround it with a buttered paper to stand about two inches above the paper case, using a little sealing-wax to fix the paper band; take half a sheet of foolscap, make it into a cylinder about three inches in diameter, also using a little sealing-wax to hold it, and stand it in the center of the souffle-case. Take four large tomatoes, peel them, and remove the pips, and pass them through the tammy; to this puree add one half pint of aspic jelly while liquid, a few drops of carmine and about one tablespoonful of tarragon vinegar; well whip these together until spongy, then add a good half pint of whipped cream, half a large breast of finely chopped chicken and three or four finely chopped small truffles; when well mixed, pour this into the papered case between the two paper bands, and put it aside to set. Take half a pint of whipped cream, season with a little finely chopped tarragon and chervil, one salt-spoonful of mignonette pepper, a dust of pepper, a pinch of salt, one small or half a large breast of shredded chicken, two or three chopped truffles, four large or six small chopped mushrooms and some shredded tongue in quantity about the same amount as the chicken, four or five shredded cocks-combs and a fourth of a pint of aspic jelly while liquid; mix all well, and pour the mixture into the cylinder of foolscap, so as to stand one and one half to two inches higher than the mixture already between the two paper bands; place the souffle in an ice-cave or souffle-case surrounded with ice and salt for about one hour; when ready, take it out, remove the paper bands, sprinkle some

chopped truffle over the higher and inner part, and garnish the outer part with little bunches of chervil. The outer ring should stand one and one half to two inches higher than the souffle-case, and should be of a pale reddish color, the inner and higher part being whitish. Dish on a dish-paper or napkin. Instead of the cylinder of paper in which the second mixture is poured, a jar could be used at first, but the jar would have to be removed and a cylinder of paper substituted when the second mixture is ready to be poured in.

CREAM À L'INDIENNE.
Crème à l'Indienne.

Line a large egg-mold with aspic jelly, and ornament it with truffle, shreds of white of hard-boiled egg, French red chilli and French gherkin; set this garnish with more jelly, and line the mold completely with aspic cream; fill up the mold with a cream, as below; put aside until set, then dip the mold into hot water and turn out the egg onto a bed of chopped aspic on an entree-dish; arrange around the egg some small eggs prepared as below, and between each of these place a little finely chopped aspic, and garnish the eggs with small hatelet skewers. Serve for an entree for dinner or luncheon or for any cold collation.

CREAM FOR MOLD FOR CREAM A L'INDIENNE.—Take half a pound of cold cooked chicken, half a pound of lean cooked ham and one ounce of fresh butter; pound together until quite smooth, then mix it with one half pint of sauce, as below, and rub all through a tammy or fine hair-sieve; mix with one fourth of a pint of stiffly whipped cream, and pour into the mold.

SAUCE FOR CREAM A L'INDIENNE.—Cut up four peeled onions into little dice shapes, and put them into a stew-pan, with one ounce of good butter, two bay-leaves and a sprig of thyme; fry until a nice golden color; then mix with one

teaspoonful of chutney, one chopped capsicum, one dessert-spoonful of tam-arinds, one teaspoonful of curry paste, one dessert-spoonful of curry-powder, one teaspoonful of turmeric, the juice of one large lemon, two tablespoonfuls of grated fresh cocoanut, one salt-spoonful of salt and one ounce of glace; mix with one pint of white stock, one wine-glassful of sherry and the same of white wine, then simmer until tender; dissolve it in one fourth of an ounce of gelatin, tammy, and use.

SMALL EGGS FOR GARNISH.—Line some little egg-molds with aspic jelly, fill up with cooked vegetables, and pour in some aspic jelly. When this is set, dip into hot water, turn out, and use.

ARTICHOKES, PLAIN.

Artichauts, Naturels.

Trim the tops, and cut off the stalks evenly of some nice fresh artichokes, put them into cold water, with a little salt, and let them remain in this for two or

three hours; then put them into plenty of slightly salted boiling water, and let them simmer gently for fifty to sixty minutes; then take them up with a slice, drain them on a clean hair-sieve, place them on a hot dish on a paper or napkin, and serve for a second-course vegetable or for breakfast or for luncheon, either as a hot or cold dish, with mayonnaise sauce handed in a sauce-boat.

Salads

CHAPTER XII.

Salads should be served the day they are prepared.

In using oil as a mixture, always use it before putting in the vinegar, to avoid curdling. Then add the vinegar, stirring all the time.

Melted butter can be substituted if oil is disagreeable, or the fat rising to the surface in boiling your fowl.

Use the best olive-oil, always.

Vegetable salads should be stirred only lightly with a fork, and never packed.

To fringe celery, cut it into pieces two inches long, stick several needles into a cork, and comb the celery with it, or split it down into several parts with a sharp knife. Throw into cold water to curl. This is a very appetizing relish, also, with vinegar, pepper and salt.

Always use a wooden spoon or fork to stir salad.

If fresh celery cannot be had, use celery-seed to flavor your salads.

All lobster salad should be eaten as soon as possible after the dressing is added, else it becomes unwholesome.

When canned lobster is used, open a few hours before using, to allow the confined odor to pass away.

Rings made of the whites of hard-boiled eggs, laid around the dish on small lettuce-leaves, garnish a dish of salad nicely.

CHICKEN SALAD.

One finely chopped boiled chicken, one head of cabbage and an equal amount of finely chopped celery, the whites of twelve hard-boiled eggs chopped with it. Take the yolks and rub them fine, then add two tablespoonfuls of sugar, one tablespoonful of butter, one tablespoonful of mustard, one cupful of cider vinegar; mix it all, and serve.

Mrs. D. R. Connell, North Lewisburgh, Ohio.

CHICKEN SALAD.

9 eggs.	2 tablespoonfuls of sugar,
½ pound of butter or	1 teaspoonful of black pepper,
1 teacupful of olive-oil,	3 cold cooked chickens or
1 teacupful of vinegar,	1 medium-sized turkey,
4 tablespoonfuls of mixed mustard,	2 or 3 bunches of celery.

Beat the eggs well, adding all the ingredients but the chicken and celery; put it into a kettle to cook, stirring it all the time until it cooks almost as thick as mush; when cold, add one half cupful of strong vinegar, and pour the dressing over the chicken and celery chopped together and salted to suit the taste; mix well, leaving out enough dressing to cover the top.

Mrs. Carrie Bell, Eminence, Kentucky.

HAM SALAD.

Chop fine the remains of a boiled ham; add the heart and inside leaves of a head of lettuce; pour over it a dressing made as follows:

1 tablespoonful of salt,	1 teaspoonful of mustard,
1 tablespoonful of butter,	½ pint of vinegar,
1 teaspoonful of sugar,	1 teaspoonful of pepper,
The yolks of three well-beaten eggs.	

Boil until it creams; when cold, pour over the ham and lettuce, and mix well; lastly stir in a cupful of sweet cream.

Mrs. Van Cartmell, Springfield, Ohio.

SALMON SALAD.

Four hard-boiled eggs, the yolks of two rubbed fine, and mixed with one raw yolk, a pinch of sugar, salt and mustard (a teaspoonful of made mustard will do), one half teaspoonful of melted butter, one half teaspoonful of vinegar. If not sour enough, use more vinegar. Chop salmon or chicken fine; also the same quantity of celery or white cabbage; mix well, and just before using, pour the mixture over.

Mrs. Robert Pickett, Fair Haven, Ohio.

SALMON SALAD.

Open the can, drain off all the oil, fill the can with vinegar, and set in a pan of boiling water, to remain an hour; drain off all the liquor, and set in a cool place. Dressing: To one can of salmon beat two eggs until very light; pour over them half a teacupful of boiling vinegar, and set over the fire until it thickens; add a teaspoonful of butter, some mustard and cayenne pepper, set away to cool. When ready for the table, add five tablespoonfuls of sweet cream, and dress with lettuce.

H. F. C , College Hill, Ohio.

LOBSTER SALAD.

Put a large lobster over the fire in boiling water slightly salted; boil rapidly for about twenty minutes; when done, it will be of a bright red color, and should be removed, for if boiled too long it will be tough; when cold, crack the claws, after first disjointing, twist off the head (which is used in garnishing), split the body in two lengthwise, pick out the meat in bits not too fine, saving the coral separate; cut up a large head of lettuce slightly, and place on a dish, over which lay the lobster, putting the coral around the outside. For dressing, take the yolks of three eggs, beat well, add four tablespoonfuls of salad-oil, dropping it in very slowly, beating all the time; then add a little salt, cayenne pepper, one half teaspoonful of mixed mustard and two tablespoonfuls of vinegar; pour this over the lobster just before sending to the table.

LOBSTER SALAD.

One can of lobsters; press out the juice, and chop (not too fine). Boil five eggs until hard, and let them cool; rub the yolks to a jelly, and add to the lobster; then add the chopped whites. Make a dressing of

2 beaten eggs,	1 tablespoonful of olive-oil,
1 small tablespoonful of mustard,	1 cupful of vinegar,
½ teaspoonful of black pepper,	Butter half the size of an egg,
½ teaspoonful of cayenne pepper,	A pinch of salt.

Put on the stove, and stir until it thickens; when cool, put over the lobster.

Grace E. Millar, Lancaster, New York.

FISH SALAD.

Take cold fish left from dinner; remove all bones, and separate in small pieces with two forks; pour over, and mix it well with the following sauce:

1 well-beaten egg,	1 tablespoonful of mixed mustard,
1 tablespoonful of sugar,	3 tablespoonfuls of vinegar,
Small piece of butter.	

Let it boil just to a cream, then pour over the fish and some lettuce-leaves chopped fine and well mixed. Arrange small lettuce-leaves nicely upon a platter, and put a large spoonful of the salad upon each leaf. Cut hard-boiled eggs into slices, and lay one upon each leaf. In serving, just slip the leaf and contents off upon the plate.

OYSTER SALAD.

Cold stewed oysters make a very nice salad if combined with cut celery, and laid upon fresh lettuce-leaves, with a salad dressing laid upon each leafful, a spoonful to each leaf.

EGG AND CHEESE SALAD.

Slice a dozen hard-boiled eggs, and put a layer of eggs into the dish; grate on a thick covering of cheese, then another layer of eggs, alternating with the cheese until the eggs are used up; sprinkle over the top a few capers and finely chopped pickles; pour over it mayonnaise sauce, and again cover with grated cheese.

Mrs. J. S. Crowell, Springfield, Ohio.

POTATO SALAD.

One quart of cold potatoes, sliced very thin, one half cupful of olive-oil, one tablespoonful of finely minced parsley, one tablespoonful of chopped onion, one level teaspoonful of salt, scant salt-spoonful of white pepper, a few grains of cayenne or a few drops of celery pepper; shake the salt and pepper over the potatoes, and stir lightly so as not to break them, then pour over the oil, and lightly stir again, then the onion, then one half teaspoonful of mustard mixed with three tablespoonfuls of vinegar, lastly the parsley. Very nice if mixed in the order given.

Miss Emily E. Squire, Author of "Woronoco Women's Wisdom," Westfield, Mass.

IRISH-POTATO SALAD.

Boil six potatoes until very soft; peel, and mash them while hot; season to taste with salt, pepper and spice; add one tablespoonful of butter. Boil two eggs, and dissolve the yolks in two tablespoonfuls of vinegar; pour it over the potatoes, and mix well; put them on a plate. Slice the whites of the eggs in circles, and place over the potatoes.

Lidie Roberts, Pickens Station, Mississippi.

TOMATO SALAD.

Twelve medium-sized tomatoes, peeled and sliced, four hard-boiled eggs, one teaspoonful of salt, one teaspoonful of white sugar, two teaspoonfuls of made mustard, one raw well-beaten egg, one half teaspoonful of cayenne pepper, one tablespoonful of salad-oil, one teacupful of vinegar. Rub the yolks to a smooth paste, adding by degrees the salt, pepper, sugar, mustard and oil; beat the raw egg to a froth, and stir in lastly the vinegar; peel the tomatoes, slice them one fourth of an inch thick, and set the dish on ice while the dressing is being made. After the dressing is mixed, stir in lumps of ice until it is very cold; then take it out and pour it over the tomatoes. Set it on the ice until ready to serve.

ONION SALAD.

Take cold biscuit or light-bread crumbs, put into the stove, and let remain until quite brittle; then run through a sieve. To two teacupfuls of crumbs add two small, finely cut onions. Have ready four hard-boiled eggs; cut up the whites of two eggs, and mix with the crumbs; pour on two tablespoonfuls of melted butter; season with vinegar, black pepper and salt; add lukewarm water enough to work up smooth; then put into a glass dish, and press down smooth. Take the yolks of the eggs, and press through the sieve, letting it fall on the salad until it is entirely covered by it; take the two whites, and cut into rings and half circles, and place about over the top. A few parsley-leaves put on top add to its appearance.

Mrs. D. F. Gaston, Boiling Springs, Virginia.

BEET SALAD.

Boil until tender three good-sized beets, skin them, and chop up fine; also chop fine a small head of cabbage; mix them, add enough salt to season, one half cupful of sugar, two tablespoonfuls of mustard, and cover all with cold vinegar.

CELERY SALAD.

1 hard-boiled egg,	½ teaspoonful of salt,
1 raw egg,	½ teaspoonful of pepper,
1 tablespoonful of olive-oil,	4 tablespoonfuls of vinegar,
1 teaspoonful of white sugar,	1 teaspoonful of made mustard,
4 large bunches of celery.	

Cut the celery into half-inch pieces; rub the cooked egg to a smooth paste; add the salt, sugar, pepper, mustard and oil; beat the raw egg to a froth, and stir in; then add the vinegar last; mix this well with the celery, and serve at once, or the vinegar will spoil the celery.

LETTUCE SALAD.

Cut four or five nice heads of lettuce; salt it, and let it stand one half hour; then add to the lettuce the powdered yolks of four hard-boiled eggs, one half teaspoonful of mustard and one half teaspoonful of pepper; add a small piece of melted butter. Heat one half pint of vinegar, and pour over; mix all, and garnish the dish with the whites of the eggs.

May Frey, Bucyrus, Ohio.

SALSIFY SALAD.

Boil the salsify until perfectly tender, drain it, and cut it into inch lengths; put it on a dish, and pour over it any simple salad dressing, or toss it up lightly with oil, vinegar, salt, pepper and chopped ravigote. Garnish as fancy dictates. Time to boil the salsify, one hour.

SALSIFY IN SALAD OR ASPIC.

Take salsifies enough to fill a mold of the size of the dish, then boil them in the same way as the others; drain, and cut them the length of the mold; dress them like a chartreuse, dip them into a little aspic to stick them together all around the mold, and fill the middle with a salad of small bits of salsifies all the same size; then season with salt, pepper, a little oil, vinegar and aspic; also put in some very finely chopped parsley; toss the whole, and put it into the mold into ice. At dinner, dip a rubber into hot water, rub the mold all around with it, and turn the salad out on the dish to serve up. If you can procure a few very green French beans, they will make the salad appear better; while haricot beans are likewise very useful.

ARTICHOKE SALAD.

Wash thoroughly and quarter some very young artichokes; remove the chokes, and eat them like radishes, with pepper, salt, vinegar and oil. They taste like nuts, and make a nice relish. Time to prepare, ten minutes.

STRAWBERRY SALAD.

Select the heart-leaves of head-lettuce, arrange four leaves, the stems crossed, heap a few strawberries in the center of the leaves, dust lightly with powdered sugar. Lay one teaspoonful of mayonnaise dressing on each portion, serve with a bit of freshly cut lemon on each. Very delicious for lunch.

Miss Emily E. Squire, Author of "Woronoco Women's Wisdom," Westfield, Mass.

DRESSING FOR CHICKEN SALAD.

Put three well-beaten eggs over the fire, with a piece of butter the size of a hen's egg, one teacupful of strong vinegar, one tablespoonful of home-made mustard, salt and pepper to suit the taste.

M. L. Hann, Wellington, Kansas.

SALAD DRESSING.

3 eggs, the yolks,	3 tablespoonfuls of olive-oil,
3 teaspoonfuls of mixed mustard,	2 teaspoonfuls of salt,
3 tablespoonfuls of white sugar,	1 dessert-spoonful of flour.

Mix this well, and pour it into a teacupful of boiling vinegar; let it cook until it thickens, stirring all the time.

CREAM DRESSING FOR A PINT OF COLD SLAW.

Two tablespoonfuls of whipped sweet cream, two tablespoonfuls of sugar and four tablespoonfuls of vinegar. Beat well, and pour over the cabbage previously cut fine and seasoned with salt.

Mary A. Smith, Mentor, Ohio.

MAYONNAISE DRESSING.

Beat a raw egg, with half a teaspoonful of salt, until it is thoroughly smooth; add one teaspoonful of mixed mustard, made thicker than usual; when smooth, add (a little at a time) half a pint of olive-oil; rub smooth to a thick paste, then dilute with vinegar until the consistency of thick cream. This sauce keeps well if bottled, and corked with a glass stopper, and may be made in advance when yolks are left over from baking. This is very nice on cold sliced tomatoes.

SWEET SLAW.

Cut the cabbage fine, then take sufficient strong vinegar, sweeten it, and season with salt and pepper; add sweet cream enough to make it nice and thick; pour it over the cabbage, and set away in a cool place for several hours.

Lewisburg, Ohio.

WARM SLAW.

2 eggs, the yolks,	1 cupful of vinegar,
2 tablespoonfuls of sugar,	2 tablespoonfuls of sour cream,
Butter the size of a walnut.	

Boil this all together, and pour over finely cut cabbage; then serve.

Mrs. Louisa Ash, Mount Vernon, Ohio.

COLD SLAW.

1 head of cabbage, cut fine,	One teaspoonful of celery-seed.
1 egg,	A little flour,
1 teacupful of vinegar,	Salt to suit the taste.
Butter the size of a hickory-nut.	

Sprinkle the flour, salt and celery-seed over the cabbage; warm the vinegar and butter in a skillet; put the cabbage into it; beat the egg, and pour it over all; mix well, and cook two minutes. Let it get cold before serving.

A. M. Harriet, Henry Clay, Delaware.

Pies and Puddings

CHAPTER XIII.

To be a good pie-baker can only be accomplished by continual practice. One may take the best recipe and fail; but do not let this discourage you.

The secret of making good pies is to use as little water as possible to get the dough into shape.

Put a cupful of lard to a quart of flour and a teaspoonful of salt. This should make four crusts, either two pies with covers or four without. Work the lard into the flour with your fingers until it is thoroughly mixed through before adding the water, then only a little, and press the dough together hard, then turn out on a well-floured board, and roll only one way.

The under crust should be a little the thickest.

If it is a fruit pie, dust a little flour on the bottom before putting your fruit in; and in making pies of fresh fruit, put your sugar in the bottom.

When you make a pie without an upper crust, it is always desirable to have a very heavy edge; make this by wetting the edge and laying on a narrow strip; pinch it up together, or when cutting the crust around the edge of the pan, hold the knife well under the outer edge of the pan, and pinch it between the thumb and finger right on top of the pan.

A rolling-pin is best not washed; scrape the dough off well, and rub with a dry towel. In this case it will always by dry, and if well floured, it will never stick.

In warm weather keep the paste on ice until wanted to bake. It improves pastry very much to lie on ice a couple of hours before using.

Puff paste should always be made of sweet, solid butter.

215

A well-beaten egg rubbed with a bit of cloth over the lower crust of pies will prevent the juice from soaking through it.

The juice of fruit pies, if thickened with a level teaspoonful of corn-starch to a pie, will not boil over.

Always beat eggs separately.

If a mold is used for boiling puddings, be sure to have it well greased.

A bag or cloth should be wrung out of hot water and well floured.

In boiling puddings, always put them into boiling water.

Boiled and steamed puddings require nearly twice as much time as baked.

When a pudding is boiled in a mold, take it from the water, and plunge it immediately into cold water, then turn it out immediately; this will prevent it sticking.

Pumpkin flour can be had at any grocery, which makes as nice pies as the fresh pumpkin, with less trouble, and full directions are on each box.

It is well in all cooking to take advantage of all the modern improvements; oftentimes agents bring things to your door that cannot be had at the stores; if you see it is going to be useful to you, it is well to provide it, as when you want it you may be unable to find it.

In baking pies the time of cooking varies, also the heat of the oven; where green-apple pie takes from thirty to forty minutes, a rich lemon pie would take only about twenty.

A very flaky, nice pie-dough is made by adding a level half teaspoonful of baking-powder to a quart of flour, in which case lessen the quantity of shortening.

Some always grease their pie-pans; this is the safest if the pie is to be removed to a plate before putting on the table. Others only dust the pan with flour. One's own experience must be the judge which is the best way.

A marble slab is very desirable to have, as it keeps the dough cold and firm—in fact, it is almost impossible to make puff paste without it.

PIE-CRUST.

One heaping teaspoonful of baking-powder, two quarts of flour, one teacupful of lard, two teacupfuls of water, a pinch of salt; mix well, and sift a little flour on the molding-board before rolling it out. This will make enough crust for four or five pies.

Mrs. W. E. Broughton, Bronson, Michigan.

MRS. E.'S PIE-CRUST.

4 cupfuls of flour.	1 cupful of water.
2 cupfuls of butter and lard mixed.	A pinch of salt.

This makes enough dough for four pies.

PIE-SHELLS.

Make a rich pie-crust, and line the pans or old saucers; prick them with a fork, and bake in a quick oven; put them into a crock or bread-box, and when needed, fill with cranberry sauce, apple sauce or any canned fruit you may have open. Another way to use them is to make a custard of any kind, put one of the shells into a pie-pan, fill it with the custard, and bake. These are convenient to have in case of unexpected company.

APPLE PIE.

Take ripe apples that will bake well, cut into halves, and core; line a pan with crust as for any pie; then place in the apples round side down. Make a paste of sugar, butter and nutmeg, fill the cores of the apples, and bake to a light brown.

A. M., Greenville, Virginia.

GREEN-APPLE PIE.

Peel and core moderately tart and ripe apples, cut them into very thin slices; fill the under crust, and put a small teacupful of brown sugar over it; add one half teacupful of hot water and a little flour dusted over all; add the upper crust, and bake in a moderate oven about forty minutes. Never use sweet apples for pies.

SLICED-APPLE PIE.

Line your plate with paste, and to each pie allow one cupful of sugar, one half lemon, apples, peeled, sliced and cored; put a layer of tart, juicy apples, then sugar, bits of butter, and lemon cut into little pieces; make two or three layers, cover with an upper crust, and bake. Use no water; it will form a syrup.

Mrs. A. E. Kirtland, Author of "Mrs. Kirtland's Cook Book," Montgomery, Alabama

CHERRY PIE.

Stem and stone the cherries. Cover the bottom of a long tin with the paste, then put in the fruit, to which add one teacupful of sugar and one teacupful of flour; bake with two crusts.

Hattie E. Davison, Grovedale, Missouri.

PEACH PIE.

Line a pie-pan with a rich paste; peel, halve and seed peaches enough to fill the pan, then sprinkle over the pie two tablespoonfuls of flour, one cupful of sugar, or more, to suit the taste; fill the pan with thick, sweet cream, and bake until done.

Mrs. Louisa Ash, Mount Vernon, Ohio.

CURRANT PIE.

1 egg,   1 cupful of ripe currants.
1 cupful of sugar,

Beat the egg and sugar together, and pour it over the currants; bake with two crusts.

Mrs. H. E. D., Clarks, Pennsylvania.

LEMON PIE.

1 egg,	2 teacupfuls of boiling water,
2 teacupfuls of white sugar,	2 small tablespoonfuls of corn-starch,
1 tablespoonful of butter.	2 lemons.

Dissolve the corn-starch in a little cold water, then put it into the boiling water; add the sugar, and let it boil a few minutes; set aside, and when cool, add the butter, egg and the juice and grated rinds of the lemons. This makes three pies; by adding more water to the above quantity it will be enough for four.

Mrs. A. Winger, Springfield, Ohio.

CUSTARD PIE.

3 eggs,	1 cupful of sugar,
1 quart of milk.	1 tablespoonful of corn-starch,
1 teaspoonful of vanilla,	A small pinch of salt.

Beat the eggs and sugar together; mix in the other ingredients well, and bake on one crust. This makes two pies.

Mrs. A. A. Davidson, Milan, Tennessee.

APPLE-CUSTARD PIE.

Peel, core and stew sour apples; mash them very fine, and for each pie allow

| 1 egg, the yolk. | ½ cupful of butter, |
| 1 cupful of sugar, | ¼ of a grated nutmeg. |

Bake with only one crust, the same as pumpkin pie, and use the white of the egg as frosting, to be spread on after the pie is done; brown it nicely by returning it to the oven for a few minutes.

Mrs. Louisa Ash, Mount Vernon, Ohio.

LEMON-CUSTARD PIE.

Two eggs, one cupful of water, one lemon, one tablespoonful of butter, one cupful of granulated sugar, one tablespoonful of corn-starch dissolved in water. Grate the rind; then peel off the thick, white skin, and grate the rest of the lemon, being careful to remove the seeds. Save out one of the whites, and beat to a stiff froth, with one tablespoonful of sugar; put this on the top after it is baked, and return to the oven until it is a delicate brown.

PINEAPPLE CUSTARD.

1 can of grated pineapple,	1 cupful of milk,
1 tablespoonful of flour.	¼ pound of butter,
1 pound of sugar,	5 eggs, beaten separately.

Mix as usual. Makes four pies.

Mrs. A. E. Kirtland, Author of "Mrs. Kirtland's Cook Book," Montgomery, Alabama.

CREAM PIE.

| 1 cupful of sweet cream, | 2 heaping spoonfuls of sugar, |
| 2 heaping spoonfuls of corn-starch or flour. | |

Flavor with lemon; bake as custard pie.

Mrs. K. A., St. Clair, Nevada.

CORN-STARCH PIE.

1 quart of milk,   2 eggs, yolks,
2 tablespoonfuls of corn-starch,   2 cupfuls of sugar.

Mix the starch in a little milk, boil the rest of the milk to a thick cream; beat the yolks and add the starch, put in the boiled milk and sugar; bake with an under crust only; beat the whites with two tablespoonfuls of sugar, and put on the top of the pie; when done, return to the oven, and brown.

COCOANUT PIE.

2 eggs,   3 tablespoonfuls of sugar,
1 cupful of grated fresh cocoanut, 1 pint of milk,
1 tablespoonful of corn-starch,   Small piece of butter.

Bake with one crust. One half cupful of desiccated cocoanut, soaked in the milk three or four hours, may be used if you cannot get the fresh.

Mrs. Geo. H. Knight, Mexico, New York.

PUMPKIN PIE.

4 eggs,   1 quart of strained pumpkin,
3 cupfuls of sugar,   1 teaspoonful of ginger,
3 pints of milk,   4 teaspoonfuls of cinnamon.

This is enough for two pies.

L. H. B., Postville, Iowa.

RASPBERRY PIE.

Line the pan with a good crust, and fill with ripe berries, regulating the quantity of sugar required by the sweetness of the berries; dredge a little flour and small bits of butter over the top; wet the edge of the crust, put on the upper crust, and pinch the edges close together, taking care to prick holes in the upper one to allow the air to escape. Bake half an hour.

HUCKLEBERRY PIE.

Make crust as for any berry pie; fill with nicely prepared berries, sprinkle with flour and sugar, add a little water and two tablespoonfuls of vinegar; then add a top crust, and bake well.

Mrs. E. Cowles, Perryville, Michigan.

RHUBARB PIE.

Line a pie-tin with rich paste. Wash the rhubarb, and cut up into inch pieces without peeling off the skin; mix with sugar, and put into the crust, being careful to sprinkle flour upon the bottom first; put on the upper crust, and pinch the edges firmly together. No water should be put in, as the fruit makes sufficient juice itself.

RAISIN PIE.

Boil one pound of raisins, one cupful of molasses and one quart of water together for one hour; then add one tablespoonful of flour, a small piece of butter, spice to suit the taste, and bake with two crusts. This quantity makes three pies.

Mrs. W. Damon, Leominster, Massachusetts.

GRAPE PIE.

One egg, one teacupful of sugar, one heaping teacupful of grapes. Beat the egg and sugar together; then add the grapes, one tablespoonful of flour and a little butter. Bake with two crusts.

Mrs. M. DePouter, New Haven, Vermont.

BOILED-CIDER PIE.

1 egg.	½ cupful of boiled cider,
1½ cupfuls of sugar,	3 tablespoonfuls of flour,
2 cupfuls of cold water.	

This makes two pies; baked with only one crust.

Mrs. G. H. T., Manlius, New York.

VINEGAR PIE.

1 cupful of molasses,	1 cupful of flour,
1 cupful of sugar,	3 cupfuls of water,
1 cupful of vinegar,	Boil all together, and let it cool.

Flavor with lemon, and make it as you would custard pie.

Mrs. E. M. Y., Herndon, Virginia.

JELLY PIE.

Five eggs, reserving the whites of two; beat together one cupful of sugar, one cupful of jelly and one third of a cupful of butter; mix all, and bake on one crust. Beat the whites of the eggs with sugar enough to make it as thick as icing, and spread this over the pie when it is done; if desired, brown it a little in the oven.

L. F. C., Seal, Alabama.

TRANSPARANT PIE.

3 eggs,	1 cupful of rich cream,
2 tablespoonfuls of sugar.	3 tablespoonfuls of jelly,
Flavor with lemon.	

This makes one pie. Bake with one crust.

Mrs. Dr. H., Pilot Grove, Missouri.

CHEESE-CAKE PIE.

3 eggs,	1 cupful of sugar,
1 quart of soft smear-kase.	

Mix well, and pour into a rich pie-crust, and bake without an upper crust. This makes two pies.

Christie Irving.

CHESS PIE.

4 eggs,	1 cupful of sweet cream,
2 cupfuls of sugar.	2-3 of a cupful of butter,
1 tablespoonful of flour.	

Flavor with nutmeg; cover the pans with crust, pour in the mixture, and grate nutmeg over it. There is no upper crust. Bake as custard pie,

Mrs. James Gladden, Stockwell, Indiana,

SQUASH PIE.

Boil the squash until well done; add a little salt, and press through a coarse sieve; then to every teacupful of squash add one egg, one half cupful of sugar, one teaspoonful of flour, and nutmeg to season; line a deep pie-plate with paste, thin the squash with milk, and fill the plate; sweet cream or a small piece of butter adds to the flavor of the pie.

Mrs. A. L. Fish, South Deerfield, Massachusetts.

PINEAPPLE PIE.

5 eggs,	1 cupful of sweet cream,
1 cupful of sugar,	½ cupful of butter,
1 grated pineapple.	

Beat the butter and sugar to a cream, add the beaten yolks of the eggs, then the pineapple and cream, and lastly the beaten whites, whipped in lightly. Take each section out with a steel fork, and cut off the blossom, then chop them up very fine, and add them to the grated core, or heart. Bake with an under crust only.

Mrs. M. P., Chesterfield, Ohio.

TOMATO PIE.

Remove the skins from four large, ripe yellow tomatoes; slice thin into your pie-crust; add

4 tablespoonfuls of sugar,	A small lump of butter,
1 tablespoonful of vinegar,	1 tablespoonful of flour.

Put strips across the top; bake slowly until thoroughly done.

GREEN-TOMATO PIE.

Pare and slice five or six green tomatoes; have the under crust ready, and put them in it; add

½ teacupful of vinegar,	1 cupful of sugar,
A small piece of butter.	

Sprinkle over it a little allspice and flour; put on the top crust, and bake in a moderately hot oven.

Mrs. Jane M. Page, Baldwin, Michigan.

IRISH-POTATO PIE.

Prepare fine mashed potatoes the same as for the table; add to a quart of the mixture two eggs, one half cupful of milk, sweeten to taste; pour into the paste, and grate nutmeg over the top; bake without an upper crust.

SWEET-POTATO PIE.

Slice cold boiled sweet potatoes as thick as bread, and lay them in a pie-plate that is covered with paste; put in one tablespoonful of vinegar, two tablespoonfuls of sugar; fill the plate with water, and sprinkle bits of butter and a little flour; season with allspice, and bake with an upper crust.

Mrs. W. B. Reid, Jackson, Michigan.

CHICKEN-PIE CRUST.

Take a quart measure full of flour, and mix with it four teaspoonfuls of baking-powder, a pinch of salt and one teacupful of lard; moisten with sweet milk sufficient to roll; roll out once, spread with butter, lap it over, and roll again. It is then ready to put on the pie.

Mrs. A. H. T., Berlin Heights, Ohio.

POT-PIE.

Cut veal, beef or chicken into pieces, and put into enough boiling water to cover, with two slices of bacon; cover closely, and boil an hour, and season to taste. Make a batter of two well-beaten eggs, two cupfuls of milk, one teaspoonful of baking-powder and flour, drop in separate spoonfuls while boiling, and cook five minutes; serve immediately.

BEEFSTEAK PIE.

Take some fine, tender steaks, beat them a little, season with a salt-spoonful of pepper and a teaspoonful of salt to a two-pound steak; put bits of butter the size of a hickory-nut over the whole surface, dredge a tablespoonful of flour over, then roll it up, and cut it into pieces two inches long; put a rich pie-paste around the sides and bottom of a tin basin; put in the pieces of steak, nearly fill the basin with water, add a piece of butter the size of a large egg, cut small, dredge in a teaspoonful of flour, add a little pepper and salt, lay skewers across the basin, roll a top crust to one half inch in thickness, cut a slit in the center; dip your fingers into flour, and neatly pinch the top and side crust together all around the edge; bake one hour in a quick oven.

MOCK MINCE PIE.

½ cupful of molasses,	1 cupful of chopped raisins,
2-3 of a cupful of water,	1 tablespoonful of cloves,
2-3 of a cupful of vinegar,	1 tablespoonful of cinnamon.
1 cupful of sugar,	1 grated nutmeg.
1 cupful of bread-crumbs,	Butter the size of a hen's egg.

Mix this, and put it on the stove to heat thoroughly, stirring often; bake with two crusts.

Mrs Mollie I. P. Boone, New Carlisle, Ohio.

MINCE-MEAT FOR PIES.

3 pounds of boiled beef,	1½ pounds of currants,
1 pound of suet,	1 pound of citron,
3 pounds of brown sugar,	1 grated nutmeg,
½ peck of apples,	Mace—5 cents' worth of powdered,
2 pounds of raisins,	Allspice and cinnamon to suit the taste.

Chop the meat, suet and apples fine; then put them with the seasoning; slice the citron fine; pour on sweet cider to make a thick batter of it, and warm thoroughly. It is seasoned through much better.

Mrs. A. K., Springfield, Ohio.

MINCE-MEAT FOR PIES.

The wife of General Fitzhugh Lee, of Virginia, is a famous housekeeper, and this is how she says she makes the mince-meat for her Thanksgiving pies:

2 pounds of beef,	2 pounds of sugar,
2 pounds of currants,	2 grated nutmegs,
2 pounds of raisins,	¼ ounce of cloves,
1 pound of citron,	½ ounce of cinnamon,
2 pounds of beef suet,	⅓ ounce of mace,
1½ pounds of candied lemon-peel,	1 teaspoonful of salt,
4 pounds of apples,	2 lemons, the juice and rind.
2 pounds of sultana raisins,	2 oranges, the juice and rind.

Simmer the meat gently until tender, and when perfectly cold, chop it fine; stone the raisins, shred the citrons, pare, core and chop the apples, chop the suet fine; mix the dry ingredients, then add the juice and rinds of the oranges and lemons; pack in a stone jar, cover closely, and keep cool. This mince-meat will keep all winter. The rule is an old one, and is said to have come from the Custis family in the beginning. According to Virginia tradition, the widow Custis who became Mrs. Washington made famous mince pies.

TARTS.

Make crust as for pies; roll very thin, and cut with a biscuit-cutter, pricking half of the number with a fork to keep them from blistering; in the remaining half cut three holes with your thimble; bake in a quick oven. Will need close watching, as they scorch easily. Prepare for the table by placing jelly on the pricked crust, and placing the one with holes over it.

S. F. Mills, Rosetta, Illinois.

CRUST FOR TARTS.

Rub one teacupful of lard into three teacupfuls of flour and a pinch of salt; beat the white of one egg slightly, add five tablespoonfuls of water to it, and mix it into the flour. Do not mix more than necessary, and it will be a flaky crust.

SWEET-POTATO TARTS.

5 eggs,	1 teacupful of butter,
1 teacupful of sugar,	A little nutmeg or cinnamon.

One pound of boiled and mashed potatoes, with a pinch of salt, and milk to make it moist; beat the butter and sugar first, and then add the potato, a little at a time; beat up the eggs, and stir them in, then add the flavor. Line the pie-pans with a crust; fill, and bake the same as pumpkin pie. This quantity will make three or four tarts.

L. G., Cuckoo, Virginia.

APPLE TARTLETS.

Cut from puff paste twelve round pieces two inches in diameter, place in tart-pans, and press firm into the scallops, lay in each some chopped apple and a little sugar; bake them in a moderate oven, and let them cool. Whip a little cream very stiff, add a little sugar and a drop of essence of lemon or vanilla; just before wanted, place a little cream on each tartlet, and two strips of red-currant jelly in the form of a cross.

Mrs. J. S. Crowell, Springfield, Ohio.

NOUILLES.

Nouilles are made of delicate pastry, cut into ribands and various shapes, and used as a substitute for vermicelli and macaroni, either in making fritters or puddings or for serving with cheese or in soup. They are made as follows: Take half a pound of fine flour, put it on the pastry-board, make a hole in the center, and in this put two eggs; add a pinch of salt, one half ounce of butter, one teaspoonful of cold water; mix all into a very firm, smooth paste; leave it a little while to dry, then roll it out as thin as possible, and cut it into thin bands about one and one fourth inches in width; dredge a little flour upon these, and lay four or five of them one above another, then cut them through into thin shreds, something like vermicelli; shake them well to prevent their sticking together, and spread them out to dry. Nouilles cannot be made without a straight rolling-pin and smooth pastry-board. When wanted for use, drop them gradually into boiling water, stirring gently with a wooden spoon to keep them from getting lumpy; let them boil for six to twenty minutes, then take them up with a strainer, drain them well, and spread them out on a coarse cloth. Besides thread-like nouilles, a few may be made the size and shape of scarlet-runner beans or small birds' eggs, or they may be cut broad like macaroni. If thoroughly dried, they will keep any length of time stored in tin canisters.

PUFF PASTE.

To each pound of flour allow one pound of butter; use half of the butter with the flour and cold water enough to mold it; roll it out quite thin, and put on half the butter that remains in small bits; dredge this with flour, roll up the paste, then roll it out again, thin; put on the rest of the butter, and roll up as before; repeat this until the butter is all used. It must be done quickly; be careful not to handle it any more than you can help. Put in a cool place until you are ready to use it.

DROP DUMPLINGS.

Sift together one cupful of flour, one half teaspoonful of salt and one teaspoonful of baking-powder; add, stirring with a knife, about one half cupful of milk or water; divide into five parts, and drop on the top of any nice stew, being careful not to let the gravy cover them; lay a cloth over the top of the kettle before putting on the lid; it will absorb the steam and prevent its falling back in drops upon the dumplings, and thus making them heavy. Cook, closely covered, for exactly twelve minutes; do not look at them during the time.

Miss Marion L. Campbell, Friendly Inn Cooking School, Cleveland, Ohio.

STEAMED APPLE DUMPLINGS.

Mix up a dough with

1 quart of flour,	1 pint of sour cream,
1 teaspoonful of soda,	A little salt.

Slice the apples, and put them into a pot; put enough water in to cook the apples; roll the dough out so as to cover the apples closely; make an opening in the center of the dough, so as to let the steam escape; when done, the dough will be raised up several inches thick. Eat with sauce.

Mrs. J. A. R., Woodrow, Pennsylvania.

BAKED APPLE DUMPLINGS.

Peel and cut into halves good cooking-apples, and remove the cores from each half; then fill the vacancies with sugar, and place the halves together again. Prepare dough as or biscuit, roll thin, and cut into pieces large enough to wrap around each apple. Bake slowly; when done, serve with sauce.

Sarah J. Carter, Cynthiana, Indiana.

BAKED APPLE PUDDING.

4 eggs, the yolks of,	3 tablespoonfuls of butter,
6 large grated pippins,	½ cupful of sugar,
The juice and half the peel of one lemon.	

Beat the sugar and butter to a cream, stir in the yolks and lemon, with the grated apples; pour into a deep pudding-dish to bake. Whip the whites, and add them last; grate a little nutmeg over the top. Eat cold with cream.

S. E. R., Chesterfield, Virginia.

CHERRY PUDDING.

2 eggs,	1 cupful of sweet milk,
2 teaspoonfuls of baking-powder.	

Flour enough to make a stiff batter, and as many cherries as can be stirred in; bake one half hour, and serve with sugar and cream.

LEMON PUDDING.

4 eggs, the yolks,	1 pint of bread-crumbs,
1 cupful of sugar,	1 teaspoonful of butter,
1 quart of milk,	The grated rind of one lemon.

When well done, spread over the top a layer of jelly, and add the whites of the eggs whipped to a stiff froth, sweetened with one cupful of sugar and flavored with the juice of the lemon; then set in the oven to brown lightly. Allow half an hour for baking the pudding.

Mrs. M. E., Creston, Iowa.

PINEAPPLE PUDDING.

1 can of grated pineapple,	½ cupful of milk,
¼ cupful of butter,	2 tablespoonfuls of corn-starch,
1 cupful of sugar,	6 well-beaten eggs.

Cream butter and sugar until light, add the other things, and bake in a pan.

Mrs. A. E. Kirtland, Author of " Mrs. Kirtland's Cook Book," Montgomery, Alabama.

ORANGE OR PINEAPPLE PUDDING.

Peel and cut into pieces four oranges; add one cupful of sugar, and let it stand over night; take one quart of milk, nearly boiling, two tablespoonfuls of corn-starch wet with cold milk, three beaten yolks of eggs; bring this to a boil; when cold, spread over the oranges; beat the whites of the eggs, with one half cupful of sugar, to a stiff froth, spread over, and brown. Can be eaten warm or cold.

Mrs. B. F. A., Providence, Rhode Island.

ORANGE PUDDING.

Peel and slice four large oranges, lay in your dish, sprinkle over them one cupful of sugar. Take

3 eggs, yolks only beaten,	2 tablespoonfuls of corn-starch,
½ cupful of sugar,	1 quart of boiling milk.

Let this boil and thicken; then let it cool a little before pouring over the oranges; beat the whites of the eggs, and pour over it; set in the oven to brown.

Mrs. McKinstry, Jackson, Michigan.

ENGLISH PLUM PUDDING.

9 eggs.	1 pound of dried currants,
1 pound of sugar,	¼ of a pound of dried citron,
1 pound of chopped suet,	1 pound of flour.
1 pound of stoned raisins,	1 tablespoonful of mixed spice.

Add sufficient milk to mix it quite stiff. Have a strong cloth, well floured, ready, and in tying it, leave plenty of room for it to swell; put it into boiling water, and let it boil nine hours, keeping it well covered; sauce to suit the taste. This one is most used:

2 quarts of milk,	1 teaspoonful of butter,
¾ of a cupful of sugar,	1 heaping tablespoonful of corn-starch.

Leave out enough milk to moisten the corn-starch, sugar and butter to a thick batter, and pour in the rest of the milk when boiling. Let it cook three minutes.

Mrs. E. C. W., Mount Vernon, Ohio.

PLUM PUDDING.

1 pound of finely cut raisins,	¼ pound of citron,
½ pound of butter.	3 ounces of flour,
3 ounces of bread-crumbs,	3 eggs.
4 ounces of sugar.	

Season with cinnamon, mace and nutmeg; pour one tumblerful of milk over the bread-crumbs to soften, a little salt, some finely cut orange-peel; mix all, and boil two hours. Serve with sauce.

Mrs. A. E. Kirtland, Author of "Mrs. Kirtland's Cook Book," Montgomery, Alabama.

RICE PUDDING.

3 eggs,	¼ of a pound of butter,
1½ cupfuls of sugar.	1½ cupfuls of raisins,
1 cupful of boiled rice.	

After the rice has cooled, mix in the rest of the ingredients, and enough sweet milk to nearly fill a six-quart pan; bake one half hour.

Mrs. T. K. M. B., Chelsea, Vermont.

CRANBERRY PUDDING.

1½ cupfuls of sour milk,	¾ of a cupful of molasses,
1 teaspoonful of soda,	1 teaspoonful of salt,
3 cupfuls of flour.	

Stir well together, and add two cupfuls of raw cranberries; pour into a buttered tin, and steam one and one half hours. Eat with sauce.

Mrs. S. L. B., Lynnfield, Massachusetts.

DELICATE RICE PUDDING.

Wash four tablespoonfuls of rice, and cook in one quart of milk until very soft; take from the fire, add one heaping tablespoonful of butter, one half cupful of sugar and half a teaspoonful of salt; when cool, add the beaten yolks of four eggs and the grated rind of a lemon, cook until firm; beat the whites of the eggs to a stiff froth, sweeten to taste with powdered sugar, and flavor with lemon-juice; pile lightly on the pudding, and brown slightly.

Mrs. Althea Somes, Teacher of Cookery, Manual Training School, Boston, Mass.

RICE AND TAPIOCA PUDDING.

3 tablespoonfuls of rice,
2 tablespoonfuls of tapioca,
1 quart of milk.

4 tablespoonfuls of sugar,
A little grated nutmeg.

Bake in a slow oven two or three hours, stirring occasionally during the first hour. This pudding is better than with rice only.

Mrs. E. Garthwaite, Pluckemin, New Jersey.

TAPIOCA PUDDING.

Soak over night in a bowl one cupful of tapioca covered with lukewarm water; next day, put into a quart of milk four well-beaten eggs, one half cupful of sugar, one half teaspoonful of salt; put in your tapioca, boil in a double vessel, stirring constantly with a wooden spoon; when it creams, remove from the fire; beat the whites of the eggs to a froth, and stir in like float; add gelatin jelly, laid on in spoonfuls. This should be made the day before. Eat cold. The addition of three tablespoonfuls of desiccated cocoanut, cooked with the tapioca, and some of it mixed in with the whites of the eggs as frosting, is very nice.

Christie Irving.

TAPIOCA FRUIT PUDDING.

Take one half teacupful of tapioca; wash nicely, and let it soak in a pint of water over night, or until it swells; then add boiling water and a little salt, and let it simmer slowly until clear like starch and of about the same consistency; add a little white sugar; take a pudding-dish, and put in a layer of tapioca while hot, then a layer of fruit, until the dish is full; bake until clear. Unless the fruit is of a kind that bakes quickly, it will be found better to stew it tender first. Eat cold with cream.

Mrs. R. W. Mills, Webster Groves, Missouri.

INDIAN TAPIOCA PUDDING.

Soak one fourth cupful of pearl tapioca until soft in one cupful of milk. Mix two tablespoonfuls of corn-meal with a little cold milk, put tapioca, meal, etc., into a buttered pudding-dish, add one half teaspoonful of salt, one tablespoonful of butter and one cupful of molasses, pour over this one quart of boiling milk, mix well, and when placed in an oven, add one cupful of cold milk without stirring; bake one hour.

Mrs. Althea Somes, Teacher of Cookery, Manual Training School, Boston, Mass.

TAPIOCA INDIAN PUDDING.

Soak one third of a cupful of pearl tapioca in enough cold water to cover, over night; add one fourth of a cupful of Indian meal, one teaspoonful of butter, one teaspoonful of salt; mix with it one quart of scalded milk in which one cupful of molasses has been added; bake slowly for one and one half hours.

Miss Angeline M. Weaver, Instructor Hyde School Kitchen, Boston, Massachusetts.

APRICOT PUDDING.

Pouding de Apricot.

Put into a basin one half pound of good butter, with the finely chopped peel of one lemon and as much ground cinnamon as will cover a five-cent piece, and a salt-spoonful of apricot yellow; work these together with a clean wooden spoon for about ten minutes, then add one half pound of fine sugar, and work these together again for about five minutes, and by degrees add one half pound of whole fresh eggs, and one half pound of fine flour that has been passed through a wire sieve, mixing these into the other ingredients thus: One egg and one tablespoonful of flour sprinkled in until all are united; to this add four preserved apricots that have been cut into little dice shapes and one half ounce of baking-powder. Take a plain or fancy timbal-mold with a pipe, butter it well with warmed butter by means of a paste-brush, and while the butter is

warm, sprinkle it all over with browned bread-crumbs, and then fill the mold three fourths with the prepared mixture; place in the pipe a band of buttered paper in which a peeled potato or carrot is placed, to prevent the mixture running away through the pipe, and fix also a band of buttered paper around the outside of the mold, and standing about three inches above it; put the pudding into a moderate oven on a baking-tin, and bake it for a little over one hour; turn out on a pastry-rack with a dish under it, and pour over it some cherry syrup, then dish the pudding up on a hot dish, on which it has to be served, and cover it entirely with yellow apricot sauce (see recipe), pouring some of the sauce also around the base of the dish; sprinkle lightly over it some finely shredded blanched almonds and pistachio-nuts, and serve. Enough for eight to ten persons.

STALE-CAKE PUDDING.

Take pieces of cake that are getting dry, and toast in the oven, then break into dishes, and pour cream over it. It is a good way to use up dry cake.

J. M. R., Eagle Lake, Minnesota.

BIRD'S NEST PUDDING.

Pare six large, tart apples, cut them into two pieces, take out the cores, and lay them in a pudding dish or pan; fill the center of the apples with sugar, cinnamon and nutmeg. Make a rich custard, and pour it over the apples; bake one half hour, and serve with sauce.

Mrs. C. S. K., Springfield, Ohio.

BROWN BETTY.

Pare and core one dozen large, juicy apples, chop fine with a hash-knife. Butter a deep pudding-dish, place first a layer of chopped apples, some bits of butter strewed over them, then sprinkle with white sugar, flavor with nutmeg, lemon essence or the juice and a little of the rind of a lemon, next a layer of bread-crumbs, then a layer of apples, and so on until the dish is full, finishing with a layer of bread-crumbs. Send it to the table hot or cold; eat with cream sauce.

COLLEGE PUDDING.

3½ cupfuls of flour,
1 cupful of molasses,
1 cupful of sour milk,
1 cupful of chopped, seeded raisins.

1 cupful of finely chopped suet,
1 level teaspoonful of soda,
½ teaspoonful of salt,

Boil in a pudding-mold for three hours.

Miss Emily E. Squire, Author of "Woronoco Women's Wisdom," Westfield, Mass.

CHOCOLATE PUDDING.

Stir four tablespoonfuls of grated chocolate into a quart of boiling milk; when it is beaten smooth, add the yolks of five eggs and two tablespoonfuls of corn-starch dissolved in a little milk; stir until it thickens, and flavor with vanilla; pour the mixture into a pudding-dish, and bake until well set; beat the whites of five eggs very light, add five tablespoonfuls of pulverized sugar, and spread over the top; bake to a delicate brown.

H. F. C., College Hill, Ohio.

STEAMED SPICE PUDDING.

To one beaten egg add one third cupful of brown sugar, one third cupful of molasses and one third cupful of cold coffee; sift together one cupful of flour, one third teaspoonful of soda, one fourth teaspoonful of cloves, one half teaspoonful of cinnamon; slowly add the liquid to the dry mixture; add one tablespoonful of melted butter and two thirds of a cupful of stoned raisins and floured with one fourth cupful of flour; steam in greased, tightly covered mold for two hours.

Miss Marion L. Campbell, Friendly Inn Cooking School, Cleveland, Ohio.

SNOW PUDDING.

Dissolve one boxful of gelatin in one pint of cold water for one half hour; then add one pint of boiling water; when this is cold, add two cupfuls of sugar and the whites of six eggs, well beaten together; flavor with almond or vanilla, and beat all together with an egg-beater until very stiff; then pour it into molds. Make a custard of the yolks of six eggs and one quart of milk to pour over it when served.

Mrs. Alex. Murray, Twenty-Mile Stand, Ohio.

FRENCH PUDDING.

Dissolve one cupful of tapioca farina in a quart of cold milk for an hour, then boil it eight or ten minutes in a double boiler; take it off the fire, and when cool, add

1 dessert-spoonful of sugar,
4 eggs, well beaten,
½ teaspoonful of vanilla.

A small piece of butter,
A little salt.

Serve cold, with the following sauce:

2 eggs, yolks of,
1 cupful of sugar.

½ pint of milk,

The whites are whipped, and put on top of the pudding.

KENTUCKY PUDDING.

3 eggs,
¾ of a cupful of butter,
3 tablespoonfuls of flour,

2½ cupfuls of sugar,
1 cupful of cream,
1 teaspoonful of lemon essence.

Bake in one crust as for custard pie.
Mrs. Carrie Bell, Eminence, Kentucky.

NEAPOLITAN PUDDING.

Soak one cupful of bread-crumbs in one cupful of sweet milk until you can rub it smooth, rub three fourths of a cupful of sugar and one tablespoonful of butter together, add the juice and grated rind of one lemon to it; beat separately six eggs, add the yolks to the creamed sugar and butter, then put in the soaked bread-crumbs; now stiffen the whites. Butter a tin bucket, put a layer of this mixture on the bottom, on this a layer of macaroons that have been dipped into wine, laid closely together, cover with the bread mixture, then slices of sponge-cake spread with jelly or delicate jam, then the bread mixture, and so on until you have sufficient, having the bread on top; cover closely, and boil one hour; turn out carefully, and serve with wine sauce. This is delightful.
Mrs. A. E. Kirtland, Author of "Mrs. Kirtland's Cook Book," Montgomery, Alabama.

NEW MINUTE PUDDING.

To one quart of milk add one pint of water, and set over the fire; just before it begins to boil, put in one cupful of raisins and a little salt; as soon as it boils, stir in flour enough to make it of the proper consistency. Eat with cream and sugar.
Mrs. M. J. Prince, Detroit, Maine.

QUEEN OF PUDDINGS.

6 eggs, 2 whole and the yolks of 4,
Butter the size of an egg,
1 quart of bread-crumbs,
1 teaspoonful of lemon extract.

1 cupful of white sugar,
1 quart of milk,
½ teacupful of raisins,

Soak the bread-crumbs in the milk; bake slowly one hour; when done, spread the top with currant jelly and the whites of four eggs beaten to a stiff froth.
Mrs. J. Kyle, Springfield, Ohio.

GRITS PUDDING.

4 eggs,	½ pint of sugar,
1 tablespoonful of butter,	½ teaspoonful of ginger,
1 pint of cold grits,	Enough sweet milk to soften.

Beat together, and bake in a buttered pan. Serve with or without sauce.

Mrs. S. C. Davidson, Wooten, Alabama.

DELICIOUS PUDDING.

Bake a common sponge-cake in a flat-bottom pudding-dish; when ready for use, cut into six or eight pieces; split, and spread with butter, and return them to the dish. Make a custard with four eggs to a quart of milk, flavor and sweeten to the taste; pour over the cake, and bake one half hour. The cake will swell and fill the custard.

COTTAGE PUDDING.

2 eggs,	1½ cupfuls of flour,
1 cupful of sugar,	½ cupful of milk.
Butter the size of a walnut,	2 teaspoonfuls of baking-powder.

Bake twenty minutes, and serve with lemon sauce.

FIG PUDDING.

Beat three eggs, add one cupful of sugar, one half cupful of milk., Chop fine one half pound of figs and one half pound of suet, add two heaping cupfuls of soft bread-crumbs, then add the first mixture, pour into a mold, steam three hours. Serve with wine or lemon sauce.

Miss Ida M. Foster, City Hospital, Wilkesbarre, Pennsylvania.

HASTY PUDDING.

Put a quart of milk into a crock, and set it on the stove to cook; as soon as it comes to a boil, sift in the flour, a little at a time, stirring it well until it is thick and stiff. Serve with sweetened cream or thickened milk made in this way: Take a piece of butter the size of a walnut, one heaping tablespoonful of sugar and one of flour; cream this together, and pour on it a pint of milk; let this cook ten minutes. Flavor to suit the taste.

RICH RASPBERRY PUDDING.

Beat one fourth of a pound of butter to a cream; add one spoonful of sugar, three tablespoonfuls of cream, the beaten yolks of four eggs and one tablespoonful of raspberry jam. Line a shallow pie-dish with puff paste; pour in the mixture, and bake in a well-heated oven until the pastry is done enough. Sufficient for three or four persons.

PALAC SINT.

Make a rich biscuit-dough, and roll it out on the molding-board about as thick as pie-crust; spread with hot butter, then use cherries, strawberries or any kind of fruit for the filling, and sweeten it well; then roll it up the same way you do a jelly-cake, and cut into strips or pieces about five inches long; pinch the ends together to keep the fruit from cooking out, then put the pieces into a well-buttered pan, and bake them well, turning them so they will brown delicately on both sides.

Professor Emile Sago.

RICE À L'IMPERIAL, WITH COMPOTE OF PINEAPPLE.

Wash four tablespoonfuls of rice thoroughly in cold water, let it soak one hour, then throw it into a large kettle of boiling water; boil rapidly for twenty minutes, drain, throw it into a clean towel or napkin, and shake it out so that it will dry each grain separately; put two tablespoonfuls of granulated gelatin into a saucepan, and cover it with one fourth cupful of milk. Whip one pint of cream to a stiff froth, turn it into a basin, stand it on a pan of cracked ice, or ice-water, sprinkle over two thirds of a cupful of powdered sugar, one dessert-spoonful of vanilla, and then the boiled rice. Stand the gelatin over the tea-kettle, and stir until dissolved; add it to the cream, and begin at once to stir, and stir constantly until it begins to thicken; turn at once into a border-mold—a plain mold will answer—stand aside to cool. While this is cooling, pare, and pick with a silver fork one pineapple, saving all the juice; put this juice with one half cupful of water into a saucepan, add one half cupful of sugar, bring to the boiling-point, take from the fire, and stand aside to cool; when ready to serve the pudding, if you have a border-mold, turn it out on a round dish, heap the pineapple in the center, and baste the pudding with the syrup. If a round mold or an ordinary pudding-mold, heap the pineapple around the base, and pour the syrup over. Serve icy cold. Any other delicate fruit may be substituted for pineapples.

Mrs. S. T. Rorer, Author of "Mrs. Rorer's Cook Book," and Principal Philadelphia Cooking School, Philadelphia, Pennsylvania.

STRAWBERRY SHORT-CAKE.

Make a pie-crust with

¾ of a pound of flour,	2 eggs, the yolks of,
¼ of a pound of butter,	A little sugar,
A pinch of soda.	

Then beat the whites of seven eggs to a stiff froth; add

¼ pound of finely chopped almonds,	½ pound of sugar,
A plateful of strawberries.	

Mix with the stiff froth, and spread on the baked crust.

Mrs. Sloan, Vienna, Virginia.

STRAWBERRY SHORT-CAKE.

3 tablespoonfuls of white sugar.	3 teaspoonfuls of baking-powder,
4 tablespoonfuls of butter.	1 quart of flour.

Make this into a soft dough with sweet milk; roll out, and bake in three jelly-cake pans; mash two quarts of berries, and sweeten them well; when the cakes are done, let the first and third ones be whole, but split the middle one, and put the berries between each layer, after they have been buttered; dust white sugar over it, and eat it as soon after making as you can. To make it still richer, before mashing the berries reserve a dozen or more of the largest and best to place on the top of the cake; then between the layers, after the berries are put on, cover them with whipped sweetened sweet cream; cover the top cake with a thick coating of the cream, and place the berries on it in clusters or otherwise. This makes a beautiful dish.

Mrs. C. S. K., Springfield, Ohio.

FRENCH STRAWBERRY SHORT-CAKE.

1 egg,	3 tablespoonfuls of milk,
1 tablespoonful of sugar,	1 teaspoonful of baking-powder,
1 tablespoonful of butter,	Flour to stiffen.

Roll out one half inch thick, and bake in a deep cake-tin; when done, fill with whole well-sweetened strawberries; on top of this put the white of an egg, beaten stiff and sweetened the same as frosting.

PEACH COBBLER.

To one pint of sour cream add lard or butter the size of a hen's egg, one teaspoonful of soda, a pinch of salt, and flour enough to make a stiff dough; roll out thin, and line a dish. Take ripe peaches, pare and quarter, put a layer into the dish, and sprinkle on sugar; cut some dough into small pieces, and put over the peaches, then a layer of sugared peaches, and lastly the dough for an upper crust; cut a hole into the middle, and pour in one and one half pints of water and a lump of butter the size of a hen's egg, and serve while hot with cream or sweetened milk. Apples can be used in the same way.

Sarah Jane Marshall, Augusta, Ohio.

STRUDEL.

Strudel is the national pastry dish of the Bohemians and Hungarians. It is delicious if properly made. Never attempt to make a strudel with baking-powder; this is entirely unknown to either country. Take one and one half pounds of sifted flour, use enough lukewarm water to make a stiff dough, work it well for one half hour. The success of this dish lays in working the dough sufficiently. When this is accomplished, flour the board, put the dough on it, and cover it by upsetting a large iron crucible thoroughly hot, and let it remain there until cold; in the meantime flour a table-cloth, put the dough in the center, and with the aid of another person pull the dough as thin as possible, taking good care not to tear it, the thinner the better; paint the whole with melted butter, and cover with the following mixture, one fourth of an inch thick: Chop some peeled apples finely, add enough sugar and powdered cinnamon to suit the taste, and use it as directed above; lift one side of the table-cloth, and the dough will roll into one round roll; cut this into pieces to suit the baking-sheet, egg on top, and bake in a moderate oven.

Eugene Stuyvesant Howard, Member of the Universal Cookery and Food Association, London, England, and Chef de Cuisine, Louisville Hotel, Louisville, Kentucky.

MODERN POTATO PASTY.

In order to make this properly, a pasty-pan must be procured which has a well-fitting, perforated plate, and a valve-pipe to screw on. This can be had at almost any tin-store, and will cost from one dollar to one dollar and twenty-five cents. The meat, seasoning and gravy are put into the lower part. The plate is then laid on the meat, the valve-pipe screwed on, and mashed potatoes spread equally on the top. The pasty should be baked in a moderate oven, and sent to the table in the same tin in which it was baked, which should have a neatly folded napkin pinned around it. The cover should not be removed until the meat is to be served, and an empty dish should be placed in readiness for it. If properly baked, the potatoes will be nicely browned, and will be flavored like the meat. The contents of this pie may, of course, be varied indefinitely. Mutton or veal cutlets, pork chops, chickens or rabbits, cut into neat joints, and fish of various kinds may all be used, and will be found excellent. The meat should be neatly trimmed and nicely seasoned, and a small quantity of gravy poured over it. The mashed potatoes should form a crust at least three inches thick. Two pounds of meat and three pounds of potatoes will make a moderate-sized pasty. Sufficient for four persons. It will need at least one hour to cook it well. In serving it, dish the meat first, then lay a section of the potato pasty upon it, and the gravy beside it. Never put gravy over a serving unless requested to do so.

POTATO PATTIES.

Take as many large, well-shaped potatoes as it is intended there should be patties, wash well, and bake them; take them out before they are quite done enough, so that the skin may not be injured, carefully cut off the top, and scoop out the inside with a spoon; mix with the floury part two or three spoonfuls of thick cream, a little piece of butter and a pinch of salt, together with sugar, lemon or cinnamon flavoring, and the yolks and whites of two or three beaten eggs, added separately; put this mixture into the hollow potatoes, place them upright side by side in a buttered dish, and bake them in a hot oven. If liked savory, instead of potatoes, patties can be made by mixing with the potato flour a little pounded veal and ham, and cream, salt, lemon-peel, grated nutmeg and mushroom catsup added in suitable proportions. Time to bake, twelve to fifteen minutes. When meat is used, cook them a little longer.

Custards and Desserts.

CHAPTER XIV.

The great art of making a custard lies in well stirring, and when this is properly managed, a custard made with milk and the quantity of eggs given in this recipe will be as rich as one made with cream and additional eggs.

Boil a pint of milk, stir in two ounces of lump-sugar, or sufficient to make the custard sweet enough for the purpose required. Have ready the yolks of three eggs, beaten up, pour the boiling milk on them. Put the stew-pan containing the custard over a slow fire, stir with a wooden spoon as briskly as possible for twenty minutes, or until thickening has commenced, then put the stew-pan on the coolest part of the range, so that it is impossible for the custard to simmer, and let it stand for a quarter of an hour, stirring it occasionally. When the custard is ready, pour it into a basin; flavor with vanilla, almond or lemon. Stir the custard until cool, which will prevent a skin forming on top.

This recipe is the groundwork for all creams made with custard.

For creams and custards, eggs should never be beaten in tin, but always in stone or earthen ware, as there is some chemical influence about tin which prevents their attaining that creamy lightness so desirable.

When gelatin is used for creams, it is better to soak it for an hour in luke-warm water kept in a warm place.

The rule for custard to bake is four eggs, one cupful of sugar and one half teaspoonful of salt to a quart of milk.

Custard should always be baked slowly in a moderate oven, as too much heat will turn it to whey.

Boiled custard must have the closest attention until off the stove.

Peach-leaves or vanilla-beans give a fine flavor, but must be boiled in the milk, and then taken out before the other ingredients are added.

In boiling custard, always use a double vessel.

Custards are nice baked in small cups to serve to each person.

In the use of spices, remember that allspice and cloves are used with meats, and nutmeg and cinnamon in combination with sugar.

The white part of the lemon under the rind is exceedingly bitter, and only the yellow part should be grated. A good way is to rub the rind off with hard lumps of sugar. The sugar thus saturated with the oil of the lemon is called "zest," and is used, when pounded fine, for creams, etc.

CHANTILLY BASKET.

Make a cement of sugar boiled to a crackling height; dip the edges of some macaroons into it, and line a mold shaped like a basket with them, taking care

that the edges of the macaroons touch each other; when wanted, take it out of the mold, fill it up with whipped cream, and it is then ready for the table. Time, two or three hours to set.

LEMON CUSTARD.

Six eggs, beaten separately, three cupfuls of sugar, one half cupful of butter, four cupfuls of water, five tablespoonfuls of corn-starch, two large lemons; slice the lemons, and put them into the water to boil until the strength is extracted, then dip them out, and drain the water, beat the yolks, butter and sugar together, and pour the water over them; return to the jar, and when ready to boil, stir in the starch; beat the whites to a stiff froth, and stir in lightly after it is taken off the stove.

Mrs. Carrie Bell, Eminence, Kentucky.

HAMBURG CREAM.

Take the rind and juice of two large lemons, the yolks of eight eggs and one cupful of sugar; put all into a bucket, and set it in a pan of boiling water; stir for three minutes; take from the fire, add the well-beaten whites of the eggs, and serve when cold in custard-glasses.

Mary E. Arnginst, Star Prairie, Wisconsin.

SPANISH CREAM.

1 quart of milk,	4 eggs, beaten separately,
½ box of gelatin,	4 level teaspoonfuls of vanilla,
1 cupful of sugar.	

Soak the gelatin in the milk for one half hour, then put it over the fire in a double boiler; beat the yolks of the eggs and the sugar together, and when the milk is boiling, stir in the eggs, and cook until it begins to thicken; beat the whites of the eggs very light, and stir into the mixture when it is taken off the fire; flavor, and pour into the mold to cook; beat the whites well into the custard.

Lola Rust, Winnepeg, Maine.

ITALIAN CREAM.

2 eggs,	1 tablespoonful of corn-starch,
4 tablespoonfuls of sugar,	1 quart of milk.

Boil slowly a few minutes, stirring it to keep it smooth; take the whites of

6 eggs, beaten stiff,	½ teacupful of powdered sugar,
1 teaspoonful of lemon.	

Drop this float from a spoon on the custard. If put into a glass dish, add small teaspoonfuls of jelly, dropped on the top of the float.

Rosa A. Willey, Deer Fork, Illinois.

MINCE PIE À LA FRANCAISE.

Prepare one pound of puff paste, roll it out about one half inch thick, and cut it into two pieces; place one piece on a wetted baking-tin, brush it over with

cold water, and place in the center of it about one pound of mince-meat, forming this in a round, flat shape; then place the other piece of paste on the top, press both pieces together, put a meat-plate on the top, face downward, and with a sharp-pointed knife cut the paste to the size; remove the plate, brush the pie over with raw beaten-up whole egg, and mark around the edge and in the center with a pretty design similar to that shown in the engraving; put the pie into a quick oven for about ten minutes, then take up, dust it all over with icing-sugar with a dredge, return it to the oven, and bake for about thirty-five to forty minutes, when the pie should be a pretty, bright golden color; dish up on a hot dish on a dish-paper, and use for luncheon or dinner. The remains of the paste can be used for small mince pies or any dish where puff paste is needed.

TAPIOCA CREAM.

Soak three tablespoonfuls of tapioca in one half cupful of water over night; bring one quart of milk to a boil, then put in the tapioca; when cool, add the beaten yolks of four eggs and one cupful of sugar; pour into a dish, and add the beaten whites.

Stella.

APRICOTS À LA CONDÉ.

Apricots à la Condé.

Put one half pound of Carolina rice into a saucepan, with enough cold water to cover it, let it come to a boil, then strain, and wash in cold water, and put it back into the saucepan, adding a little finely cut lemon-peel or one half stick of split vanilla-pod, one and one half pints of new milk, two ounces of castor-sugar and one ounce of fresh butter; when it comes to a boil, cover over with a piece of buttered paper cut to fit the pan; let it simmer gently without being stirred until it has nearly absorbed all of the milk, then add another fourth of a pint of milk; when the rice is quite cooked and all the grains are separate, have a wide round border-mold well buttered, and press the rice well down into the shape; have a saute-pan with about one pint of boiling water in it, and

stand the border in it, then place it in the oven for about fifteen minutes; when the rice is dry at the top, turn it out onto the dish it is to be served on; have a hot compote of apricots ready, and place them neatly on top of the rice; garnish between the halves of the apricots with shreds of uncrystallized cherries and narrow strips of uncrystallized angelica that is cut into lengths of two and one half to three inches, place the angelica around the edge of the rice, and serve apricot sauce around the base of the dish, and use for a hot sweet.

PINEAPPLE.

They are best cut into dice and saturated with sugar, then piled loosely in a glass dish, with a row of ladyfingers around the edge of the dish. Or slice on a slaw-cutter or very thin with a knife, and mix with finely powdered sugar. Set on ice until ready to serve.

Winnie Bassett.

CODDLED APPLES.

Make a syrup of white sugar and water; throw in some stick cinnamon; have sour apples pared and quartered, and when the syrup boils, put in the apples, and boil until tender.

Mrs. J. A. H., Paris, Kentucky.

APPLE FLOAT.

Peel and core one dozen large apples; let them cook until they can be pierced with a straw; then take them off, and beat with an egg-beater until very smooth, sweeten to taste, and add the well-beaten white of one egg to every cupful of apple; flavor with grated nutmeg; put into a dish, and dot over with small specks of red jelly.

Miss Rosa Sellers, Lexington, Virginia.

BAKED APPLES.

Select tart apples, pare, cut into halves, remove the cores; bake until tender. For a large panful of apples, take two thirds of a pint of thin cream; stir in one tablespoonful of sugar and one level tablespoonful of flour, add a little nutmeg · or lemon; cook this syrup a short time; when the apples are done, pour it over them. Serve warm or cold.

Mrs. Nathan Burgess, Bartlett, Ohio.

APRICOT MERINGUES.

Meringues d'Abricots.

Take one half pound of finely sifted castor-sugar, and mix with it one teaspoonful of apricot yellow and one salt-spoonful of vanilla essence; rub it well together, and allow it to thoroughly dry; put into a whipping-tin four large fresh whites of egg and a pinch of salt, whip them quite stiff, then add the pre-

pared sugar by degrees, taking care not to stir the mixture more than possible after adding the sugar. Take a hot baking-tin, rub it all over with white wax, then leave it until cold; put the meringue mixture into a forcing-bag with a plain pipe, and force it out onto the tin in portions of about the size of apricots, dust them over with castor-sugar, and put into a moderate oven until quite dry and crisp on the top, but the under side should be somewhat soft; then take them from the tin, and by means of an egg work a little well in the bottom of each, holding the top of the meringue in the hand; return them to the tin, and place them in the oven (care must be taken that the meringues are not hurried in the cooking or they will lose their color); when quite dry, remove from the tin, and set aside until cold, then place in each of the little wells a small round of cooked apricot; place another meringue on the top of this, mask them over with maraschino glacé colored with a little apricot yellow, and dish up around a pile of stiffly whipped cream, sweetened, and flavored with vanilla; serve as a dinner or luncheon sweet or for any cold collation. These meringues can be kept ready for use if put into a dry place.

BANANA FLOAT.

Take a small box of gelatin, and dissolve it in a teacupful of cold water for an hour; boil three pints of sweet milk and two and one half teacupfuls of sugar together, dip out a little of the boiling milk, and stir it into the gelatin, then stir this into the rest of the milk, and boil ten minutes; when cool, stir in six bananas that have been broken to pieces with a silver fork, mix thoroughly, and set it on ice. The next day, an hour before serving, take a quart of rich cream, sweeten to taste, flavor with vanilla, and whip it well; put the frozen bananas into a glass dish or bowl, with the whipped cream on top.

Mrs. C. S. K., Springfield, Ohio.

BASKET À LA ROSSLYN.

Corbeille à la Rosslyn.

Take a basket-mold, oil it well, and line it with nougat paste about one fourth of an inch thick, pressing the mixture well into the shape of the mold; trim the edges evenly, and when the nougat is somewhat cool, remove it from the mold, glaze the outside with pink-colored maraschino glacé, and leave until set. Prepare some cutlets of Genoise paste (see recipe), also a round of the same cake the size of the interior of the basket, and fill up with raw fruits, such as

apricots, bananas, melon, etc., cut into slices, and flavor with a little maraschino or other liquor and sweetened with castor-sugar; arrange the cutlets around the top of this, as shown in the engraving, garnish the edge of the nougat with pink royal icing, using a forcing-bag and small rose-pipe for the purpose, pile up in the center of the cutlets some sweetened whipped cream flavored with vanilla, dish up on a dish-paper, garnish the base with any nice crystallized fruits or composition chocolates, and serve as a sweet for dinner or luncheon or for any cold collation.

PINEAPPLE TRIFLE.

Pare and chop finely a pineapple; mix well with it one cupful of sugar, and put to stand in a cool place from two to three hours. Collect all bits of stale light cake, and put a layer of the cake in a pretty glass dish, then a layer of pineapple, and so on, having a pineapple as the last layer; whip cream, and pile on it lightly; sprinkle over it bits of pineapple cut into fancy shapes.

Miss Angeline M. Weaver, Instructor Hyde School Kitchen, Boston, Massachusetts.

TRIFLE.

One half pound of ladyfingers, one half pound of almond macaroons, one half pound of blanched almonds, one half pound of crystallized cherries, some delicate jelly or jam, a little wine, one pint of cream, some rose-water, two quarts of milk. Make a custard of the milk, eight eggs, two cupfuls of sugar and one full tablespoonful of flour; when the milk comes to a boil, have the eggs and sugar beaten very light, put the flour into it, and stir in the hot milk; stir constantly over the fire until quite thick; set off to cool, then flavor with vanilla. Spread the ladyfingers with jelly, and put into a large bowl; next come the macaroons dipped into wine and spread with jelly. Blanch, and cut up the almonds, pour over some rose-water, scatter the almonds and cherries between and over the layers of cake, then pour over the custard; sweeten and flavor the cream; churn it as in the syllabub; when done, beat stiff the whites of two eggs, add a little sugar to them, mix with the whipped cream (it is more solid for it), pour over the top of the bowl, garnish with crystallized cherries. This is enough for twenty people, and very fine.

Mrs. A. E. Kirtland, Author, Montgomery, Alabama.

TRIFLES.

Cut into slices some stale cakes, and spread with jelly; lay them in a glass dish, and cover them with whipped cream.

Mrs. L. E. R., Chesterfield, Virginia.

VANILLA BAVAROISE, WITH FRUITS.

Bavaroise Vanille aux Fruits.

Put into a stew-pan three fourths of a pint of new milk, three ounces of castor-sugar, a split pod of vanilla, and bring to a boil; stand the pan in the

bain-marie for about fifteen minutes to infuse; then remove the pod, and add one half ounce of gelatin, and when dissolved, stir it onto three raw yolks of eggs that are mixed up in a basin; then return the mixture to the stew-pan, and stir over the fire until it thickens, but don't let it boil; then wring it through the tammy, and set away until somewhat cool, but not set; then mix with it rather more than one half pint of stiffly whipped cream, and one teaspoonful of vanilla essence and one wine-glassful of brandy; pour into any fancy mold, and leave until set; turn out on a dish, and garnish with a macedoine of fruits, using fresh fruit when in season. Serve for dinner, luncheon, etc.

PLAIN TRIFLE.

Cut stale sponge-cake (or plain cake without fruit) into slices one fourth of an inch thick; put a layer of cake on the bottom of a glass dish, then a thin layer of any kind of jam (raspberry or strawberry are the best), then another layer of cake; pour over the cake two tablespoonfuls of sherry or any other sweet white wine, with two tablespoonfuls of cold water; then add more jam and cake, piling it up to a point in the center of the dish, having a layer of jam on top; add enough wine and water to moisten the whole; set it away until half an hour before serving it. Make a custard with one half pint of milk, one egg, one tablespoonful of sugar and one half teaspoonful of vanilla; when the milk is scalded, add it by degrees to the well-beaten egg and sugar; cook in a double boiler about five minutes, or until it thickens on a spoon; it must be slowly stirred all the time; strain the custard when done, add the flavoring, and when nearly cold, pour it over the cake. Decorate with little diamond shapes of currant jelly.

Miss Amabel G. E. Hope, Teacher Boston School Kitchen No. 1, Boston.

AMERICAN MERINGUES.

Meringues à l'Americaine.

Prepare an almond icing, and form it into little cone shapes; place these on lightly waxed cool baking-tins, then mask over with the meringue mixture, as below, using two separate forcing-bags and plain pipes for the purpose, and

make them in two colors; dust over the meringues with icing-sugar, and place them in the oven, which must be of very moderate heat, for about one and one half to two hours, when they should be quite dry and a pretty pale color; put them aside until cold, then glaze over with maraschino or noyau glace, one in red, one in white or brown colors, as liked; let them dry again on a pastry-rack, and then dish up on a dish-paper or napkin, and serve for a dinner or luncheon sweet or for any cold collation, or they can be served for dessert. They also form a nice sweet without the glace, being then served with whipped cream.

MERINGUE MIXTURE FOR MERINGUES A L'AMERICAINE.—Put whites of two eggs into a pan with a pinch of salt, and whip until quite stiff, then mix with one fourth of a pound of castor-sugar; place a similar quantity of eggs into another pan, add a few drops of carmine, whip until quite stiff, then mix with one fourth of a pound of castor-sugar, and use.

MUSHROOM MERINGUES.

Champignons Meringues.

Whip four whites of eggs very stiff, with a pinch of salt, and mix with it one half pound of castor-sugar, taking care not to work the eggs more than possible after the sugar is mixed in; then put it into a forcing-bag with a plain pipe about one half inch in diameter, and have two baking-tins warmed and rubbed over with a little white wax; when the tins are cool, take one of them and force the meringue out onto it in little rounds for making the tops of the mushrooms, and then dust them over immediately with icing-sugar, and put them into a very slow oven to dry for three or four hours; put some more of the mixture into a forcing-bag with a pipe about one eighth of an inch in diameter, and force it out into shapes to form the stalks of the mushrooms, and then dust these over with icing-sugar, and cook them in the same way as the others; when they are quite dry, take the large pieces of meringue, and make a little round hole about the size of a pea in the center, using a small knife for the purpose; force inside this a little royal icing, and then very lightly brush over the part of the meringue

that was on the baking-tin with a little raw white of egg, and dip into it some finely grated chocolate, and brush over the flat part of the larger pieces with a little raw white of egg, and then dip into powdered chocolate; let this get quite dry, stick the small part of the meringue as a stalk into the space formed by the knife, and then dish-up the mushrooms on a basket partly filled with spun sugar, artificial moss or maiden-hair-fern leaves, and serve for dessert; or the mushrooms can be dished up on a pile of very stiffly whipped cream that is sweetened and flavored with vanilla essence, which can be colored, if liked, with a little carmine. The mushrooms, if kept in a dry place, will keep for a considerable time.

STRAWBERRY CHARLOTTE.

Make a boiled custard with one quart of milk, yolks of six eggs and three fourths of a cupful of sugar, flavored to taste. Line a glass dish with slices of sponge-cake dipped into sweet cream, lay on them ripe strawberries sweetened to taste; then a layer of cake and strawberries as before; when the custard is cold, pour over the whole; then beat the whites of the eggs to a stiff froth, add a little sugar and pour over the top. Decorate with some ripe berries.

CHARLOTTE RUSSE.

Line a plain mold with a well-oiled paper all over, trim some finger sponge-cakes, and place them all around the mold close together; then prepare a custard to fill up the center, put in rather more than one fourth of a pint of milk, just bring it to a boil, with two ounces of sugar and a piece of split vanilla-pod, then stand in the bain-marie to infuse; or the custard can be flavored with vanilla or other essence; when cool, dissolve in it one fourth of an ounce of finest gelatin leaf, stir it onto two raw yolks of egg; thicken over the fire, but do not let the custard boil after the eggs are added; strain, and when cool, add a good one fourth of a pint of thickly whipped cream and two tablespoonfuls of maraschino or noyau syrup, fill up the mold with it, and when set, turn out and remove the oiled paper; serve on a dish-paper. The charlotte can be garnished with whipped cream around the dish by means of a bag and fancy pipe.

Gustave Beraud, Chef of Calumet Club, Chicago, Formerly Chef of William Aston New York.

TIMBAL OF CHESTNUTS À LA CANNES.

Timbale de Merrons à la Cannes.

Take one and one half pounds of chestnuts prepared as for puree of chestnuts; mix quickly into this puree two ounces of castor-sugar, one good tablespoonful of thick cream, eight to ten drops of essence of vanilla, one raw white

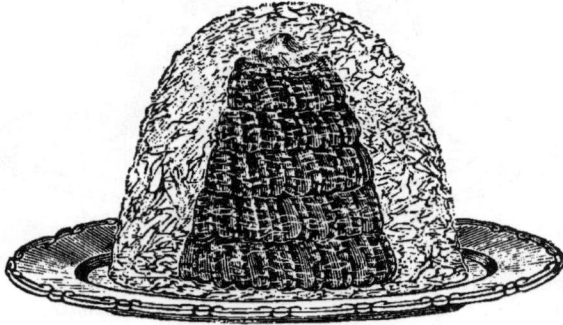

of egg, two tablespoonfuls of orange-flower water and one tablespoonful of brandy, and work up into a ball; then carefully roll it out about one fourth of an inch thick, sprinkling it with little icing-sugar, and stamp out in small heart shapes or rounds or rings; place these on a baking-tin in a screen until they are quite dry on the surface; then dip each piece separately into boiled sugar (see recipe), let this set; then stick the pieces together, as shown, to form a shape, and garnish it in some pretty design with pink and white icing, using a forcing-bag and pipe for the purpose; then, when cold, fill up with cream, as below, and garnish with spun sugar (see recipe), and use for a fancy sweet.

VANILLA CREAM FOR TIMBAL OF CHESTNUTS A LA CANNES.—Whip stiff one pint of double cream, sweeten it with four ounces of castor-sugar, and flavor with eight or ten drops of vanilla essence. Part of this can, if liked, be colored brown or red before using.

LITTLE MOKAS.

Petits Mokas.

Put into a stew-pan four whole fresh eggs, six ounces of castor-sugar, the finely chopped peel of one lemon and a few drops of vanilla essence; whip these over boiling water until warm, then remove the pan from the fire, and whip the contents until cold and thick. Have four ounces of fine flour passed through a sieve and warmed, and mixed with the above ingredients, stirring the mixture as little as possible after the flour is added. Brush over a saute-pan with warm butter, line it with a buttered paper, dust this over with fine flour and castor-sugar mixed in equal quantities, and then put in the prepared mixture; bake it in a moderate oven for one half hour, then turn it out of the pan, and leave it until cold; cut the cake into square pieces, and very lightly mask these over with coffee icing, then dip each into almonds prepared as below, ornament the top with Vienna icing colored with a little black coffee; sprinkle with

chopped pistachios, and dish up the mokas on a dish-paper, as shown in the engraving, and serve for luncheon, dinner, etc.

ALMONDS FOR LITTLE MOKAS.—Take some blanched Valencia almonds, cut them into small dice shapes, and bake until a nice golden color.

DISH OF SNOW.

Grate a cocoanut, leaving out the brown part; heap it up in the center of a handsome dish, and ornament with fine green leaves, such as peach or honeysuckle. Serve it up with snow cream made in this way: Beat the whites of five eggs to a stiff froth, add two large spoonfuls of fine white sugar, one large spoonful of rose-water or pineapple; beat the whole well together, and add one pint of thick cream; put several spoonfuls over each dish of cocoanut.

Mrs. T. V. R., Sedalia, Missouri.

FLOATING ISLAND.

Beat the yolks of three eggs until very light; sweeten and flavor to taste; stir into a quart of boiling milk, cook until it thickens; when cool, pour into a low glass dish; whip the whites of the eggs to a stiff froth, sweeten, lay them in spoonfuls upon boiling water for two or three minutes, then put upon the custard far enough apart so that the "little white islands" will not touch each other. A pleasing effect will be produced by dropping little specks of bright jelly on each island; also, filling glasses with it, and arranging around the stand, adds to the appearance of the table. Set upon ice to get cold.

Mrs. Ellen K. B., Bellevue, Ohio.

FARINA MELUSINE, WITH APPLES.

Bring one quart of milk to a boil, add, stirring constantly, one cupful of farina, and stir until it forms into a stiff paste and loosens itself from the bottom of the saucepan; transfer it to a dish; when cold, stir two tablespoonfuls of butter to a cream, and add alternately the yolks of six eggs, the farina, four tablespoonfuls of sugar, the rind of one lemon and lastly the beaten whites; pare and core eight large, tart apples, put them into a long pan over the fire, add one quart of boiling water, cover with another pan of the same size, and steam them five minutes—no longer; then remove carefully, lay them in a long-shaped pudding-dish, put one tablespoonful of jelly into each apple, and pour the farina mixture over so that the apples are entirely covered; bake in a medium-hot oven about three quarters of an hour, and serve with the following sauce: Stir two tablespoonfuls of butter with one cupful of powdered sugar to a cream, add the yolks of two eggs, two tablespoonfuls of rum or cognac, a little nutmeg, and lastly the whites beaten to a stiff froth. Sufficient for family of eight persons.

Mrs. Gesine Lemcke, Principal of the German-American Cooking College, Brooklyn.

FRUIT ON CAKES À LA PARISIENNE.

Croûtes aux à la Parisienne.

Cut some cake into slices about one half inch thick, and stamp out in rounds about three inches in diameter, place them on a buttered tin, dust them over with

icing-sugar, and place them in the oven until quite crisp. Arrange on the croûtes half peaches or sliced pineapple, and dish them around the dish for a border, and pile up in the center any nice fruits, such as cherries, strawberries, skinned and stoned grapes or any other fruit you may have, and when ready to serve, pour over all the fruits a sauce of apricots or any other nice fruit; garnish with spun sugar, and serve for a dinner sweet or for luncheon or for a cold collation.

SAUCE FOR FRUIT ON CAKES A LA PARISIENNE.—One pot of apricot jam, four ounces of castor-sugar, one salt-spoonful of apricot yellow, one salt-spoonful of liquid carmine, one fourth of a pint of water; boil together for about ten minutes, rub through a sieve or tammy, add a large wine-glassful of maraschino or chartreuse liquor, and use.

CHARLOTTE À LA PRINCESSE.

Charlotte à la Princesse.

Line a plain mold with lightly oiled paper, arrange sponge or vanilla cakes all around it, then fill up with good vanilla bavaroise, as below, mixed with two ounces of any nice fruits cut into shreds; when set, turn out, and ornament with Vienna icing in pink and white, using forcing-bags with fancy pipes; serve on a fancy dish-paper for a dinner or luncheon sweet.

VANILLA BAVAROISE FOR CHARLOTTE A LA PRINCESSE.—Take one and one half gills of boiled milk, with vanilla-pod and two ounces of castor-sugar, mix when boiling with one fourth of an ounce of gelatin; then stir onto two raw

yolks of eggs, return to the stew-pan, and stir over the fire until it thickens; then tammy, and when cool, add one half pint of whipped cream, one wine-glassful of brandy and one of any other liquor, and use.

STEWED PEARS, WITH VANILLA SAUCE.

Peel the stewing-pears, and put them into a stew-pan, with enough cold water to cover them, add twelve ounces of sugar to each quarter of water, a little piece of cinnamon, a little lemon-peel and a few drops of liquid carmine; cook for two and one half hours, gently simmering, take them up, and let them cool; reduce the syrup in which they were cooked to the consistency of a single cream; when the pears are cold, stamp out the cores with a long vegetable-cutter, and fill up the centers with stiffly whipped cream flavored with vanilla and sweetened, using a forcing-bag and rose-pipe for the purpose; sprinkle them with finely shredded, blanched sweet almonds or pistachios; dish up, and pour the syrup around them. This is a nice luncheon or dinner sweet.

Gustave Beraud, Chef of Calumet Club, Chicago, Formerly Chef of William Astor, New York.

BLACKBERRY FLUMMERY.

To one pint of blackberries add one pint of water; boil until tender, and then add

1 cupful of sugar.   4 tablespoonfuls of corn-starch.
A pinch of salt.

Stir until it boils; flavor to taste. To be eaten with cream and sugar.

Mrs. J. B. Schoonover, Bush Hill, Pennsylvania.

ORANGE DESSERT.

Pare five or six oranges, cut into thin slices; pour over them a coffee-cupful of sugar; boil one pint of milk; add, while boiling, the yolks of three eggs, one tablespoonful of corn-starch (made smooth with a little cold milk); stir all the time; as soon as thickened, pour over the fruit; beat the whites of the eggs to a froth, add two tablespoonfuls of powdered sugar, pour over the custard, and brown in the oven. Serve cold.

Lulu Plummer, New Athens, Ohio.

TIMBAL À LA CHRISTINA.

Timbale à la Christina.

Well oil a timbal or turban mold, and line it with nougat paste, trim off the edges, and set aside until cold, remove the case from the mold, mask it over on the outside with maraschino glace, using a forcing-bag and small rose-pipe for the purpose, and garnishing around the edges with shredded pistachio-nuts; fill up the inside with chestnut cream prepared as below, using a forcing-bag

and large, plain pipe for the purpose; garnish the top of this with whipped cream colored red and white, forming it into roses by means of a forcing-bag with a large rose-pipe; sprinkle lightly with shredded pistachio and crystallized rose-leaves, garnish the center with spun sugar (see recipe), and serve for a dinner-party sweet.

CHESTNUT CREAM FOR TIMBAL A LA CHRISTINA.—Prepare one pound of chestnut puree, mix with it four ounces of castor-sugar, one tablespoonful of brandy, the same of orange-flower water, one teaspoonful of vanilla essence and the finely chopped peel of a lemon, one half pint of stiffly whipped cream, and use.

BAVARIAN CREAM, WITH STRAWBERRY.

Pick over two quarts of strawberries, squeeze them through a colander, and add two level cupfuls of white sugar; when the sugar is all dissolved, add one ounce or three tablespoonfuls of gelatin that has been soaking an hour in one half cupful of tepid water; place it on the ice, stir it smooth, and when it begins to set, stir in one pint of whipped cream, put it into molds, and serve with the whole strawberries around it.

"Hazel Kirk."

PILAU À LA GRECQUE.

Pilau à la Grecque.

Take one half pound of Patna rice, blanch it, and wash well in cold water, put it back into the stew-pan, with two ounces of warm butter and one and one half pints of light stock, put a bunch of herbs on the top, cover with a buttered paper, and simmer gently until tender, which will take about one hour, adding a little more stock if needed; then turn out some of the rice to form a border; put the ragout in the center, then pour around the edge of the dish a puree of tomatoes, and sprinkle over a little saffron shreds and raw chopped parsley, and some thinly cut slices of raw lemon all around as a border. Serve for luncheon or dinner.

RAGOUT FOR PILAU A LA GRECQUE.—Take some cold game or poultry, cut into neat dice shapes, and season with salt and one and one half ounces of grated

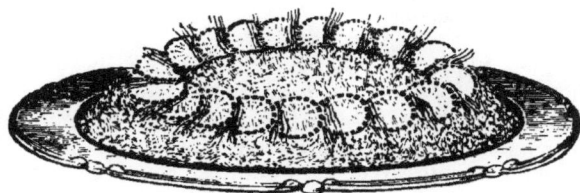

Parmesan cheese and a dust of pepper, and mix. Take four onions, peel, and cut them into tiny dice shapes, two ounces of butter, two ounces of lean raw bacon cut into dice shapes, fry together until a nice golden color; mix with one ounce of fine flour, add three fourths of a pint of good-flavored stock, and simmer until tender; add the cut chicken, etc., boil up, and use.

APPLE CHARLOTTE.

Select six medium-sized Newton pippins, peel, core, and cut them into quarters; put them into a large saucepan, with two ounces of fresh butter and four ounces of powdered sugar, and place over a moderate fire; toss them for two minutes, then moisten with a gill of white wine, and grate with the peel of one half lemon; cover the saucepan, and let it cook for ten minutes, so that the liquid be almost entirely absorbed by the apples; remove from the fire, and put aside to cool. Take a three-pint charlotte-mold, line it, beginning at the bottom, with cut slices of American bread the thickness of a silver dollar; glaze them well with melted butter, using a brush for the purpose, and sprinkle powdered sugar lightly over; then line the sides to the edge in the same way; fill the mold with prepared apples, and cover with slices of bread; lay it on a baking-pan, and place it in a brisk oven for forty-five minutes, or until the bread be a golden color, then take it out, lay a hot dessert-dish on top, turn it over, and remove the mold. Heat in a saucepan two ounces of apricot marmalade, with two table-spoonfuls of maraschino and one of water; mix well, pour it over the charlotte, and serve very hot.

Gustave Beraud, Chef of Calumet Club, Chicago, Formerly Chef of William Astor, New York.

SEA-MOSS FARINE.

This comes in small packages in a fine powder. Take one level tablespoonful to one quart of milk; set on the milk to boil, with one cupful of sugar and a pinch of salt; mix the moss farine smooth with a little cold milk, stir into the milk, and stir constantly until it boils; it must cook in a double vessel; let it boil only ten minutes; pour into a mold, and let it get cold. Eat with cream. Flavor with vanilla. ·

Christie Irving.

BISQUE GLACÉ.

Make a rich ice-cream in the proportion of one half gallon of cream and three fourths of a pound of sugar. Take one and one half dozen of stale macaroons or one dozen stale egg-kisses, pour a little cream over them, and allow them to stand until they soften; beat until very fine. As the cream freezes, stir in the moistened cakes.

Mrs. C. S. K., Springfield, Ohio.

LITTLE BASKETS À LA LAVANUE.

Petites Corbeilles à la Lavenue.

Prepare some Genoise paste (see recipe), and fill about three parts full some little molds; place the tins on a baking-sheet, and bake in a moderate oven for twenty-five to thirty minutes; then turn out, and when cool, cut out the inside

with a small knife to make a hollow, leaving the edges one eighth of an inch thick; place inside the space thus formed one teaspoonful of apricot jam or other nice preserve; mask the outside of the molds with a little apricot jam, and then sprinkle over the jam some blanched and finely chopped pistachio-nuts; ornament the edges with a little icing by means of a forcing-bag and small rose-pipe; cut some uncrystallized angelica in lengths of about five inches, and about one fourth of an inch thick, and place these over the molds, lodging them between the cake and the jam, so as to form handles; whip some cream very stiffly, sweeten it, and flavor with vanilla essence, and by means of a forcing-bag and a large rose-pipe partly fill up the inside of the molds, cover the jam entirely, and form the cream into a rose pattern, on which sprinkle very lightly a little red-colored sugar made by mixing a little liquid carmine with some castor-sugar; dish up, and serve for a dinner or luncheon sweet or for any cold collation.

FLEUR, WITH MERINGUE.

Fleur au Meringue.

Have a plain or fancy fleur-ring buttered, and place it on a buttered paper on a baking-tin, line the ring with short paste, prick it well on the bottom to prevent it blistering, trim it off evenly around the edges of the ring with a knife, and partly fill up the inside with a pastry custard; put a few little pieces of butter here and there on the top to keep it moist, and bake in a moderate oven for twenty-five to thirty minutes, when the custard should be a pretty golden color; then remove the fleur-ring, and mask the top of the custard over with a layer of any nice jam; fill up the fleur with a stiff meringue mixture, putting it on ornamentally by means of a forcing-bag and pipe, then dust over with icing-sugar from a dredge, and place it in a moderate oven for twelve to

fifteen minutes to dry; then arrange neatly on the top some nice dried or fresh fruits, such as strawberries or cherries, dish on a paper or napkin, and serve for a dinner or luncheon sweet or for any cold collation.

FRENCH RICE.

Cook slowly in a double boiler

¼ pound of rice,	1 teacupful of sugar,
1 tablespoonful of butter,	1 lemon, the grating,
½ teaspoonful of salt,	½ pint of milk,
1 pint of water.	

When quite soft, remove from the fire, and stir in two well-beaten eggs; bake twenty minutes in a pudding-dish, with crumbs on top of the mixture.

APPLE DAINTY.

Wipe, quarter, pare and core apples; to each pint allow one third of a cupful of sugar, one third of a cupful of cold water, a speck of cloves; put into an earthen dish, cover tightly, and bake slowly eight or ten hours; when candied and deep red in color, pile lightly on a dish, pour over it a boiled custard made with three yolks, two tablespoonfuls of sugar, one half teaspoonful of vanilla and one pint of scalded milk; pile lightly over this the three whites beaten with one tablespoonful of powdered sugar and a drop of vanilla.

Miss Angeline M. Weaver, Instructor Hyde School Kitchen, Boston, Massachusetts,

ORANGE SOUFFLÉ.

Peel and slice six oranges; put into a glass dish a layer of oranges, then one of sugar, and so on until all the orange is used, and let stand two hours; make a soft-boiled custard of yolks of three eggs, one pint of milk, sugar to suit the taste, with grating of orange-peel for flavor; pour over the orange when cool enough not to break the dish; beat the whites of the eggs to a stiff froth, stir in sugar, and put over the pudding.

Kate Kilbourne, Indianapolis, Indiana.

FLOWER CASES À LA CRÈME.

Bouquetiers à la Crème.

Make some nougat; when cooked, turn the mixture onto an oiled slab, roll it out with an oiled rolling-pin, and line some oiled dariol-molds with it very thinly, pressing well to the shapes; trim the edges, and when cool, turn out of the molds, and mask them lightly over the outsides with royal icing which is colored with a little carmine or cherry red; sprinkle this over with red-colored

sugar, and ornament the edges of the bouquetiers with white royal icing by pistachio-nuts, and when ready to serve, fill up the centers with whipped cream, and garnish the top with crystallized rose-leaves and violets. Serve on a dish-paper or napkin for a dinner or luncheon sweet or for any cold collation.

BAKED PEARS.

Place in a stone jar first a layer of pears (without paring), then a layer of sugar, then pears, and so on until the jar is full; then put in as much water as it will hold; bake three hours.

Nettie R., Wyoming.

BLANC-MANGE.

One quart of sweet milk, three tablespoonfuls of sugar, and boil together; then pour into this five tablespoonfuls of corn-starch, two eggs; beat the eggs with the corn-starch; flavor to suit the taste, and stir quickly before pouring into the molds.

Mrs. N. A. P., Ridgeway, South Carolina.

CHARLOTTE RUSSE.

I suppose every one has a syllabub churn. If not, procure one from your tinner. It is also called a whip churn. Take one pint of sweet, fresh cream, churn it, and as the froth rises, skim off into a bowl, as much liquid cream will run from it which can be churned again. You will find, too, it will become too thick to churn; then pour in sweet milk to thin the cream, and it will churn beautifully. After it is all churned and skimmed off into another bowl to avoid the settlings, stir gently through it one half cupful of sugar; have ready in soak one box, or a little less, of gelatin in very little water for at least one hour; drain from it the water, and dissolve in one half cupful of hot sweet milk; while cooling, beat separately two eggs, adding one half cupful of sugar to the yolks; when very light, add the stiff whites and two tablespoonfuls of vanilla. If the gelatin has cooled, mix thoroughly with the egg, and pour at once into the whipped cream. Line the bowl with ladyfingers, and pour in the charlotte. This is delightful, and sufficient for ten people.

Mrs. A. E. Kirtland, Author, Montgomery, Alabama.

TIMBAL À LA MATHILD.

Timbale à la Mathilde.

Prepare some choux paste, say one pint for twelve to fourteen persons, put it into a forcing-bag with a large, plain pipe, and force the mixture out onto an ungreased baking-tin in rings about four inches in diameter; brush these all

over the top with whole beaten-up egg, and bake in a moderate oven for about thirty-five to forty minutes; then take them up, and arrange them one on the other in a pile on a paste bottom, fixing them together with a little icing or boiled sugar, and then prepare a meringue mixture, and completely cover the timbal with this, as shown in the engraving, with a bag and pipe, forming it in little ball shapes, and forcing them out quite close together; dust it over with icing-sugar, using a dredge for the purpose, and then place it in a moderate oven, and let the meringue get perfectly dry without getting discolored, then dish up, and fill up the center with pastry custard, and serve chocolate sauce in a boat. Serve hot or cold for dinner sweet or cold collation.

ROSAMOND TIMBAL.

Prepare some Florence paste, and with it line a plain timbal or charlotte mold; put it aside until cold, then by means of a palette-knife loosen it from the mold, turn it out, and ornament it, as shown in the engraving, with rose-colored Vienna icing and very stiffly whipped cream, using a large rose-pipe, and small rose-pipe with a leaf-shaped pipe for the top edge; fill in the center of the timbal with alternate layers of chocolate, strawberry and maraschino ice-cream, smooth this over, and on the top of the shape arrange some stiffly whipped cream flavored with vanilla essence and sweetened, using a forcing-

bag and rose-pipe for the purpose; place here and there some chocolate varieties, arrange the timbal on a dish on a paper, and serve for a dinner or ball supper sweet.

CHARLOTTE À LA CORA.

Take a plain charlotte-mold, oil it, and line it with oiled paper, and arrange around it some vanilla or sponge finger-biscuits, trimming them as may be necessary to fix them nicely and evenly in the mold, then fill the mold up with a chocolate bavaroise, and put the mold aside in a cool place or on ice until the bavaroise is set; when ready to serve, dip the charlotte-mold into hot water for a moment, pass a cloth over the bottom to absorb any moisture, and turn the charlotte out on a dish; remove the paper, and pour a thick apricot sauce over and around the charlotte, and sprinkle it with some blanched and shredded kernels of the pistachio-nut. This is a very nice sweet, and is suitable for either luncheon or dinner.

BAVAROISE FOR CHARLOTTE CORA.—Take one fourth of a pound of chocolate, cut up small, add a few drops of essence of vanilla, and put it into a saucepan, with two ounces of sugar and rather more than one half pint of milk; let it boil for about ten minutes, then dissolve in it one half ounce of finest leaf gelatin, and pour into it three raw yolks of eggs in a basin, keeping it stirred; then pour it back into the saucepan, and stir it over the fire until it thickens, but do not let it boil, pass it through the sieve, and when it is getting cool, add to it one half pint of whipped cream and one wine-glassful of maraschino syrup, and pour it into the mold to set.

Gustave Beraud, Chef of Calumet Club, Chicago, Formerly Chef of William Astor, New York.

MELON À LA DUCHESSE.

Take one half pound of baked almonds, chopped fine, six ounces of rice cream, two salt-spoonfuls of apple-green, six whole eggs, four ounces of sugar, two salt-spoonfuls of essence of vanilla; work the butter until like a cream, then add the rice cream, sugar, coloring and the eggs by degrees, and finally the almonds, and work all together for about fifteen minutes. Butter and flour the two halves of a melon-mold, and half fill them with the above paste; bake for about one half to three quarters of an hour in a moderate oven; turn the cakes out of the mold; when they are cool, trim them off evenly, so that when put together they will form a ball; scoop out the centers, and fill the spaces with apricot or strawberry jam and whipped cream, sweetened, and flavored with vanilla, place the two parts together, glaze the cake with noyau or maraschino glace colored with a little apple-green; dish on a border of nougat on a paper, garnish with leaves, and serve.

Gustave Beraud, Chef of Calumet Club, Chicago, Formerly Chef of William Astor.

LITTLE NOUGAT BASKETS À LA DUCHESSE.

Petites Corbeilles de Nougat à la Duchesse.

Line some little oiled oval dariol-molds with nougat paste about one eighth of an inch thick, trim them, and turn out the nougat cases to form the base of the baskets, and when quite cold, fill up the insides with whipped cream, using a bag and pipe for the purpose, form the lids and handles from the boiled sugar

or angelica, garnish with small quarters of orange, whole ripe strawberries and cherries, or any nice fresh ripe fruit that is dipped into clear boiled sugar; if fresh fruits are not in season, dried ones may be used; arrange on a dish-paper or napkin, and serve for a dinner or luncheon sweet or for any cold collation.

PRINCE OF WALES CHARLOTTE.

Lay thick slices of any kind of delicate cake in a deep pudding-dish; over this pour hot boiled custard made from the yolks of three eggs and one pint of milk, sweetened and flavored to taste. Do this several hours before the dish is to be served; just before serving, put a layer of sliced peaches or oranges over the cake; have the whites of the eggs beaten to a stiff froth, with a little sugar, and put over the fruit; put into the oven a few minutes to brown.

Mrs. P. P. Mast, Springfield, Ohio.

ALMOND CHARLOTTE À LA BEATRICE.
Charlotte d'Amandes à la Beatrice.

Take one pound of nougat paste, then turn it out onto an oiled slab or board, and roll out the mixture; cut up a portion into strips four or five inches long and one and one half inches wide; cut two plain rounds about four inches in diameter, and put these aside to use, one for the top and the other for the bottom of the charlotte; also stamp out some small rounds about the size of a quarter to garnish the top and bottom; let these cool, then have some boiled sugar, and join the strips together in a well-oiled mold; leave these until set, then fill up the inside with a bavaroise mixture, as below; let this set, then turn out, and fasten on the bottom and top made of prepared paste, using the boiled sugar for the purpose; garnish tastefully with the little rounds of the paste, and ornament

the charlotte with royal icing, using a small rose-pipe and forcing-bag for the purpose. This is a nice sweet to serve for a dinner or any cold collation.

BAVAROISE FOR ALMOND CHARLOTTE A LA BEATRICE.—Put into a stew-pan one half pint of milk, with two ounces of castor-sugar and half a split pod of vanilla, stand in the bain-marie to infuse for about ten minutes, then mix with it one half ounce of gelatin, and stir until this is dissolved; mix three yolks of eggs in a basin, and stir the above mixture onto them, return to the bain-marie, and stir until it thickens, then tammy, and when cool, mix in a wine-glassful of cherry syrup, one half wine-glassful of rum or brandy and one half pint of stiffly whipped cream; divide this mixture into three parts, color one with a little sap-green, one with carmine, and leave the other part white; then pour these mixtures into the charlotte-case in alternate layers as they are getting set.

TIMBAL À LA FLORENCE.
Timbale à la Florence.

Put more than one half pound of Valencia almonds into a stew-pan, with sufficient cold water to cover them; bring to a boil, then rinse them in cold water; strain this off, and rub them in a cloth to take off the skins; chop up the almonds quite fine, and put them into a stew-pan, with one half pound of fine sugar, two tablespoonfuls of brandy, one tablespoonful of strained lemon-juice, and sufficient liquid carmine to make it a nice red color; stir these all together over the fire for seven or eight minutes, when they will be almost dry; then take a well-oiled mold, and arrange in it the above mixture about three fourths of an inch thick, quickly pressing it to the mold with a slightly oiled lemon; trim the top evenly, then put aside until quite cold; remove from the mold (loosening it with a small-pointed knife), and put the almond case on a dish-paper on the dish in which it will be served; fill up the inside with a bavaroise mixture, putting this into the case when it is beginning to set. Take some Vienna icing flavored with chocolate in the proportion of one ounce of the chocolate to one half pound of icing-sugar, and some more flavored with vanilla essence; put them separately into forcing-bags with rose-pipes, and ornament the case with these mixtures, as in the engraving, then arrange some crys-

tallized violets here and there on the icing (these give a very pretty effect to the dish); when ornamented, put the timbal into a cool place for several hours to allow the icing to become set; then serve for a dinner sweet or for a ball supper, etc.

VOL-AU-VENT À LA PRINCE GEORGE.

Vol-au-vent à la Prince George.

Prepare some puff paste, say three fourths of a pound, for a vol-au-vent for eight persons, and roll it out about one half inch thick; stamp out four pieces with a vol-au-vent cutter which has been dipped into boiling water, so that it cuts the paste evenly; wet a baking-tin all over with cold water, place the pieces of paste on it, leaving two pieces whole, and removing the centers from the other two pieces by means of a small-sized vol-au-vent cutter; put the center pieces likewise on the baking-tin; brush the paste over with the whole beaten-up egg, and bake in a quick oven for fifteen to twenty minutes; take up, place the two whole pieces one on the other, and fasten them together with the luting-paste, and then on top of them place the two pieces from which the centers were removed, and fasten them together with the paste; whip three or four whites of eggs stiff, with a pinch of salt, put it into a forcing-bag with a rose-pipe, and ornament the vol-au-vent with it, as shown in the engraving, in lines up the sides and on the top, and on the whipped egg arrange alternately little

9

bunches of chopped cooked ham or tongue and blanched and chopped pistachios; put the vol-au-vent in a very moderate oven for about fifteen minutes to dry the white of egg and fixing-paste; then dish up on a hot dish on a dish-paper or napkin, fill up the hollow center with the ragout, as below, place one of the center pieces of paste on the ragout, and serve either hot or cold.

RAGOUT FOR VOL-AU-VENT A LA PRINCE GEORGE.—Take three fourths of a pound altogether of cooked chicken, rabbit, sweetbread, cooked ham or tongue, calves' brains left from any previous meal, cut all into pieces about the size of a nickel, and mix them with a thick veloute sauce; make all hot in the bain-marie, and fill in the vol-au-vent case with it.

LITTLE NOUGAT BASKETS À LA DÜRER.

Petites Corbeilles de Nougat à la Dürer.

Well oil some fluted basket-molds, and line them thinly with nougat paste; when this is cool, turn the nougats, and stick the two parts of the baskets together with a little boiled sugar; mask the bottom part of the basket with a

little royal icing, sprinkle this with a few finely shredded pistachio-nuts, and fill up the inside of the baskets by means of a forcing-bag and pipe with colored garnishing-cream, garnish with fruits, such as strawberries, cherries, etc., that have been first dipped into boiling sugar and allowed to get cold; dish up on a dish-paper, and serve for a sweet for dinner or any cold collation.

SPUN SUGAR.

Put one half pound of water and one pound of best cane loaf-sugar into a perfectly clean copper sugar-boiler or thick stew-pan, cover the pan over, bring to a boil, remove any scum as it arises from time to time, and continue boiling until the liquid forms a thick-bubbled appearance (commonly called the crack); then take a small portion on a clean knife or spoon (or the finger may be used, but it

must be well wetted with cold water and used quickly), and plunge it immediately into cold water, and if it is then quite brittle, and leaves the knife or spoon or finger quite clear, it is ready for spinning. If it clings or is at all soft or pliable, continue the boiling until as above. When ready, take a small portion on a fork or spoon, and rapidly throw it to and fro over a slightly oiled rolling-pin; continue until sufficient threads of sugar are obtained,

FLEUR À LA FLORENCE.

Fleur à la Florence.

Take a square fleur-mold, oil it well, and line it about one fourth of an inch thick with Florence paste, pressing this well to the mold; trim off the edges neatly, and when the paste is cold and firm, remove the pegs from the mold, take away the fleur-tin, and ornament the edges of the paste by means of a

forcing-bag and small rose-pipe with royal icing; place the case on the dish in which it is to be served, arrange around the inside, as in the engraving, cornets prepared as in recipe, page 274, but color the cornet paste with six or eight drops of liquid carmine, and fill up the center with a macedoine of fruits; fill the cornets with vanilla-flavored whipped cream for garnishing, using a forcing-bag and rose-pipe for the purpose, and arrange some of the same cream on the top of the macedoine of fruits. Serve for a dinner sweet or for ball supper.

PASTRY POTATOES.

Pommes de Terre Pâtisseries.

Put into a stew-pan three ounces of castor-sugar, one ounce of finely powderd chocolate rubbed through a wire sieve, four large eggs, and whip these

together over boiling water until the mixture is quite warm, then remove the pan, and whip the contents off the water until the mixture is like a thick batter and quite cold; add to it three ounces of fine flour that have been passed through a sieve and warmed. Have a baking-tin brushed over with warm butter, and then lined with paper, brush the paper also over with butter, and dust it over with fine flour and castor-sugar mixed in equal quantities; pour the mixture into this pan about one fourth of an inch thick, and bake it in a moderate oven for about one half hour; then turn out, and when cold, rub it all into crumbs, and mix with it two tablespoonfuls of apricot, strawberry or raspberry jam, which should be first rubbed through a sieve; add about twelve drops of essence of vanilla, and mix it into a paste in a basin; then take portions of the mixture, about one dessert-spoonful, flatten it out with the hand, using a little icing-sugar for the purpose, and inside the paste place one or two uncrystallized cherries, then roll up into the form of a very small potato. Have some almond icing, and with it completely cover the first preparation, making the almond covering perfectly smooth, and working it with icing-sugar, then roll the potato into chocolate that has been grated and rubbed through a sieve; roll the potato well into the chocolate, and then with the point of a small knife make little impressions to represent the eyes of the potato; leave them on a pastry-rack, and when the almond icing is set and feels firm, dish up the potatoes, as in the design, with a few little green leaves; these will keep well for a week or two if kept in a dry place, and are nice to use for a sweet or for dessert or any cold collation. Quantities given will be enough for fourteen to sixteen persons.

STRAWBERRY SOUFFLÉ À LA CALUMET CLUB.

Take three fourths of a pint of fresh strawberry pulp that has been rubbed through a sieve, then mix with two and one half ounces of finely sifted flour, two ounces of butter, one gill of cream, three fourths of a pound of sugar, a few drops of essence of vanilla, and enough liquid carmine to make it a pretty red color, and four yolks of raw eggs; stir together over the fire until the mixture boils, then add three fourths of a pound of sliced ripe strawberries, and six whites of eggs that are whipped stiff, with a pinch of salt; pour the mixture into a souffle-tin or pie-dish, place a band of buttered paper around the tin or dish, bake in the oven about twenty minutes; dust it with icing-sugar; when cooked, remove the paper, place a folded napkin over the dish, and serve it in a hot dish, with a puree of iced strawberries, handed in a sauce boat or glass for dinner or luncheon.

Gustave Beraud, Chef of Calumet Club, Chicago, Formerly Chef of William Astor, New York.

FRESH PEACHES.

Choose large, fresh, ripe and juicy peaches, pare, and cut them into two or three pieces, sprinkle them with granulated sugar; put them into a freezer, and half freeze them, which will take an hour or more. Do not take them from the freezer until ready to serve, then sprinkle over a little more sugar, and serve in a glass dish. Canned peaches may be used in the same way.

BANANAS.

Peel and slice them, heap them up in a glass dish, and serve raw with fine sugar and cream. Some like them sliced in with strawberries or oranges, while others eat them as you would an apple.

ICES, CREAMS, SHERBETS, ETC.

LEMON-ICE.

One gallon of water and four pounds of sugar, well boiled and skimmed; when cold, add the juice of a dozen lemons and the sliced rind of eight, and let infuse one hour; strain into the freezer without pressing, and stir in lightly the well-beaten whites of twelve eggs.

Mrs. J. B. Wood, Bellevue, Ohio.

FEDORA BOMB.

Bombe à la Fedora.

Prepare a puree of apples, as below, and when cool, freeze it, and line a bomb-mold about one fourth of an inch thick with it; then fill up the center of the mold with a cherry or maraschino mousse mixture, put the cover on the mold, and place it in the charged ice-cave for about three and one half hours, during which time turn it around occasionally; when sufficiently frozen, take out

the mold, dip it into cold water, remove the cover, pass a clean cloth over the bottom to absorb any moisture, and turn out the bomb on a paper or napkin onto a cold dish. Garnish with small shapes of chocolate or coffee ice-cream, and serve for dinner or dessert ice.

APPLE PUREE FOR FEDORA BOMB.—Take two pounds of good cooking-apples, peel and slice them, and put them into a stew-pan, with one quart of water, the peel and juice of two lemons, a piece of crushed cinnamon about one inch long, one or two bay-leaves and six ounces of sugar. Color a pale salmon with carmine, boil all together into a puree, rub this through the tammy, and when cool, partly freeze it, then mix it with one half pint of stiffly whipped cream; refreeze, and use.

ORANGE-ICE.

Boil one and one half cupfuls of sugar in a quart of water, skimming when necessary; when cold, add the juice of one half dozen oranges; steep the rinds in a little water, and strain into the rest; add the rind and juice of a lemon, and strain into the freezer, and freeze like ice-cream.

Gladys Romaine, Cleveland, Ohio.

RASPBERRY WATER-ICE.

Mix one pound of sugar and the juice of two lemons with one quart of raspberries, let stand one hour, strain, add one quart of boiling water; let cool, and freeze.

STRAWBERRY WATER-ICE.

Boil one pound of sugar and one pint of water until thick syrup, let cool, and add the juice of one quart of strawberries and the juice of one lemon, turn into the freezer, and freeze.

PRINCESS MELON.

Peel one and one half pounds of good cooking-apples, and cut them into slices; put these into a stew-pan, with one and one half pints of water, the finely chopped peel of two lemons and their juice, six ounces of sugar, a strip of cinnamon and two bay-leaves; bring this to a boil, then simmer it until tender, and color with a few drops of carmine; rub it through a tammy; put the mixture into the charged freezer, and freeze it to the consistency of a batter;

add to it one half pint of stiffly whipped and slightly sweetened cream, refreeze it, and line a melon-mold with it about one inch thick; fill up the inside of the mold with a cream prepared as below; fasten up the mold, and put it into the charged ice-cave for two and one half to three hours, during which time occasionally turn it from side to side, so that the ice becomes evenly frozen. When ready to serve, dip the mold into cold water, and turn out the melon onto a border of the ice prepared as below, that is placed in the center of a dish on a dish-paper; garnish with small assorted shapes of the cream-ice, as for the center, that have been frozen in small molds in the charged ice-cave, also with little sprigs of maiden-hair fern. Use for a dinner or dessert ice.

CREAM FOR INSIDE MELON-MOLD.— Take one pint of single cream, sweeten it with three ounces of castor-sugar and flavor it with a salt-spoonful of vanilla essence; pour it into the charged freezer, and freeze it dry; then add to it three ounces of uncrystallized cherries that have been cut into halves, and use.

ICE BORDER FOR PRINCESS MELON.— Fill a border-mold with cold water, and set it in the charged ice-cave for two and one half to three hours; when frozen, dip the mold into cold water, pass a clean cloth over the bottom to absorb any moisture, turn out the border, and use.

PRINCESS BASKET.

Take a basket-mold, as in the engraving, and put it into a charged ice-cave for about one half hour before arranging the various custards in it; remove the top of the mold, but leave it in the mouth of the cave while putting in the ice, otherwise this may run and spoil the arrangement of the colors; fill the spaces in the top of the mold which represent cherries or strawberries with a strawberry-cream ice, the apples and pears with pistachio-ice, and for the grapes use a little vanilla-ice colored lightly with damson blue; fill the pomegranate also with the latter ice, which has been made a somewhat deeper red than the strawberry-cream ice with cherry red. When the top part of the mold is complete, fill up the bottom part with layers of the different ice-creams, arranging them as evenly as possible; place the top on carefully, and let the mold remain in the cave for about two and one half hours, during which time give it an occasional turn, so that the ice will be thoroughly frozen through. When ready to serve, dip the mold into cold water, pass a cloth over the bottom to absorb any moisture, then have a dish with a serviette or paper ready; take off the

bottom part of the mold, place the ice carefully on the dish, then remove the top of the mold, take out the pegs, and open the side pieces, and remove them. A few tiny fern-leaves can, if liked, be used to garnish the ice. Serve for a dinner sweet or for a dessert ice. A large-sized mold would be sufficient for twelve to fourteen people.

LEMON WATER-ICE.

Put one pound of sugar and one pint of water on to boil; chip the yellow rind from three lemons and one orange, add to the syrup, boil five minutes, and stand away to cool; peel the lemons and orange, cut them into halves, take out the seeds and squeeze out all of the juice; mix with the syrup, strain, put into the freezer, and freeze.

CHERRY WATER-ICE.

Stone and mash one half gallon of cherries, let stand for one hour, and strain; boil a pound of sugar and one pint of water until it threads, then set aside to cool; when cold, mix with the cherry-juice, and freeze. Currant, grape and gooseberry water-ices may be made the same way.

PEACH CREAM.

Pare and stone one quart of very soft peaches; add to them one pound of sugar, and mash them thoroughly; when ready to freeze, add two quarts of rich cream, which, when frozen, will fill a dish holding four quarts.

Mrs. J. E. Timberlake, Stevenson's Depot, Virginia.

VERSAILLES PINEAPPLE CREAM.

Put a pineapple-mold into a charged ice-cave for about one half hour before using; then open it, and fill the top part, which represents the leaves, with pistachio ice-cream, and fill the body of the mold with pineapple-ice, to which add the pulp of six tangerines and the very finely chopped peels of the same; fill the bottom of the mold with pistachio-ice; close up the mold, and stand it in

the charged ice-cave for three and one half to four hours, during which time turn it occasionally, so that the ice becomes evenly frozen; when required, turn out the ice in the usual way onto a tall dessert-dish on a dish-paper; garnish it with little assorted shapes of the pistachio and pineapple ice, as shown in the engraving, and little sprigs of fern. Serve for a dinner sweet or dessert ice.

TSARINA CREAM.

One and one half pints of thick cream, three fourths of a boxful of gelatin, one fourth of a cupful of rose-water, one half cupful of chopped blanched almonds, one and one half cupfuls of powdered sugar, one fourth of a cupful of maraschino, one teaspoonful of vanilla, one fourth of a cupful of chopped blanched pistachios, green coloring. Soak the gelatin in just enough cold water to cover; when soft, add the rose-water and stand over boiling water until dissolved; whip the cream solid, stir in very carefully the sugar; strain in the melted gelatin, a little at a time, stir lightly and carefully until it begins to thicken, then add gradually the vanilla and maraschino and sufficient green coloring to give a faint tinge; add the chopped nuts, and turn into a wetted mold; cover tightly, and pack in ice and salt for three hours. Serve with iced champagne sauce.

Miss Cornelia Campbell Bedford, Superintendent New York Cooking School.

ICE-CREAM.

Two quarts of rich milk, two teaspoonfuls of corn-starch, nine eggs beaten to a froth, two cupfuls of granulated sugar, two teaspoonfuls of vanilla or any other flavor. Heat the milk boiling hot; beat the eggs, sugar and corn-starch together, and stir into the milk; cook a few moments; when cool, put in the flavoring, and freeze.

Mrs. John B. Sanderson, Groton, Massachusetts.

ROSSELINE BOMB.

Take one quart of single cream, and mix with it six ounces of sugar, eight tablespoonfuls of rose-water, one large tablespoonful of vanilla essence, one tablespoonful of cherry liquor; mix well, and freeze it in the charged freezer to the consistency of a thick batter, then add to it one half pound of preserved uncrystallized chèrries cut up into very small pieces, and two ounces

of blanched, peeled sweet almonds cut up into little dice shapes, and baked until brown; put the mixture into a bomb-mold, and leave it in the charged ice-cave for three and one half hours, during which time occasionally turn the mold, so that the contents may be evenly frozen; then turn out the bomb onto a dish on a paper; garnish with crystallized cherries that are masked with boiled sugar, blanched pistachio-nuts and spun sugar, and serve at once. Have some wafers arranged on a dish on a fancy dish-paper, and hand them with the ice.

CARAMEL ICE-CREAM.

Make a custard of two quarts of sweet milk, one cupful of sugar, six well-beaten eggs; dissolve one fourth of a box of gelatin in one cupful of milk, put in hot custard; put one pound of sugar into the frying-pan, let melt and brown a little, put two or three tablespoonfuls of water into it; after it browns, set off to cool a little, then add to the custard; stir until dissolved; when ready to freeze, add one pint of cream, and vanilla to flavor.

Mrs. A. E. Kirtland, Author of "Mrs. Kirtland's Cook Book," Montgomery, Alabama.

GINGER ICE-CREAM.

Scald three pints of cream, add two cupfuls of sugar and three tablespoonfuls of Sicily Madeira wine, and freeze; when partly frozen, stir in three fourths of a cupful of finely chopped crystallized ginger, and finish freezing. To make a smooth ice-cream, the ice should be chopped as fine as the rock-salt.

Mrs. Althea Somes, Teacher of Cookery, Manual Training School, Boston.

EMPRESS FREDERICK TIMBAL.

Cook some Genoise paste, and cut it into rings about four inches in diameter, arrange about six of these one on top of the other, spreading between the layers a very little apricot jam that has been rubbed through a sieve; mask over the outside with white icing, put the timbal aside until it is cold and the icing is firm and dry, then arrange all over it some button meringues, sticking them to the cake with a little icing; garnish the top edge with tiny roses of royal icing,

and stick in here and there strips of angelica or blanched and peeled pistachionuts; arrange the timbal on a paper on a dish, then fill it up with alternate layers of burnt almond, strawberry and cinnamon cream ices; smooth over the top, and garnish by means of a forcing-bag and rose-pipe with garnishing-cream mottled with a few drops of carmine. It may be garnished with spun sugar, if liked, as in the engraving. Serve for a dinner sweet or for luncheon, ball supper, etc.

ICE-CREAM, WITHOUT EGGS.

Take equal parts of cream and milk, and sweeten it very sweet; flavor with any extract desired; pour it into a freezer, with plenty of rock-salt and ice around it, and let it stand fifteen minutes before stirring. After stirring it for fifteen minutes, it will be a nice cream.

E. A. Loring, Cordaville, Massachusetts.

PISTACHIO ICE-CREAM.

Scald one pint of cream and one cupful of milk, add three fourths of a cupful of sugar; cool, and add a little spinach coloring, and flavor with almonds; freeze.

Mrs. Althea Somes, Teacher of Cookery, Manual Training School, Boston.

SORBET.

Boil together twenty minutes one pint of sugar, one quart of water, one pint of chopped pineapple; add one half cupful of lemon-juice and one cupful of orange-juice; cool, strain, and freeze to a mush.

Miss Ida M. Foster, City Hospital, Wilkesbarre, Pennsylvania.

PINEAPPLE SHERBET.

Take one large pineapple, grate, and mix with three quarts of water, one ounce of dissolved gelatin, four lemons and the whites of six eggs; sweeten, and freeze.

CAMBRIDGE BOMB.

Put into a stew-pan one and one half pints of new milk, the peel of two lemons, two bay-leaves, a split pod of vanilla and four ounces of sugar; bring to a boil, then stir it onto twelve raw yolks of eggs, a salt-spoonful of apricot yellow, the same quantity of carmine and one fourth of an ounce of ground ginger; return the mixture to the stew-pan, and stir it over the fire until it

thickens, then rub it through the tammy, put it aside until cold, add one fourth of a pound of very finely cut up preserved ginger, two ounces of glace cherries, two ounces of finely chopped blanched and baked almonds, one wine-glassful of noyau and one teaspoonful of vanilla essence. Freeze it in the charged freezer to a semi-solid consistency, mix with it two and one half gills of stiffly whipped cream that is sweetened with one ounce of sugar; refreeze, and put it into a tall bomb-mold; place it in the charged ice-cave for about three and one half to four hours; then turn out the bomb in the usual way onto a clean, dry cloth, and dish up on paper on a dish, garnish around with little assorted shapes of the same ice, and serve for a dinner sweet.

LEMON SHERBET.

Squeeze the juice from one dozen lemons; then slice them, and pour one gallon of boiling water over them; mix three pounds of sugar with the lemon-juice and one half teacupful of arrowroot, and stir all together; when half frozen, stir in the whites of ten eggs, beaten stiff; freeze again, and set to mellow.

ORANGE SHERBET.

One gallon of water, one dozen oranges, juice of six lemons, whites of six eggs; mix, and freeze.

SULTANA ROLLS.

Line one-half-pound baking-powder cans with pistachio ice-cream, sprinkle with sultana raisins soaked in brandy; fill the centers with thick, whipped cream, sweetened, and flavored with vanilla; freeze, and serve with claret sauce.

Mrs. Althea Somes, Teacher of Cookery, Manual Training School, Boston.

ICED STRAWBERRY PURÉE.

Pound together one pound of strawberries, one half pound of sugar, the juice of one lemon and a few drops of liquid carmine; rub through a sieve, and stand on ice until wanted for use.

Gustave Beraud, Chef of Calumet Club, Chicago, Formerly Chef of William Astor, New York.

ICE-WATER CUPS.

Fill the ice-water cups three parts full with plain or colored cold water, fix on the covers, and put the molds on the bottom of the charged ice-cave for two and one half to three hours; then take up, dip each shape separately into cold water, and turn out the cups onto a clean, dry cloth, and use for a sorbet; or they can also be filled with custard or fruit-ices if liked.

PASTES, ICINGS, ETC.

FIG PASTE FOR CAKE.

1 pound of figs,   ¾ of a large cupful of sugar,
½ cupful of water.

Chop the figs, and then cook with the sugar and water until thick as paste.
H. A. E., Rockford, Illinois.

GELATIN ICING FOR CAKES.

One scant tablespoonful of gelatin dissolved in two tablespoonfuls of hot water; mix with powdered sugar until quite stiff, spread on the cake, and smooth with a knife dipped into hot water.

CHOCOLATE ICING.

½ cake of finely grated chocolate,   2-3 of a cupful of sugar,
½ cupful of milk or cream.

Boiled and stirred to a paste.

BOILED ICING.

One and one half cupfuls of sugar; put to this two tablespoonfuls of water; let it boil on the back of the stove until it is waxy or stringy; then add the whites of two eggs.

FILLING.

Two cupfuls of sugar, one half cupful of water boiled until it will make a stiff thread, pour on the stiff whites of two eggs, beat until stiff, flavor, and spread over the cake; sprinkle with freshly grated cocoanut each layer and over the top.

Mrs. A. E. Kirtland, Author of "Mrs. Kirtland's Cook Book," Montgomery, Alabama.

RAISIN FILLING FOR LAYER CAKES.

One teacupful of coffee-sugar and three tablespoonfuls of water boiled five minutes; beat the whites of two eggs to a stiff froth, and pour the boiling syrup over it; seed and chop one half pound of raisins, and beat all together until cold.

Stella.

FROSTING.

Break the whites of two eggs into a bowl without beating; add one tablespoonful of corn-starch and pulverized sugar enough to make it quite stiff. It will dry sufficiently in a few minutes.

CHOCOLATE FROSTING.

Melt one square or one ounce of plain chocolate in a bowl over the tea-kettle, then add two and one half tablespoonfuls of cold water, one cupful of confectioners' sugar and one fourth of a teaspoonful of cinnamon; spread on the cake while warm. Enough for one small sheet.

Mrs. G. L. Green, Formerly Principal Boston Y. M. C. A. School of Cookery, now Teacher of Cooking in the High School, Concord, New Hampshire.

FROSTING FOR A SMALL SHEET OF CAKE.

Two tablespoonfuls of cold water, with confectioners' sugar (not powdered) enough to make it spread nicely without running, and a little of any kind of flavoring added, makes a much nicer, softer frosting than when the whites of eggs are used. Do not spread until the cake is entirely cold. If you wish a very handsome as well as toothsome finish for the top of the cake, sprinkle the icing thickly, while moist, with chopped English walnuts, citron and candied cherries, mixed.

Mrs. G. L. Green, Formerly Principal Boston Y. M. C. A. School of Cookery, now Teacher of Cooking in the High School, Concord, New Hampshire.

TUTTI-FRUTTI FROSTING.

Boil one half teacupful of water with three cupfuls of white sugar until it is very thick and waxy; beat the whites of two eggs to a stiff froth, and pour the syrup over them, beating until it is cool; then add one half pound of finely chopped almonds, one small half teacupful of large raisins and a little citron, sliced thin. This is very nice for sponge-cake.

SHORT PASTE FOR FRUIT TARTS, ETC.

One half pound of flour, one ounce of creme de riz, four ounces of butter, one ounce of castor-sugar, one yolk of egg; rub the flour and butter together until smooth, then add the sugar and the egg and one fourth of an ounce of baking-powder; mix with cold water into a very stiff paste, roll out, and use.

PUFF PASTE.

For one pound of flour take one pound of butter, or part butter and part lard; mix a pinch of salt with the flour, and make it into a stiff paste with cold water; the paste should be as near as possible to the consistency of the fat; roll the paste out to about the size of a large meat-plate; press any water from the fat, and then work it with the hand into a ball, using a very little flour; put the fat into the paste, and press it out to about half the size of the paste; then wrap the fat up in the paste, and put it away in a cool place for about one hour, then roll it out straight four times; repeat the rolling twice; let the paste lie for the same time between each turn, then use.

SHORT PASTE FOR CROUSTADES.

Four ounces of butter rubbed into one half pound of fine flour, mixed with one raw yolk of egg and a pinch of salt, then made into a stiff paste with cold water; roll out, and use.

CHOUX PASTE.

Put one half pint of water into a stew-pan, with four ounces of butter and two ounces of castor-sugar, bring to a boil, then mix into it five ounces of fine flour that has been rubbed through a sieve, stir well together, and stand on the stove to cook for ten minutes, occasionally stirring it; when cooked, remove from the stove, and let the mixture cool, then mix in by degrees three whole eggs and six or eight drops of essence of vanilla, and use.

ANCHOVY BISCUIT PASTE.

Rub two ounces of flour with three fourths of an ounce of butter until quite smooth, then add to it a salt-spoonful of essence of anchovy, about eight drops of carmine, a tiny dust of red pepper, a pinch of baking-powder and half an egg; mix all with one teaspoonful of cold water, then roll out thin, and use.

LUTING-PASTE.

Mix half a white of an egg into a sticky paste with a little flour, color with a few drops of saffron, and use.

NOUGAT PASTE.

Take one half pound of blanched and finely chopped or shredded dried almonds, one half pound of castor-sugar and two tablespoonfuls of strained lemon-juice; put the sugar and lemon-juice into a stew-pan together, and boil them until a nice golden color, stirring all the time, then mix in the almonds, stir on the fire until the mixture reboils, then use at once.

FLORENCE PASTE.

Take one half pound of blanched and finely chopped almonds, put them into a stew-pan, with one half pound of sugar, three tablespoonfuls of brandy, or any liquor, the juice of one large lemon and one tablespoonful of liquid carmine; stir this continually all together over the fire for seven or eight minutes, then use at once while hot.

GENOISE PASTE.

One half pound of good butter and the finely chopped peel of one lemon, and work them in a basin with a wooden spoon until white and like cream; then add one half pound of sugar, and work them together for about ten minutes, and then mix by degrees five small whole raw eggs and one half pound of sifted fine flour, adding one egg and about one tablespoonful of flour at a time, and lastly one eighth of an ounce of baking-powder; put it into a buttered saute-pan, and bake for about thirty minutes, then turn out, and when cool, stamp out, and use.

ALMOND ICING.

To two and one half pounds of very finely chopped almonds add three and three fourths pounds of finest icing-sugar, mix in seven or eight raw whites of eggs, one wine-glassful of white rum and one teaspoonful of essence of vanilla; work into a stiff, dry paste, and use.

ROYAL ICING.

To two and one half pounds of icing-sugar put seven or eight whites of fresh eggs and one half tablespoonful of strained lemon-juice, work for fifteen to twenty minutes with a clean wooden spoon into a smooth, thick paste, and put onto the cake with a clean palette-knife, occasionally dipping this into cold water. Cakes should be covered one day, and ornamented the next.

VIENNA ICING.

Ten ounces of icing-sugar and one fourth of a pound of butter worked with a wooden spoon until smooth; mix with one small wine-glassful of mixed white rum and maraschino, work it until like cream, then use. This may be flavored and colored according to taste.

VIENNA CHOCOLATE ICING.

To three fourths of a pound of icing-sugar add one half pound of fresh butter, one fourth of a pound of finely powdered chocolate, a little coffee brown and about one half wine-glassful of brandy or liquor; mix all with a wooden spoon for about fifteen minutes, when it will present a creamy appearance, and is ready for use.

GLACÉ.

Take three fourths of a pound of icing-sugar, one and one half tablespoonfuls of noyau or noyau syrup, one and one half tablespoonfuls of orange-flower water; mix just warm, and use, coloring to any desired shade.

COFFEE GLACÉ.

Mix three fourths of a pound of icing-sugar with one and one half tablespoonfuls of strong coffee or essence of coffee and one and one half tablespoonfuls of hot water; just mix, and warm, then use at once.

MARASCHINO GLACÉ.

Put into a stew-pan three fourths of a pound of icing-sugar, then mix in three tablespoonfuls of maraschino, stir over the fire until just warm, then use. Noyau or any other liquor can be used similarly.

GARNISHING-CREAM.

Whip one half pint of double cream until stiff, then add to it one ounce of castor-sugar and a little vanilla essence, and use. It can be colored or left plain, or mottled by adding a few drops of carmine drops or sap-green, and then drawing a fork through it.

SNOW CREAM.

Put one pint of cold water into a basin or stew-pan, with one fourth of a pint of double cream, the strained juice of one lemon and two ounces of castor-sugar; whip this mixture quickly with a whisk until the top is frothy like snow, remove the froth with a slice, and place it on a hair-sieve to drain; repeat the whipping while any froth is obtainable; then when ready to serve, take it gently from the sieve with a slice or spoon, and use.

MARASCHINO MOUSSE.

Put into a whipping-pan ten raw yolks of eggs, three whites of eggs, one wine-glassful of sherry liquor, two ounces of castor-sugar and one dessert-spoonful of vanilla essence; whip these over boiling water until the mixture is warm, then remove the pan from the fire, and continue the whipping until the mixture is cold and thick; add to it one half pint of slightly sweetened, stiffly whipped cream, and put it into a mousse-mold that has been in the charged ice-cave for about a quarter of an hour; put the cover on the mold, place it on the bottom of the cave, and freeze the mousse for about four and one half hours, giving the mold an occasional turn around so that the mousse becomes evenly frozen; when frozen, dip the mold into cold water, remove the cover, pass a clean cloth over the bottom to absorb any moisture, and turn out onto a cold dish on a paper. Serve for a dinner sweet or for dessert.

CAKE-BOTTOM.

Rub two ounces of butter into half a pound of flour until smooth, then add two ounces of sugar and one egg, and mix with cold water into a very stiff paste; roll out, cut into square shape, and bake in a moderate oven for about half an hour, then put to press, trim, and use. When these are used for savory turbans the sugar should be left out.

BAVAROISE MIXTURE.

Take a good one half pound of new milk, and put into it one half stick of vanilla-pod and two ounces of sugar, let it infuse for about ten minutes, standing the pan in the bain-marie, remove the pod, and dissolve in the milk one half ounce of gelatin; put three raw yolks of eggs into a basin, and stir the milk onto them; return the mixture to the stew-pan, and stir on the stove until the contents thicken, but do not allow it to boil; strain it through the tammy, and let it cool, then mix into it two large tablespoonfuls of orange-flower water, one wine-glassful of rum, the same of maraschino or noyau syrup and one half pint of stiffly whipped cream, stir well together, and pour into an ornamented mold; when set, turn it out on a dish on a paper or napkin, and serve for a sweet for dinner, luncheon or for any cold collation.

ALMOND MERINGUE MIXTURE.

Put into a whipping-tin two whites of eggs, with a pinch of salt, and whip them until quite stiff, then add one fourth of a pound of castor-sugar and one ounce of blanched and finely shredded almonds, put into a forcing-bag with a large, plain pipe, force it onto cold waxed tins, arranging the shape according to taste, dust over by means of a dredger with a little icing-sugar, put into a moderate oven, and bake until a nice brown color, then take up; dress when cold with whipped and sweetened and flavored cream, place on a dish on a paper, and serve for a dinner or luncheon sweet or plainly for dessert. These can also be used for filling cakes, etc.

PANARD.

One half pint of water put to boil with one ounce of butter and a pinch of salt; then, when boiling, mix in four large tablespoonfuls of fine flour, and cook on the stove for about five minutes, giving the panard an occasional stir while it is cooking; when cool, use.

CUSTARD FOR PROFITEROLES, PASTRY, ETC.

Put into a stew-pan one ounce of fine flour, one raw yolk of egg, two ounces of butter, one ounce of castor-sugar and one and one half gills of cold milk; stir these over the fire until the mixture boils, then flavor with a few drops of vanilla, mix into it one tablespoonful of whipped cream, and use.

CORNETS, WITH CREAM.

Mix into paste four ounces of finely chopped almonds, two ounces of fine flour, two ounces of sugar, one large raw egg, a pinch of salt and a tablespoonful of orange-flower water. Put one or two baking-tins into the oven, and when they are quite hot, rub them over with white wax, let the tins get cool, then spread the paste smoothly and thinly over the tins (say one tenth of an inch thick), and bake in the oven for three or four minutes; take out the tins, and quickly stamp out the paste with a plain round cutter about two and one half to three inches in diameter, and immediately wrap these rounds of paste on the outside of the cornet-tins, which have been slightly oiled inside and out, pressing the edges well together, so that the paste takes the shape of the cornet; then remove the paste, and slip it inside the tin, and put another one of the tins inside the paste, so that it is kept in shape between the two tins; place them in a moderate oven, and let them remain until quite crisp and dry; take them out, and remove the tins. These can be kept any length of time in a tin box in a dry place. Ornament the edges with royal icing by means of a bag and pipe, and then dip the icing into different colored sugars; fill them with whipped cream, sweetened, and flavored with vanilla, using a forcing-bag and pipe for the purpose, and arrange them in a pile on a dish-paper or napkin. These cornets can also be filled with any cream or water-ice or set custard or fruits, and served for dinner, luncheon or supper dish.

Cakes, Cookies and Fritters

CHAPTER XV.

CAKE-MAKING.

In cake-making, as indeed in all other branches of cookery, the best results are obtained only by using the best materials. It is a great mistake to think, as many do, that butter not good enough for the table is yet just as good for cake as the best, or that a coarse quality of granulated sugar will make the same light, fine-grained cake that a finer grade will. In all the rules which follow use only the best butter, fine granulated sugar, not powdered, good pastry-flour and always the best extracts obtainable. Well-made cake, eaten in moderate quantities, is not harmful, but, on the contrary, is beneficial, containing as it does so much of necessary material for the nourishment of the body.

The cup used in my rules is the one in general use everywhere in cooking-schools, made of tin, holding one half pint, and of two kinds—one for measuring fourths and the other thirds. All dry materials are measured by dipping with a spoon into the cup, not by dipping with the cup itself, as nine out of ten will do, unless they have been cooking-school pupils. Butter is measured packed solidly into the cup, but always scant, sugar level, and flour just a little rounding, always sifting before measuring, and putting it lightly into the cup with a spoon. Measure the baking-powder rounding on top just as the spoon rounds underneath, and mix well with the flour. Spices for cakes are measured level.

Before beginning to put cake together, see that the fire is ready. The baking cannot be done successfully with a new coal fire, neither must it be put into a cool oven and the fire replenished then. Perfect baking is obtained only by having a fire that will last through the whole time, with no more care than opening and closing the drafts. More depends on the baking than the mixing in successful cake-making, and it can only be learned by experience.

With an oven not hot enough, the cake rises without becoming firm, and at the last falls, while with too great a heat the cake browns before it rises, and as it must expand in some way, it does so by means of a yawning crack in the middle of the loaf.

Mix cake always in earthenware, never in tin. If obtainable, use wooden spoons made especially for the purpose, flat and broad, made with three perforations lengthwise. The old-fashioned way of mixing with the hand is preferable, however, to tin or iron spoons.

In putting cake together, cream the butter first, then add the sugar gradually, beating all the time, then the flavoring, and the yolks of the eggs beaten until light and thick. The milk and flour are added, a little of each together at a time, beating well between each, adding until all are in. Beat the whites of eggs to a stiff froth and add last, stirring in as lightly as possible.

Do not make the mistake of thinking that stirring and beating mean the same thing. Stirring is blending or mixing the materials, while articles of food are made lighter by beating, as a certain amount of air is inclosed, which expands on being heated.

Mrs. G. L. Green, Formerly Principal Boston Y. M. C. A. School of Cookery, now Teacher of Cooking in the High School, Concord, New Hampshire.

SUGGESTIONS.

In warm weather lay the eggs in cold water, as they will froth better.

Always use lard to grease your cake-pans, as the salt in the butter causes it to stick to the pans.

Sweet milk and baking-powder go together, sour milk and soda; also, saleratus combines the properties of soda and cream of tartar, and is always used alone.

In all these recipes, except gingerbread, where soda is used, double the amount of cream of tartar. Where you substitute baking-powder, take just the quantity of soda and cream of tartar combined. To one quart of flour use two and one half teaspoonfuls of baking-powder; or one teaspoonful of soda and two teaspoonfuls of cream of tartar.

Keep cakes in the cellar, in a tin box, to keep them from drying out.

Keep the oven closed for ten minutes after putting in your cake.

Gingerbread should always be baked with a very moderate fire.

In making cookies, put them into the pan as soft as possible.

Where you want to put sugar and spice on them, lay it on the board, and roll your dough over it.

Never try to ice a cake hot, and let layer cakes get nearly cold before putting together.

All lard to fry fritters and doughnuts must be very, very hot before putting them in.

In using almond essence, be careful to use only from four to five drops, as it is very poisonous.

A new kind of cake-pan, with removable bottom, will be a great boon to the young housekeeper, as it takes a great deal of experience to be able to turn cake out of the pan in a neat manner; the tin bottom can be left on the cake if desired, and used to cook on.

BLANCHED ALMONDS.

Crack the nuts, and put the meats into a crock, with cold water over them. Let them cook until they just come to a boil, then pour off the hot water, and put on very cold water. Remove the shells, and dry the almonds on a cloth in the oven, where there will be very little heat. They are pounded, and used in macaroons, meringues, etc.

TO PREPARE RAISINS FOR CAKE.

First take out all the stems and seeds; then put them into a dish, with just water enough to cover them; let them boil slowly one half hour, or until the water is nearly gone; then stir them in your cake as usual. In this way they will not be tough, and tear the cake in cutting.

Another way is to take off all the stems, and wash them well; then spread them on a towel laid in a pan, and set them in the oven to dry thoroughly. Before stirring into the cake or pudding, roll in flour.

FOR COLORING CAKES AND ICES.

¼ ounce of pulverized cochineal,	½ ounce of cream of tartar,
½ pint of boiling water,	¼ ounce of salts of tartar.
¼ ounce of alum,	

Let it stand until the color is extracted, then strain and bottle.

Mrs. A. E. Webster, Knowlesville, New York.

WHITE CAKE.

½ cupful of butter,	1 cupful of sugar,
1-3 cupful of milk,	1¾ cupfuls of flour,
1 tablespoonful of any extract,	1 teaspoonful of baking-powder,
Whites of four eggs.	

Specially nice flavored with almonds and with blanched and chopped almonds mixed in the frosting. Bake thirty or forty minutes.

Mrs. G. L. Green, formerly Principal of Boston Y. M. C. A. School of Cookery, now Teacher of Cooking in the High School, Concord, New Hampshire.

WHITE LAYER CAKE.

8 eggs, the whites,	¾ of a cupful of corn-starch,
2½ cupfuls of sugar,	3 cupfuls of flour,
1 small cupful of butter,	2½ teaspoonfuls of baking-powder,
1 cupful of milk,	1 teaspoonful of vanilla.

Follow the general rule for mixing cakes. This makes four layers. Spread between each layer a soft icing, with a tablespoonful of some kind of a bright red jelly stirred into it. This makes a very pretty cake when cut. Bake in deep pie-pans.

Mrs. T. L. Arthur, Springfield, Ohio.

MOKA CAKE.

Gâteau Moka.

Prepare a Genoise paste mixture (see recipe), put it into a forcing-bag with a large, plain pipe and with it three parts fill a plain timbal-mold; place a well-buttered paper (cut sufficiently deep to stand four inches above the mold) around the outside of the mold; put it into a moderate oven, and bake one and a quarter hours, then turn out, and when cold, mask over with coffee glace; let this glace set, then stand the cake on a cake-bottom, and garnish, as in the engraving, with Vienna icing in pink and white; arrange around the edge some icing, then

sprinkle with blanched and chopped pistachio-nuts or colored sugar, and when the cake is ready to serve, fill up the center with stiffly whipped, sweetened and flavored cream and a nice compote of fruits. This is an excellent dinner or luncheon sweet, or it can be served for any cold collation.

MARBLE-CAKE.

Dark part—

7 eggs, the yolks,
2 cupfuls of brown sugar,
1 cupful of butter,
1 cupful of molasses,
1 cupful of sour cream,
1 tablespoonful of cloves.

5 cupfuls of flour,
1 teaspoonful of soda,
1 teaspoonful of pepper,
2 tablespoonfuls of cinnamon,
1 tablespoonful of allspice.

White part—

7 eggs, the whites,
2 cupfuls of white sugar,
1 cupful of butter,
½ teaspoonful of soda.

1½ cupfuls of sweet milk,
3 cupfuls of flour,
1 teaspoonful of cream of tartar,

Put alternate layers of the mixture, beginning with the dark and ending with the white; bake one hour.

Mrs. E. C. W., Mount Vernon, Ohio.

RED AND WHITE MARBLE-CAKE.

White—

3 eggs, whites,
1½ cupfuls of sugar,
½ cupful of butter,
½ teaspoonful of soda.

½ cupful of milk,
2 cupfuls of flour,
1 teaspoonful of cream of tartar,

Red—

1 egg, yolk,
½ cupful of red sugar,
2 tablespoonfuls of butter,
2 tablespoonfuls of milk.

1 cupful of flour,
½ teaspoonful of cream of tartar,
¼ teaspoonful of soda,
Flavor to suit the taste.

Mix the colors according to your choice. This makes a medium-sized loaf.
H. W. H., Corinth, New York.

FRUIT-CAKE.

7 eggs,
1 cupful of sugar,
1 cupful of butter,
½ cupful of molasses with
½ teaspoonful of soda in it,
½ pound of citron,
1 pound of raisins,

1 pound of currants,
1 pound of blanched almonds,
1 tablespoonful of nutmeg,
1 tablespoonful of cinnamon,
½ tablespoonful of cloves,
1 quart of sifted flour,

Flavor with about five drops of almond essence.

Beat the eggs separately; put whites in the last thing before putting it into the pan; have the currants washed and dried the day before; seed and chop the raisins. Bake two hours in a moderate oven.
Christie Irving.

WHITE FRUIT-CAKE.

The whites of twelve eggs, two cupfuls of powdered sugar, one cupful of butter, one cupful of sweet cream, five cupfuls of flour, one and one half teaspoonfuls of soda or four teaspoonfuls of cream of tartar, five teaspoonfuls of baking-powder, two pounds of chopped almonds, one pound of finely cut citron, one pound of grated cocoanut, two tablespoonfuls of rose-water, one teaspoonful of lemon extract, one slice of sugared orange-peel, sliced. Bake carefully in a moderate oven until it is thoroughly done.
Mrs. C. S. K., Springfield, Ohio.

BLACK FRUIT-CAKE.

Cream one pound of sugar and one pound of butter until light; then add ten well-beaten eggs and one pound of flour, reserving some of it to flour the fruit; spice the batter with nutmeg, cinnamon and cloves, two pounds of raisins, two pounds of well-washed currants, one pound of small-cut citron, one pound of small-cut English walnuts (in shell), one pound of dried figs, cut small; seed and cut small the raisins. Mix all your fruit, add part of one pound of flour to it, and flour the fruit well, so it does not stick together; stir into your batter; now add one cupful of cold water in which one teaspoonful of soda has been dissolved. You will find this very fine. The water prevents its being dry.
Mrs. A. E. Kirtland, Author of " Mrs. Kirtland's Cook Book," Montgomery, Alabama.

WEDDING FRUIT-CAKE.

10 eggs,
5 level cupfuls of brown sugar,
½ pint of molasses,
3 teacupfuls of soft butter,
1 lemon,
1 pound of figs,
1 pound of citron,
2 pounds of currants,
1 quart of flour.

3½ pounds of raisins,
1 heaping tablespoonful of ground cinnamon,
1 heaping tablespoonful of ground cloves,
1 heaping tablespoonful of mace,
1 grated nutmeg,
½ teaspoonful of soda,

This is a large recipe, and makes two large cakes. Bake carefully in a moderate oven for two or three hours.

Kate McL , Springfield, Ohio.

PROGRESS CAKE.

Gâteau Progrès.

Put into an egg-bowl eight whole eggs, twelve ounces of sugar and the finely chopped peel of one lemon; whip these over boiling water until the mixture is quite warm; then remove from the fire, and continue the whipping until the contents are thick and cold; add to it eight ounces of fine flour that has been

sifted and warmed, mixing this in gently with a wooden spoon. Prepare a cake-tin for baking by rubbing it over with warm butter, and lining it with buttered kitchen-paper, then dusting it over with fine flour and castor-sugar mixed in equal quantities; put the prepared mixture into the tin, and bake it in a moderate oven for one and one quarter hours, then take up, turn out the cake onto a pastry-rack, and let it remain until cold; then cut it into rounds about one half inch thick; spread the slices alternately, one with chocolate icing, and so on until all are masked; then arrange the cake again in its original form, trim the outside neatly, and mask it over entirely with maraschino glacé; let this remain until set, and then with forcing-bags and rose-pipes ornament the cake, as in the engraving, with the same icings, and dish up on a fancy dish-paper. Serve for a sweet for dinner or luncheon or for a ball supper.

JELLY-CAKE.

Take the whites of eight eggs, two cupfuls of sugar, one half cupful of butter, three fourths of a cupful of sweet milk, two and one half cupfuls of flour, two heaping teaspoonfuls of baking-powder. Beat the whites of the eggs to a froth; beat the butter and sugar to a cream; divide into three or four equal parts, and bake in jelly-pans; when done, spread with jelly, and pile one cake above the other.

L. H. Beedy, Postville, Iowa.

LEMON-JELLY CAKE.

½ cupful of butter,
3 eggs,
3 cupfuls of flour.
1 teaspoonful of lemon extract.

2 cupfuls of sugar,
1 cupful of milk,
2 teaspoonfuls of baking-powder.

Bake in four or five layers, as you choose, and put between them lemon jelly made as follows: The grated rind of one and the juice of two lemons, one cupful of sugar, one egg, one half cupful of water, one teaspoonful of butter and one heaping tablespoonful of flour cooked over hot water until they thicken; cool before spreading.

Mrs. G. L. Green, Formerly Principal Boston Y. M. C. A. School of Cookery, now Teacher of Cooking in the High School, Concord, New Hampshire.

FIG CAKE.

½ cupful of butter,
2 cupfuls of flour,
¾ cupful of milk,

1½ cupfuls of sugar,
1½ teaspoonfuls of baking-powder,
Whites of four eggs.

FILLING.

¾ pound of finely chopped figs,
1 tablespoonful of lemon-juice,

¾ cupful of orange-juice or water.
¾ cupful of sugar.

Cook until smooth enough to spread; split the cake, and fill; cover with a boiled icing.

Miss Ida M. Foster, City Hospital, Wilkesbarre, Pennsylvania.

RIBBON FIG CAKE.

White part—
  2 cupfuls of sugar,
  2-3 of a cupful of butter,
  2-3 of a cupful of milk,
Bake in layers.
Gold part—
  ½ cupful of butter and
  1 cupful of sugar beaten to a cream,
  1 whole egg and 7 yolks,

3 cupfuls of flour,
2 teaspoonfuls of baking-powder,
8 eggs, whites.

½ cupful of milk,
1½ cupfuls of flour,
1 teaspoonful of baking-powder.

Season strongly with cinnamon and allspice; put half the gold cake into a pan, and lay on it halved figs closely; dust with a little flour, and then put on the rest of the cake, and bake; put the gold cake between the white cakes, using frosting between them, and cover with frosting.

FIG CAKE.

6 eggs, the whites,   1 cupful of milk,
2 cupfuls of sugar.   ½ cupful of corn-starch,
¾ of a cupful of butter,   2 cupfuls of flour,
3 teaspoonfuls of baking-powder.

Take one third of the batter, and add

1 teaspoonful of cinnamon,   1 teaspoonful of allspice or cloves,
1 dozen figs, cut into small pieces.

Bake in layers, two white and one dark one, and spread them with the following icing: Three eggs, the whites, beaten to a stiff froth, two teacupfuls of granulated sugar, level full, four tablespoonfuls of water; boil the sugar and water together five minutes, then pour it on the whites, and beat until cold. One half pound of blanched almonds pounded to a paste is an addition.

Mrs. J. Kyle, Springfield, Ohio.

DELMONICO CAKE.

Gâteau à la Delmonico.

Butter a bomb-mold, dust it over with finely chopped dried cocoanut, and fill it with the cake mixture, as below; bake in a moderate oven for about one hour, then turn out the cake, cover it all over with almond icing, dust it over with

icing-sugar, place it again in a moderate oven until a nice golden color, then remove; set it aside until cold, and mask it over with icing, smoothing the surface of this over with a wet palette-knife; take some very finely shredded blanched pistachio-nuts, also some finely sliced uncrystallized cherries, and with these ornament the cake in six alternate divisions, as shown in the engraving; garnish lengthwise between each division with pink and white Vienna icing by means of a forcing-bag and a pipe; dish up on a cake-bottom, and garnish the base of this with icing and angelica, and the top of the cake with the Vienna icing; place the cake on a dish-paper, and serve for a sweet for dinner or for any cold collation.

CAKE MIXTURE FOR DELMONICO CAKE.—Take four whole raw eggs, one dessert-spoonful of black coffee, six ounces of castor-sugar, a few drops of vanilla essence and the finely chopped peel of one lemon; whip all together over boiling water until warm, then remove, and continue whipping until cold, then add four ounces of fine warmed flour that has been sifted; mix well, and use.

CHOCOLATE LAYER CAKE.

3 eggs, the whites,	2 large tablespoonfuls of butter,
2 cupfuls of sugar,	3 cupfuls of flour,
1 cupful of sweet milk,	2 heaping teaspoonfuls of baking-powder.

Bake half of the batter in two pans, and to the remaining half add one half cupful of grated chocolate; then bake; when done, pile up the layers alternately light and dark, spreading chocolate icing between.

Mrs. Louisa Ash, Mt. Vernon, Ohio.

CHOCOLATE LOAF CAKE.

Grate one half cake of baker's chocolate, and mix it with one half cupful of milk and the yolk of one egg; put it on the back part of the stove to dissolve and heat through; when thoroughly warmed, set it off to cool while preparing the cake. Take two eggs, the yolk of one having been used, two cupfuls of sugar, one cupful of butter, one teaspoonful of soda dissolved in a little water; add the chocolate, and flour enough to make a thin batter that will pour smooth. Bake carefully.

Mrs. J. Willis, Springfield, Ohio.

JELLY OR CHOCOLATE CAKE.

4 eggs,	½ cupful of milk,
2 cupfuls of sugar,	1 teaspoonful of soda,
1 cupful of butter,	2 teaspoonfuls of cream of tartar or
3 cupfuls of flour,	2 teaspoonfuls of baking-powder.

Bake in jelly-tins, and spread with jelly or chocolate prepared in this way: Take one fourth of a cake of grated baker's chocolate, one half cupful of milk, one half cupful of sugar, one teaspoonful of vanilla, one heaping teaspoonful of corn-starch; put the chocolate, sugar and milk on the stove in a saucepan, and just let it boil; add the corn-starch, and after taking it off the stove, add the vanilla; when cool, spread between the cakes; ice the top or sift powdered sugar over it.

SPONGE-CAKE.

Beat the yolks of two eggs until thick and the whites to a stiff froth; mix nearly all of one cupful of sugar with the whites, the remainder with the yolks, and then beat the two together; add one fourth of a teaspoonful of salt, one teaspoonful of lemon extract, and one cupful of flour in which has been mixed one generous teaspoonful of baking-powder; lastly add one half cupful of boiling water. Bake thirty minutes.

Mrs. G. L. Green, Formerly Principal of Boston Y. M. C. A. School of Cookery, now Teacher of Cooking in the High School, Concord, New Hampshire.

WHITE-MOUNTAIN CAKE.

Yolks of three eggs, whites of two, two cupfuls of flour and one and one fourth teaspoonfuls of baking-powder. Use the third white for making your frosting; bake in small cups or pans, filling them half full; put half an English walnut on each before baking; frost over the nuts after taking from the pans. This rule makes eighteen cakes.

Miss Harriott T. Ward, Scientific and Special Teacher of Cooking, Boston.

IMPERIAL CAKE.

Gâteau à l'Impériale.

Whip twelve whole eggs, one pound of castor-sugar and two ounces of vanilla sugar over boiling water until the mixture is warm, then remove it from the fire, and whip it until cold and thick; add twelve ounces of finely sifted flour, four ounces of finely chopped desiccated cocoanut, and mix well; then divide the mixture into three parts; color one part with carmine, and flavor it with six or eight drops of essence of almonds; color the second portion with sap-green, and flavor it with essence of lemon, and leave the third portion white; sprinkle over each a little more cocoanut, place each portion separately in a saute-pan or round baking-tin about eight inches wide by two inches deep, and bake in a moderate oven for about one half hour; when cooked, turn out, and leave until cold, then cut each into two slices horizontally, spread a layer of Vienna icing flavored with chocolate over each of the red-colored portions, arrange a layer of Vienna icing over the green-colored portions and a layer of rose-colored Vienna icing over the white parts; then place each slice of the

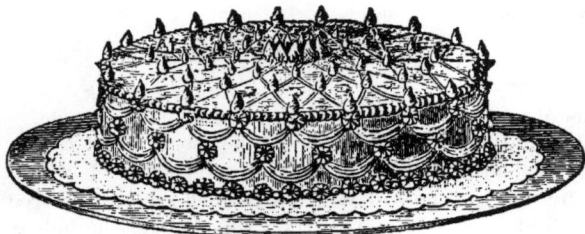

cake one on top of the other, arrange the different colors effectively. Prepare a paste bottom about one inch thick and the same size as the cake, and bake it until a nice golden color; then place the prepared cakes in this, glaze it with maraschino glace, and leave it until set; then by means of a forcing-bag and rose and plain pipes ornament the top and sides, as in the engraving, with Vienna icing and rose-colored Vienna icing, and put it aside until the next day to dry. Dish up on a round silver dish on a gold or silver dessert-paper, and serve for a ball supper or afternoon party, etc.

ANGEL'S-FOOD.

11 eggs, the whites,	1 teaspoonful of cream of tartar,
1½ cupfuls of sifted powdered sugar,	1 teaspoonful of vanilla,
1 cupful of flour,	A pinch of salt.

Sift the flour, cream of tartar, sugar and salt together four or five times; beat the eggs in a large platter to a stiff froth, then add the sifted flour gradually on the platter with the eggs. Don't let it stand a minute after it is thoroughly mixed; bake forty minutes in a moderate oven. Try it with a straw, and if not done, let it bake a few minutes longer. Do not open the oven door until the cake has been in the oven fifteen minutes.

Miss Stella Reid, Jackson, Michigan.

ANGEL'S-FOOD.

1 pound of pulverized sugar,	3 teaspoonfuls of cream of tartar,
¼ pound of corn-starch,	¼ pound of flour,
½ teaspoonful of essence of vanilla,	15 whites of eggs.

Whip the whites to a stiff froth, add one third of a pound of pulverized sugar, and whip well; the remaining two thirds of a pound of sugar, the flour and corn-starch must be mixed thoroughly and sifted three times, add all at once to the froth, mix well, add the vanilla, and put it into a perfectly dry pan. Bake in a moderate oven about forty-five minutes, then turn the pan upside down on a clean sheet of paper, and within a few hours the cake will drop on the paper.

N. B.—Never grease the pan, or attempt to remove the cake while warm.

Eugene Stuyvesant Howard, Member of the Universal Cookery and Food Association, London, England, and Chef de Cuisine, Louisville Hotel, Louisville, Kentucky.

CREAM CAKE.

Beat two eggs in a teacup, and fill the cup with sweet cream.

1 cupful of sugar,	1 teaspoonful of cream of tartar.
1 teaspoonful of baking-powder or	1 cupful of flour,
½ teaspoonful of soda,	

Flavor with lemon, and bake in a moderately heated oven.

M. C. A. Gould, Rock Rift, New York.

LAYER CREAM CAKE.

6 eggs,	2 cupfuls of flour,
2 cupfuls of sugar,	2 tablespoonfuls of cream of tartar,
2 tablespoonfuls of water,	1 teaspoonful of soda.

Bake twenty minutes with a quick fire, and when cold, cut it in two; then spread on the cream made after the following recipe:

2 eggs,	1 cupful of sugar,
½ cupful of corn-starch.	

Beat these ingredients well, and pour it into one pint of boiling milk; flavor with the grated rind and juice of a lemon or a teaspoonful of the extract of lemon. Half of the above quantity makes a nice cake for a small family.

Mrs. M. E., Creston, Iowa.

MARY'S COCOANUT CAKE.

6 eggs, the whites,	3 cupfuls of flour,
2 cupfuls of powdered sugar,	2 teaspoonfuls of baking-powder
¾ of a cupful of butter,	1 cupful of sweet milk,
1 teaspoonful of lemon essence.	

Bake this as loaf cake, and the next day cut off the upper and lower crusts, trim the brown off the sides, and slice it into four layers; grate two cocoanuts, and put in the icing; spread each layer, the top and sides, with plenty of the icing. When cut, it will be perfectly white all through, and a very handsome cake.

Mrs. A. Winger, Springfield, Ohio.

CARAMEL CAKE.

Two cupfuls of sugar, one cupful of butter, one cupful of milk, three and one half cupfuls of flour, the whites of seven eggs, two heaping teaspoonfuls of baking-powder; flavor with vanilla; bake in three layers.

Filling—One cupful of dark brown sugar and one cupful of white sugar, mixed; cover it well with water, and let it boil to a candy that will break against the cup when you try it in cold water; then add two tablespoonfuls of sweet cream and one heaping teaspoonful of butter, beat it very thoroughly in a cool place until the mixture is cool enough to spread; flavor with vanilla just before spreading.

NEAPOLITAN CAKE.

Gâteau Napolitaine.

Take one pound of fine flour that has been sifted, rub into it one half pound of good butter until quite smooth, and mix into it one half pound of castor-sugar, one half pound of very finely chopped blanched sweet almonds, four raw yolks of eggs, three large tablespoonfuls of orange-flower water and about twelve drops of essence of vanilla, and work it into a very stiff paste with cream or

milk; roll the mixture out about one fourth of an inch thick, and stamp out of it rings about six inches in diameter outside; place these rings on a wetted baking-tin, and prick them all over with a pricker or fork, brush over lightly with new milk, put them into a moderate oven, and bake for fifteen to twenty minutes until a pretty fawn color; take them from the tin, and put them separately on the table to be pressed under a board with a heavy weight on top, and leave them until cold; arrange them one on top of the other with a little apricot or any nice jam between each ring; when all the pieces are placed together, trim off all around any irregular pieces from the outside. Prepare an apricot glacé, or of any other nice jam, and by means of a paste-brush brush the cake all over with it; let this get set, and then place it on a paste bottom ornamented with icing, and then ornament the cake with the icing by means of a forcing-bag and pipe, and garnish with little pieces of dried cherries and angelica, or any other nice fruit, and dish up on a pretty dish-paper. This cake can be served for a dinner sweet or for any cold collation, and may be filled with whipped cream sweetened and flavored, or with ice or iced soufflés.

NUT-CAKE.

½ cupful of butter,
1½ cupfuls of sugar,
3 eggs,
1 cupful of the meats of any kind of nuts.
Mrs. J. E. C., Springfield, Ohio.

½ cupful of milk,
2½ cupfuls of flour,
1½ teaspoonfuls of baking-powder,

HICKORY-NUT CAKE.

4 eggs,
2 cupfuls of sugar,
2 teaspoonfuls of baking-powder.

2½ cupfuls of flour,
½ cupful of cream or butter,

Bake in jelly-tins, and between the layers spread the following cream: Two eggs, one cupful of sugar, two heaping tablespoonfuls of corn-starch, one coffee-cupful of chopped hickory-nut meats, one pint of milk. Beat the eggs, sugar, corn-starch and nuts together, and stir it into the pint of milk while it is boiling; let it cook as thick as a custard, and when cold, spread it between the layers.
" Hazel Kirk," Cozy Nest.

MARSHMALLOW CAKE.

1½ cupfuls of sugar,
½ cupful of sweet milk,
½ cupful of corn-starch,
2 even teaspoonfuls of baking-powder.

½ cupful of butter,
1½ cupfuls of pastry-flour,
Whites of six eggs,

Flavor with one half teaspoonful of extract of anise. Bake in two large layers or three small ones. Make a rule of boiled icing; when ready to cool, add to one third of it four fresh marshmallows, cut into small bits, and a few drops of the anise; stir until perfectly smooth and the mallows are dissolved, then put between the layers; add a few drops of anise to the remainder of the icing; when cool enough to spread, cover the entire cake; then split in half a sufficient number of the mallows to lay around the top edge of the cake, toast them slightly on top, and arrange them while the icing is soft; arrange three halves in the center, and twist a bit of the mallow for a stem, forming a clover-leaf; take more halves, not toasted, fold them together, and lay them around the base of the cake. This is a most delicious and elegant-looking cake, and is my favorite specialty.
Miss Emily E. Squire, Author of " Woronoco Women's Wisdom," Westfield, Mass.

MRS. DEAN'S CUSTARD-CAKE.

2 eggs,
½ cupful of sugar,
1 heaping teaspoonful of baking-powder.
Cream—
½ cupful of sugar,
¾ of a cupful of milk,

4 tablespoonfuls of water,
1 cupful of flour,

1 tablespoonful of corn-starch,
1 teaspoonful of essence of lemon.

Boil until thick as jelly; bake the cake in jelly-cake pans, and when cool, put the cream between each one, and ice it or not, as you choose.

CAKE À LA PRINCESSE MAUD.

Gâteau à la Princesse Maud.

Put six ounces of castor-sugar into a stew-pan, with four whole eggs and one teaspoonful of vanilla essence, add a little carmine to make it a pretty pink color, and whip over boiling water until the mixture is warm; then remove the pan from the water, continue the whipping until cold and stiff, and mix into it four ounces of fine flour that has been sifted and warmed. Prepare a tin for baking the mixture by brushing it over with warm butter, then paper it, and butter this paper also; dust it over with flour and sugar that have been mixed in equal quantities, pour in the prepared mixture, and bake it in a moderate oven for one and one quarter hours; then turn out the cake, and scoop out the inside so as to form a case; line this case with almond icing, and fill up the center with the chocolate meringue mixture (see recipe); replace the cake on a baking-tin, and put it into a moderate oven to dry for one half hour; then when firm, remove it to a pastry-rack, pour over it a strawberry or red maraschino

glace; let this cool, then place it on a cake-bottom ornamented with icing, and ornament the cake, as in the engraving, with icing in two colors, one colored brown with coffee. Serve it on a dish-paper for a dinner sweet or for luncheon or ball supper.

ORANGE CAKE.

Bake a simple sponge-cake in a round, deep pan, and when cold, cut it with a sharp knife into four layers; peel and slice six or eight oranges, and put a layer of oranges on the first layer of cake, and cover them with sugar, then another layer of cake, then oranges and sugar until they are all used. Make a soft icing, and just let it brown in the oven.

CHRISTMAS CAKE.

2 pounds of powdered sugar,	1 pound of butter,
24 eggs, whites,	1 teacupful of sweet cream,
2 pounds of sifted flour,	1 tablespoonful of lemon extract.

Mix all, and beat thoroughly for one half hour. Have a fancy, high mold, grease, fill three fourths full, and bake in a steady oven; when done, remove from the mold. Make a thin icing; place the cake on the plate; with a spoon put the icing on top, and allow it to run down the sides until every part is covered. Ornament with flowers, leaves or bonbons.

CITRON CAKE.

Beat separately the whites and yolks of four eggs, three cupfuls of sugar, one cupful of butter, one half cupful of sweet milk, three cupfuls of flour, two and one half teaspoonfuls of baking-powder, one half pound of citron, chopped and rolled in flour. Bake in long, narrow pans.

Mrs. D. C. Young, Larrabee, Pennsylvania.

SILVER CAKE.

Beat the whites of seven eggs to a stiff froth, two cupfuls of powdered sugar, two thirds cupful of butter, one half cupful of milk, two teaspoonfuls of baking-powder or one teaspoonful of cream of tartar, one half teaspoonful of soda, three cupfuls of flour, one teaspoonful of vanilla or four drops of almond essence. Bake in a loaf for one half hour.

GOLD CAKE.

Take the yolks of seven eggs, add another egg, and make just the same as silver cake, with a little more butter added; flavor with lemon essence.

Mrs. W. W. Pitman, Brooklyn, New York.

TEXAS CAKE, OR SILVER CAKE.

Cream one cupful of butter and three cupfuls of sugar until light, add one cupful of sweet milk and five cupfuls of sifted flour with two teaspoonfuls of baking-powder in it; sift two or three times to distribute the baking-powder; lastly stir in gently the whites of twelve eggs, beaten stiff, and one teaspoonful of almond extract.

Mrs. A. E. Kirtland, Author of "Mrs. Kirtland's Cook Book," Montgomery, Alabama.

SPICE-CAKE.

1 egg,	½ cupful of butter,
½ cupful of sugar,	½ cupful of molasses,
½ cupful of sweet milk,	⅓ cupful of chopped raisins,
½ cupful of citron, cut small,	2½ cupfuls of flour,
½ teaspoonful of soda.	

Spice with nutmeg, cloves and cinnamon; bake in patty-pans, and ice. They are so nice.

Mrs. A. E. Kirtland, Author of "Mrs. Kirtland's Cook Book," Montgomery, Alabama.

SPICE-CAKE.

4 eggs, leaving out the whites of 2,	2 cupfuls of brown sugar,
½ cupful of melted butter,	½ cupful of sour milk,
1 teaspoonful of soda,	2 teaspoonfuls of cinnamon,
1½ teaspoonfuls of cloves,	½ teaspoonful of nutmeg,
2 cupfuls of flour.	

Dissolve the soda in the sour milk. Bake in layers. Make the icing to spread between with the whites of two eggs and one cupful of sugar.

Mrs. Jos. Kyle, Springfield, Ohio.

10

LITTLE BEATRICE CAKES.

Petits Gâteaux à la Béatrice.

- Line some little boat-shaped molds very thinly with short paste, as below, trim off the edges, and place inside each case three dried cherries; cover these entirely with a layer of almond mixture, as below, and place the case on a baking-tin, and cook in a moderate oven for about fifteen minutes; then remove them from the tins; allow them to cool, and mask each over with maraschino glace; let this get cold, then by means of a forcing-bag and little, plain pipe ornament the tops with a little royal icing in any pretty design in two colors, brown and pink—for the former color a portion of the icing with coffee brown, and for the latter use a little carmine. When ready to serve, dish up on a dish-paper or napkin, and serve for a sweet for dinner or luncheon or for any cold collation.

SHORT PASTE FOR BEATRICE CAKES.—Rub three ounces of fine flour into one and one half ounces of butter until quite smooth, add one ounce of fine sugar

and one raw yolk of egg, and mix with orange-flower water into a stiff paste, then use. This quantity is sufficient for twelve to fifteen cases.

ALMOND MIXTURE FOR BEATRICE CAKE.—Take one fourth of a pound of very finely chopped blanched almonds or pistachio-nuts, and mix with them four ounces of castor-sugar, one dessert-spoonful of orange-flower water, six or eight drops of essence of vanilla, one half raw white of egg and a little of apple or sap green to make it a nice pistachio color.

DONNA'S POUND-CAKE.

1 pound of eggs,	1 pound of butter,
1 pound of sugar,	1 pound of flour,
Flavor to suit the taste.	

Beat well, and bake three quarters of an hour.

Mrs. L. P. W., Laurens C. H., South Carolina.

CORN-STARCH CAKE.

1½ cupfuls of sugar,	½ cupful of corn-starch,
6 eggs, whites,	½ cupful of butter,
½ cupful of milk,	2 teaspoonfuls of baking-powder,
1½ cupfuls of flour,	Lemon to flavor.

After all is well mixed, add one half cupful of cold water.

NEW-YEAR'S CAKE.

1½ pounds of butter, creamed,
15 eggs, beaten yolks,
1½ pounds of sugar,

Beat well, and sift in
2 (scant) pounds of flour, with
3 tablespoonfuls of baking-powder.

Mix in the beaten whites of the eggs. Grate two lemons in one half cupful of molasses, add it with two pounds of finely chopped almonds, one pound of seeded raisins, one pound of chopped citron. Bake two hours in a moderate oven; when cold, ice nicely.

THANKSGIVING CAKE.

2½ pounds of flour, in which mix
3 pounds of sugar,
2 pounds of butter,
3 teaspoonfuls of baking-powder,
2 tablespoonfuls of extract of lemon.

18 eggs,
½ pound of beaten almonds,
1 grated cocoanut.
1 teacupful of preserved lemon-peel.

Bake in a moderate oven two hours; when cool, ornament handsomely with icing and fancy bonbons.

DUTCH CAKE.

Take a piece of light bread-dough the size of a large teacup, a piece of butter the size of a hen's egg.

2 eggs,
1 cupful of sugar,
Flavor with cinnamon or lemon.

1 teacupful of dried currants,
1 teaspoonful of soda,

Mix until of the consistency of cake-batter, and bake in a moderately quick oven.

Sallie E. Ruff, Kingville, Mississippi.

PORTUGAL CAKE.

¾ pound of flour,
8 eggs,
The grate of one lemon.

1 pound of sugar,
½ pound of butter.

One fourth teaspoonful of soda dissolved in one tablespoonful of sour cream improves it, though not necessary, as it is very nice without it.

Miss Harriott T. Ward, Scientific and Special Teacher of Cooking, Boston, Mass.

VANITY CAKE.

6 eggs, the whites,
1½ cupfuls of sugar,
½ cupful of butter,
½ cupful of milk.

½ cupful of corn-starch,
1½ cupfuls of flour,
1 teaspoonful of baking-powder.
Flavor to suit the taste.

Follow the usual directions for mixing, and bake carefully.

Mrs. Markley, Dayton, Ohio.

BUTTER SPONGE-CAKE.

2 cupfuls of flour,
1 cupful of butter,
Juice and grate of one lemon.

2 cupfuls of sugar,
5 eggs,

Miss Harriott T. Ward, Scientific and Special Teacher of Cooking, Boston, Mass.

DARK CAKE.

Three cupfuls of molasses, one cupful of butter (or part of beef-drippings or lard may be used; if they are, be sure to add salt), one teaspoonful of each kind of spice, four eggs, three cupfuls of stoned raisins, one cupful of citron, one teaspoonful of soda, one cupful of brown sugar, one half grated nutmeg, one cupful of milk, three cupfuls of currants, seven and one half cupfuls of flour. One square of plain chocolate, melted and stirred in, makes a darker, richer cake. Bake slowly one hour. This rule makes two loaves, and keeps excellently.

Mrs. G. L. Green, Formerly Principal Boston Y. M. C. A. School of Cookery, now Teacher of Cooking in the High School, Concord, New Hampshire.

BRETON CAKE.

Gâteau Breton.

Prepare five or six of the Breton border-molds of various sizes; partly fill each one of the molds with cake mixture, as below, then stand the molds on baking-tins, and bake in a moderate oven for twenty-five to thirty minutes, then turn out, and leave until cold; mask over the top part of each piece with apricot jam

that has been rubbed through a sieve, and place the pieces together, resting one on the other, and putting the larger ones at the bottom; glaze over with maraschino glace, leave until cold, then arrange together, ornament with Vienna icing, place the cake on a dish-paper, and serve for dinner, handed with a compote of fruits, or it may be served alone for afternoon tea or for dessert.

BRETON-CAKE MIXTURE.—Take eight whole eggs, twelve ounces of castor-sugar, the finely chopped peel of a lemon, one teaspoonful of vanilla essence, sufficient carmine to make it a pale salmon color, one salt-spoonful of ground ginger, and as much ground cinnamon as would cover a nickel; whip over boiling water until warm, then take up, and whip until cold and thick, then mix with eight ounces of warmed fine flour that has been passed through a sieve, and use.

WATERMELON CAKE.

White part—

5 eggs, whites,	2-3 cupful of sweet milk,
2 cupfuls of white sugar,	3 cupfuls of flour,
2-3 cupful of butter,	1 tablespoonful of baking-powder.

Red part—

5 eggs, whites,	2 cupfuls of flour,
1 cupful of red sugar,	1 tablespoonful of baking-powder,
1-3 cupful of butter,	1-3 cupful of sweet milk,

½ pound of seeded raisins, rolled in flour.

First put the white part into a cake-pan, keeping it away from the center and well around the sides; then pour the red part into the center, and bake. The sugar should be bright red, not solferino. This makes a good-sized loaf.

Mrs. I. C. Souders, Dayton, Ohio.

ICED ORANGE CAKE.

Put six whole eggs into a saucepan, with a salt-spoonful of vanilla essence, ten ounces of powdered sugar, the very finely chopped peel of three oranges and a teaspoonful of liquid carmine; whip this mixture with a whisk over boiling water on the stove until it is warm, then remove from the fire, and continue the whipping until the ingredients are cold and thick like stiffly whipped cream; mix into it with a wooden spoon six ounces of fine flour that has been rubbed through a fine wire sieve, and put into the screen to get warm. Brush over a charlotte-mold with warm butter, paper it, butter this also, and dust over with flour and sugar mixed in equal proportions; pour the cake mixture into the mold, and bake in a very moderate oven for one and one quarter hours; then turn out the cake onto a pastry-rack or sieve, and let it get quite cold; cut it into slices, and mask each slice with orange marmalade that has been rubbed through a sieve, place the slices together in their original form, and glaze over the cake with maraschino and orange glace. When the glace is beginning to set, sprinkle all over it some finely shredded pistachio-nuts, and dish on a dish-paper. Serve for a dinner sweet, with ice or a macedoine of fruit, or it can be served for dessert or afternoon tea. The mixture may also be baked in any small fancy molds.

Gustave Beraud, Chef of Calumet Club, Chicago, Formerly Chef of William Astor,

MAIDETTE'S CAKE.

4 eggs, well beaten,	1 cupful of milk,
2 cupfuls of sugar,	4 cupfuls of flour,
1 cupful of butter,	2 teaspoonfuls of baking-powder.

Flavor with four drops of almond essence; stir well. Bake in a solid loaf.

Mrs. Wm. W. Pittman, Brooklyn, New York.

PRINCESS CAKE.

The whites of ten eggs, three cupfuls of powdered sugar, one cupful of butter, one cupful of milk, four and one half cupfuls of flour, one teaspoonful of baking-powder, level full, one teaspoonful of lemon essence or some sliced citron. Bake carefully one hour in a moderate oven. This is nice used as a layer cake.

"Hazel Kirk," Cozy Nest.

RICE CAKE.

Work one half pound of good butter in a basin until of creamy appearance, then one half pound of sugar, four drops of essence of almonds and four drops of vanilla, and work all together with the hands or a wooden spoon for ten minutes; then work in six whole eggs (one at a time), five ounces of fine flour mixed with three ounces of ground rice, working in about a tablespoonful of this with each egg; it will take about fifteen minutes to work these in properly; brush over the inside of two pint cake-molds with a little warm butter, and line them with buttered kitchen-paper, fill them with the cake mixture, and put them to bake for about an hour in a moderate oven. If the paper is kept on these cakes when turned out of the mold, and they are put into a tin box, they will keep for a week or two. The same mixture can be baked in little fancy-shaped molds, in which case the buttered paper may be dispensed with, but the mold should be dusted over with a little flour after it is brushed with warm butter.

Gustave Beraud, Chef of Calumet Club, Chicago, Formerly Chef of William Astor.

CHEVALIER CAKES.
Choux à la Chevalier.

Prepare some choux paste, and put it into a forcing-bag with a plain pipe; force the mixture out onto a baking-tin in the form of horseshoes, and brush these over with whole beaten-up egg. Bake in a moderate oven for thirty-five to

forty minutes, remove from the oven, and when cool, split open the underneath part of the shoes, and fill up the inside with pastry custard or stiffly whipped cream that is sweetened, and flavored with vanilla essence; mask over the tips of the shoes with coffee glace, and the remaining part with vanilla glace; garnish, as in the engraving, with chopped almonds that are colored with a little carmine, or with chopped pistachio-nuts, and dish up ten or twelve on a dish. Serve for a dinner or luncheon sweet or for a cold collation.

GINGERBREAD.

One egg, one cupful of sugar, one cupful of molasses, one cupful of lard, one cupful of sour milk, four teaspoonfuls of soda, two tablespoonfuls of ginger, flour enough to roll soft. To be eaten when warm. This recipe will make three loaves; baked in broad, shallow pans.

Mrs. R. D. Bullock, Jackson, Michigan.

COFFEE-CAKE.

1 egg,
1 cupful of brown sugar,
1 cupful of molasses,
1 cupful of butter,
1 cupful of strong cold coffee,
4 or 5 cupfuls of flour.

1 pound of raisins,
1 tablespoonful of cloves,
1 tablespoonful of cinnamon,
1 grated nutmeg,
1 heaping teaspoonful of soda,

Mix it very stiff, and bake in a moderate oven for an hour.

M. C., Troy, Pennsylvania.

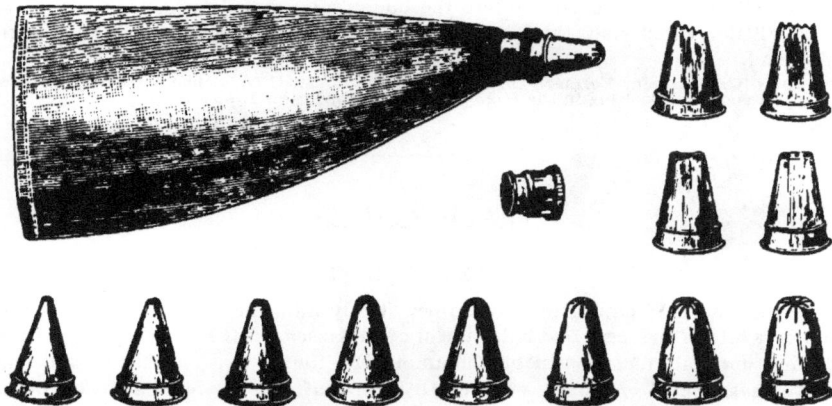

TIN ICING PIPES AND BAG FOR ORNAMENTAL ICING. (See page 206.)

DUTCH GINGERBREAD.

Two cupfuls of flour, one half cupful of butter, two eggs, one slightly rounding teaspoonful of yellow (African) ginger, one cupful of sugar, one half cupful of milk, one rounding teaspoonful of baking-powder. Sift, and mix flour, baking-powder and ginger; cream butter and sugar, and add yolks beaten until light; add milk and flour mixture alternately, and lastly the whites beaten to a stiff froth. Bake in a moderate oven forty-five minutes.

Miss Angeline M. Weaver, Instructor Hyde School Kitchen, Boston, Massachusetts.

COFFEE-CAKE.

Three eggs, two cupfuls of sugar, one half cupful of molasses, one cupful of butter, one cupful of cold strong coffee, four cupfuls of flour, four teaspoonfuls of baking-powder, one tablespoonful of cinnamon, one tablespoonful of cloves, one grated nutmeg, one pound of raisins, chopped and seeded, one pound of dried English currants, one fourth of a pound of finely cut citron. This makes a very large cake or two medium-sized ones. Bake slowly one hour or more.

Mrs. T. L. Arthur, Springfield, Ohio.

PLAIN CAKE.

½ cupful of butter,	1 cupful of sugar,
2 eggs,	½ cupful of milk,
2 cupfuls of flour,	1 teaspoonful of baking-powder,
1 teaspoonful of vanilla.	

Bake for thirty to forty minutes. This rule admits of many variations. Add to it one cupful, mixed, of chopped raisins and English walnuts, and the result is delicious. One square of plain chocolate can be melted and stirred in half the dough, and the two parts baked as marble-cake. Chopped almonds sprinkled thickly over the top before baking will form so nice a top that you will prefer it to frosting when once tried, and still another variation is to grate a little of the yellow rind of an orange into the dough, and make an icing of the juice, with a little grated rind, thickened with confectioners' sugar until stiff enough to spread.

Mrs. G. L. Green, Formerly Principal Boston Y. M. C. A. School of Cookery, now Teacher of Cooking in the High School, Concord, New Hampshire.

SMALL CAKES.

CINNAMON COOKIES.

Cream one half cupful of shortening, slowly add one half cupful of sugar, yolk or white of one egg, one half cupful of molasses. Sift together two cupfuls of flour, one half teaspoonful of cinnamon, one fourth teaspoonful of salt, one fourth teaspoonful of cloves, one eighth teaspoonful of allspice, a little grated nutmeg and one level teaspoonful of soda; add these materials to the butter mixture; add one teaspoonful of vinegar; roll out a little at a time, cut out, grease, and bake on the wrong side of the pan, as they will brown more uniformly than when baked in the usual way.

Miss Marion L. Campbell, Friendly Inn Cooking School, Cleveland, Ohio.

COCOANUT COOKIES.

¼ cupful of butter,	1 cupful of sugar,
1 tablespoonful of milk,	2 eggs,
1 cupful of grated cocoanut,	1 teaspoonful of baking-powder.
Lemon to flavor,	Flour enough to roll out.

Roll thin, and cut out. It makes thirty-two, and they are elegant.

Mrs. A. E. Kirtland, Author of "Mrs. Kirtland's Cook Book," Montgomery, Alabama.

CLOVE COOKIES.

Mix one level teaspoonful of saleratus, one level teaspoonful of salt, one half level teaspoonful of ginger and two level teaspoonfuls of cloves; mix one cupful of molasses, one tablespoonful of vinegar, one fourth of a cupful of cold water and one half cupful of melted drippings; add the dry ingredients, stir in flour to make a soft dough, roll one fourth of an inch thick, and bake in a hot oven.

Miss Angeline M. Weaver, Instructor Hyde School Kitchen, Boston, Massachusetts.

COOKIES WITHOUT EGGS.

1 cupful of sugar,	2 teaspoonfuls of cream of tartar,
½ cupful of butter,	1 teaspoonful of soda,
1 cupful of water,	Flavor with nutmeg.

Flour enough to roll out, and cut into any shape you prefer.

Bettie Ferguson, Stockton, Alabama.

MOTHER CRISTIE'S COOKIES.

3 eggs,	1 cupful of butter,
2 cupfuls of sugar,	1 quart of flour,
1½ teaspoonfuls of baking-powder.	

Use more flour if necessary to make it stiff; roll thin, and bake in a pretty hot oven.

PHOEBE'S POVERTY CAKES.

1 pint of sour milk,	1 teaspoonful of soda,
1 teaspoonful of salt.	

Flour enough to roll; cut into narrow strips, and fry in hot lard. They are nice for breakfast, eaten with the coffee.

MAPLE-CAKES.

1 egg,	1 teaspoonful of soda,
1 teacupful of butter and lard, mixed.	1 teaspoonful of salt,
3 pints of flour.	

Rub well together, and mix with buttermilk; turn out on your kneading-board, and work them until quite smooth; roll very thin, cut like crullers, and fry in lard.

Mrs. Lashells.

MOTHER'S TEA-CAKES.

1 egg,	¼ cupful of water,
1 cupful of sugar,	1 teaspoonful of soda.
½ cupful of butter or beef suet,	Flavor with a little cinnamon,
Flour enough to roll.	

Cut into fancy patterns, and cook in a quick oven.

Mrs. W. B. Reid, Jackson, Michigan.

MARGARETHA FRIED CAKES.

2 eggs,	1 pint of sour milk,
1 cupful of sugar,	½ cupful of lard,
1 teaspoonful of soda.	

Spice and salt to suit the taste, and flour to roll; fry a rich brown in hot lard.

"Hazel Kirk."

DROP-CAKES.

4 eggs, beaten separately,	½ cupful of butter,
1 cupful of sugar,	1 cupful of corn-starch,
2 teaspoonfuls of baking-powder.	

Bake in small tins; place a large raisin in the top of each one after they are put into the tins.

Mrs. M. A. Long, Philadelphia, Pennsylvania.

SOFT GINGERCAKES.

1 pint of molasses,   1 cupful of butter,
1 cupful of lard,   1 tablespoonful of saleratus,
1 tablespoonful of ginger.

Allow flour enough to roll as soft as possible, and bake quickly, but not with a very hot fire, as they burn easily.

Mrs. E. C. W., Mount Vernon, Ohio.

BAKER'S CREAM CAKES.

Boil one half pint of water and one cupful of butter together, and pour it into one and one half cupfuls of flour; when nearly cold, pour in six well-beaten eggs; drop this, in small spoonfuls, on buttered tins, and bake in a quick oven. Open them at the sides, and put in the following custard:

½ pint of milk,   1 teaspoonful of corn-starch,
1 teaspoonful of flour,   1 egg,
2 tablespoonfuls of sugar.

Boil the milk, and add the beaten egg, sugar, flour and corn-starch; let it cook until it thickens, stirring all the time; when cold, put it in the cakes.

Mrs. E. D. J., Waupaca, Wisconsin.

MACAROONS.

Take the whites of two eggs, one coffee-cup level full of powdered sugar, one half pound of sweet almonds; pour boiling water over the almonds to take off the brown skin, then put them into the oven to dry; when cold, pound them to a paste; beat up the eggs and sugar to a stiff froth, and add them to the almond paste, mixing them thoroughly with the back of a spoon; roll the preparation in your hands into little balls the size of a nutmeg, and place them on a piece of white paper an inch apart. Bake them in a cool oven until a light brown.

GINGERSNAPS.

Take one egg, one cupful of molasses, one cupful of sugar, one cupful of butter and lard mixed, one half cupful of boiling water, one level tablespoonful of soda dissolved in the water, one tablespoonful of ginger, and flour enough to mold out rather soft; roll out thin, and bake in a quick oven.

Mrs. T. L. Arthur, Springfield, Ohio.

MERINGUES.

Whip the whites of four eggs to a stiff froth with a wooden spoon, stir in quickly half a pound of powdered sugar. Cut strips of white paper about two inches wide, place on a thin board, drop a tablespoonful of the mixture at a time on the paper, taking care to have all the meringues the same size, strew over some sugar and finely chopped almonds, and bake in a moderate oven half an hour. As soon as they begin to color, remove from the oven, take each slip of paper by the two ends, turn gently on the table, and with a spoon take out the soft part of each meringue; spread some clean paper on the board, turn the meringues upside down, and put them into the oven to harden and brown on the other side. When ready to use, fill with whipped cream flavored with vanilla and sweetened. Join two meringues together, and pile them high in a dish.

LADYFINGERS.

Two eggs, one cupful of sugar, one half cupful of butter beaten to a cream, four tablespoonfuls of sweet milk, two tablespoonfuls of baking-powder, enough flour to stir stiff with a spoon; flavor with lemon or vanilla; flour your molding-board, take a little piece of dough, roll with your hands as large as your fingers, cut off in four-inch lengths, and put closely on buttered ladyfinger-tins. Bake in a quick oven.

Mrs. F. C. K., Douglas, Michigan.

CINNAMON-DROPS.

One egg, one cupful of sugar, one cupful of molasses, one half cupful of butter, one cupful of water, two teaspoonfuls of cinnamon, one heaping teaspoonful of soda, five cupfuls of flour; bake in small cups nearly half full.

Grace H. Johnson, North Madison, Connecticut.

COCOANUT PATTIES.

Two large cupfuls of sugar and a piece of butter the size of an egg, braided together; beat six eggs with another cupful of sugar, mix all with one cupful of milk; stir into this mixture six large cupfuls of fresh grated cocoanut; bake in little scalloped patty-pans lined with puff paste.

Miss Harriott T. Ward, Scientific and Special Teacher of Cooking, Boston.

KISSES.

Beat the whites of four eggs to a stiff froth; then stir in one and one half pounds of powdered loaf-sugar; flavor with vanilla or lemon extract; continue to beat until it will lie in a heap; lay the mixture on letter-paper in the size and shape of half an egg and about an inch apart; then place the paper on a piece of hard wood, and put into a quick oven without closing the door. Watch them, and when they turn yellowish, take them out, and let them cool for three or four minutes; then slip a thin-bladed knife under one and transfer it to your hand; then take off another, join the two by the sides that lay on the paper, and place the kisses thus made on a dish. They are delicious.

Miss M. A. Dorin, Oak Ridge, Indiana.

SNOWBALLS.

Cream one half cupful of butter, add one cupful of fine granulated sugar, beat well; mix two level teaspoonfuls of baking-powder with two cupfuls of flour, add alternately with one half cupful of milk; beat the whites of four eggs to a stiff froth, add lightly. Fill buttered cups half full, and steam half an hour; roll in powdered sugar.

Mrs. Althea Somes, Teacher of Cookery, Manual Training School, Boston.

SUGARSNAPS.

1 cupful of sugar,	1 cupful of butter,
1 cupful of water,	1 teaspoonful of soda,
1 teaspoonful of cream of tartar.	

Flour enough to mix stiff, and roll thin.

"Stella," Jackson, Michigan.

MUSTARD WAFERS.

½ cupful of butter,	½ cupful of sugar,
1 egg,	1 cupful of milk,
3 cupfuls of flour,	1 level teaspoonful of saleratus,
1 level teaspoonful of mustard.	

Sift and mix flour, saleratus and mustard; cream butter and sugar, add beaten yolks, then milk and flour mixture alternately, lastly the beaten whites. Roll thin, and bake in a hot oven; sprinkle with granulated sugar when taken from the oven.

Miss Angeline M. Weaver, Instructor Hyde School Kitchen, Boston.

JUMBLES.

Three fourths of a cupful of butter, three tablespoonfuls of milk, one and one half cupfuls of sugar, three eggs, one teaspoonful of baking-powder. Roll, sprinkle with granulated sugar, mix with sufficient flour to roll thin; cut out with a hole in the center, and bake.

CRULLERS.

Take one egg, one cupful of sugar, one cupful of sour cream, one small teaspoonful of soda, a small pinch of salt, spice to suit the taste. Mix soft, roll nearly an inch thick, cut out with a cake-cutter that has a hole in the center; fry in hot lard.

WAFERS.

One fourth pound of butter, one half pound of pulverized sugar and three level tablespoonfuls of flour; flavor with rose-water and spread in thin cakes on dripping-pans; bake, and while hot, roll them up, and powder with white sugar. They are very pretty with mixed cakes. They bake quickly, and must be rolled quickly.

RAISED DOUGHNUTS.

3 eggs,	1-3 of a cupful of butter,
1 cupful of sugar,	3 pints of bread-sponge.

Mix with the hand as soft as possible; let it rise; mold again; have the bread-board floured, put the dough on it, roll out half an inch thick, and cut out; let them raise half an hour; fry in moderately hot lard.

SAND-TARTS.

2 eggs, reserving the white of one,	1 cupful of butter or beef drippings,
2 cupfuls of sugar,	3 cupfuls of flour.

Roll out thin; spread the white of the egg on top of each cake cut out, sprinkle with sugar and cinnamon, and press a blanched almond or raisin in the center of each. Cook in a quick oven.

Mrs. P. P. Mast, Springfield, Ohio.

FRITTERS.

3 eggs,	1 teaspoonful of soda,
2 tablespoonful of sugar,	A pinch of salt,
1 pint of sour milk,	Flour enough to make a stiff batter.

Beat thoroughly; drop a large spoonful in hot lard; fry brown, and roll in powdered sugar when done.

M. C., Troy, Pennsylvania.

Pickles— and Catsups

CHAPTER XVI.

In getting vinegar for pickles, always try to get cider vinegar, as the other kinds frequently eat up the pickles entirely or cause them to turn soft. Too strong vinegar should be partly diluted with water.

All pickles should be tightly sealed, to prevent air reaching the vinegar, as this kills it. It should always be poured on hot as it comes to the first scald—never allow it to boil.

Never put up pickles in anything that has held any kind of grease, and never let them freeze.

If pickles are put into brine, it should always be strong enough to bear an egg. Use coarse salt, in proportion of a heaping pint of salt to a gallon of water.

The nicest way to put up pickles is to put them into bottles, and seal while they are hot.

Always select perfect fruit for catsups. Cook in porcelain, never in metal.

Always use glass or stone ware to bottle in, never tin.

If on opening there is a leathery mold on top, carefully remove every particle of it, and the catsup will not be injured.

To prevent this molding, some do not fill the bottles quite to the top with catsup, but fill up with hot vinegar.

If on opening and using a part there is danger that the rest may sour, scald; and if too thick, add vinegar.

Always stir in the vinegar the last thing before putting on to boil.

TO CLARIFY PICKLES.

The scum which often rises on the top of pickles can be remedied by putting a slice or two of horse-radish in the jar, which soon sinks to the bottom, taking all the scum with it, thus leaving the vinegar clear.

TO KEEP PICKLES FROM GETTING SOFT.

To one barrel of pickles, when in brine, add one half bushel of grape-leaves. This will keep them sound and firm.

BOTTLED PICKLES.

Pour boiling water over them, and let stand four hours; to every gallon of vinegar take

1 teacupful of sugar.
1 teacupful of salt,
¼ ounce of whole cloves.
1 teaspoonful of pulverized alum,
1 ounce of cinnamon-bark,

Boil spice and vinegar, and pour over the pickles. Seal while hot.

Mrs. W. B. Reid, Jackson, Michigan.

CHOPPED PICKLES.

Chop fine
1 gallon of cabbage,
1 gallon of green tomatoes,
1 quart of onions,
2 or 3 green pepper-pods.

Sprinkle salt over the tomatoes, and let them stand awhile; then drain off the water, put with the other ingredients, and to this add four tablespoonfuls of ground mustard, two tablespoonfuls of powdered ginger, one tablespoonful of powdered cloves, one tablespoonful of powdered mace, one tablespoonful of powdered cinnamon, three pounds of sugar, three ounces of turmeric-powder and one ounce of celery-seed; mix well, cover with good vinegar, and boil slowly until done.

Mrs. D. D. H., Marion, Virginia.

CUCUMBER PICKLES.

One hundred green cucumbers about two inches long will fill four glass quart jars. Soak twenty-four hours in rather strong brine; then pour off the brine, and rinse in clear water. To this number of cucumbers use three quarts of pure cider vinegar, one cupful of sugar, one ounce of whole cloves, one ounce of stick-cinnamon, one ounce of small black peppers, a little sliced horse-radish, a few small red peppers; scald the cucumbers in the vinegar. As soon as the vinegar is scalding hot, dip them out, fill the jars, and then pour the vinegar over them until the jar is full. Seal while hot.

Clara C., Springfield, Ohio.

RIPE CUCUMBER SWEET PICKLES.

Pare twelve large cucumbers, and take out the pulp; cut them into strips about two inches wide and three or four inches long; let them stand a few minutes; take

2 pounds of sugar,	1 ounce of cinnamon,
1 pint of vinegar,	½ ounce of cloves.

Boil together, and skim; then put in the cucumbers; let them cook until tender; then take them out, and let the liquor cook fifteen minutes; pour this over the cucumbers, and cover tightly.

Libbie Kent, Genoa, Ohio.

GREEN-TOMATO PICKLE.

Chop a peck of green tomatoes, and stir in half a teacupful of salt; drain over night; add

3 green chopped peppers,	2 quarts of vinegar,
1 teacupful of grated horse-radish,	1 teacupful of sugar.

Let it boil, gently stirring occasionally, until the tomato is tender, then add a great spoonful each of cinnamon and cloves.

SWEET MANGO PICKLES.

Select young muskmelons or cantaloups (the former preferred) when they are large enough to make a nice pickle, cut a slit in the side, put into strong brine for one week, then they will be soft enough to remove the seed; wash them well, soak in weak alum-water for twenty-four hours, lay them in the sun for a few hours to dry; then scald in weak vinegar with a little alum in it; when nicely greened, dry again. Make a stuffing thus: One pound each of white and black mustard-seed, one teacupful of celery-seed, one half teacupful each of cloves, allspice and mace, one tablespoonful of turmeric. Slice some cucumber pickle, add to the spices or cabbage pickle some sliced onions cut very small—I think an improvement—three pounds of brown sugar; stuff each mango, tie securely, and place in a large stone jar, slit side up, with a few slices of lemon between. Prepare a second vinegar, sweeten to taste, pour hot over the mangos, tie up tightly for a week or two before using; the longer the better. They are delicious.

Mrs. A. E. Kirtland, Author of "Mrs. Kirtland's Cook Book," Montgomery, Alabama.

CANTALOUP SWEET PICKLE.

Take seven pounds of melons not quite ripe, lay them in a weak brine over night; then boil them in weak alum-water until transparent; lift them out, and put them into a jar.

1 quart of cider vinegar,	1 ounce of cloves,
2 ounces of stick cinnamon,	3 pounds of granulated sugar.

Let this boil, and add the fruit, cooking it twenty minutes longer; pour it into a jar, and cover closely; scald it over for two mornings; then seal tightly.

Mrs. J. A. H., Paris, Kentucky.

PICKLED PEPPERS.

Select large green peppers (those called sweet peppers are the best), cut a small slit on one side so as not to cut off any part; take out all the seeds carefully; soak the peppers in salt-water for six days, changing the brine several times. Chop onions, red cabbage, tomatoes, small cucumbers, green grapes, beans, okra, a few slices of carrots, some green corn cut from the cob, some horse-radish, whole mustard-seed, celery-seed and a little curry-powder. Regulate the quantity of each ingredient by your own taste. Prepare as much of the stuffing as will fill to the natural size, all the peppers you desire to pickle. Before filling the peppers, sprinkle all over the inside of them a little ground cinnamon, cloves and allspice; then fill in the stuffing, all well mixed; sew up the slit neatly, place in a stone jar, cover with cold spiced vinegar, cover the jar closely, and set aside.

Mrs. F. Anthony, Providence, Rhode Island.

ONION PICKLE.

Peel very small onions (button onions are the best), pour over boiling brine, let stand one week; take from the brine, and sun one day on a cloth. To each gallon of onions add one ounce of turmeric, two pounds of brown sugar, twenty-five cloves and a small quantity each of allspice, cinnamon, mace and ginger; season the vinegar, cool, and pour over the onions. Fit to use as soon as the vinegar strikes through.

Mrs. A. E. Kirtland, Author of "Mrs. Kirtland's Cook Book," Montgomery, Alabama.

SWEET-PICKLED PEACHES.

The clingstone peaches are best for pickling, though many use the free-stone as well. Some peel them, while others rub the down off with a coarse towel, and leave the skin on.

8 pounds of fruit,	1 quart of vinegar,
4 pounds of sugar,	2 ounces of stick-cinnamon,
2 ounces of cloves.	

Boil the sugar and vinegar with the cinnamon for five minutes, then put in the peaches, a few at a time, with one or two cloves in each peach; when they are done enough to prick easily with a fork, take them out of the jar, and put in others to cook until they have all been cooked; boil the syrup down to one half the original quantity, and pour it over the peaches. Seal while hot. Plums may be pickled in the same way.

PICKLED LEMONS.

6 lemons,	2 quarts of cider vinegar,
1/2 pound of fine salt,	1/4 ounce of ground cloves,
1/4 ounce of grated nutmeg,	2 ounces of black mustard-seed.

Cut the lemons three fourths of an inch down into two cross-cuts at the stem-end, put them into a covered jar with the vinegar, spices and salt, set the jar in a kettle of water, and boil until they are tender enough to pass a knitting-needle through them. The vinegar in which they are cooked is very nice for fish and veal.

Miss Harriott T. Ward, Scientific and Special Teacher of Cooking, Boston.

PICKLED ARTICHOKES.

In pickling artichokes, if you wish to have them hard, gather them as soon as they are dug; cover them with vinegar; add red pepper to suit the taste. To make them soft after gathering, let them freeze before putting them into the vinegar.

Mrs. C. V. Smith, Conyors, Georgia.

TIPTOP PICKLE.

Take one peck of green tomatoes and one dozen large onions, slice both on a slaw-cutter; have them in separate vessels, sprinkle salt between the tomatoes, and let them stand two hours; pour scalding water over the onions, and let stand until wanted; then squeeze both out, and arrange them in a crock in alternate layers, sprinkle between them celery-seed, white and black mustard-seed; pour over this one quart of vinegar and one pint of sugar brought to a boil. Ready for use when cold.

Bettina Hollis.

PICCALILLI.

2 dozen large chopped cucumbers,
2 quarts of whole small onions,
1 head of chopped cabbage.

1 peck of chopped green tomatoes,
1 dozen chopped green peppers,

Sprinkle one pint of salt over this, and let it stand over night; then squeeze out very dry. Put into a kettle one gallon of vinegar, one pint of brown sugar, one fourth of a pound box of mustard, one half ounce of turmeric-powder, one half ounce of cinnamon, one tablespoonful each of allspice, mace, celery-seed and a little horse-radish. Cook the mess slowly two hours, then add two hundred small pickles just as it is to come off the stove. Add the mustard last, as this thickens it, and it is apt to burn.

Mrs. Jas. Leffel, Springfield, Ohio.

CHOW-CHOW.

¼ peck of small string-beans,
¼ peck of tomatoes,
1 dozen green peppers,
1 quart of small white onions,
3 dozen ears of sugar-corn,
2 dozen very small cucumbers,
2 tablespoonfuls of salad-oil.

1 head of cauliflower,
¼ pound of white mustard-seed,
¼ pound of black mustard-seed,
½ pound of English ground mustard,
1 tablespoonful of celery-seed,
2 teaspoonfuls of turmeric-powder,

Salt the beans, tomatoes, peppers and onions, and let them stand under pressure for twelve hours. Make a pickle for cucumbers and cauliflower, and pour over for the same time. When ready to mix, remove the corn from the cob; mix everything well in a large kettle, excepting the oil and turmeric-powder, cover the whole with strong cider, and boil it one hour. As soon as it is lifted from the stove add the turmeric, mixing it thoroughly, and add the oil last of all, mixing that well with the other ingredients. Do not make it until the last of September or the first of October.

Carrie K. Inglis, Philadelphia, Pennsylvania.

TOMATO CATSUP.

This we make in winter. We can the juice left from canning tomatoes in summer. In the winter we take one can of juice or one can of tomatoes, boil and strain; add

½ cupful of sugar,	½ teaspoonful of salt,
1 cupful of vinegar,	½ teaspoonful of cayenne pepper,
1 tablespoonful each of cloves, cinnamon and nutmeg.	

Boil one hour, and put into a bottle for use.

GREEN-TOMATO CATSUP.

Chop one gallon of green tomatoes, one half gallon of cabbage and one pint of onions, with six pods of red pepper; sprinkle with salt, and let stand over night; drain, and add two tablespoonfuls each of mustard, ginger and black pepper, with one tablespoonful each of cinnamon, cloves, allspice, horse-radish and mace and one cupful of brown sugar; pour over the catsup; put into a preserve-kettle, and boil four hours, when it becomes thick and smooth.

CUCUMBER CATSUP.

Pare large, ripe cucumbers, and take out the seeds; grate fine, and to one dozen cucumbers add ten small onions, two tablespoonfuls of grated horse-radish, one half teaspoonful of cayenne pepper, one teaspoonful of white sugar, a little salt and black pepper; cover with cold vinegar, and seal.

SLICED-CUCUMBER CATSUP.

Take three dozen large, ripe cucumbers, two dozen white onions, one tablespoonful of pepper, one of salt and three red peppers; cut fine, and let drain over night; then spice, put into glass jars, and cover with boiling vinegar.

CHOPPED-CUCUMBER CATSUP.

Peel and chop three dozen cucumbers and one dozen onions together; sprinkle with salt, put into a sieve, and let drain over night, add

1 teacupful of mustard-seed,	½ ounce of whole cloves,
2 tablespoonfuls of black pepper,	½ ounce of allspice.

Mix well, and cover with cider vinegar.

CABBAGE CATSUP.

Chop one gallon of winter cabbage, one quart of onions and six pods of green pepper together. Boil one half gallon of vinegar, one ounce of mustard, ginger and allspice, one tablespoonful each of cinnamon, cloves, mace and horse-radish and one pound of brown sugar; pour over the cabbage.

RED-PEPPER CATSUP.

Take four dozen red peppers; put over the fire in a quart of vinegar and water each, with two roots of grated horse-radish and six sliced onions; season with salt, pepper, mustard-seed and spice; boil ten minutes, and strain; then add one teacupful of brown sugar, two ounces of celery-seed and one of mace, with a pint of strong vinegar; boil one hour, and bottle.

WORCESTERSHIRE CATSUP.

One quart of vinegar, one half ounce of cayenne pepper, four heads of bruised garlic, one half dozen mashed anchovies, ten whole cloves and one blade of mace; cover, and stand aside for eighteen hours; strain through a sieve, add one gill of walnut catsup and one tablespoonful of made mustard; put into a stone jug, and stand aside for two weeks; bottle and seal. This catsup is an excellent substitute for Worcestershire sauce.

MIXED CATSUP.

4 dozen sliced cucumbers,　　　　　　2 dozen onions,
4 green peppers,　　　　　　　　　　4 dozen large green tomatoes.

Sprinkle with one pint of salt, and let stand over night, then drain; put the whole into a preserve-kettle, and add sliced horse-radish, one ounce of mace, one ounce of white pepper, one ounce of turmeric, one ounce of white mustard-seed, one ounce of cloves, one ounce of celery-seed and one and one half pounds of brown sugar in one gallon of vinegar; boil one hour.

CURRANT CATSUP.

To three quarts of currant-juice add

3 pounds of sugar,　　　　　　　　1 tablespoonful of cloves,
1 pint of vinegar,　　　　　　　　1 tablespoonful of pepper,
1 tablespoonful of cinnamon,　　　1 tablespoonful of nutmeg.

Boil together twenty minutes, then seal, and cork tightly.
　　Mrs. G. C., Winterset, Iowa.

GRAPE CATSUP.

Stew five pounds of grapes over a slow fire until soft; then strain through a sieve; add

2½ pounds of sugar,　　　　　　　1 tablespoonful of cloves,
1 tablespoonful of cinnamon,　　　1 tablespoonful of pepper,
1 tablespoonful of allspice,　　　½ tablespoonful of salt,
1 pint of vinegar.

Boil until a little thick, and then bottle. This makes an excellent sauce for cold meats.
　　Mrs. L. C., Fair Haven, New Jersey.

SPANISH CATSUP.

Half a gallon of green cucumbers. After being peeled and cut up, sprinkle with salt, and let stand six hours; press the water from them, and scald in vinegar. Prepare half a gallon of cabbage in the same way. Chop one dozen onions, and let stand in boiling water half an hour; also chop one quart of green tomatoes and one pint of green beans with one dozen small, young ears of corn; scald and drain, then mix two tablespoonfuls of grated horse-radish, one tea-cupful of ground mustard, two cupfuls of white mustard-seed, three tablespoon-fuls of turmeric, one tablespoonful of mace, three tablespoonfuls of celery-seed, one tablespoonful of cinnamon, one tablespoonful of cayenne pepper, two table-spoonfuls of olive-oil and one pound of sugar; put into a jar with the prepared articles for catsup, and cover with boiling vinegar.

MUSHROOM CATSUP.

Take freshly gathered mushrooms, wipe, but do not wash them; put a layer of mushrooms in the bottom of an earthen dish, sprinkle with salt, then put another layer of mushrooms and salt alternately; cover with a damp, folded cloth, and stand in a warm place for thirty-six hours; then mash, and strain through a coarse bag. To every quart of juice add one ounce of peppercorns; put into a kettle, and boil one half hour, then add one ounce of whole allspice, one half ounce of ginger-root, two dozen whole cloves and a blade of mace; let simmer gently fifteen minutes longer, then take from the fire, and stand in a cool place; when cold, strain through a flannel bag, put into glass bottles, and seal.

COLD CATSUP.

One half peck of finely cut ripe tomatoes, one teacupful of finely cut onions, one teacupful of finely cut nasturtium-seeds, one teacupful of grated horse-radish, two finely chopped red peppers, three finely chopped large stalks of celery, one teacupful of whole mustard-seed, one half teacupful of salt, one large tablespoonful each of black pepper, cloves, mace and cinnamon, one half cupful of sugar, one quart of vinegar. This needs no cooking.

L. K. E., Lebanon, Ohio.

MUSTARD.

Take one half cupful of mustard flour; stir in enough water to make a smooth paste, add one half teaspoonful of salt and one tablespoonful of sugar. For another variety stir into this one half cupful of currant jelly.

TOMATO MUSTARD.

One peck of tomatoes and one teaspoonful of salt; boil in a preserve-kettle one half hour; strain it through a colander, and return it to the kettle with the following: One dessert-spoonful of ground cloves, one dessert-spoonful of all-spice, one dessert-spoonful of black pepper, one dessert-spoonful of ginger, one dessert-spoonful of cayenne pepper, some onions and a little curry-powder. Let it boil down considerably; then strain it through a sieve, and add flour of mustard until the proper thickness is obtained, and simmer for a short time. Bottle for use.

AROMATIC MUSTARD.

6 tablespoonfuls of ground mustard,	1 teaspoonful of salt,
1 tablespoonful of flour,	1 teaspoonful of pepper,
2 tablespoonfuls of sugar,	1 teaspoonful of cloves,
1 teaspoonful of cinnamon.	

Mix with vinegar in which one onion has been boiled. Let stand before using.

FRENCH MUSTARD.

Slice an onion in a bowl; cover with good vinegar, and leave two or three days; pour off the vinegar into a basin, and put into it

1 teaspoonful of pepper,	1 tablespoonful of brown sugar, and
1 teaspoonful of salt,	Mustard enough to thicken.

Smooth the mustard with a little of the vinegar as you would flour for gravy; mix it, set on the stove, and stir until it boils, when remove, and use it cold.

Ella Edgerton, Turin, New York.

MAITRE D'HOTEL BUTTER.

One fourth of a pound of butter, two small tablespoonfuls of minced parsley, one tablespoonful of lemon-juice and pepper to taste; mix well, but do not stir. Pack in small jars, cover closely, and set away for use.

SPICED CUCUMBERS.

Two dozen cucumbers pared and sliced as for the table, put them into a stone jar in layers, sprinkle each layer with fine salt, let them stand in a cool place twenty-four hours; drain well through a sieve, add two large onions sliced very thin and cut up very fine. Put the cucumbers into glass preserve-jars in alternate layers of cucumbers and onions; sprinkle each layer with celery-seed, cayenne and black pepper, and to each jar add two or three small red pepper-pods; pour over all one large bottle best lucca-oil and one pint of cider vinegar. Screw the cover on tightly, so as to exclude all air. In three days they will be ready for use.

Miss Harriott T. Ward, Scientific and Special Teacher of Cooking, Boston, Mass.

SPICED SALT.

¼ ounce of thyme,
¼ ounce of bay-leaf,
¼ ounce of pepper,
½ ounce of grated nutmeg.
⅛ ounce of marjoram,
⅛ ounce of cayenne pepper,
½ ounce of cloves,

Dry, powder and sift these, thoroughly mixed. To every four ounces of this mixture add one ounce of salt. Keep in an air-tight box or can. This is an excellent seasoning for soups, dressings, veal loaf, etc. One ounce to three pounds of dressing is sufficient.

Mrs. E. D. Buss, Springfield, Ohio.

SPICED CHERRIES.

9 pounds of fruit,
4 pounds of sugar,
½ ounce of whole cloves.
1 pint of cider vinegar,
½ ounce of cinnamon-bark,

Let the syrup come to a boil before putting in the fruit; cook the fruit until the skins break; then take out the fruit, and boil the syrup down until thick; pour over the fruit hot.

Mrs. Geo. H. Knight, Mexico, New York.

SPICED VINEGAR FOR PICKLES.

1 gallon of vinegar,
1 pound of sugar,
2 tablespoonfuls of allspice,
2 tablespoonfuls of salt,
1 tablespoonful of mace,
3 onions,
2 tablespoonfuls of mustard-seed,
2 tablespoonfuls of celery-seed,
1 tablespoonful of turmeric-powder,
1 tablespoonful of black pepper,
2 grated nutmegs,
1 handful of grated horse-radish.

Mrs. L. F. LeClercq, Springfield, Ohio.

SPICED TOMATOES.

Take red and yellow pear-shaped tomatoes, prick two or three times with a fork, sprinkle with salt, let stand over night, pack in a glass jar, and cover over with vinegar prepared as follows for a half-gallon jar:

1 pint of vinegar,	1 teaspoonful of allspice,
1 teaspoonful of cloves,	1 teaspoonful of pepper,
1 teaspoonful of cinnamon,	1 tablespoonful of sugar.

The spices should be ground. Let this come to a boil, and pour it over the tomatoes; after they get cold, tie strong paper over them.

Mrs. J. H. Calder, Briggs, Ohio.

TARRAGON VINEGAR.

Put into a wide-mouthed bottle one cupful of freshly grated tarragon-leaves, cover with one quart of good cider vinegar, cork the bottle, and stand aside for a week; strain through a bag, pour into small bottles, cork, and keep in a cool place.

CELERY VINEGAR.

Pound one gill of celery-seed; put into a bottle, and fill with strong vinegar.

NASTURTIUM VINEGAR.

Gather nasturtium flowers which are fully blown, put them into large glass bottles, and shake them well together; fill the bottle with cold vinegar, and put a finely minced shallot and one third of a clove of garlic with each quart. Let the vinegar remain for two months. At the end of that time strain it through a tamis, and add one half ounce of cayenne and one half ounce of salt. Put the vinegar into small bottles, and cork securely.

Preserves and Jellies

CHAPTER XVII.

For jelly, select your fruit before it is too ripe, if possible, as it is always of a much better flavor.

It should be put on and brought to a heat, as the juice can be much better extracted.

Have a bag made of flannel, in a funnel shape, to put the juice through. For straining it through the first time use a wire sieve, with a revolving wire to crush the fruit.

Jelly should always be strained twice, and comes much clearer by allowing it to hang over night and drip. Put on the juice and allow it to come to a heat, then put in the sugar, which should be put into the oven and heated. Jelly should always boil rapidly, and in a pan with a very large bottom, so that as much surface can be on the stove as possible. If it is desired to keep the color light, use a very little gelatin, so that it need not cook so long. From fifteen to twenty minutes is long enough for it to cook after it begins to boil, and it should not stop until done. Better success can be had by making it in small quantities. After putting it into the glasses, set them in a hot sun until cold, then cover with a piece of writing-paper directly on the jelly, another to cover the top of the glass. This can be confined with a tiny rubber band, which is better, as you can easily lift your covers and inspect your jellies. Some seasons

311

more mold will accumulate upon things than others, and if once removed, will not return.

To prevent preserves from sugaring, add a little tartaric acid when cooked.

If corn-starch be put into the juice before adding the sugar, it will make it clearer; two teaspoonfuls in two tablespoonfuls of water to three pints of juice. A teaspoonful of sugar put upon the top of jelly in the glass prevents molding.

Preserves need only tying up with several thicknesses of paper, over which put a cloth; but they should be looked over occasionally, and if signs of fermentation appear, just heating them again will correct it. Stone jars of small capacity are best for these.

We would recommend all young housekeepers in buying their jars, etc., for canning fruits to get nothing but glass or stone ware. Everything is better put up in these, as the acids in so many fruits acting upon tin are apt to make them very unwholesome, if not positively injurious. Tomatoes, peaches and other canned fruits may then be wrapped with paper to keep the light from them.

TO SEAL UP CANS OR JARS.

Scald the fruit thoroughly, pour into the cans; have ready three or four pieces of paper (a thin, tough tea-paper is best), cut about one inch larger around than the top of the can; wet the under side with the white of an egg, press on quickly, and put two or three more pieces on top of this, wet the same as the first; tie a string around over these, to be sure they are close.

Mrs. Rose C. Havenor, Centralia, Wisconsin.

TO FILL JARS WITH HOT FRUIT WITHOUT WARMING THEM.

Place the jar in a bowl of cold water, and pour into it one cupful of the boiling fruit. This will heat the jar without breaking it, and it must be taken out of the water to finish filling it. Care must be taken not to fill the hot fruit higher than the water on the outside of the jar before removing it, or it will be sure to break. This will also answer for filling jelly-glasses.

M. B. Patterson.

LIST OF FRUIT IN PRESERVES.

Seven and one half pounds of cherries and seven and one half pounds of sugar make one gallon of preserves; fourteen pounds of blackberries and fourteen pounds of sugar make five quarts of jam; six quarts of steamed grapes make five and one half pints of juice, which, with five and one half pounds of sugar, make nine tumblerfuls of jelly; two quarts of stemmed currants make two pints of juice, added to nearly two pounds of sugar, make three tumblerfuls of jelly.

WATERMELON PRESERVES.

Select one with a thick rind; cut into any shape desired; lay the pieces in strong salt-water for two or three days; then soak them in clear water for twenty-four hours, changing the water frequently; then put them into alum-water for an hour to harden them. To every pound of fruit use one pound of sugar; make a syrup of the sugar and a few small pieces of white ginger-root and one sliced lemon; take out the lemon and root, after the syrup has been boiled, and add the watermelon; let it boil until transparent. Carefully lift it, and put it into the jars, pouring the syrup over it.

Mrs. N. A. P., Ridgeway, South Carolina.

CITRON PRESERVES.

Select sound fruit, pare it, divide into quarters, carefully take out the seeds, and cut into very small pieces any shape you desire, and weigh it; to every pound of fruit allow one half pound of loaf-sugar. Put the citron on to cook until it is quite clear, then remove it from the kettle where it can drain, and pour out the water it was cooked in; then put on the weighed sugar, with water enough to wet it through; let it boil until very clear, and before putting in the citron again add to the syrup two large sliced lemons and a small piece of ginger-root to give it a fine flavor; then add the citron, and let all cook together about fifteen minutes; fill the jars with citron, and pour over the hot syrup, then seal up.

Miss Bettie Ferguson, Stockton, Alabama.

CITRON AND QUINCE PRESERVES.

Pare, and cut the citron into inch pieces; boil hard in middling strong alum-. water thirty minutes; drain, and boil in fresh water until the color is changed and they are tender. Wash carefully the quinces; pare, quarter, core and halve the quarters; boil one and one half hours the cores and parings in water to cover them; remove them, and add the prepared quince to the liquid; boil, and when they begin to be tender, add the citron and three fourths of a pound of white sugar to every pound of the fruits.

C. M. Hulbert, Almont, Michigan.

PRESERVED PEARS.

Select smooth, sweet pears of a kind which will not break when cooked; pare, halve, and remove the cores; drop into cold water as you pare, to prevent turning black. Put a little over one quart of granulated sugar into your preserving-kettles; add just water enough to moisten the sugar; when warm, put into this two quarts of pears; let them cook very slowly several hours; when the syrup is thick, dip the preserves into glass cans, and seal.

Emma Morrison, Winchester, Indiana.

PINEAPPLE PRESERVES.

Pare and slice the apples; then weigh them, and to every pound of fruit use one pound of sugar; put a layer of the slices into a jar, and cover them with a layer of sugar; and thus proceed until the apples and sugar are used up; let them stand over night; then take the apples out of the syrup, cook the syrup until it thickens, replace the apples, and boil fifteen minutes; take the apples out of the syrup, and let them cool; then put them into jars, and pour the syrup over them. A few pieces of ginger-root boiled in the syrup will improve it.

Mrs. N. A. P., Ridgeway, South Carolina.

TOMATO PRESERVES.

Scald and peel carefully small, pear-shaped tomatoes, not too ripe; prick with a needle to prevent bursting, and put their weight in sugar over them; let them lie over night, then pour off all the juice into a preserve-kettle, and boil until it is as thick as syrup, clarifying it with the white of an egg; add the tomatoes, and boil until they look transparent. A piece or two of ginger-root or one lemon to one pound of fruit, sliced thin and cooked with the fruit, will improve it.

PRESERVED STRAWBERRIES.

Remove the hulls from your berries, and put into a colander a couple of quarts only at a time; pour water over to cleanse them; have on the stove a pan of syrup made of two pounds of white sugar and one half cupful of water, drop the berries into it, allow them to cook rapidly for twenty minutes, remove all the scum that rises, but do not stir the fruit; pour into tumblers, and when you are all done, cook your syrup and juice to a jelly, and fill up your glasses; let stand until next day, and tie up with thin paper, over which put a cloth. Keep in a dry place.

CANNING STRAWBERRIES.

Wash the berries thoroughly before picking off the stems, and weigh them; to each pound of berries allow one fourth of a pound of sugar. Let them cook fifteen minutes after they come to a boil; then they are ready for the cans.

Bettie Ferguson, Stockton, Alabama.

CANNING APPLES AND QUINCES.

Pare and cut equal quantities of apples and quinces. First cook the quinces in sufficient water to cover them until they are tender, then take them out, and cook the apples in the same water; put into a jar or kettle a layer of quinces, then of apples until all are used; pour over them a syrup made of one half pound of sugar to one pound of quinces, dissolved in a little water, and let it stand over night. The next day heat them thoroughly, and seal in cans.

Mrs. A. P. K., St. Charles, Missouri.

CANNED PLUMS.

Twelve pounds of damsons and three pounds of sugar will fill six quart cans, and the same of pears and peaches.

CANNED PEACHES.

Pare the peaches with a silver knife, if possible, cut into halves, and lay in cold water until ready. Put on the stove one pound of sugar, with one and one half quarts of hot water turned over it; let it cook to a syrup. Set your jars on a cloth in hot water; fill your jars with the cold peaches, putting a layer of sugar between the peaches; when the jar is full of peaches, fill up with the hot syrup, and seal immediately. The water the jars set in should come nearly to the top.

CANNED GRAPES.

Carefully pick from the stems, and wash the grapes; remove the skins, dropping the pulp into one vessel and the skins into another. When all are thus prepared, put the pulps into a preserving-kettle over the fire, and stir constantly until the seeds come out clean; then press the mass through a colander, add the skins to the pulp, weigh them, and to one pound of grapes allow one half pound of sugar; boil one and one half hours, and put into glass jars while hot, and seal. Thirteen pounds of grapes and six and one half pounds of sugar will fill six quart cans.

Russie Feagan, Palmyra, Missouri.

CANNED PEARS.

Ten pounds of fruit, peeled, halved and cored, five pounds of sugar, one sliced lemon, one teaspoonful of ground cinnamon, one teaspoonful of grated nutmeg, a piece of ginger-root three inches long; tie the cinnamon and nutmeg loosely in a thin muslin bag; cook all together until the pears turn pink, then bottle, and seal hot.

BLACKBERRY JAM.

Two quarts of blackberries, one quart of finely cooked apples and two quarts of sugar; boil twenty minutes.

L. K. E., Lebanon, Ohio.

RED OR BLACK RASPBERRY JAM.

To use one third of currants to two thirds of raspberries is better than the berries alone. Mash the fruit well, and let it boil twenty minutes; weigh the quantity; allowing for the weight of the kettle, and to every pound of fruit use three fourths of a pound of sugar. After this is put in, let it boil until, by taking some out on a plate to try it, no juice gathers about it; then it is ready to put away, as you would jelly, in glasses; or stone jars are nice.

Mary McAllister, Mechanicsville, Iowa.

PLUM AND APPLE JAM.

After canning plums there is often some left, not enough to fill a can; a very nice jam can be made of this by putting it through a sieve, and adding the same quantity of good cooked apples; sweeten to taste, and put in a very little cinnamon and cloves; cook one hour, then tie up in jars when cold.

APPLE BUTTER.

Three gallons of cooked apples, one quart of cider vinegar and five pounds of brown sugar; boil this down to about two gallons, and season with cinnamon.

Sallie E. Ruff, Kingsville, Mississippi.

TOMATO BUTTER.

Five quarts of tomatoes and six quarts of apples; stew separately; mix well, put into a kettle, and add six pounds of sugar, two tablespoonfuls of ground cloves and three tablespoonfuls of cinnamon.

Mrs. E. W. Thomas, Fetterman, Pennsylvania.

CRANBERRY JELLY.

To three quarts of cranberries take two pounds of good white sugar and one quart of water; cook thoroughly, mashing all the berries fine, then put all through a fine sieve; return the juice to the stove, and cook fifteen minutes more. Pour into glasses, and seal when cool.

SPICED GRAPE JELLY.

Take grapes half ripe, crush all the juice out well, and strain; take equal quantities of juice and sugar; to each quart add one half teaspoonful of cloves and one tablespoonful of cinnamon; cook hard twenty minutes, then remove from the stove, and pour into glasses.

Christie Irving.

CURRANT JELLY.

Wash, and strip the currants from the stems, and put them into a preserving-kettle; mash them as they get hot, and let them boil one half hour; then turn them into a coarse hair-sieve or jelly-bag, and let them drip; when through dripping, without squeezing, measure, and pour into the kettle to cook. After it has boiled about ten minutes, put in the heated sugar, allowing one pound of sugar to one pint of jelly, and the jelly will set as soon as the sugar is dissolved—about three quarters of an hour.

Mary McAllister, Mechanicsville, Iowa.

GRAPE JELLY.

To every eight pounds of fruit take one coffee-cupful of water; put them into a porcelain-lined kettle, and boil until quite soft; strain through a cloth strainer; measure the juice; measure and set aside an equal quantity of granulated sugar; then boil the juice one half hour; add the sugar, and let it boil five or eight minutes longer. All jellies, to be good, should have nearly all of the boiling done before the sugar is added. Fruit that is partially ripe makes the prettiest jellies.

Mrs. Thos. Morgan.

RHUBARB AND APPLE JELLY.

Cut up your rhubarb, and wash it; put over the fire without any water at all; take good sour apples, pare and quarter, and cook in a very little water; strain the juice from both, and put them on the stove to cook for fifteen minutes; then add the heated sugar, three fourths as much sugar as juice; boil hard for twenty minutes. Turn into glasses, and set in the sun, if possible, for half a day; seal the next day.

CHAPTER XVIII.

ALKATHREPTA AND BROMA.

Two preparations of cocoa, which can be obtained at the drug-stores, with full directions upon the package for making into drink. It is very delicate, and can be used in illness.

COCOA-SHELLS, OR NIBS.

Cocoa-shells are the thin coverings of the cocoa-kernel, and can be bought at a very low price. They form a light food for an invalid when taken warm. Soak them in water during the night, and then boil them in the same water until it is reduced to half the quantity. They should boil two hours, and then be mixed with milk.

COFFEE.

Grind the necessary amount of coffee, and put it into the pot with just enough water to boil it; let it boil five or six minutes, and then set it on the back of the stove; a few minutes before serving, pour enough boiling water into the pot to make the required quantity of coffee.

Mary A. Rush, Claysville, Arkansas.

COFFEE.

Carefully roast good coffee, grind it, and for every teacupful of ground coffee put one egg; shake it well in the coffee-pot, and add a few spoonfuls of boiling water, mix this well, then pour on as much water as the coffee requires; let it cook fifteen or twenty minutes.

Mrs. Charles Van F., Westerville, Ohio.

317

TEA-BALLS.

These useful articles are made in different shapes, of plated and also solid silver. They are opened, the tea is put inside, then closed, and boiling water poured over them into the teacups; the perforations allow the water to reach

the leaves, making the tea any strength desired without the annoyance of the floating leaves. The ring is placed upon the finger, and the ball dipped up and down through the water. The tea can be changed when fresh is desired. This will also serve for afternoon teas.

TEA.

People must consult their own tastes as to the kind of tea. Mixed is the best to use with ice. Allow one teaspoonful for each person. Use boiling water, but do not boil the tea, and use while fresh. Tea is best made in an earthen

tea-pot. It should never be made in tin. Iced tea should be made several hours before it is needed, and then set upon ice. When ready to use, sweeten, and drink without milk or cream. Use cracked ice to put into the glass.

TEA.

Allow one teaspoonful of tea for three cupfuls; pour on nearly one quart of boiling water, and set it where it will keep warm, but not cook. Some put a pinch of tea-leaves into the cup, and fill it up with hot water. It is ready to use after standing a few moments.

CHOCOLATE.

One cupful of milk, one cupful of water, one tablespoonful of grated chocolate; sweeten to taste; boil for five minutes; scalding will not do. This makes two cupfuls.

Helen F. Dawley, Jordansville, New York.

CHOCOLATE.

Allow a heaping tablespoonful of grated chocolate to one pint of fresh milk; let it come to a boil, and sweeten to taste.

LEMONADE.

This is invaluable in fevers, and also in rheumatic affections. Rub two medium-sized lemons soft; cut them through the center, and squeeze out the juice; take out the seeds; put two tablespoonfuls of white sugar to each lemon and one pint of cold or boiling water, according as you desire the lemonade—hot or cold.

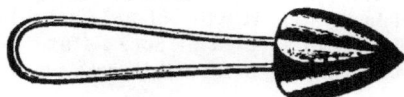

LEMON-EXTRACTOR.

AUNT ELLEN'S SODA-WATER.

3 pounds of sugar,
1½ pints of molasses,
2 quarts of boiling water.

¼ of a pound of tartaric acid,
½ ounce of sassafras,

After these have boiled together, bottle, and cork well. It will keep a long time in a cool, dark place. Use two tablespoonfuls of this syrup and one half teaspoonful of soda to a glassful of water.

E. C., Hoosac, New York.

SODA-CREAM.

Dissolve one pound of lemon-sugar in one pint of water, and let it boil; add the whites of three eggs, beaten to a stiff froth, boil four minutes, stir, and strain; when cold, add four teaspoonfuls of lemon extract, and bottle. When wanted for use, put four tablespoonfuls into a glass of ice-water, add to it one third of a spoonful of soda, stir, and drink.

STRAWBERRY ACID.

Dissolve four ounces of tartaric acid in two quarts of water, and pour it over two gallons of ripe strawberries; let stand twenty-four hours, and drain the liquor off; to every pint of juice add one and one half pounds of loaf-sugar; boil, let stand three days, and bottle. A few spoonfuls in a glassful of ice-water make a delightful drink.

LEMON VINEGAR.

Keep a jar of vinegar, into which put lemon-peel not used in cooking. A few spoonfuls of it will make a pleasant and refreshing drink added to ice-water well sweetened.

RASPBERRY VINEGAR.

Put ripe raspberries into a stone jar, cover with cider vinegar, let stand twenty-four hours; pour the liquor over a gallon of fresh berries, and let stand over night; allow one pound of loaf-sugar to one pint of juice; boil, and skim; bottle. Add one half glassful of the vinegar to one of ice-water.

HARVEST DRINK.

1 quart of water,	1 tablespoonful of sifted ginger,
3 tablespoonfuls of sugar,	½ pint of vinegar.

SWEET-GRAPE CORDIAL.

Take twenty pounds of Concord grapes, add three quarts of water, crushing the grapes in the water, and put them into a porcelain kettle; stir them well until it reaches boiling heat, let them cook fifteen or twenty minutes, then strain through a cloth; add three pounds of white sugar; when the sugar is dissolved, strain again through a cloth; heat to the boiling-point again, pour it into pint or quart bottles, and seal instantly. It will not keep after being opened, so it is best to put up only enough to be used at once. Have the bottles thoroughly heated, and use new corks; dip the necks, with corks in, into hot sealing-wax.

Candies

CHAPTER XIX.

ICE-CREAM CANDY.

1 cupful of sugar,	¼ teaspoonful of cream of tartar,
1-3 cupful of water,	Butter the size of an egg.

Boil all together about fifteen minutes, not stirring until taken from the fire, when the extract is added.

ICE-CREAM CANDY.

6 pints of white sugar,	1½ pints of water,
2 teaspoonfuls of cream of tartar.	

Boil until it ropes, or when dropped into a glass of ice-water will stand up in it; pull until very white.

Miss Belle Mast, Springfield, Ohio.

CREAM CANDY.

Three cupfuls of white sugar; a little more water than enough to cover. Do not stir it while cooking. Let it boil until it ropes, then before taking it off the stove, add one teaspoonful of cream of tartar moistened with the flavoring you choose. When cold, pull until perfectly white.

Mrs. Lizzie K., Springfield, Ohio.

11   321

NUT CANDY.

Boil together until it "snaps" when dropped into cold water, two cupfuls of dark brown maple sugar and one cupful of milk or cream; remove from the fire, and stir rapidly until it begins to sugar; add one cupful of chopped shagbarks; pour into a buttered tin.

Mrs. Althea Somes, Teacher of Cookery, Manual Training School, Boston, Mass.

NUT CANDY.

Take a well-buttered plate, and spread on it about one half pint of hickory-nut kernels; then take one pint of maple molasses, boil it until it becomes thick, and try it by dropping some into cold water; when it hardens in the water, pour it over the kernels, and stir up quickly.

Lewisburg, Ohio.

COCOANUT CANDY.

2 teacupfuls of white sugar,   ½ teacupful of sweet cream,
Butter the size of a walnut.

Let it boil fifteen minutes; then stir in as much cocoanut as you think best; flavor to taste.

Carrie L., Austin.

VANILLA SUGAR CANDY.

2 pounds of granulated sugar,   Butter the size of an egg,
2-3 of a cupful of water,   1 tablespoonful of glycerin,
1-3 of a cupful of vinegar,   2 tablespoonfuls of vanilla.

Boil all except vanilla, without stirring, twenty minutes or one half hour, or until crisp when dropped into water. Just before pouring upon platters to cool, add one small teaspoonful of soda or cream of tartar. After pouring upon platters, pour over it the vanilla. This can be pulled beautifully white. Make in strips, and cut with shears.

WHITE-SUGAR CANDY.

4 pounds of white sugar,   4 tablespoonfuls of cream,
1 pint of water,   4 tablespoonfuls of vinegar,
Butter the size of an egg.

Boil all together slowly for about three quarters of an hour.

Weldon W., Springfield, Ohio.

UNCOOKED CANDY.

Into the whites of two eggs stir as much confectioners' XXXX sugar as will make the mixture like a soft dough. This is used as a foundation for a great many kinds of candy. Put it out on a molding-board, and form into balls, which can be dipped into melted chocolate, and made into chocolate creams. A piece put between a split date, with the seed removed, and the whole rolled in either pink or white granulated sugar, forms another. A piece put between two half kernels of English walnut makes another. Chopped nuts mixed in the dough, and then cut into squares, forms another. Putting a little red sugar in the mixture as you stir it makes a lovely pink color, which you can arrange in layers between the white, and cut into squares. These are only a few of its uses. Use any flavoring extract desired, but in very small drop quantities.

L. A. C.

MOLASSES CANDY.

Two cupfuls of Orleans molasses, one cupful of brown sugar, butter the size of a walnut; boil twenty minutes; when done, add to the candy two teaspoonfuls of cream of tartar, one teaspoonful of soda, one tablespoonful of vinegar; let it stand until cool enough to pull.

L. C. W., Port Kennedy, Pennsylvania.

MAPLE-SUGAR CANDY.

1 cupful of maple sugar,
Small bit of butter.

½ cupful of water,

Boil about ten minutes; when done, add one teaspoonful of vanilla, and pour into buttered tins. It must not be stirred.

Mrs. E. L. Clark, Skaneateles, New York.

WALNUT TAFFY.

1 cupful of granulated sugar,
1 scant cupful of milk,

1 scant cupful of molasses,
1 level teaspoonful of butter.

Boil twenty minutes, or until the mixture becomes brittle when dropped into cold water; add two level teaspoonfuls of cocoa and one teaspoonful of vanilla; pour it over one half pound of English walnuts which have been shelled, quartered and spread evenly over a buttered tin.

Miss Angeline M. Weaver, Instructor Hyde School Kitchen, Boston, Massachusetts.

VANILLA TAFFY.

1 cupful of vinegar,
3 cupfuls of sugar,

Butter the size of a walnut,
½ teaspoonful of vanilla.

VINEGAR TAFFY.

2 tablespoonfuls of vinegar,
6 tablespoonfuls of sugar.

4 tablespoonfuls of water,

Boil twenty minutes, then pour onto a buttered plate.

"Lollypops."

FRENCH VANILLA CREAM.

Break into a bowl the white of one or more eggs; add to it an equal quantity of cold water; then stir (do not beat it) in the confectioners' sugar until you have it stiff enough to mold in shape with the fingers; flavor with vanilla. After it is formed into balls, cubes or any other shape desired, lay them upon sheets of waxed paper upon plates, and set aside to dry. This is the foundation of all French creams.

PARISIAN CREAMS.

Make the French cream (see recipe), and divide into three parts, leaving one part white, color one part pink with a few drops of fruit coloring, and the third part brown with grated chocolate; make a cake about one half inch thick of the white cream, which may be done by rolling on a platter or marble slab. Take the pink in the same manner, and lay it upon white cream, then the chocolate in the same manner, pressing it all together; trim the edges smooth, and cut into squares. Each layer may be flavored differently

CHOCOLATE CREAMS.

Two cupfuls of white sugar and one half cupful of water; put on the fire, and boil about three minutes, stirring constantly; then stir in one large half cupful of corn-starch; flavor with lemon; work up very quickly into little cones. Have ready one half cake of melted chocolate; dip in the cones, and place on a plate to harden.

Mrs. G. W. Dains, East Litchfield, Connecticut.

FRENCH CREAM.

These candies are made with XXXX confectioners' sugar, and can be made without boiling. The sugar can be obtained at any large grocery, and is as fine as flour.

CREAM WALNUTS.

Crack English walnuts carefully, so as to take the meat out whole. Take the white of an egg, half as much water, and stir in powdered sugar until the paste is stiff; put the paste between the pieces of walnut.

CHOCOLATE CARAMELS.

2 cupfuls of brown sugar,	½ cupful of butter,
1 cupful of molasses,	½ pound of grated chocolate,
1 cupful of cream or milk,	2 tablespoonfuls of flour.

Boil the molasses, butter, sugar and flour for fifteen minutes; stir the chocolate into the cream, and pour in the boiling syrup, and boil until done; drop a little into cold water; if it piles up and hardens, then it is done. Before pouring it out on buttered pans or plates, add one teaspoonful of vanilla, and as it cools, crease it into small squares.

Mrs. E. W., Mount Vernon, Ohio.

BUTTER-SCOTCH.

3 cupfuls of brown sugar,	Butter the size of a walnut,
¾ of a cupful of water,	A pinch of soda,
Flavor to suit the taste.	

Cook until it begins to harden when dripping from a spoon. Pour it out into buttered pie-pans. As it cools, mark it off into squares with a knife dipped into water to keep it from sticking. When wanted for eating, turn the pan bottom side up, knock on it, and the candy will come out without any trouble.

Lizzie Mast, Springfield, Ohio.

CHAPTER XX.

A majority of the ailments of the human race are caused by a "disordered stomach," and the greatest danger to our system is the non-assimilation of food. In a good many cases this has been caused through injudicious food, or by food partaken of in too great a hurry. "Peptonized diet" is the only remedy. The food must reach the stomach in a prepared state, and will be readily absorbed by the system and strengthen the debilitated organs so that they will be able again to perform their duties. In cases of convalescence and consumption this treatment will be of great value. We will make a few suggestions for these preparations.

BROTH, QUICKLY MADE.

Take a bone or two of a neck or loin of mutton, and take off the fat and skin, set it over the fire in a small tin saucepan that has a cover, with three fourths of a pint of water, the meat being first beaten and cut into thin bits; put in a bit of thyme and parsley, and if approved, a slice of onion. Let it boil very quickly, skim it nicely; take off the cover if likely to be too weak, else cover it. Half an hour is sufficient for the whole process.

325

CLEAR BROTH.

The following is a clear broth that will keep long: Put the round of beef, a knuckle-bone of veal and a few shanks of mutton into a deep pan, and cover closely with a dish or coarse crust; bake until the beef is done enough for eating, with only as much water as will cover. When cold, cover it closely in a cool place. When to be used, give what flavor may be approved.

CHICKEN BROTH.

Put the body and legs of the fowl of which chicken panada was made, after taking off the skin and rump, into the water in which it was boiled, with a blade of mace, one slice of onion and ten peppercorns. Simmer until the broth be of a pleasant flavor; if there is not water enough, add a little. Beat fine one fourth of an ounce of sweet almonds, with a teaspoonful of water, boil it in the broth, strain, and when cold, remove the fat.

VEAL BROTH.

Put the knuckle of a leg or shoulder of veal with very little meat to it, an old fowl and four shank-bones of mutton extremely well soaked and bruised, three blades of mace, ten peppercorns, an onion, a large bit of bread and three quarts of water into a stew-pot that covers closely, and simmer in the slowest manner after it has boiled up and been skimmed; or bake it; strain, and take off the fat; salt as wanted. It will require four hours.

VEAL BROTH FOR INVALIDS.

Cut two pounds of lean veal into small pieces; sprinkle a little salt upon these, and put them into a saucepan with one quart of cold water. Let the liquor boil, skim carefully, then simmer as gently as possible. Strain it, let it get cold, and remove the fat from the surface; thicken with a little arrow-root before serving. Time to simmer the veal, three hours.

WHITE BROTHS, WITH VERMICELLI.

Light and delicate white broths may be produced by stirring the yolks of two or three fresh eggs with two tablespoonfuls of cold water, which must then be poured into the hot broth, gently stirring it all the time, without allowing the broth to boil after the eggs are put in, or they will be curdled.

PEPTONIZED BROTH.

Take one quart of consomme (as stated under "Consomme"), boil it down to one pint, and when nearly cool, add two tablespoonfuls of essence of pepsin; put on the ice at once. Ready for use as soon as cold.

Eugene Stuyvesant Howard, Member of the Universal Cookery and Food Association, London, England, and Chef de Cuisine, Louisville Hotel.

WATER GRUEL.

Rub smooth a large spoonful of oatmeal with two of water, and pour it into one pint of water boiling on the fire; stir it well, and boil quickly, but take care that it does not boil over. In a quarter of an hour strain it off, and add salt and a bit of butter when eaten. Stir until the butter be incorporated.

SAGO GRUEL.

Take two tablespoonfuls of sago, and place them in a small saucepan; moisten gradually with a little cold water; set the preparation over a slow fire, and keep stirring until it becomes rather stiff and clear; add a little grated nutmeg and sugar to taste; if preferred, half a pat of butter may also be added with the sugar.

INVALIDS' SOUP.

Split a calf's foot, and cut one pound of good, lean, juicy beef and one pound of lean mutton into small pieces; put them, together with one half gallon of water, into an earthenware jar, and bake in a slow oven for from six to seven hours, adding another quart of water, a small teaspoonful of whole allspice and a leaf or two of sage when the mixture has been stewing three or four hours. When the soup is reduced to half the quantity, strain through a sieve, and when cold and a jelly, remove the fat. This soup may be taken cold, or warmed up with a little vermicelli, and pepper and salt to taste. Sufficient for three pints.

BEEF TEA.

Cut into small pieces two pounds of fresh, lean beef; add three pints of cold water; when on the eve of boiling, carefully remove the scum; the moment it boils add one pint of cold water; then let it boil up again, and remove the scum as before. If by this time it is not perfectly clear, the same quantity of water may be added the second time, which will cause more scum to rise. The same remarks apply to all other broths and gravies, which will always be transparent and finely flavored if the same rule be observed. Beef tea should be allowed to simmer not less than three quarters of an hour, and not more than one hour from the time it is last skimmed.

CHICKEN PANADA.

Take the breast of a cold chicken, and pound it in a mortar to a very fine paste, then put it into a very small stew-pan, and add to it, gradually, as much boiling-hot broth as will make it of the required consistency; season with a little salt; place the stew-pan over the fire, stir the contents, but do not let them boil.

TOAST AND WATER.

Toast slowly a thin piece of bread until extremely brown and hard, but not the least black; then plunge it into a jugful of cold water, and cover it over an hour before using. It should be of a fine brown color before drinking it.

APPLE-WATER.

Cut two large apples into slices, and pour a quart of boiling water on them, or on roasted apples; strain in two or three hours, and sweeten slightly.

BARLEY-WATER.

Wash a handful of common barley, then simmer it gently in three pints of water with a bit of lemon-peel.

INVALIDS' LEMONADE.

Put about half of a sliced lemon, pared and divested of the inner skin, or pith, with the parings and an ounce or two of lump-sugar, into a jug; pour boiling water over these ingredients, and cover closely. In two hours strain for use. To the above quantity of lemon add one pint of water, which will make a refreshing lemonade.

ORANGEADE.

Take the thin peel of two oranges and of one lemon; add the water and sugar the same as for lemonade; when cold, add the juice of one lemon and of four or five oranges, and strain off.

FLAXSEED LEMONADE.

Four tablespoonfuls of whole flaxseed, one quart of boiling water poured on the flaxseed, and the juice of two lemons, leaving out the peel; sweeten to taste; steep three hours in a covered pitcher. If too thick, put in cold water, with the lemon-juice and sugar. Ice for drinking. It is splendid for colds.

TAPIOCA JELLY.

Choose the largest sort, pour cold water on to wash it two or three times, then soak it in fresh water five or six hours, and simmer it in the same until it becomes quite clear; then put lemon-juice and sugar in. The peel should have been boiled in it. It thickens very much.

MULLED JELLY.

Take one tablespoonful of currant or grape jelly; beat with it the white of one egg and a little loaf-sugar; pour on it one half pint of boiling water, and break in a slice of dry toast or two crackers.

CALVES'-FEET JELLY.

Boil two calves' feet in four quarts of water for five hours, then strain the liquor through a hair-sieve, and the next day take off all the fat. Whisk the whites and shells of three eggs in a stew-pan, then put in the jelly, and add a small piece of cinnamon, the thin peel of two lemons and the juice of three, with about six or seven ounces of loaf-sugar; put the stew-pan over a brisk fire, and whisk its contents until on the eve of boiling, then remove the stew-pan, cover it closely, and let it remain near the fire for fifteen minutes, taking care not to allow the jelly to boil. Pass it through the bag in the usual way.

INVALIDS' CUTLET.

Get a cutlet from the loin or neck of well-fed mutton, but cut away all the fat, and leave nothing but the lean, which put into a stew-pan with just enough water to cover it, and a very little salt; stew gently, and add a small quantity of celery cut into thin shavings. Carefully skim off any fat that may appear on the top, and when it has stewed about two hours, without boiling, the meat will be easy of digestion. Add pepper and salt to taste. Time to stew celery, thirty to thirty-five minutes.

ARROWROOT PUDDING.

Take one tablespoonful of arrowroot and one half pint of milk, one tablespoonful of which add cold to the arrowroot, stirring it until it is well mixed, then boil the remainder of the half pint of milk, sweeten to taste with loaf-sugar, and while it is boiling hot, add it by degrees to the arrowroot, then boil the whole, stirring it all the time, until it becomes thickened, and have ready the yolks and whites of six eggs beaten together, which stir into it. Put all into a buttered basin, and cover with paper; then steam it for one half hour. A pudding may be made in the same way, baked in a dish with a light crust around, and flavored with any approved ingredient.

MINCED CHICKEN.

Take the breast of a cold roasted chicken, and mince it finely; add one half teaspoonful of fine flour, together with five or six tablespoonfuls of broth; season with a pinch of salt. If broth is not at hand, substitute new milk.

SCRAPED BEEF.

Take a good piece of raw steak, lay it on a meat-board, and with a knife scrape into fine bits; after removing all hard and gristly parts, put it into a pan over the fire, and let it remain just long enough to become thoroughly heated through, stirring it up from the bottom occasionally. Season with a little salt. This is very nutritious and quite palatable. As a food for infants this is unsurpassed. It should be fed raw—in quantities of one half teaspoonful at a time. This, in connection with cod-liver oil as a tonic, will build up a child in delicate health who is unable to retain milk in any form. It should be freshly prepared whenever used.

DRIED FLOUR FOR INFANTS.

Take one teacupful of flour, tie it up tightly in a close muslin bag, put it into a pot of cold water, and let boil three hours; then take it out, and dry the outside. When used, remove the outer skin, and grate it. One tablespoonful is enough for one teacupful of milk (which would be better with a little water); wet the flour with a little cold water, and stir into the milk; add a very little salt, and boil five minutes. This is a good food for a child suffering with summer complaint or any kind of loose bowels.

FLOUR CAUDLE.

Into five large spoonfuls of water rub smooth one dessert-spoonful of fine flour; set over the fire five spoonfuls of new milk, and put two bits of sugar into it; the moment it boils, pour into it the flour and water, and stir it over a slow fire twenty minutes. It is a nourishing and gently astringent food. This is an excellent food for babies who have weak bowels.

WHEY.

That of cheese is a very wholesome drink, especially when the cows are fresh in herbage.

JUNKET.

Take one tumblerful of sweet milk (not cold), add enough sugar to suit the taste, a few drops of essence of vanilla and one tablespoonful of essence of pepsin; mix well, and let it remain in a warm place until it commences to thicken, then put on ice, and serve when thoroughly cold.

PEPTONIZED MILK.

Take one imported quart bottle (champagne), clean it thoroughly, mix two tubes of pepsin in one fourth of a teacupful of water, put it into the bottle, and fill the same three fourths full, shake well, cork, and fasten the cork well. Have a pailful of hot water—hot enough to bear your hand in—ready, put the bottle into it. The water should be as high on the outside of the bottle as the milk on the inside. Let it remain there for fifteen minutes; then put the bottle on the ice at once. When cold, it is ready for use. It is advisable to take small doses very often.

ORGEAT.

Beat two ounces of almonds, with one teaspoonful of orange-flower water and a bitter almond or two; then pour one quart of milk and water into the paste. Sweeten with sugar.

SIPPETS.

On an extremely hot plate put two or three sippets of bread, and pour over them some gravy from beef, mutton or veal, if there is no butter in the dish. Sprinkle a little salt over it.

Practical Suggestions to young Housekeepers.

CHAPTER XXI.

BY CHRISTIE IRVING.

All good housekeepers know the advantage to be derived from a "good start" in the morning. To insure this, make all preparations for breakfast the evening before. Give especial attention to your match-box, kindling-basket and coal-receiver; and if all things are ready, it will take but a short time to have breakfast ready.

Never use the first water that comes from a pump or hydrant; it has been in a lead or iron pipe all night, and is not healthful.

Much hurry and confusion would be prevented if housekeepers would do little tedious jobs during leisure moments.

Study your cook-book as you would any other lesson—not at the very moment you wish to use it, but some time when you are sitting down for an hour's leisure or rest.

All groceries and household supplies should be put away in their own proper receptacles, and not left standing around in paper bags. Keep rice, oatmeal, cracked wheat, tapioca, etc., in closely covered glass jars, tea and coffee in tin canisters, meal and flour in covered wooden buckets.

Never set coal-oil near butter or lard.

If corn-meal is bought by the quantity, it should be spread out upon an old sheet in a room where the air passes, and thoroughly dried before putting it away, to keep it from getting musty.

331

When you buy raisins for cooking purposes, seed them, wash, and thoroughly dry them, and put into glass jars with tight lids; currants also. If you prefer, you can buy the seedless raisins, but they are a little more expensive.

During the oyster season always have rolled crackers ready. You can save the crushed crackers and crumbs from your crackers in a glass jar, and so avoid using your whole ones.

It is best to buy hominy, beans, rice, etc., in quantities.

Five or six quarts of biscuit-flour can be prepared at a time by taking one teaspoonful of soda and two of cream of tartar, or three of baking-powder, to every quart of flour, sifting it thoroughly three times, and put away for use.

Burn all egg-shells, coffee-grounds, sweepings, etc.

If you keep chickens, cook all your vegetable parings, and feed them; if not, burn them.

Never throw tin cans into the alley or street. Wash them, and set aside for use. They will often be handy.

Never set aside a bottle dirty. Wash clean, and turn with the neck down, that it may dry, and no dust be in it when you want it.

Never wrap steel or silver in a woolen cloth; use soft tissue-paper.

Never let any kind of food remain in copper or brass vessels after it is cooked.

Never wash your rolling-pin. Scrape off the dough that adheres, and wipe with a dry towel.

In cleaning any vessel in which strong-smelling vegetables have been cooked, use half a teaspoonful of soda in a little hot water, washing it well afterward in hot soap-suds.

A brass kettle can be cleaned, if discolored by cooking in it, by scouring it well with soap and ashes first, then put in half a pint of vinegar and a handful of salt, and let them boil on the stove a short time; then wash, and rinse it out in hot water.

Never use a metal spoon for stirring stewed fruit or tomatoes. A wooden one is best, and those with short handles are preferable for stirring thick messes.

Never let the handles of knives be put into hot water. If possible, buy silver knives when you begin your housekeeping. You will not find it an extravagance in the end.

Never allow your carving-knife to be used to cut bread; provide a separate knife.

Never throw water on burning oil; use flour.

If your clothes take fire, do not run about, but lie down, and roll over and over until the flame is smothered.

Never buy sweet potatoes in large quantities.

Always keep a stick wrapped with old muslin to grease hot pans and all baking-tins.

Always put your griddle-cake batter into a pitcher, and pour it out to bake.

Old bleached muslin is of no use except for carpet-rags. They will not do for dusters, as they will not hold dust, nor for cleaning, as they will not absorb moisture, while old unbleached stuff does nicely.

For dish-towels some use crash, which should be of the very best quality, though old drilling or a poor quality of ticking makes better ones; and many ladies prefer a light-weight unbleached muslin, as a cotton cloth does not leave the lint that linen does when a little worn. '

For dish-rags buy white mosquito-netting—a quarter of a yard is sufficient for one—which should be folded back and forth as many times as the width will allow, and tack as a comfort. Some make them of a ball of candle-wick, knit on two wooden needles the size of a lead-pencil. Set up twenty stitches. Knit in plain garter knitting until the ball is used up. These are easily kept clean if washed in hot soap-suds after each meal; also wash the dish-towels at the same time. A half dozen are quite sufficient.

Provide also several soft holders to use in taking up hot dishes; these should be made six inches by eight, slightly caught through and a brass ring in one corner to hang upon a nail close to the stove. Old stockings are good for this, or two thicknesses of pants cloth.

Every housekeeper should provide herself with little conveniences for doing her work. A short-handled, broad paint-brush to wash the outside of window-sills, and an old tooth-brush for washing around the glass.

Begin housekeeping on the cash basis. If you cannot pay cash for an article, do not get it.

Among the first things you learn to do, let it be your own marketing.

Every wife should have a certain weekly allowance to use for household expenses.

Have a flour-sack in which to put all clippings from sewing, all waste paper, etc., which save to dispose of to the ragman for articles you need.

Save yourself steps by having a broom, dust-pan and dusters up-stairs to do the chamber work.

Have all new steel knives well sharpened, also chopping-knives; use these only in the kitchen. Time is saved by using silver-plated ones on the dining-table.

A rubber window-cleaner is a very convenient article to have; also a hair-brush for outside cleaning.

Jelly-bags are made of flannel.

If possible, have your kitchen table made to order, with an ash top and three deep drawers—two in partitions.

Ticking makes the nicest kitchen aprons. Some prefer ginghams or denim. Large, plain white ones, to reach to the bottom of the dress, should always be ready to put on when going to the table, or to tie quickly over the other if called to the door.

If ladyfingers are wanted, get special tins to bake them the proper shape.

Bread-crusts should be dried in the oven, and put away in paper bags until wanted for use.

India-rubber gloves are used by many ladies for washing dishes, as the hot, soapy water is very injurious to some skins, also causing some finger-nails to split and get sore. These would seem an extravagance at first, but are not if looked upon as a preservative for the hands; and it is right to take as good care of one's self in every way possible.

After washing the hands, dip them in weak vinegar-water before wiping them. This will keep them nice, and often prevent chapping.

The best china and glass are the cheapest, even for every-day use, if the outlay can be afforded, as they are annealed before leaving the manufacturers' hands, and may be washed in boiling water without injury, and do not crack and chip from usage like the common ware. China and glass should be gently washed in hot water with a little soap, rinsed in cold water, and carefully wiped with a clean, soft towel. All articles with gilding must be handled with great care, never rubbed or polished if the gilding becomes tarnished; chamois-skin, with a little whiting on it, may be used to polish it.

When warming plates and dishes for meats, extreme caution must be used to prevent them getting hot, as heat cracks the glazing, and if it does not show at the time, it will soon crack or break.

Cut glass will not look clear unless washed in very hot water, but does not require soap. If it is in any way blurred or tarnished, it must be cleaned with a soft brush dipped in whiting, and then polished with a soft piece of newspaper; this gives it a brilliant, clear appearance, and no lint remains as when rubbed with a linen towel.

BILL·OF·FARE· FOR ·FAMILY·DINNER·

SUNDAY.

Tongue.

Lettuce, with Eggs.   Saratoga Potatoes.   Canned Corn.

Currant Jelly.   Pickles.   Peach Pie.

Tea or Coffee.

MONDAY.

Roast Beef.

Parsnips.   Potatoes (baked with the meat).   Spinach.

Apples.   Baked Custard.   Raisins.

Nuts.   Coffee.

TUESDAY.

Roast Lamb, with Caper Sauce.

Peas.   Potatoes (mashed, and browned in oven).   Cresses.

Canned Peaches.   Tapioca Pudding, Hard Sauce.   Chocolate Cake.

Coffee.   Nuts.

WEDNESDAY.

Breaded Veal.

Baked Corn.   Mashed Potatoes.   Cold Slaw.

Steamed Peach Dumplings.

Chocolate.   Cake.   Confectionery.

THURSDAY.

Stewed Veal.   Potatoes.

Carrots.   Vegetable Rice.   Chocolate.

Tapioca Pudding.   Sponge-cake.

FRIDAY.

Corned Beef.   Potatoes (whole).

Turnips.   Apple Sago.   Carrots and Rice.

SATURDAY.

Fried Chicken, Cream Gravy.

Macaroni.   Mashed Potatoes.   Asparagus.

Lettuce.   Cheese.   Currant Jelly.

Pound-cake.   Ice-cream · Meringues.   Apple Pie.   Coffee.

A WHITE DINNER.

Codfish.

Macaroni, with Cheese.

Water-cresses.   Mashed Potatoes.   Rice Pudding.

BILLS OF FARE FOR SPECIAL DAYS.

❀ ❀

NEW-YEAR'S DINNER.

Soup.

Oysters.   Wafers.

Turkey, with Cranberries.

Mashed Potatoes.   Sweet Potatoes.

Hubbard Squash.

Pickled Watermelon.   Gooseberry Catsup.

Cold Slaw.   Onions.

Apple Pie.   Grated Cheese.

Coffee.   Milk.   Tea.   Chocolate.

Nuts.   Raisins.   Figs.

THANKSGIVING DINNER.

Oyster Soup.

Crackers.   Pickles

Roast Turkey, with Cranberries.

Chicken Pie.

Turnips.   Mashed Potatoes (browned).   Onions.

Squash.   Celery.

Mince Pie.   Pumpkin Pie.   Cheese.

Chocolate.   Cake.

Ice-cream.

Raisins.   Nuts.

CHRISTMAS DINNER.

Soup.

Turkey, with Oyster Dressing.

Turnips.   Mashed Potatoes.   Sauer-kraut.

Boiled Sweet Corn.

Cranberries.   Plum Sauce.

Mince Pie.   Cheese.   Custard Pie.

Tea.   Coffee.   Chocolate.

Nuts.   Bonbons.

DINNER TO THE SUPREME COURT, AT THE WHITE HOUSE.

February 1, 1894.

❀ ❀

Blue Points.
Bisque of Crabs aux Quenelles.
Chicken Consomme Royal aux Perles.

Hors-d'oeuvres.

Fish.
Cassolettes des Gourmets Bechamel
Escallops of Bass en Bordure.

RELEVEES.
Fillet of Beef, Larded, Braise, Madeira Sauce.
Fonds d'Artichauts and Champignons Farces.

ENTREES.
Petites Timbales de Macaroni (Puree of Grouse).
Sauce Supreme aux Truffes.

Terrapin Maryland Style.

Cotelettes of Poulardes a la Demidoff.

Punch Glace.

Cold Dish—Chaudfroid de Reed Birds a la Gelee.
Roast—Canvasback Duck.
Water-cress and Tomato Salad.

Fruits Glaces.
Paniers Garnis, Varies.
Ice-cream.
Amandes Salees.
Petits Fours.
Two Pieces Nougat Garnies, Historiees.
Coffee

Paul Resal, Chef of White House (Executive Mansion), Washington, D. C.

DINNER TO MEMBERS OF THE CABINET, AT THE WHITE HOUSE.

January 18, 1894.

❦ ❦

Blue Points.

Creme de Volaille aux Quenelles.

Green Turtle.

Cannelons, Puree de Gibier.

Fillet of Striped Bass a la Cardinale.

Selle de Chevreuil, Sauce Poivrade.

Puree de Marrons Croutonnee.

Mousse de Chapon a la Perigord.

Sauce Supreme.

Terrapin a la Maryland.

Game Pie a la Cleveland.

Imperial Punch.

Roast Canvasback Duck, Molded Cranberry.

Tomato and Lettuce Mayonnaise.

Cheese and Crackers.

Glaces Varies.

Cafe.

Two Pieces Montees.

Petits Fours.

Amandes Salees.

Fruit Glaces.

Paul Resal, Chef of White House (Executive Mansion), Washington, D. C.

DINNER SERVED IN PARIS,
IN THE LEGATION OF THE UNITED STATES,
TO MINISTERS OF ALL NATIONS.

Creme d'Asperges.

Printanier Royal.

Croustades de Crevettes.

Bouchees Lucullus.

Saumon, Sauce Venitienne.

Timbale de Laitauce de Carpe.

Fillet de Boeuf, Richelieu.

Mousse de Tambon a la L. P. Morton.

Cailles aux Laitues.

Galatine d'Anguilles en Bellevue.

Poularde du Mans Truffee.

Sarcelles Roties.

Salades Suedoises.

Asperges en Branche.

Corbeille de Fruits Glaces.

Gateaux des Tles.

Cafe.

Paul Resal, Chef of White House (Executive Mansion), Washington, D. C.

Glossary of Cooking Terms.

Aspic.—A savory jelly of meat.

Assiettes.—Small entrees not more than a plate will contain.

Au Bleu.—A French term applied to fish boiled in white wine with flavor.

Au Gras.—Dressed with meat gravy.

Au Jus.—In the natural juice or gravy.

Au Naturel.—Plain, simple cookery.

Baba.—Very light plum cake, or sweet, French yeast cake.

Bain-marie.—An open vessel which has a loose bottom for the reception of hot water. It is used to keep sauces nearly at the boiling-point without reduction or burning.

Barbecue.—To roast whole.

Barde.—A thin slice of bacon-fat placed over any substance specially requiring the assistance of fat without larding.

Batterie de Cuisine.—Complete set of cooking apparatus.

Bavaroise a l'eau.—Tea sweetened with syrup of capillaire, and flavored with a little orange-flower water.

Bavaroise au Lait—Made in the same way as the above, but with equal quantities of milk and tea.

Bechamel.—A rich white French sauce.

Beignet, or Fritter.—(See fritter.)

Bisque.—A soup made of shell-fish.

Blanc.—White broth, used to give a more delicate appearance to the flesh of fowl, lamb, etc.

Blanch.—Placing anything on the fire in cold water until it boils, and after straining it off, plunging it into cold water for the purpose of rendering it white. Used to whiten poultry, vegetables, etc.

Blanquette.—A fricassee usually made of thin slices of white meat, with white sauce thickened with egg yolk.

Blonde de Veau.—Double veal broth used to enrich soups and sauces.

Boerguingote.—A ragout of truffles.

Boudin.—A delicate compound made of quenelle forcemeat.

Bouilli.—Beef which has been boiled in making broth.

Bouillie.—A French dish resembling that called hasty pudding.

Bouillon.—The common soup of France.

Bouquet Garni.—The same thing as fagot, which see.

Bouquet of Herbs.—Parsley, thyme and green onions tied together.

Braise.—Meat cooked in a closely covered stew-pan to prevent evaporation, so that the meat retains not only its own juices, but those of any other article, such as bacon, herbs, roots and spices put with it.

Braisiere.—A saucepan with ledges to the lid so that it will contain firing.

Brider.—To truss fowls with a needle and thread.

Brioche.—A sponge-cake similar to Bath buns.

Buisson.—A cluster or bush of small pastry piled on a dish.

Callipash.—The glutinous portion of the turtle found in the upper shell.

Callipee.—The glutinous meat of the turtle's under shell.

Cannelons.—Small rolls or collars of mince-meat, or of rice and pastry with fruit.

Capilotade.—A hash of poultry.

341

Casserole.—The form of rice to be filled with a fricassee of white meat or a puree of game; also a stew-pan.

Civet.—A dark, thickish stew of hare or venison.

Compiegne.—Sweet French yeast cake, with fruit.

Compote.—Fruits stewed in syrup. There are also compotes of small birds.

Confitures.—Sweetmeats of sugars, fruits, syrups and essences.

Consomme.—Strong, clear gravy obtained by stewing meat a considerable length of time.

Coulis.—A rich, smooth gravy used for coloring, flavoring and thickening certain soups and sauces.

Couronne, En.—To serve any prescribed article on a dish in the form of a crown.

Croquant.—A kind of paste or cake.

Croquettes.—A savory mince of fish, meat or fowl, made with a little sauce into various shapes, rolled in egg and bread-crumbs, and fried crisp.

Croustacles.—Also known as Dresden patties. They are composed of mince incased in paste, and molded into various forms.

Croustades.—Fried forms of bread to serve minces or other meats upon.

Crouton.—A sippet of bread, fried, and used for garnish.

Cuisine Masquee.—Highly seasoned or usually mixed dishes.

Cuisson.—Method of cooking meats, or the liquor in which they have been boiled.

Curried.—Flavored with curry-powder.

Dariole.—A sweet pate baked in a mold.

Daube.—Meat or fowl stewed in sauce.

Daubiere.—An oval stew-pan.

Desosser.—To bone.

Deviled.—Highly seasoned.

Diced.—Cut in cubes.

Dorure.—Yolks of eggs, well beaten, for covering meat and other dishes.

Entree.—A corner dish for the first course.

Entremet.—A side-dish for the second course.

Escalopes.—Collops.

Espagnole.—A rich brown Spanish sauce.

Fagot.—A small bunch of parsley and thyme tied up with a bay-leaf.

Farce.—Forcemeat.

Feuilletage.—Puff paste.

Financiere.—An expensive, highly flavored mixed ragout.

Flamber.—To singe fowl or game after picking.

Flan.—A French custard.

Flancs.—The side-dishes of large dinners.

Fleur.—Cases made of a particular kind of short crust, either sweets or second-course savories.

Foncer.—To put into the bottom of a sauce-pan thin slices of veal or bacon.

Fondue.—A light and pleasant preparation of cheese.

Fricandeaux.—May be made of any boned pieces of veal, chiefly cut from the thick part of the fillet, and of not more than two or three pounds weight.

Fricassee.—Chickens, etc., cut into pieces in a white sauce, with truffles, mushrooms, etc., as accessories.

Fritter.—Anything incased in a covering of batter or eggs, and fried.

Galantine.—Meat freed from bones, tied up in a cloth and boiled, and served cold.

Gateau.—A pudding or baked cake.

Gauffres.—A light, spongy sort of biscuit.

Glace.—Stock boiled down to the thickness of jelly, and used to improve the appearance of braised dishes.

Godiveaux.—Various varieties of forcemeats.

Gras.—With, or of, meat; the reverse of *maigre.*

Gratin, or *Au Gratin.*—A term applied to certain dishes prepared with sauce, and baked.

Gratiner.—To cook like a grill.

Gumbo.—Okra.

Haricot.—So called from the French word for beans, with which the dish was originally made. Now understood as any thick stew, or ragout of mutton, beef or veal, cut into pieces and dressed with vegetables and roots.

Hatelet.—A small silver skewer.

Hors-d'œuvres.—Small dishes of sardines, anchovies and other relishes.

Lardiniere.—Vegetables stewed down in their own sauce.

Lardon.—The piece of bacon used in larding.

Liaison.—The mixture of egg and cream used to thicken white soups, etc.

Lit.—Thin slices in layers.

Luting.—A paste to fasten lids on pie-pans for preserving game.

Macedoine.—A garnish of vegetables of various kinds, a mixture of fruits of different sorts, dusted with sugar and tossed in a little wine or liquor.

Madeleines.—Small plum cakes.

Maigre.—Without meat.

Marinade.—The liquor in which fish or meat is steeped.

Mask.—To cover meat with any rich sauce, ragout, etc.

Mayonnaise.—Cold sauce or salad dressing.

Mazarines, or *Turbans.*—Ornamental entrees of forcemeat and fillets of poultry, game or fish.

Menu.—The bill of fare.

Meringue.—Light pastry made of sugar and the whites of eggs, beaten to "snow."

Mignonette Pepper.—Coarsely ground peppercorns.

Miroton.—Small, thin slices of meat about as large as a silver dollar, made into ragouts of various kinds, and dished up in a circular form.

Mouiller.—To add broth, water or other liquid while the cooking is proceeding.

Nougat.—Almond candy.

Nouilles.—Strips of paste made of eggs and flour.

Panada.—Soaked bread used in the preparation of French forcemeat.

Paner.—To cover with bread-crumbs, fried, or baked food.

Papillote, En.—The pieces of paper greased with oil and butter, and fastened around a cutlet, etc., by twisting it along the edge.

Pate.—A small pie.

Paupiettes.—Slices of meat rolled.

Piece de Resistance.—The principal joint of the dinner.

Pilau.—A dish of meat and rice.

Piquer.—To lard with strips of bacon-fat, etc.

Poelee.—Stock for boiling turkeys, fowls, vegetables, instead of water, so as to render them less insipid.

Potage.—Soup.

Printaniers.—Early spring vegetables.

Profiteroles.—Light pastry, creamed inside.

Puree.—The name given to a soup the ingredients for thickening which have been passed through a sieve, then thinned with broth to the proper consistency. Meat and fish are cooked, and pounded in a mortar, roots and vegetables are stewed until soft in order to prepare them for being thus converted into a smooth pulp.

Quenelles.—Forcemeat of various kinds composed of fish or meat, with bread, yolk of egg and some kind of fat, seasoned in different ways, formed with a spoon to an oval shape, then poached in stock and used either as garnish to entrees, or served separately.

Ragout.—A rich sauce, with sweetbreads, mushrooms, truffles, etc., in it.

Relevees.—The remove dishes.

Remoulade.—Salad dressing.

Rifacimento.—Meat dressed a second time.

Rissole.—A mince of fish or meat inclosed in paste, or formed into balls and other shapes. Used either as side-dishes or garnish. (See also fricassee.)

Roti.—Roast meat.

Roux.—A mixture composed of butter and flour used for thickening white soups and gravy.

Salmi.—A hash of game cut up and dressed when only half roasted.

Santon.—To dress with sauce in the saucepan by keeping it in motion.

Sauce Piquante.—A sharp sauce in which lemon and vinegar predominate as a flavor.

Saute-pan.—A thin-bottomed, shallow pan for quick frying.

Sauter.—To toss over the fire in a saute-pan with a small quantity of fat only.

Serviette, a la.—Served in a napkin.

Sippets.—Small pieces of bread cut into various shapes, either soaked in stock, toasted or fried, to serve with meats as garnishing or borders.

Souffle.—A light pudding.

Stock.—The broth of which soups are made.

Tammy, or *Tamis.*—A strainer made of fine woolen canvas used for straining soups and sauces.

Timbale.—A sort of pie made in a mold.

Tourte.—A tart baked in a shallow tin.

Trifle.—A second-course dish, made of sponge-cake, macaroons, jams, etc.

Trousser.—To truss a bird.

Turbans.—(See mazarines.)

Vanner, To.—To make a sauce smooth by rapidly lifting it high in large spoonfuls, and allowing it to fall quickly again for some time.

Veloute.—Rich sauce used to heighten the flavor of soups and made dishes.

Vol-au-vent.—A light puff paste, cut round or oval, inclosing any delicate mince-meat.

The following suggestions may not be out of place concerning the treatment of new cooking-utensils:

Iron pots should always be boiled out first with wood ashes and cold water, then thoroughly washed, and they are ready for use. Skillets, griddles, iron gem-pans and waffle-irons should be well greased, and allowed to burn off once or twice before using.

Sheet-iron pans for cake and bread are preferable to tin.

Earthen and stone ware jars or crocks should be filled with cold water, and put over a slow fire, and allowed to come to a boil once or twice before using to cook in.

In washing greasy skillets, the addition of a little soda to the first water will neutralize the grease and make it much easier to clean. These are best cleaned when hot.

Always keep the inside of your coffee-pot bright to insure good coffee. Boil it out occasionally with soap, water and wood ashes and scour thoroughly.

All bottles and cruets are best cleaned with shot and soap-suds. Save the shot in a small bottle to use again.

Where sand cannot be obtained, bath brick can be used to scrub wooden articles, tables, floors, etc.

In lime-water localities, keep an oyster-shell in your tea-kettle to receive the lime deposits, or egg-shells.

Have a folding rack to screw against a window-frame or near the stove to dry the dish-towels on.

A small folding table to use as a side-table is a great convenience when your family is larger than common.

344

Apple-corer
Aprons, 6
Ash-bucket (tin or iron)
Baskets, 3
Beefsteak-pounder
Biscuit-cutter
Bowls, 2
Bread-box
Bread-pans, 3
Brooms, 2
Cake-cutter, 2 shapes
Cake-pans, 2 sizes
Cake-turner
Candlesticks, 2
Can-opener
Chopping-knife
Clock
Coal-hod
Coal-tongs
Coffee-canister
Coffee-mill
Coffee-pot, tin
Corkscrew
Dish-pans, 2 sizes
Dish-rags, 3
Dish-towels, 6
Double Kettle for cooking grains
Dredging-boxes, 3, labeled salt, sugar, flour
Drippers, 2
Dripping-pans, 3; 1 large, 2 small
Dusters
Dust-pans, 2
Egg-beater
Egg-poacher
Fish-kettle (a luxury)
Flour-scoop
Flour-sieve
Forks, 3 small two-tined, 1 meat-fork, 1 toaster

Funnels, 2; large and small
Gem-iron
Glass Funnel
Graters, 2; large and small
Griddle
Gridiron
Hammers, 2
Hand-towels, 6
Hatchet
High Stool
India-rubber Gloves
Jars, 3 one-gallon
Jelly-bags
Jelly-cake Tins, 4
Jelly-mold
Jugs, 3
Kettle, 1 porcelain
Kettles, 3 iron; small, medium, large
Kitchen Chairs, 3
Kitchen Tables, 2
Knives; 1 shoe, 3 case, 1 bread, 1 chopping, 1 carver
Ladles, 3; 1 perforated
Lantern
Lemon-squeezer
Match-box
Meat-board
Meat-cleaver
Meat-saw
Milk-pans
Mouse-trap
Movable Sink
Muffin-rings, 1 dozen
Mustard-pot
Nutmeg-grater
Patty-pans
Pepper-box
Pie-board
Pie-crimper
Pie-pans, 4
Porcelain Saucepan

Potato-masher
Potato-slicer
Pot-cleaner
Pudding-mold
Refrigerator
Rolling-pins, 2; 1 glass
Rubber Window-cleaner
Salt-box
Scrubbing-brush
Shovel
Sieve, wire-basket
Skillets, 3; 2 iron, 1 sheet-iron, long handle
Slaw-cutter
Spice-box
Spoons; 2 long-handled iron, 2 short-handled large wooden
Stand to put under roast meat
Steamer
Step-ladder
Stove
Sugar-box and Scoop
Tea-canister
Tea-kettle
Tin Bread-box
Tin Cake-box
Tin Pails, 2
Tin Pail, two-quart
Tin Pint
Tin Quart
Tubs, 2 small
Waffle-iron
Wash-keeler
Whisk-broom
Wire Basket for boiling vegetables
Wire Screens, assorted sizes
Wire Strainer
Wire Toaster
Wooden Bowl
Wooden Buckets, 2; 1 cedar
Wooden Starch-box

NAPERY.

Dinner napkins should be about twenty-eight inches broad and thirty inches long. They may be folded in a variety of ways, which impart a style to a table without adding much to the expense, and may be readily accomplished with a little practice and attention to the following directions and diagrams:

THE EXQUISITE.—Fig. 1.

Fold the napkin into three parts longways, then fold down two fifths of the length from each side as in Fig. 2 at A; roll up the part B toward the back,

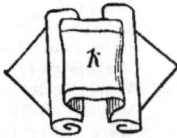

FIG. 1.

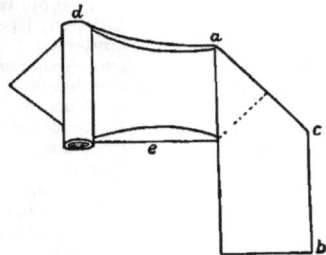

FIG. 2.

repeat on the other side, then turn up the corner toward the corner A, and it will appear as D. The center part, E, is now to be turned up at the bottom and down at the top, and the two rolls brought under the center piece, as in Fig. 1. The bread is placed under the center band, K, Fig. 1.

THE CINDERELLA.—Fig. 3.

Fold the napkin into three parts longways, then turn down the two sides as in Fig 12; turn the napkin over and roll up the lower part as in Fig 4, A, B. Now turn the corner B upward toward C, so that it shall appear as in D; repeat on the other side, and then bring the two parts E together so that they shall bend at the dotted line, and the appearance will now be as Fig. 3. The bread is placed under the apron part, K, Fig. 3.

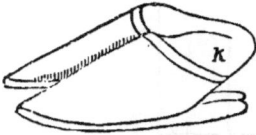

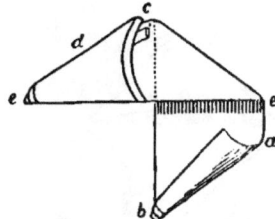

Fig. 3.

Fig. 4.

THE MITER.— Fig. 5.

Fold the napkin into three parts longways, then turn down the right-hand corner, and turn up the left-hand one, as in Fig. 6, A and B. Turn back the point A toward the right, so that it shall lie behind C; and B to the left, so as to be behind D. Double the napkin back at the line E, then turn up F from before

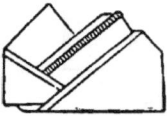

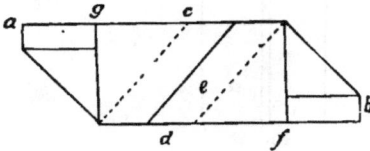

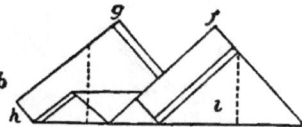

Fig. 5.

Fig. 6.

Fig. 7.

and G from behind, when they will appear as in Fig. 7. Bend the corner H toward the right, and tuck it behind I, and turn back the corner K toward the left at the dotted line, and tuck it into a corresponding part at the back. The bread is placed under the miter, or in the center at the top.

THE FLIRT.—Fig. 8.

Fig. 8.

Fold the napkin into three parts longways, then fold across the breadth, commencing at one extremity and continuing to fold from and to yourself in folds about two inches broad until the whole is done; then place in a tumbler, and it will appear as in the illustration.

THE NEAPOLITAN.—Fig. 9.

Fold the napkin into three parts longways, then fold one of the upper parts upon itself from you; turn over the cloth with the part having four folds from you, and then roll up the part A underneath until it appears as in the dotted lines in Fig. 10 at B. Now turn up the corner B toward C, so that the edge of the rolled part shall be even with the central line; repeat the same upon the opposite side, and turn the whole over, when it will appear as in Fig. 9. The bread is placed underneath part κ, as represented in the illustration.

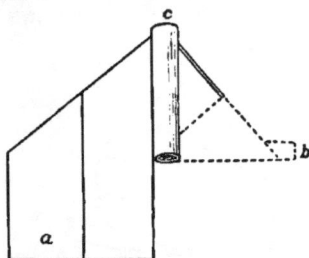

FIG. 9.   FIG. 10.

THE COLLEGIAN.—FIG. 11.

Fold the napkin into three parts longways, then turn down the two sides toward you, so that they shall appear as in Fig. 12; then roll up the part A underneath until it looks like B, Fig. 13. Now take the corner B and turn it up toward

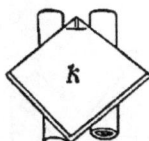

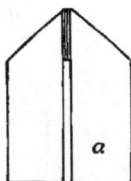

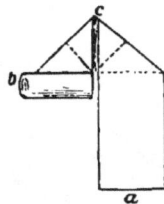

FIG. 11.   FIG. 12.   FIG. 13.

C, so that the edge of the rolled part shall be even with the central line; repeat the same on the other side, and turn the whole over, when it will appear as in Fig. 11. The bread is placed underneath the part κ.

THE FAVORITE.—FIG. 14.

Fold the napkin into three parts longways, then turn down the two edges as in Fig. 12, and roll up the part A on both sides until as represented on the right-hand side in Fig. 15; then turn it backward (as A, B) on both sides; now fold

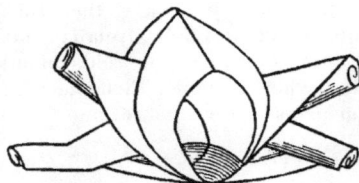

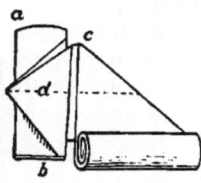

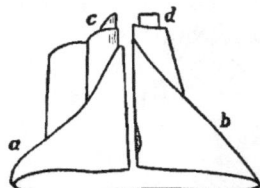

FIG. 14.   FIG. 15.   FIG. 16.

down the point c toward you, turn over the napkin and fold the two other parts from you, so that they shall appear as in Fig. 16. Turn the napkin over, thus folded, and raising the center part with two thumbs, draw the two ends A and B together, and pull out the parts c and D until they appear as in Fig. 14.

Suggestions on Carving

The art of carving is a very requisite branch of domestic management. It not only belongs to the honors of the table, but it is important from an economical point of view, for a ham or a fowl or a joint of meat ill carved will not serve so many persons as it would if it were properly carved. And it does seem to me that the most careless and commonplace person can at once discern the difference in the taste (to say nothing of the looks) of a fowl that is well carved and one that is awkwardly handled.

Ladies ought especially to make carving a study. In their own homes they grace the table, and should be enabled to perform the task allotted them with sufficient skill to prevent remark or the calling forth of eager proffers of assistance from good-natured visitors, who probably would be mortified by a complete failure. It is true that the mode adopted of not sending meats, etc., to the table, but having them served on a side-table by servants, is rapidly banishing the necessity for promiscuous carving from the elegantly served boards of the wealthy; but in the homes of the less wealthy, where the refinements of cookery are not adopted, the utility of skill in the use of a carving-knife is sufficiently obvious.

In the first place, whatever is to be carved should be set in a dish sufficiently large for turning it if necessary; but the dish itself should not be moved from its position, which should be close before the carver, only leaving room for the plates. The carving-knife should be light, sharp, well tempered and of a size proportioned to the joint, strength being less required than address in the

349

manner of using it. Large, solid joints, such as ham, fillet of veal and corned beef, cannot be cut too thin; but mutton, roast pork and other joints of veal should be served in very slender slices. There are certain choice cuts or delicacies with which a good carver is acquainted. In helping fish, silver should always be used, and care taken to avoid breaking the flakes, which should be kept as entire as possible. Salmon and all short-grained fish should be cut lengthwise and not across, portions of the thick and thin being helped together.

TO CARVE SIRLOIN OF BEEF.

A sirloin should be cut with one good, firm stroke from end to end of the joint, at the upper portion, making the cut very clean and even from A B to C. Then disengage it from the bone by a horizontal cut exactly to the bone, B to D, using the tip of the knife. Bad carving bears the hand away to the rind of

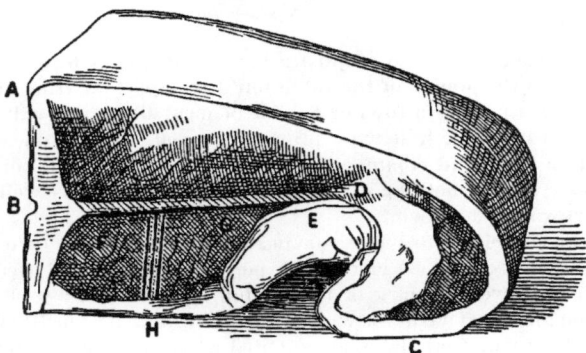

the beef eventually after many cuts, peeling it back to the other side, leaving a portion of the best of the meat adhering to the bone. Every slice should be clean and even, and the sirloin should be cut fairly to the very end. Many persons cut the under side while hot, not reckoning it so good cold; but this is a matter of taste, and so is the mode of carving it. The best way is, first of all, to remove the fat, E, which chops up well to make puddings, if not eaten at the table. Then the under part can be cut, as already described, from end to end, F to G, or downward, as shown by the marks at H.

BONING TURKEY.

Boning poultry is a difficult business for the inexperienced, and, generally speaking, is best left to the poulterer. Written instructions for its accomplishment are almost valueless, and the knowledge gained from them is worth very little compared to that which may be derived from once watching an experienced cook perform the operation. Turkeys are usually boned without the skin being cut up the back. To do this, the joints are loosened inside the bird, the flesh raised with a short, sharp-pointed knife, and the bones drawn out gradually, the flesh being laid back until the body is turned inside out, when the boning may be easily finished. When a turkey has been boned, the legs and wings are generally drawn into the body of the bird, and care must be taken to simmer, and then to cool the bird very gently for fear the skin should burst.

CARVING OF TURKEY.

The breast of a turkey is so large that slices taken neatly from it and from the wings generally suffice for all the company. They should be taken from

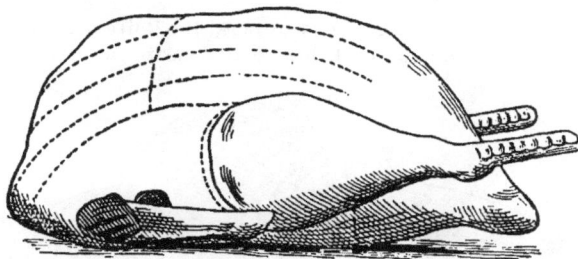

each side alternately, beginning close to the wings; and a little forcemeat and a small portion of liver ought to be served to each guest. When it is necessary for the legs to be used, they should be separated from the body with a sharp knife, and cut into slices, but it should be remembered that they, with the gizzard, will make an excellent devil.

TO CARVE HAUNCH OF VENISON.

In carving a haunch of venison, first cut it across down to the bone in the line A B; then turn the dish with the knuckle farthest from you, put in the point of the knife, and cut down as deep as you can in the direction shown by the

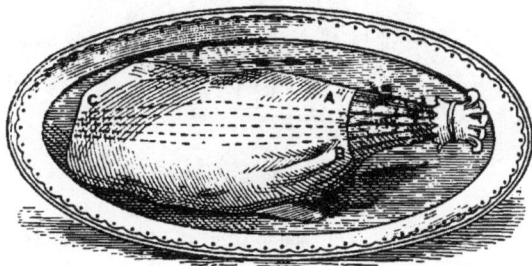

dotted lines. You may take out as many slices as you please on the right and left. The knife should slope in making the first cut, and then the whole of the gravy will be received in the well. It is held by genuine epicures that some parts of the haunch are better flavored than others, but it is doubtful whether ordinary palates will detect any difference. Slices of venison should not be cut thick, and plenty of gravy should be given with them. The fat is very apt to get cool soon, and become hard and disagreeable to the palate; it should, there-fore, always be served upon a water-dish.

STEAK.

Steak is cut into thin slices, the tenderloin being served first, the other part after that is finished. Veal cutlet is usually cut up into small pieces before being cooked; if not tender, it should be cut into pieces by the carver, and served with gravy or sauce.

TO CARVE LEG OF ROAST PORK.

In carving either the roast leg or loin of pork, the knife must follow the direction of the lines scored by the cook before the meat was roasted, on the skin

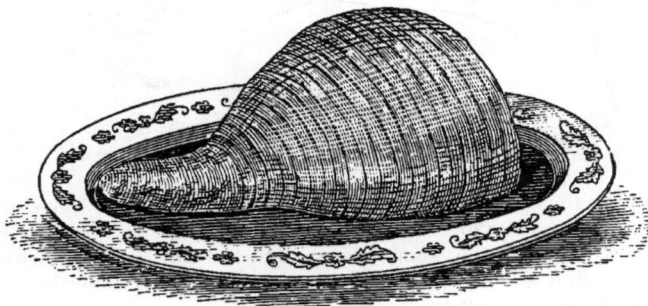

which forms the crackling. This skin is too crisp to be conveniently cut through. It usually happens that the lines scored on the roasted leg of pork are placed too far apart for single cuts. In order, therefore, to cut thin slices from the

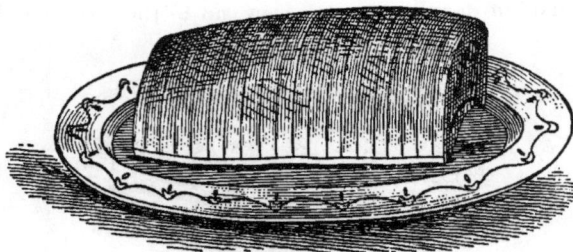

meat, raise up the crackling. The seasoning should be placed under the skin around the shank-bone. Often, however, sage and onion are sent to the table separate from the joint.

TO CARVE CALF'S HEAD.

Commence by making long slices from end to end of the cheek, cutting quite through to the bone, according to the dotted lines from A to B. With each of these slices serve a cut of what is called the throat-sweetbread, which lies at the fleshy part of the neck-end. Cut also slices from G to D (they are gelatinous and delicate), and serve small pieces with the meat. A little of the tongue and a spoonful of the brains are usually placed on each plate. The tongue is served on a separate plate, surrounded by the brains, and is cut across in rather thin slices. Some persons prefer the eye. It is removed by a circular cut marked by dotted lines at E. First put the knife in slanting at F, inserting the point at the part of the dotted line, and driving it into the center under the eye; then turn the hand around, keeping the circle of the dotted line with blade of the knife, the point still in the center. The eye will come out entire, cone-

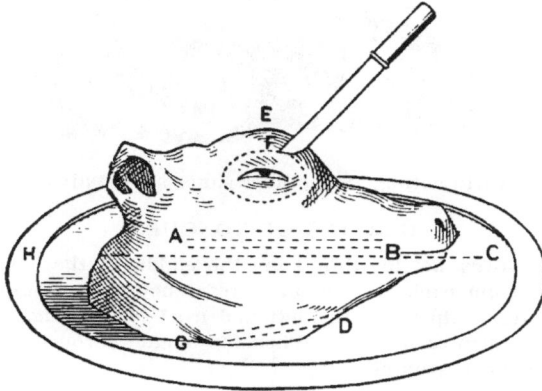

shaped at the under part, when the circle is completed by the knife. The lower jaw must next be removed, beginning at C; and to do this properly the dish must be turned. The palate is also considered a dainty, and a little of it should always be offered to each guest.

HAM.

Ham, if whole, should be cut through to the bone upon the upper side in thin

slices. It is by many thought to be a more economical way of cooking it than in a piece.

12

TO CARVE BOILED RABBIT.

First separate the legs and shoulders; then cut the back across into two parts. This may readily be accomplished by inserting the knife in the joint, and raising up the back with the fork. As in the case of the hare, the back of

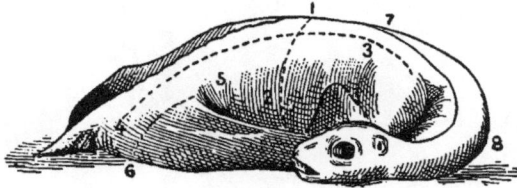

the rabbit is best worth eating. Some liver sauce should always be served with boiled rabbit.

CARVING OF TONGUE.

Begin to take slices, not too thin, from the middle of the tongue, and afterward cut slices from each side, being careful not to cut quite through the tongue. The extreme tip is usually left and used for grating. A little of the fat should be put upon each plate. When the tongue is rolled, it should be cut into very thin slices horizontally.

TO CARVE ROAST PARTRIDGE.

The partridge is cut up in the same way as a fowl. The prime parts of a partridge are the wings, breast and merry-thought. When the bird is small,

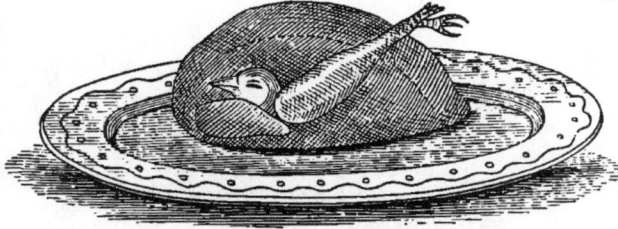

the two latter are not often divided. The wing is considered the best, and the tip of it considered the most delicate morsel of the whole.

SUGAR

- 2 heaping teaspoonfuls equal 1 heaping tablespoonful.
- 1 heaping tablespoonful of granulated, A coffee, or best brown equals 1 oz.
- 2 heaping tablespoonfuls of powdered equal 1 oz.
- 2 heaping teacupfuls of A coffee equal 1 ℔.
- 2 level teacupfuls of granulated equal 1 ℔.
- 2 level coffee-cupfuls of powdered equal 1 ℔.
- 2¼ level teacupfuls of best brown equal 1 ℔.
- 2¼ level teacupfuls of powdered equal 1 ℔.
- 1½ level coffee-cupfuls of granulated equal 1 ℔.
- 1 pint of A coffee equals 12 oz.
- 1 heaping pint of granulated equals 11 oz.
- 1 quart of powdered equals 1 ℔ and 7 oz.
- 1 quart of granulated equals 1 ℔ and 9 oz.
- 1 quart of any kind equals 4 teacupfuls.
- 1 teacupful equals 8 fluid oz. or 2 gills.
- 1 teacupful or 16 tablespoonfuls equal ½ a pint or 2 gills.
- A common-sized tumbler holds ½ a pint.

FLOUR

- 2 heaping teaspoonfuls equal 1 heaping tablespoonful.
- 2 heaping tablespoonfuls equal 1 oz.
- 5 heaping tablespoonfuls equal 1 teacupful.
- 5 teacupfuls of sifted flour equal 1 ℔.
- 3½ level teacupfuls of *corn-meal* equal 1 quart.
- 1 quart of sifted flour equals 1 ℔.

BUTTER

- 1 tablespoonful of soft butter, well filled, equals 1 oz.
- Size of a medium egg equals 2 oz.
- 4 heaping tablespoonfuls of soft butter equal 1 teacupful.
- 2 teacupfuls of packed soft butter equal 1 ℔.
- 1 pint of well-packed soft butter equals 1 ℔.

8 large or 10 medium-sized eggs equal 1 ℔.

GENERAL MEASURES.

16 ounces make 1 pound.	2 pints make 1 quart.
4 gills make 1 pint.	4 quarts make 1 gallon.

LAUNDRY-WORK.

In these days of so many washing helps of every variety, the old way of good soap, rain-water and elbow grease is fast disappearing.

Washing-day need not be such a terror to the housekeeper if managed right. I found it to be less of a bugbear when I got my maid to coincide with me that Tuesday was the best day to have for washing-day. Then there was no sorting of clothes on Sunday night, nor was the larder completely depleted, as it was over Sunday with the old arrangement. So we took Monday for general cleaning and sweeping, ate up the left-overs and made a little preparation for Tuesday's meals, so as not to go through the ordeal of a wash-day dinner also.

The clothes should be carefully sorted over first, then wash, boil, and rinse all that need no starch, and put these out to dry. Then give the attention to the starched ones.

Do not take boiling suds to wash your calicos unless you wish them to look badly in a few washings. A poor laundress will spoil a forty-cent gingham in one washing; a good one will keep it bright until it is worn out. It is simply impossible to use any of the washing-powders on colored clothes without fading them.

Red table-cloths and napkins lose their fresh, red color soon unless carefully handled. They should be soaked for half an hour in cold water, then put quickly through a lukewarm suds, rinsed in salt-water, and hung up immediately. Unless you have a bright day to dry your woolens, they had better be left until the sun shines, or dried over the stove, as nothing shrinks flannels as hanging too long wet and being cold.

Stockings should never be left to soak, but washed immediately in clean water, and not in the boiling suds that is left from the other clothes, and which always has plenty of lint in it. They should be pinned in pairs, and hung up by the toes. Woolen hose should not be ironed, but dried nicely, and pulled into shape.

Stains in table-linen can be taken out by pouring boiling water through them before they have been put into the boiling suds. Ink spots on white goods, if submerged immediately into new milk, will come out; but if allowed to stand until dry, an acid of some kind will have to be used. Citric is recommended by some.

IRONING-BOARD—OPEN.

Iron rust can be easily removed by the application of oxalic acid weakened with water, as it is liable to eat the goods. This cannot be used upon any kind of colored fabric without removing the color. Some use chlorid of lime to whiten their clothes, but it must be used with great care.

To starch dark-colored clothes, mix your starch with coffee liquid, and starch them on the wrong side.

SPRINKLING.

When the clothes are dry, pull them into shape, and fold so that you need only iron the ends. Table-linen should be very damp, and folded the length of the cloth first. The irons should be very hot, and it should be ironed very dry, so as to give it a gloss. It should then be hung in the sunshine or by the fire to finish. The towels should be dampened and well shaken, and folded all one way. Sprinkling and folding will often save ironing. Thin things, like handkerchiefs, can be laid between damp things, and will iron better for not being sprinkled. Starched clothes should be quite wet, and should be shaped as they are folded down. These may be left until some of the rougher things are ironed.

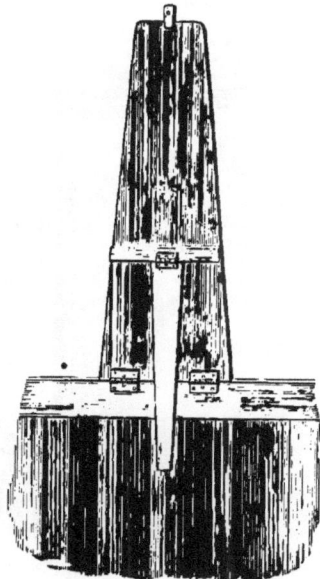

IRONING-BOARD—CLOSED.

IRONING.

If you do all of your own housework, you will not find much time to iron in the morning. Have a well-covered board, good holders, and a waxed cloth to rub off your irons, or some salt upon a paper. The irons that have wooden handles are to be preferred, as they do not spread the hand so much, and it is not so tiring. I do not know that any exact rules can be laid down for ironing,

CLOTHES-LINE HOIST.

as it is practice that makes perfect, in this as well as many other things. All irons retain their heat better after dark, and it is much better to work with them then than in the daytime. They should be washed occasionally and well

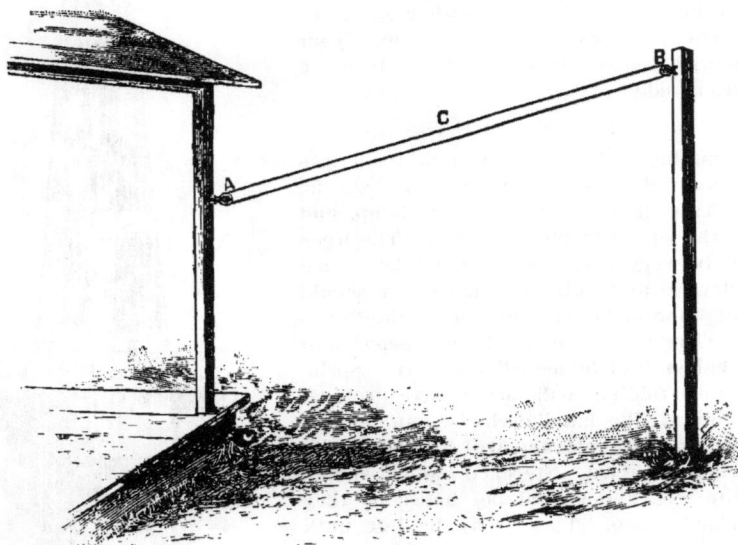

A CONVENIENT CLOTHES-LINE.

dried, and rubbed with lard to keep them from rust, and they should never set against an outside wall. As far as possible, iron with the thread of the goods, pull the article straight, and move the iron in the same direction as the weaving of the cloth. Iron embroideries on the wrong side, upon a thick piece of flannel. Pass the iron over lace only enough to dry it, then with the fingers pull it into shape. Experience is the main thing in all laundry-work, and it can only be obtained by practice.

STARCH.

This should be well mixed with cold water in the pan in which you intend to cook it, boiling water turned upon it, and stirred to keep it from lumping. I put into my starch only one teaspoonful of white sugar. I find that salt is affected by the atmosphere, and makes the clothes limpy; then I also use a preparation made of equal parts of white wax and paraffin melted together, and poured into a mold, of which I take a piece the size of a filbert to every pan of starch; this gives a nice gloss to the linen, and makes the ironing of it much easier.

Housekeeping in all its details is a wide subject, and many of us must take the best part of a lifetime to learn it. It is best to learn it gradually, and not be discouraged if it is not all accomplished in a year. There are always new ways coming up, and it is a good plan to take up with some of them. We give cuts of a good ironing-board, and also a convenient clothes-line and clothes-hoist.

A is a pulley fastened under the porch, B is a pulley fastened to a high post or on top of the barn, C is a double rope. Commencing at A and working the line toward B, you can hang up that many clothes without getting off your porch. A great saving to going through snow or wet grass. Those using them would not be without them.

HOUSEHOLD
HINTS AND RECIPES.

PASTE FOR SCRAP-BOOKS.—Put in plenty of alum. It will prevent moth or mice.

KEROSENE and powdered lime, whiting or wood ashes, will scour tins with little trouble.

TO CLEAN STOVEPIPES.—Rub well, while warm, with linseed-oil.—Hattie M. Wood, Mt. Gilead, Ohio.

MOTHS.—To keep moths out of drawers, wet a piece of cloth in spirits of turpentine, and lay in the dawers.

TO REMOVE SEWING-MACHINE OIL.—Wet the spots with spirits of turpentine, and wash out with cold water and toilet soap.

TAR may be removed from either hands or clothing by rubbing well with lard, and then washing well with soap and water.

TO KEEP LARD FRESH.—To every eight gallons of lard add one quart of strained honey.—Jennie Meek, Tahlequah, Indian Territory.

CALCIMINE.—Four pounds of Paris white, two pounds of zinc, one half pound of white glue.—Mrs. Edward A. Webster, Basking Grove, New Jersey.

BLUING.—One ounce of Prussian blue, one half ounce of oxalic acid; dissolve in one quart of warm water.—Mrs. B. F. A., Providence, Rhode Island.

ANTS.—To keep black ants from any dish or pail, draw a circle of chalk around it. This remedy has been proved.—S. E. C., South Britain, Connecticut.

CEMENT FOR CANS.—One pound of rosin, one pound of lard, one ounce of tallow, one ounce of beeswax. Melt, and stir together.—Mrs. D. S. A., Roanoke, Indiana.

TO CLEAN KNIVES.—Cut a good-sized, solid, raw potato in two; dip the flat surface into powdered brick-dust, and rub the knife-blades. Stains and rust will disappear.

TO TAKE OUT SCORCH.—If a shirt-bosom or any other article has been scorched in ironing, lay it where the bright sunshine will fall directly on it. It will take it out entirely.

To FREE THE HOUSE FROM DISAGREEABLE ODORS.—Sprinkle one tablespoonful of ground coffee on the stove while it is hot, or brown sugar sprinkled on some live coals held on a shovel.

HOW TO MAKE FURNITURE LOOK NEW.—Take three parts of sweet-oil, one part spirits of turpentine, and mix them. Rub off all the dust, and apply the mixture with a flannel cloth.

To MAKE SOUR FRUIT SWEET WITHOUT SUGAR.—To two pounds of fruit, when cooking, add one teaspoonful of soda. It will be found cheaper than sugar.— Mrs. A. F. T., Big Island, Virginia.

To TAKE OFF RUST OR STARCH FROM FLAT-IRONS.—Tie a piece of beeswax in a cloth. When the iron is almost hot enough to use, rub with the beeswax, and then with a coarse cloth.—L. J., Kingsville, Missouri.

To TAKE OUT MILDEW.—Mix soft soap with powdered starch, half as much salt, and the juice of one lemon; lay it on the part, on both sides, with a brush; let it lie on the grass day and night until the stain comes out.

COLOGNE-WATER.—One ounce of lemon, one ounce of bergamot, one ounce of lavender, one ounce of musk, one ounce of cinnamon, one ounce of orange, one half pint of alcohol.—Carrie L. Austin, Throopsville, New York.

To CLEAN COPPER KETTLES.—Wet a coarse cloth in hot water. Soap the cloth well, and sprinkle over pulverized borax. Rub the kettle well, and rinse in hot water. Some use vinegar, but this is easier, and does as well.

STARCH-POLISH.—Two ounces of gum arabic dissolved in one pint of boiling soft water; let it stand all night; drain off into bottles; use two tablespoonfuls to one pint of starch.—Mrs. E. W. Thomas, Fetterman, Pennsylvania.

CLEANING SILVER.—Two drams of aqua ammonia, two ounces of alcohol, one teaspoonful of precipitated chalk. Shake it well before using, and polish with a Canton flannel cloth.—Mrs. C. W. H., Fountain, South Dakota.

To CLEAN OSTRICH-FEATHERS.—A white or light-colored feather: Lay it on a plate, and pour over it a little warm water: then with a tooth-brush and a little soap brush it gently. Rinse it well, and it will be as good as new.

To TAKE PAINT OFF OF CLOTHES.—Rub the clothes well with spirits of turpentine. If the paint be allowed to harden, nothing will remove it but spirits of turpentine rubbed on with perseverance. Use a soft sponge or a soft rag.

TRACING-PAPER.—Mix by a gentle heat one ounce of Canada balsam and one fourth of a pint of spirits of turpentine. Spread thinly over one side of good tissue-paper with a soft brush.—E. Flora Broadman, Delaware county, Ohio.

To MAKE WASHING EASY.—Mix one tablespoonful of kerosene-oil with one pint of soft soap, and soap all the boiled clothes: put them in soak over night, and very little rubbing will be necessary.—Mary E. M. Lendon, Prairie Grove, Texas.

To CLEAN A TEA-POT.—If the inside of your tea or coffee pot is black, fill it with water, and put in a piece of hard soap. Set it on the stove, and let it boil half an hour or one hour. It will be as bright as new.—H. E. Van Deusen, Elsie, Michigan.

To CLEAN CISTERN-WATER.—Add two ounces of powdered alum and two ounces of borax to a twenty-barrel cistern of rain-water that is blackened or oily; in a few hours the sediment will settle, and the water be clarified and fit for washing.

STOVE-POLISH.—Shave up equal quantities of stove-polish and hard soap; boil slowly with enough soft water to dissolve it. Apply by moistening the mixture with a little water, and rub on with a brush.—Mrs. H. E. D., Clarks, Pennsylvania.

To BRIGHTEN TINWARE.—Wash your tinware with warm water and a little soap to get it clean. Then take a piece of soft leather, wrap it around the hand, rub it as you would to polish it, and it will be very bright.—Emma J. Cravens, Hanover, Indiana.

To REMOVE IRON RUST.—While rinsing clothes, take such as have spots of rust on them, wring out; dip a wet finger into oxalic acid, and rub on the spot; then dip into salt, and rub on, and hold on a warm flat-iron, or on the tin or copper tea-kettle if it has hot water in it.

To KEEP OFF MOSQUITOES.—Dip a piece of sponge or flannel into camphorated spirits, and make it fast to the top of the bedstead. A decoction of pennyroyal or some of the bruised leaves rubbed on the exposed parts will keep these insects away.—Sallie Cochran, Ennalls Springs, Indiana.

TURKISH CEMENT.—Put into a bottle two ounces of isinglass and one ounce of the best gum arabic; cover with proof spirits; cork loosely, and place the bottle in a vessel of water, and boil until a thorough solution is effected; then strain for use.—Mrs. Mary Shannon, Walnut Station, Minnesota.

CURRANT VINEGAR.—Bruise two quarts of ripe currants; add one quart of strong vinegar; let it stand twenty-four hours; strain it, and add four pounds of white sugar; let it boil fifteen minutes, then bottle it. A nice drink in cases of fever or in summer-time.—Mrs. H. S. Clark, La Crosse, Michigan.

BEDBUGS.—Get a bottle of the oil of cedar, and with a brush paint the cords at the eyelet-holes, and all the crevices in the bedstead, and after one or two applications housekeepers will be delighted to find that all the bugs have disappeared; and there is nothing dangerous or unpleasant in the remedy.

LIQUID GLUE.—Take a wide-mouthed bottle, and in it dissolve eight ounces of best glue in one half pint of water by setting the bottle in a vessel of water, and heating it until it dissolves; then add slowly, constantly stirring, one half ounce of strong aqua fortis (nitric acid). Keep well corked.—Mrs. T. A., Augusta, Ohio.

To CLEAN LIGHT KID GLOVES.—One quart of deodorized gasolene and one ounce of ether; mix, and cork tightly in a glass bottle. Lay the gloves on a plate, turn on enough of the mixture to dampen well, and rub gently with a soft linen or cotton rag; then expose it well to the air.—Mrs. L. O. Field, Farmington, Minnesota.

How TO KEEP WEEVIL OUT OF BEAN-SEED.—Gather them when quite dry, and sun before taking them out of the hulls; after hulling, put them into a bag, sieve or basket, and pour boiling-hot water on them; let the water run off immediately, put them in the sunshine, and dry them.—Mrs. L. Amanda Carver, Mount Juliet, Tennessee.

To CLEAN WOOLEN DRESSES.—Take corn-meal and water, and boil it the same as for mush; put the dress with enough water and the mush to wash it; rinse it in clear water, and hang it up to dry without wringing, to keep it from being wrinkled; iron it on the wrong side before it is quite dry.—Mrs. John F. Staats, Townsend, Delaware.

To Keep Lard Sweet.—When cold, cover the top with a cloth a little larger than the top of the jar; cover the cloth over with fine salt, and lay another cloth over that; tuck the edges down closely to keep out the air; put on the cover, and over this place two or three thicknesses of paper, and tie down closely. Keep it in a cool place.—A. E. M., Wilmot Flat, New Hampshire.

Raspberry Vinegar.—Two quarts of raspberries, one pint of vinegar. Let them lie together two or three days; wash them up, and strain through a bag; to every pint of juice allow one pound of sugar; boil twenty minutes; bottle when cold. Just about two tablespoonfuls to a glassful of water makes a cooling drink for warm days.—Emily R. Meads, Clyde, New York.

For Mending China.—One fourth of a pound of extra white glue, two ounces of isinglass, two ounces of gum shellac, two ounces of white lead, three fourths of a pint of alcohol, three fourths of a pint of water. Mix well, and boil twenty minutes; then bottle for use. This will stand hot or cold water.—Mrs. Mattie Stapp, Secretary Trenton High School Reading-room, Kentucky.

Cleaning Marble.—Dissolve a large lump of Spanish whiting in water which has previously dissolved a teaspoonful of washing-soda, taking only water enough to moisten the whiting, and it will become a paste; rub onto the marble with a flannel cloth, and leave it for awhile. Repeat the process two or three times, if necessary. Wash it off with soap and water; dry well, and polish.—J. McPherson, Montreal.

To Color Cotton Brown.—To four pounds of goods take one pound of catechu and one half pound of bichromate of potash. Dissolve the bichromate of potash in hot water in a boiler, and then turn out, and put the catechu in the boiler, and dissolve, having water enough on both to color the goods. Keep both dyes hot; wet the goods in hot water, and dip first into catechu, then into the bichromate of potash, until you have the desired color.

To Wash Thread-lace.—Cover a bottle with white flannel. Baste the lace carefully on the flannel, and rub with white soap. Place the bottle in a jar filled with warm suds, and let it remain two or three days, changing the water several times. Boil with the finest white clothes on washing-day. When cooled a little. rinse several times in plenty of cold water. Wrap a soft, dry towel around it, and place in the sunshine. When dry, unwind, but do not starch it.—Miss E. M., Cincinnati, Ohio.

Permanent Blue for Cotton.—For each pound of cotton use one ounce of copperas and one half ounce of prussiate of potash. Dissolve the copperas in sufficient water, put in the cloth, and let it drain twenty minutes. Then dissolve the prussiate of potash in sufficient water, and dip the cloth in for one half hour. Then add one half ounce more of prussiate of potash, dip again, and air it. Then add one ounce of oil of vitriol. Drain; dip again, and rinse with cold water.—Charles McLaughlin, West Point, Ohio.

Japanese Cream for Cleaning Black Goods.—Two ounces of white castile soap, one half ounce of ether, one half ounce of spirits of wine, one half ounce of glycerin, one and one half ounces of ammonia. Cut the soap fine, and dissolve it in one pint of rain-water; then add the other ingredients. When needed for use, shake it well, and take one half teacupful of the cream to one pint of warm water; sponge the goods with it on the right side, and press it on the wrong side.—Mrs. R. W. Mills, Webster Groves, Missouri.

To Color Rags or Yarns Yellow.—Dip four pounds of rags or yarn into hot water in which one half pound of sugar of lead has been dissolved; dissolve one half pound of bichromate of potash in enough water to take it up, then dip the material into it. It will color a beautiful orange by dipping it into boiling, air-slaked lime-water; then rinse in clear water. To color green, dip the yellow goods into a solution made with two boxes of indigo-blue, dissolved in one and one half pails of water.—D. A. H., Vernon Center, Minnesota.

To Make Extract of Lemon.—Pare or grate off the yellow rind of the lemon. It is the yellow rind that contains the essential oil of the fruit. Be very careful to avoid the white underlying skin, which is very bitter, and would spoil the delicacy of the flavor. Put the grated rind into a bottle, and cover it with alcohol or with simple syrup, or both in equal parts; then cork the bottle, and let it stand for three weeks, after which it is ready for use. If you wish it very strong, pour the same liquor over fresh peel, and let it stand three weeks longer. —F. C. White, Georgiana, Florida.

Washing Preparation.—Three pounds of bar-soap, two pounds of sal-soda, one and one third pounds of borax. Dissolve the soda and borax in three quarts of warm water, and the soap in seven quarts, without boiling: when all are dissolved, put together, pour into a tub; when cold, cut into pieces, and put into a box. When ready to wash, put into the boiler the necessary amount of water, and into this put a teacupful of the preparation; let it get scalding hot, then pour over the soiled clothes, and let them stand one half hour before rubbing.—Mrs. Emma Eggleston, Mount Riga, New York.

Vinegar.—To make six gallons, take six pints of shelled corn, and pour on cold water enough to allow the corn to swell. Let it boil until the strength is extracted. Strain this into the jar or keg, and fill it up with water, hard or soft, to make six gallons in all. Add six teacupfuls of brown sugar, two teacupfuls of molasses, and a piece of the mother of vinegar. Tie a thin piece of muslin over the top, and set in a moderately warm place. In a few weeks it will be excellent vinegar. When more is needed, leave a quart in the jar, and it will make quicker.—Mrs. M. J. S., Cannon Falls, Minnesota.

Washing Scarlet Flannel.—A handful of flour mixed with a quart of cold water and boiled for ten minutes. Add it to the water you have ready to wash in. The articles will require many rinsings in clean water after being washed in this mixture; but if carefully done, the most brilliant scarlet will lose none of its brightness. If flannel is soaked in pure, cold water before making it up, it never shrinks at all. Get a washing-trough filled from the pump, and in this the flannel is placed. As soon as it sinks to the bottom it is taken out, and hung up without any squeezing. It drains itself, and does not lose the appearance of new flannel when dry.

Washing Compound.—Two and one half pounds of sal-soda, one half pound of borax, one fourth of a pound of resin, two ounces of salts of tartar, one ounce of liquid ammonia. Dissolve the soda, borax and resin in four quarts of water, and let it boil ten minutes. When cold, add salts of tartar and the ammonia, with four gallons of water. Keep well corked. Soak the clothes over night in clear water. In the morning, wring them out into a tub. Pour five gallons of water, one half pint of the washing compound and one half pint of soft soap into the boiler. When hot, but not boiling, pour it over the clothes, letting them stand covered twenty minutes. Then look them over, rub out the streaks of dirt, and put them into the boiler, with the same quantity of water, soap and compound as before mentioned. Let them come to a boil, then rinse, starch, and hang them up to dry.—Mrs. D. A. H., Vernon Center, Minnesota.

REMEMBER that the wings of turkeys, geese and chickens should never be thrown away. Many people, especially in the country, keep them to brush off the stove or range, but there is nothing better to wash and clean windows. Chamois or buckskin is very good, but wings are better, costing nothing; and their use is an economy—utilizing that which would otherwise have been thrown away. They are excellent to clean the hearth or stove, to dust furniture, but best of all, to wash windows, because the corners can be easily and perfectly cleaned by them, leaving no lint behind, as when cloths are used. Use these wings also to spread on paste when papering walls. There is nothing does that kind of work better.—Mrs. Stowe.

SPIRITS OF AMMONIA.—There is no telling what a thing will do until you try it. I knew ammonia diluted in water could restore rusty silks and clean coat-collars, but when I got a green spot on the carpet I tried half a dozen things before I thought of that, and that was just what did the work effectually. I put a teaspoonful into about one teacupful of hot water, took a cloth, and wet the spot thoroughly, just rubbing it slightly, and the ugly spot was gone. It is splendid for cleaning your silver. It makes things as bright as new without any expenditure of strength, and for looking-glasses and windows it is best of all. One day when I was tired and my dish-cloths looked rather gray, I turned a few drops of ammonia into the water, and rubbed them out, and found it acted like a charm; and I shall be sure to do so again some day. I suppose housewives have a perfect right to experiment and see what results they can produce; and if they are not on as large a scale as the farmers', why, they are just as important to us, and may make our work lighter, and brighter, too. Now, I do not believe in luxuriating in a good thing all alone, and I do hope all the housekeepers will send and get a ten-cent bottle of spirits of ammonia and commence a series of chemical experiments and see what they can accomplish with it. Take the boys' jackets, the girls' dresses, and when you have cleaned everything else, put a few drops into some water, and wash the little folks' hoods.

GARNISHED SKEWERS.

Skewers are made use of either as an ornament or as a garnish. They are applied alike to removes and entrees, if they be cold or warm, meat or fish. Yet it will not prove useless to observe that skewers as a garnish ought only to be applied in rare cases; by making too frequent use of them their value is considerably diminished.

Garnished skewers should be used only if playing a part agreeing to their natural luxury; from the moment they cease to be surrounded by the brilliant cortege which constitutes the sumptuous part of a well-served dinner they produce no effect.

The twelve skewers represented in the following pages are all of a different character.

Fig. 1 is composed of different pieces of turnips and carrots, cut with the aid of a small knife; the oval and crescent are in turnip, hollowed out in the center and studded with a thin slice of carrot; the vegetables must not be boiled, and are scarcely blanched.

Fig. 2 represents a skewer composed of a truffle and a cockscomb; the truffle is boiled with its peel on. The cockscomb must be of a nice white color.

Fig. 3 represents a skewer composed of a decorated quenelle and two truffles, one small, the other large.

Figs. 4, 5 and 6 represent vegetables imitating vases of various kinds. These vases are cut out with the knife, and formed of several pieces, and are garnished with flowers imitated in vegetables—roses, camellias and dahlias—and with cloves, peppercorns, etc. Flowers imitated in these materials cannot be of perfect likeness, but if managed tastefully they have, notwithstanding, a fine effect.

These six skewers are applicable to hot removes.

Figs. 7, 8 and 9 represent transparent skewers destined for cold pieces; they are formed in tin cases, which are either round, hexagonal or channeled; the interior of these ornaments is decorated with details of truffles, very red pickled tongue or with very white poultry-fillets. The truffles applicable to transparent ornaments may be boiled without being peeled, yet there is no impropriety in peeling them, the chief point being that they be large, of a nice black color and of as round a shape as possible.

Figs. 10, 11 and 12 are applicable to cold fish removes. These differ from the others only by the large prawns or crayfish joined to them in order to dis-

FIG. 1.

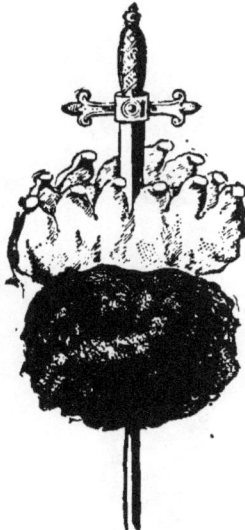

FIG. 2.

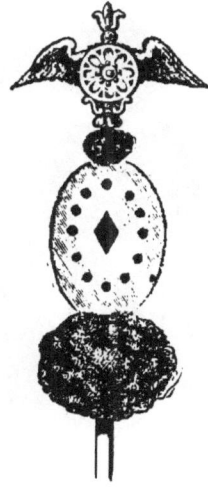

FIG. 3.

FIG. 4.

FIG. 5.

FIG. 6.

tinguish them; moreover, truffles and mushrooms may be admitted into their composition, only the cockscombs being inadmissible. In many cases ornaments destined for fish are composed only of large shrimps or prawns; but cray-fish are always better joined with truffles or mushrooms, which by their color give an agreeable relief to the eye.

FIG. 7.

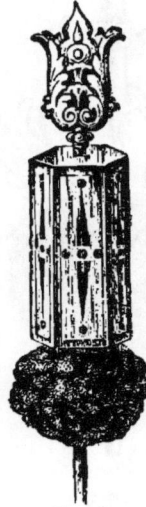

FIG. 8.

FIG. 9.

FIG. 10.

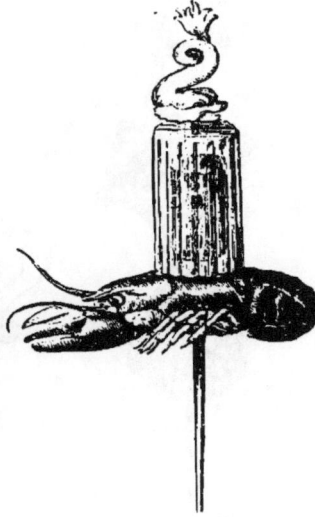

FIG. 11.

FIG. 12.

Figs. 10 and 11 are composed of truffles, mushrooms and crayfish; they are simply disposed in a different order.

MOLDS FOR CREAMS AND ICES.

—

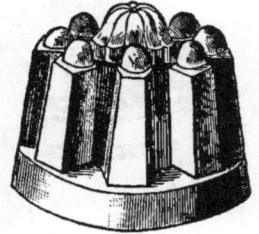

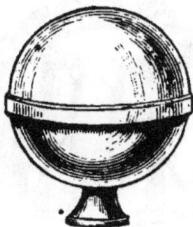
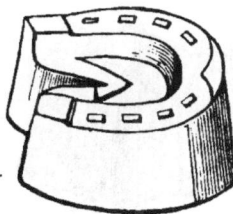

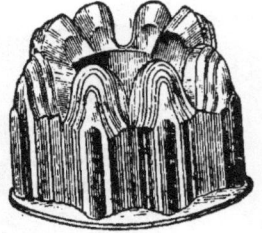

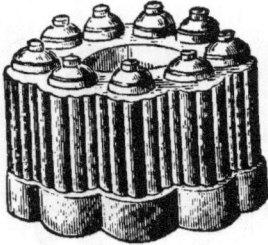

INDEX....

PAGE

Acid, strawberry 319
Alkathrepta 317
Almond.
  Blanched 277
  Charlotte 256
  Icing 272
  Forcemeat 34
  Meringue mixture.. 274
Ammonia, spirits of. 365
Anchovies 73
Anchovy.
  Biscuit paste...... 271
  Butter 53
Angel's-food ... 284, 285
Ants, to drive away. 360
Apple.
  And quinces, canning
    314
  Baked 190, 239
  Butter 315
  Charlotte 249
  Coddled 238
  Dainty 251
  Dumplings, baked.. 225
  Dumplings, steamed 224
  Float 239
  Fried 189
  Omelet 177
  Pie 217, 218
  Pudding, baked.... 225
  Sauce 11
  Stuffing 95
  Tartlets 223
  Water 327
Apricot.
  a la Conde........ 238
  Jam sauce........ 24
  Meringues 239
  Pudding 228
Arrowroot pudding... 329
Artichoke.
  Bottoms, stewed... 156
  Pickled 305
  Plain 208
  Salad 213
  Sauce 12
Ash-cake, southern... 168

PAGE

Asparagus 153
  Peas 30
  Sauce 12, 188
  Upon toast........ 153
Aspic.
  Chicken in........ 84
  Cream sauce....... 12
  Jelly 12
  Mayonnaise 20
  Salsify in......... 213
  Tomato 34
Bacon-ham, to boil... 136
Bain-marie sauce or
    stew pan 12
Baking-powder 172
Banana float........ 240
Bananas 261
Barley.
  Soup 41
  Water 273
Baskets.
  a la Rosslyn...... 240
  Chantilly 236
  Larks in 105
  Little, a la Lavanne 250
  Little nougat.. 255, 258
  Princess 264
Bass.
  Black 52
  Fillets of.......... 58
Beans.
  Boston baked...... 185
  Lima 149
  String 149
  To keep out weevil 362
Bedbugs 362
Beef.
  Corned 117
  Creams of......... 118
  Dried......... 118, 183
  Farce for border.... 30
  Farce for stuffing.. 30
  Fillet of...114, 115, 116
  Forcemeat of...... 35
  Loaf 114
  Pot-baked 116
  Patties 184

PAGE

Beef—Continued.
  Potted 117
  Scraped 329
  Sirloin 113
  Smothered 114
  Soup 38
  Steak, baked...... 117
  Steak pie......... 222
  Tea 327
  Tenderloin of 112
  Tongue 116, 119
Beet salad 212
Beverages 317, 320
  Alkathrepta 317
  Broma 317
  Chocolate 319
  Cocoa-shells, or nibs 317
  Coffee 317
  Cordial, sweet-grape 320
  Harvest drink 320
  Lemonade 319
  Lemon vinegar 319
  Raspberry vinegar.. 320
  Soda-cream 319
  Soda-water 319
  Strawberry acid ... 319
  Tea 318
Bills of fare 335-340
  Family dinners.335, 336
  Special days 337
  State dinners. 338-340
Biscuits 157
  Light 162
Birds' nests 186
  Mush 185
  Paste, anchovy 271
  Soda 163
  Suggestions for.157, 158
  Without shortening. 162
Bisque.
  Glace 250
  Of mutton (soup).. 38
Blackberry.
  Flummery 247
  Jam 315
Blanc-mange 252
Bluing 360

373

	PAGE
Boar's head	137
Bologna sausage	140
Bomb, Cambridge	268
Bomb, Fedora	262
Bomb, Rosseline	266
Border.	
Potato	32
Rice for	33
Bottom for cake	273
Bouillon	39
Brains.	
Calf's, fried	124
Calf's, little crous-	
tades of	123
Cooked	123
Forcemeat balls	55
Bread	157
Brown	162
Brown, Boston	162
Buttermilk	160
Corn	166
Corn, delicate	167
For dyspeptics	162
Fried	181
Graham	160
Hominy	161
Making, practical les-	
sons in	158
Milk-sponge	161
Pancakes	179, 180
Potato	160
Rye	162
Salt-rising	161
Sauce	14
Soft-egg	132
Soup	39
Steamed	181
Stuffing for fish	50
Suggestions for	157, 158
Whey	161
White	160
Bread, biscuit, etc.	157–172
Breakfast.	
And tea dishes	173
Dish	183
Stew	183
Vanities	186
Broma	317
Broth.	
Chicken	40, 326
Clear	326
Peptonized	326
Quickly made	325
Veal, brown	47
Veal, for invalids	326
White	326
Brown Betty	229
Brunswick stew	118
Buckwheat.	
Cakes	178
Self-raised	179
Buck, Yorkshire	186
Butter.	
Anchovy	53
Apple	315
Clarified	16
Egg	58
Green	32

	PAGE
Butter—Continued.	
Maitre d'hotel	32, 309
Montpelier	32
Sauce, drawn	17, 25
Sauce, melted	20
Sponge-cake	291
Tomato	23, 315
Cabbage.	
Boiled	149
Catsup	306
Creamed	149
Fried	149
Smothered	150
Cake	275
a la Princesse Maud	288
Angel's-food	284, 285
Bottom	273
Breton	292
Caramel	286
Chevalier	294
Chocolate	283
Christmas	288
Citron	289
Cocoanut	285
Coffee	295
Coloring for	277
Corn-starch	290
Cream	285
Custard	291
Dark	292
Delmonico	282
Dutch	291
Fig	281, 282
Fruit	279, 280
Gingerbread	294, 295
Gold	289
Hickory-nut	287
Iced orange	293
Imperial	284
Jelly	281, 283
Lemon-jelly	281
Little Beatrice	290
Maidette's	293
Making	275
Marble	278, 279
Marshmallow	287
Moka	278
Neapolitan	286
New-Year's	291
Nut	287
Orange	288
Orange, iced	293
Plain	296
Portugal	291
Pound	290
Princess	293
Progress	280
Rice	294
Silver	289
Small	296
Cookies	296, 297
Cream, baker's	298
Crullers	300
Doughnuts, raised	300
Drop	297
Drops, cinnamon	299
Fried	297
Fritters	300
Gingersnaps	298

	PAGE
Cake, Small—Continued.	
Ginger, soft	298
Jumbles	300
Kisses	299
Ladyfingers	299
Macaroons	298
Maple	297
Meringues	298
Patties, cocoanut	299
Phoebe's poverty	297
Snowballs	299
Sugarsnaps	299
Tarts, sand	300
Tea	297
Wafers	300
Spice	289
Sponge	283
Sponge, butter	291
Suggestions for	276
Texas	289
Thanksgiving	291
To prepare raisins	
for	277
Vanity	291
Watermelon	293
White	277
White-mountain	283
Cakes, cookies and	
fritters	275–300
Calcimine	360
Calf's brains	123, 124
Calf's liver	122
Calves'-feet jelly	328
Candies	321–324
Butter-scotch	324
Chocolate caramels	324
Chocolate creams	324
Cocoanut	322
Cream	321
Cream, French	323, 324
Creams, Parisian	323
Cream walnuts	324
Ice-cream	321
Maple-sugar	323
Molasses	323
Nut	322
Sugar, vanilla	322
Taffy, vanilla	323
Taffy, vinegar	323
Taffy, Walnut	323
Uncooked	322
White-sugar	322
Cans, to seal up	312
Cantaloup sweet pickle	
	303
Caper sauce	15
Caramel cake	286
Caramel ice-cream	266
Carrots	150
New	205
Stewed	150
Carving, suggestions	
on	349–354
Catsup	301
Cabbage	306
Cold	308
Cucumber	306
Currant	307
Grape	307

Catsup—Continued.
Mixed 307
Mushroom 308
Red-pepper 306
Spanish 307
Suggestions for.301, 302
Tomato 306
Worcestershire 307
Candle, flour 329
Caul 30
Cauliflower 156
Celery 189
Salad 213
Sauce 15
Stewed 156
Vinegar 316
Cement for cans 360
Cement, Turkish 362
Charlotte.
a la Cora 254
a la Princesse 247
Almond 256
Apple 249
Prince of Wales ... 255
Russe 244, 253
Strawberry 243
Cheese.
Cake pie 220
Chicken 79
Cottage (Dutch).... 192
Cream sauce 25
Fleur in surprise ... 195
Fondue 190
Pineapple 193
Potted 192
Sandwich 196
Straws 192
Chefs, celebrated ... 5, 6
Cherry.
Pie 217
Pudding 225
Spiced 309
Water-ice 264
Chestnut.
Dressing 97
Forcemeat 34
Puree or farce 31
Sauce 14, 24
Timbal of 244
Chevalier cakes 294
Chicken.
a la Bechamel 78
a la Chanceliere ... 82
a la Renaissance .. 92
a la Rubanee 89
a l'Imperiale 91
Aspic, in 84
au Gros Sel 80
au Reveil 81
au Riz 82
Boiled 81, 85
Broiled spring 81
Broth 326
Broth, clear white.. 40
Cheese 79
Creams of 84, 86
Curried 85
Cutlets 88, 184
Dormers 90

Chicken—Continued.
Escalloped 89
Farce 34
Fried 91
In jelly 185
Livers 89
Minced 329
Panada 327
Pepitoria 90
Pie 87
Pie crust 222
Pressed 88
Quenelles of 33
Roast 86
Salad 210
Salad, dressing for. 214
Salmis of 83
Saute 83, 93
Sauted mascot 93
Smothered 90
Soup 39
Steamed 92
Stewed 80, 85
Tongues and ... 77, 79
Turban of 87
Chilli sauce 15
China, to mend 363
Chocolate 319
Cake 283
Frosting 270
Icing 269
Pudding 229
Chopped pickles 302
Chops.
Lamb 128
Pork 138
Choux paste 271
Chow-chow 305
Chowder, clam 65
Christmas cake 288
Cider, boiled, pie 220
Cinnamon.
Cookies 296
Drops 299
Cistern-water, to clear 361
Citron.
And quince preserves
.... 313
Cake 289
Preserves 313
Clam.
Chowder 65
Deviled 65
Soup 39
Claret sauce 15
Clarified butter 16
Cleaning black goods. 364
Clove cookies 296
Cobbler, peach 253
Cocoanut.
Cake 285
Cookies 296
Patties 299
Pie 219
Cocoa-shells, or nibs.. 317
Codfish.
Balls 55
Browned 50
To cook 54

Coffee 317
Cake 295
Cake, breakfast ... 168
Glace 272
Rolls 182
Cologne-water 361
Consomme 40
Cookies 275
Cinnamon 296
Clove 296
Cocoanut 296
Mother Christie's.. 297
Without eggs 297
Cooking terms ..341—343
Copper kettles, to clean
.... 361
Cordial, sweet-grape. 320
Corn.
Baked 147
Bread 166
Bread, delicate 167
Canned 148
Custard 148
Fried, green 147
Fritters 148
Gems 165
Green, on the cob.. 148
Hulled 148
Meal and rice waffles
.... 169
Meal cakes 180
Meal flapjacks 168
Meal fritters 170
Meal gems 165
Meal griddle-cakes. 167
Meal mush 170
Meal pancakes 179
Meal puffs 171
Meal scones 168
Muffins 165
Omelet, green 148
Oysters 149
Pone 168
Soup 41
Starch cake 290
Starch pie 219
Sweet, dried, and
beans 148
To hull 148
Cornets, with cream. 274
Cottage cheese 192
Cotton.
Permanent blue for 363
To color brown ... 363
Crabs.
Dressed 71
Timbal of 72
Cracked wheat 182
Crackers 166
Cream 166
French 165
Soda 165
Water 166
Cracknels 132
Egg 166
Cranberry.
Jelly 315
Pudding 226
Sauce 16, 188

PAGE

Cream 265
a l'Indienne 207
Bavarian 248
Cake 285
Cake, layer 285
Cakes, baker's 298
Cheese sauce 25
Dressing for cold
slaw 214
Garnishing 273
Hamburg 236
Ice 266
Italian 237
Muffins 164
Of beef 118
Of chicken 86
Of fish 55
Of rabbit 109
Peach 265
Pie 218
Pineapple 265
Sauce 16
Sauce, hygienic ... 26
Snow 273
Spanish 237
Tapioca 238
Toast 181
Tsarina 265
Crisp, oatmeal 170
Croquettes.
Buckeye 128
Fish 52
Ham 184
Meat and rice 184
Mush 169
Salsify 152
Veal 120
Cronstades.
Little 135
Of calf's brains.... 123
Of game 106, 107
Short paste for 271
Crullers 300
Cucumbers 190
Catsup 306
Fried 155
Peas 31
Pickles 302
Stewed 155
Currant.
Catsup 307
Jelly 316
Pie 217
Sauce 16
Vinegar 362
Curry.
Forcemeat balls ... 35
Rice for 33
Custard.
Cake 287
Corn 148
For pastry 274
For profiteroles ... 274
Lemon 236
Pie 218
Pineapple 218
Sauce 25
Suggestions for 235, 236
Tomato 147

PAGE

Custards and desserts
....235—274
Cutlets.
Chicken ... 88, 184
Invalids' 328
Lamb . 129, 130, 131,
.... 132, 133
Pigeon 97
Veal 120, 121
Desserts, suggestions
for 235, 236
Dinner, Yankee boiled 156
Dormers, chicken.... 90
Doughnuts, raised ... 300
Dressing.
Chestnut 97
Cream 214
For poultry 80
Mayonnaise 214
Salad 214
Dress, woolen, to clean
.... 362
Duck.
a la Provencale.... 95
Roast 95, 96
Wild 96
Dumplings.
Apple 224, 225
Drop 224
Eclairs a la Palmers-
ton 206
Eel in jelly 72
Eels 56
Egg-plant 152
Baked 152
Fried 152
Eggs.
a la Caracas 175
a la Millais 203
a la Suisse 176
And cheese 192
And cheese salad.. 211
And gravy 174
Brouille 177
Butter 58
Forcemeat balls ... 35
For lunch 175
Fricasseed 175
Fried 175
Frothed 176
In chaudfroid 204
Pickled 174
Plovers', in aspic.. 202
Poached 174, 176
Potted 176
Sandwich 196
Sauce 17
Scrambled 175
Stuffed 176
Suggestions for ... 173
Eggs, omelets, break-
fast and tea dishes
.... 173—186
English plum pudding 226
Escallops.
Chicken 89
Salmon murillo ... 59
Sweetbread 127
Turkey 93

PAGE

Espagnol sauce 17
Farce.
Beef 30
Chestnut 31
Chicken 34
Fish 31, 32
Little creams of fish 55
Little fish, for..... 54
Liver 32
Rabbit 34
Veal 34
Farina Melusine..... 246
Farine, sea-moss 250
Fig.
Cake 281, 282
Paste for cake 269
Pudding 231
Fillets.
Bass 58
Beef 114, 115, 116
Hare 110
Herring 52, 58
Sole, of 60
Filling 270
Raisin 270
Fish 49
Anchovies 73
Bass, black 52
Bass, fillets of 58
Bread stuffing for.. 50
Broil, to 53
Cakes 61
Chartreuse of 50
Cod, balls 55
Cod, browned 59
Cod, to cook 54
Croquettes 52
Eels 56
Farce 31, 32, 55
Flounder 61
Forcemeat of 36
Fresh, to boil 51
Fried 50
Halibut, smoked and
dried 62
Herrings 52, 53, 56,
.... 57, 58
Little 54, 57
Little creams of ... 55
Little timbals of... 56
Mackerel 51, 52
Salad 211
Salmon 58
Salmon murillo, es-
callops of 59
Sardines 58
Sardine sandwiches 58
Sauce 18, 59
Sauce, excellent.... 17
Shadines 58
Shrimps 62
Smelts, fried 58
Sole and smelts, fried
.... 60
Sole, fillets of...... 60
Stocks 10
Suggestions for.... 49
Toast 55
To dress 51

PAGE

Fish—Continued.
  Trout, fried 55
  Tunny 53
  White 53
Flannel-cakes 179
Flannel, scarlet, to
  wash 364
Flapjacks, corn-meal. 168
Fleur a la Florence .. 260
Fleur, with meringue. 251
Float.
  Apple 239
  Banana 240
Floating island 245
Flounder de la creme
  blanc 61
Flour.
  Caudle 329
  Dried, for infants.. 329
Flower cases........ 252
Foie gras.
  a la Chateau Dore. 108
  Ballettes of 197
  Little bouchees of.. 199
  Mousse of 198
  Souffle of 197
  Timbals of 199
Fondue 185, 190
  a l'Italienne... 190, 191
  Cheese 190
  In cases 191
Forcemeat.
  Almond 34
  Baked pike, for 35
  Balls 35
  Beef, of 35
  Chestnut 34
  Fish, of 36
  Game, of 36
  Oyster 36
  Sausage, of 36
  Veal, of 36
Fowl sauce 18
Fresh fish, to boil ... 51
Fricassee, rabbit 110
Fritters 275, 300
  Corn 148
  Corn-meal 170
  Salsify 151
  Sauce for 170
  Squash 154
  Tomato 147
Frogs, fried 62
Frosting 270
  Cake, for small sheet
    of 270
  Chocolate 270
  Tutti-frutti 270
Fruit.
  Cake 279, 280
  List of 312
  On cakes 246
  To make sweet 361
Furniture, to make
  look new 361
Game 75
  Croustade of .. 106, 107
  Forcemeat of 36
  Pie 107

PAGE

Game—Continued.
  Stock 10
  Suggestions for .. 75, 76
Garnishes.
  Asparagus peas ... 30
  Financiere 31
  Green butter...... 32
  Green mayonnaise.. 32
  Potato border 32
  Rice 33
  Tomato aspic 34
  Tomatoes 34
Garnishes, purees, far-
  ces, etc...... 30—36
Garnishing-cream ... 273
Gelatin icing 269
Gems.
  Corn 165
  Corn-meal 165
  Graham 165
  Whole-wheat 165
Giblet soup 41, 42
Gingerbread ... 294, 295
Gingercakes, soft ... 298
Ginger ice-cream 267
Gingersnaps 298
Glace 272
  Bisque 250
  Coffee 272
  Maraschino 272
Gloves, kid, to clean. 362
Glue, liquid 362
Goose.
  Boiled 96
  Roast 96
Grape.
  Canned 314
  Catsup 307
  Cordial 320
  Jelly 315, 316
  Pie 220
Griddle-cakes.
  Breakfast 180
  Buckwheat ... 178, 179
  Corn-meal ... 167, 180
  Flannel 179
  Raised 167
  Rice 180, 181
  Rye, breakfast 180
Grits pudding 231
Gruel.
  Sago 327
  Water 326
Gumbo, or okra 156
  Soup 42
Halibut.
  Sauce 19
  Smoked and dried.. 62
Ham.
  And chicken 139
  And egg lunch loaf 135
  And eggs 138
  And veal pie 121
  Baked 135
  Boiled 135
  Croquettes 184
  Deviled 138
  Fried 135
  Mousse 136

PAGE

Ham—Continued.
  Omelet 178
  Patties 135
  Salad 210
  Sandwiches 195
  Toast 138, 181
  To boil 136
  To broil 135
Hamburg.
  Cream 236
  Steak 113
Hard sauce 26
Hare.
  Blind 110
  Fillets of 110
Harvest drink 320
Hasty pudding 231
Hash.
  Potato and beef.... 183
  Veal, egged 122
Headcheese 140
Herring.
  Fillets of 52, 58
  Loaf 56
  Marinaded 51, 57
  Marinaded fillets of. 53
Hickory-nut cake ... 287
Hoe-cake, southern .. 167
Hominy 182
  Bread 161
  Fried 182
  Steamed 182
Honey 186
Hors-d'oeuvres 71
Horse-radish.
  Sauce 19
  To prepare 189
Hotchpotch, English.. 41
Household hints and
  recipes ...... 360—365
Huckleberry pie 219
Ice-cream 266
  Caramel 266
  Ginger 267
  Pistachio 267
  Without eggs 267
Ices 262
  Cambridge bomb .. 268
  Cherry-water 264
  Coloring for 277
  Cream, peach 265
  Cream, tsarina.... 265
  Cream, Versailles
    Pineapple 265
  Fedora bomb 262
  Lemon 262
  Lemon-water 264
  Molds for .... 369—372
  Orange 262
  Princess basket .. 264
  Princess melon ... 263
  Raspberry-water .. 263
  Rosseline bomb ... 266
  Sherbet, lemon ... 268
  Sherbet, orange ... 269
  Sherbet, pineapple. 268
  Sorbet 268
  Strawberry-water .. 263
  Sultana rolls 269

PAGE

Ices—Continued.
Timbal, Empress
Frederick 267
Ices, creams, sherbets,
etc. 262
Ice-water cups 269
Icing 269
Almond 272
Boiled 269
Chocolate 269, 272
Gelatin, for cakes.. 269
Royal 272
Vienna 272
Invalid cookery..325—330
Invalids' cutlet 328
Invalids' lemonade .. 328
Invalids' soup 328
Iron rust, to remove. 362
Jam.
Blackberry 315
Plum and apple... 315
Raspberry 315
Sauce 24
Jars.
To fill 312
To seal up 312
Jelly 311
Aspic 12
Cake 281, 283
Calves' feet 328
Cranberry 315
Currant 316
Eel in 72
Grape 315, 316
Mulled 328
Pie 220
Rhubarb and apple 316
Suggestions for ... 311
Tapioca 328
Johnny-cake.
Saratoga 167
Sweet 167
Jumbles 300
Junket 330
Kidneys 141
Kisses 299
Kitchen utensils, nec-
essary 344, 245
Knives, to clean 360
Ladyfingers 299
Lamb.
Chops a la Trianon 128
Cutlets 129, 130, 131,
.... 132, 133
Spiced 130
Steaks, fried 130
Lard.
To keep fresh 360
To keep sweet 363
Larks.
a la Reyniere 104
a la Sotterville 103
In baskets 105
Laundry-work . 356—359
Lemon.
Custard 236
Custard pie 218
Extract, to make . 364
Ice 262

PAGE

Lemon—Continued.
Jelly cake 281
Pickled 304
Pie 218
Pudding 225
Sauce 20, 26, 27
Sherbet 268
Vinegar 319
Water-ice 264
Lemonade 319
Flaxseed 328
Invalids' 328
Lettuce salad 213
Lima beans 149
Liver.
Braised 122
Calf's, and bacon.. 122
Calf's, braised 122
Chicken 80
Farce 32
Fried 124
Loaf.
Beef 114
Ham and egg 135
Veal 120
Lobster.
a la Bordelaise 70
a la Boulevard 70
a la Cannes 66
a la Newburg 71
a la St. Cloud 67
Little bombs of ... 69
Salad 66, 68, 211
Sauce 20
Luting-paste 271
Macaroni.
Stewed 154
Timbal of 154
With cheese 155
Macaroons 208
Mackerel 51
Salt 52
Mango pickles, sweet 303
Maple.
Cakes 297
Syrup 27
Maraschino.
Glace 272
Mousse 273
Marble.
Cake 278, 279
To clean 363
Marshmallow cake .. 287
Mayonnaise.
Aspic 20
Dressing 214
Green 32
Sauce 20
Meat ...... 111—141
And potatoes 184
Brunswick stew .. 118
Hashed cold 184
Jellied 117
Omelet 187
Suggestions for 111, 112
Melon a la Duchesse. 255
Meringues 298
Almond, mixture .. 274
American 242

PAGE

Meringues—Continued.
Apricot 239
Mushroom 243
Mildew, to take out.. 361
Milk.
Peptonized 330
Soup 42
Sponge-bread ....: 161
Toast 181
Mince-meat 222, 223
Mince pie 237
Mince pie, mock ... 222
Mock-turtle soup ... 43
Forcemeat balls for 35
Mokas, little 245
Molds for creams and
ices ...... 369—372
Mosquitos, to keep off 362
Moths 360
Mousse.
Foie gras, of 198
Ham 136
Maraschino 273
Muffins 164
Buttermilk 164
Cream 164
Graham, Park House
.... 164
St. Charles corn ... 165
Whole-wheat flour. 164
Mush.
Biscuit 185
Corn-meal 170
Croquettes 169
Fried 169, 170
Mushrooms 185
Baked 152
Broiled 153
Catsup 308
Meringues 243
Puree of 33
Sauce 21, 29
Stewed 152
Mustard 308
Aromatic 308
French 308
Prepared 189
Relish 188
Sauce 21
Spiced 309
Tomato 308
Wafers 309
Mutton.
Double haunch 128
Leg of, baked 129
Neck of 134
Soup 43
Stew and green peas 127
Napery .... 346—348
Nasturtium vinegar . 310
Noodles for soup ... 43
Noodle soup 43
Nougat baskets 258
Nougat paste 271
Nouilles 224
Nut-cake 287
Oatmeal.
Crisp.... 170
To cook 182

PAGE

Odors, to free a house 361
Oil, sewing-machine, to
  remove 360
Okra 156
  Soup 44
Olives 64
  Braised 30
  Potatoes 143
Omelet 173
  Apple 177
  Baked 178
  Creamy 177
  French 177
  Green-corn 178
  Ham 178
  Meat 178
  Plain 178
  Puff 177
  With ham 178
Onion.
  Pickle 304
  Relish 187
  Salad 212
  Sauce 14, 188
  Stew 150
  Stuffed 150
  To boil 150
Orange.
  Cake 288
  Dessert 248
  Ice 262
  Pudding 225, 226
  Sauce 27
  Sherbet 269
  Souffle 252
Orangeade 328
Orgeat 330
Ostrich-feathers, to
  clean 361
Ox-tail soup 44
Ox-tongue, boiled ... 119
Oysters 49
  a la Dumas 63
  Broiled 74
  Corn 149
  Forcemeat 36
  Fried 65
  Little bombs of ... 62
  Pie 64
  Pot-pie 63
  Salad 211
  Sauce 21
  Scalloped 63
  Scalloped vegetable 152
  Soup 44
  Tomato........... 147
  Vegetable 151
Oysters and fish.. 49—74
Paint, to take off clothes
  361
Palae sint 231
Panada, chicken 327
Panard 274
Pancakes 179
  Bread 179, 180
  Corn-meal 179
  French 179
Paper, tracing 361
Parmesan rings 191

Parsley sauce 22
Parsnips 153
  To cook 153
Partridge, roast 101
Paste 269
  Almond meringue
    mixture 271
  Anchovy biscuit ... 271
  Choux 271
  Fig, for cake 269
  Florence 271
  For croustades 271
  Fruit tart 270
  Genoise 272
  Luting 271
  Nougat 271
  Puff 224, 271
  Scrap-book 360
  Short 270, 271
Pastes, icings, etc.. 269
Pastry potatoes 240
Patties.
  Beef 184
  Cocoanut 299
  Ham 135
  Potato 234
Peaches.
  Fresh 261
  Canned.. 314
  Cobbler 233
  Cream 265
  Pie 217
  Sauce 27
  Sweet-pickled 304
Peafowls 100
Pears.
  Baked 252
  Canned 315
  Preserved 313
  Stewed 247
Peas.
  Asparagus 30
  Cucumber 31
  Green, puree of ... 46
  Green, sauce 19
  Green, soup 42
  Soup 44
Pepitoria 90
Pepper.
  Pickled 304
  Pot (soup) 45
  Sauce 22
Pheasant.
  Beignets of 102
  Pie 102
  Supreme of 101
Piccalilli 305
Pickles 301
  Artichokes 305
  Bottled 302
  Cantaloup (sweet).. 303
  Chopped 302
  Chow-chow 305
  Cucumber 302
  Cucumber (sweet).. 303
  Lemons 304
  Mango (sweet) 303
  Onion 304
  Peaches (sweet) ... 304

Pickles—Continued.
  Peppers 304
  Piccalilli 305
  Suggestions for ... 301
  Tiptop 305
  To clarify 302
  To keep from getting
    soft 302
  Tomato, green 303
Pickles and catsups
  .... 301—310
Pies 215
  Apple 217
  Apple-custard 218
  Beefsteak 222
  Boiled-cider 220
  Cheese-cake 220
  Cherry 217
  Chess 220
  Chicken 87
  Cocoanut 219
  Corn-starch 219
  Cream 218
  Crust 216
  Crust, chicken 222
  Currant 217
  Custard 218
  Game, cold 107
  Grape 220
  Huckleberry 219
  Jelly 220
  Lemon 218
  Lemon-custard 218
  Mince 237
  Mince-meat for 222, 223
  Mock mince 222
  Oyster 64
  Peach 217
  Pheasant 102
  Pigeon 96
  Pineapple 221
  Pot 222
  Potato, Irish 221
  Potato, sweet 221
  Pumpkin 219
  Raisin 219
  Raspberry 219
  Rhubarb 219
  Shells 216
  Squash 221
  Suggestions for 215, 216
  Tomato 221
  Transparent 220
  Veal and ham..... 121
  Vinegar 220
Pies and puddings
  .... 215—234
Pigeon.
  Cutlets of 97
  Pie 96
  Roast 97
Pig's feet 138
Pilau a la Grecque.. 249
Pineapple 228
  Cheese 193
  Cream 265
  Custard 218
  Pie 221
  Preserves 313

PAGE

Pineapple—Continued.
Pudding 225
Sherbet 268
Trifle 240
Pistachio ice-cream... 267
Plum.
Canned 314
Pudding 226
Pone, corn 168
Pork.
Barbecued 139
Chops 138
Potage.
a la Royale 45
de saute 45
Julienne 45
Parmentier 45
Potato.
Border 32
Bread 160
Cakes 144
Pasty, modern 233
Patties 234
Pie, Irish 221
Pie, sweet 221
Puree 33
Salad 212
Souffle 145
Soup 46
Stuffing 97
Tarts, sweet 223
Potatoes.
a la Dumanoir 145
a l'Albert 145
And meat 184
Browned 144
Creamed 144
Cupped 144
Fried 144
Mashed Irish 143
Olive 143
Pastry 260
Puree of 33
Quirled 144
Saratoga 143
Scalloped 145
Stewed 144
Sweet, baked 146
Sweet, fried 145
Sweet, mock 146
Pot-pie 222
Oyster 63
Poultry.
Dressing for 80
Suggestions for. 75, 76
Poultry and game 75—110
Pound-cake 290
Practical suggestions
.... 331—334
Preserves 311
Citron 313
Citron and quince.. 313
List of fruit in ... 312
Pears 313
Pineapple 313
Strawberries 314
Suggestions for 311, 312
Tomato 313
Watermelon 312

PAGE

Preserves and jellies
.... 311—316
Pudding 215
Apple, baked 225
Apricot 228
Arrowroot 329
Bird's nest 229
Brown Betty 229
Cherry 225
Chocolate 229
College 229
Cottage 231
Cranberry 226
Delicious 231
Fig 231
French 230
Grits 231
Hasty 231
Kentucky 230
Lemon 225
Minute 230
Neapolitan 230
Orange 225, 226
Pineapple 225
Plum 226
Plum, English 226
Queen of 230
Raspberry 231
Rice 226
Rice and tapioca .. 227
Rice, delicate 227
Sauce 28
Snow, steamed 229
Spice, steamed 229
Stale-cake 228
Suggestions for 215, 216
Tapioca 227, 228
Puffets for tea. 171
Puff omelet 177
Puffs.
Corn-meal 171
German 170
Paste 224, 271
Pumpkin pie 219
Puree.
Iced strawberry ... 269
Mushrooms 33
Potatoes 33
Spring herbs, of... 46
Timbals of fish.... 56
Tomato 34
Tongue 34
Quail.
a la Lesseps 99
a la Tosca 98
Broiled 98
Potted 100
Roast 98
Salmis 100
Quenelles 46, 101
Chicken, of....... 33
Rabbit, of 33
Veal, of 33
White and clear soups,
for 46
Quinces and apples, can-
ning 314
Rabbit.
Cream of 109

PAGE

Rabbit—Continued.
Farce 34
Fricassee 110
Quenelles of 33
Stew 109
Stewed 123
Rags, to color yellow. 364
Raguse sauce 28
Raisin.
Filling 270
Pie 219
To prepare for cake 277
Ramekins 191
a la Parisienne ... 192
Fried 192
Rarebit, Welsh 183
Raspberry.
Jam 315
Pie 219
Pudding 231
Vinegar 320, 362
Water-ice 263
Relishes ...... 187—208
Apples, fried 189
Apples, glace, baked 190
Artichokes, plain . 208
Carrots, new 205
Celery 189
Cheese 192, 193
Cream a l'Indienne. 207
Cucumbers 190
Devonshire 187
Eclairs a la Pal-
merston 206
Eggs a la Millais.. 203
Eggs and cheese .. 192
Eggs in chaudfroid. 204
Eggs, plovers', in
aspic 202
Foie gras. 197, 198, 199
Fondue 190, 191
Horse-radish, to pre-
pare 139
Mustard 188, 189
Onion 187
Parmesan rings ... 191
Ramekins 191, 192
Rhubarb 189
Sandwiches 194, 195,
.... 196, 197
Sauces 188
Souffle a la Margue-
rite 206
Swans a la Phrygienne
.... 204
Timbals 200, 201
Water-cress 189
Rhubarb 189
Pie 219
Rice.
a l'Imperial 232
Borders, for 33
Cake 181, 294
Curry, for 33
French 251
Griddle-cakes..... 180
Pudding 226, 227
Soup 47
Waffles 180

PAGE

Roast.
Chicken 86
Duck 95
Goose 96
Partridge 101
Pigeon 97
Quail 98
Spparerib 140
Steak 117
Turkey 93
Veal 122
Rolls.
Coffee 182
Parker House 165
Spiced 163
Sultana 269
Tea 163
Roman sauce 22
Rusks 163
Dried 163
Rust, to remove from
flat-irons 361
Rye.
Bread 162
Breakfast cakes ... 180
Salad .... 209—214
Artichoke 213
Beet 212
Celery 213
Chicken 210
Dressing 214
Egg and cheese ... 211
Fish 211
Ham 210
Lettuce 213
Lobster 66, 68, 211
Onion 212
Oyster 211
Potato 212
Salmon 210
Salsify 213
Sauce, French 18
Slaw 214
Slaw, cream dress-
ing for 214
Strawberry 213
Suggestions for ... 209
Tomato 212
Sally-lunn 182
Salmagundi 140
Salmis of chicken ... 83
Salmis of quails ... 100
Salmis sauce 22
Salmon 53
Escallops murillo .. 59
Salad 210
Salsify 151
Boiled 151
Croquettes 152
Fritters 151
In salad or aspic .. 213
Salad 213
Sauce 22
Salt-rising bread 161
Salt, spiced 309
Sandwiches.
a la Fiane 196
a la Louise 195
a la Victoria 194

PAGE

Sandwiches—Continued.
Cheese 196
Egg 196
Ham 195
Sardine 53, 196
Tongue 197
Turkey 195
Saratoga johnny-cake 167
Saratoga potatoes ... 143
Sardines 53
Sardine sandwich, 53, 196
Sauces .... 11—29
American 11
Anchovy cream 11
Anchovy, for fish . 11
Angelic (sweet) ... 24
Apple 11
Apricot jam (sweet) 24
Artichoke 12
Asparagus 12
Asparagus Suedoise 188
Aspic cream 12
Aspic jelly 12
Aux quatre fruits
(sweet) 28
Bearnaise 13
Bechamel 13, 18
Bordeaux 13
Bread 14
Brown 14
Caper 15
Celery 15
Chaponay 15
Chaudfroid 15
Cheese cream (sweet)
.... 25
Chestnut 14, 24
Chilli 15
Claret 15
Clarified butter ... 16
Courte (sweet) 25
Cranberry 16, 188
Cream 16
Currant 16
Custard (sweet) ... 25
Czarina (sweet) ... 25
Devil 16
Drawn-butter 17
Drawn-butter (sweet)
.... 25
Duchess (sweet) ... 25
Dutch 17
Egg 17
Egg, for chicken .. 85
Espagnol 17
Financiere (sweet), 25
Fish 18, 59
Fish, excellent 17
Fowl 18
Fritters, for 170
German (sweet) ... 26
Green-pea 19
Halibut 19
Hard (sweet) 26
Horse-radish 19
Hubert (sweet) 26
Hygienic (sweet) .. 26
Iced champagne ... 19
Irlandaise (hot) ... 19

PAGE

Sauces—Continued.
Jam (sweet) 24
Lemon 20
Lemon (sweet).. 26, 27
Lobster 20
Magenta (sweet) .. 27
Maitre d'hotel 20
Maple syrup (sweet) 27
Mayonnaise 20
Mayonnaise aspic .. 20
Melted-butter 20
Mushroom 21
Mushroom, white
(sweet) 29
Mustard 21
Nesle (sweet) 27
Onion 14, 188
Orange (sweet) ... 27
Oyster 21
Parsley 22
Peach (sweet) 27
Pepper 22
Pudding (sweet) .. 28
Ragnse (sweet) ... 28
Rexford (sweet) ... 28
Roman 22
Rubance (sweet) .. 28
Salad, French 18
Salmis 22
Salsify 22
Shad-roe 23
Snowflake 23
Spiced (sweet) ... 29
Suedoise (sweet) .. 29
Sugar (sweet) 29
Supreme 23
Tartare 23
Tomato 23
Tomato butter 23
Vanilla (sweet) ... 29
Velonte 23
Vinaigrette 24
Vinegar (sweet) ... 29
Wellington (sweet). 29
White 24
Worcestershire... 19, 24
Sauer-krant 155
To cook 155
Sausage 140
Bologna 140
Breaded 184
Forcement of ... 36
Saute, chicken ... 83, 93
Sauted mascot, chicken
.... 93
Scones 168
Scorch, to take out.. 360
Scrapple 138
Sea-moss farine 250
Shadines 53
Shad-roe sauce 23
Sheep's tongue 119
Sherbet 268
Lemon 268
Orange 269
Pineapple 268
Shortcake, strawberry
.... 232, 233
Shrimps 62

PAGE

Silver, to clean 361
Sippets 339
Sirloin of beef 113
Skewers, garnished
  .... 366—368
Slaw.
  Cold 214
  Sweet 214
  Warm 214
Smelts, fried 58, 60
Snow.
  Balls 299
  Cream 273
  Dish of 245
  Flake sauce........ 23
  Pudding 229
Soda.
  Biscuit 163
  Crackers 165
  Cream 319
  Water 319
Sole.
  And smelts, fried.. 60
  Fillets of 60
Sorbet 268
Souffle.
  a la Marguerite ... 266
  Foie gras 197
  Orange 252
  Potato 145
  Strawberry 261
Soup .... 37—48
  Beef 38
  Bisque of mutton . 38
  Bouillon 39
  Bread 39
  Chicken 39
  Chicken broth 40
  Clam 39
  Clear 39
  Consomme 40
  Corn 41
  Cream of barley .. 41
  Crecy, with whole
    rice 41
  Giblet 41
  Giblet (German) .. 42
  Green-pea 42
  Gumbo 42
  Hotchpotch, English 41
  Invalids' 327
  Jenny Lind's 42
  Milk 42
  Mock-turtle 43
  Mongole 43
  Mutton 43
  Noodle 43
  Noodles for 43
  Okra 44
  Ox-tail 44
  Oyster 44
  Pea 44
  Pepper pot 45
  Potage a la Royale. 45
  Potage de saute ... 45
  Potage Julienne .. 45
  Potage Parmentier. 45
  Potato 46
  Puree of green peas 46

PAGE

Soup—Continued.
  Puree of spring herbs
    46
  Quenelles 46
  Rice 47
  Stock for 9
  Suggestions for . 37, 38
  Tomato 47
  Turtle 47
  Veal broth, brown. 47
  Vegetable 47
  Venison, brown .. 48
  Vermicelli 48
  White 48
Sparerib, roast 140
Spinach 156
Sponge-cake ... 283, 291
Spring herbs, puree of 46
Spun sugar 259
Squash.
  Baked 151
  Dried 154
  Fritters 154
  Hubbard, baked .. 153
  Pie 221
  Summer, to cook .. 151
Squirrel, broiled 110
Starch 359
  Polish 361
  To remove from flat-
    irons 361
Steak.
  Hamburg 113
  Roast 117
Stew.
  Breakfast 183
  Mutton 127
  Onion 150
  Rabbit 109
Stock 10
  Economic 9
  Fish 10
  Game 10
  Suggestions for ... 9
  White 10
Stocks for soup, gravy,
  etc 9, 10
Stovepipes, to clean.. 360
Stove-polish 362
Strawberries.
  Acid 319
  Cake, French 233
  Canning 314
  Charlotte 243
  Iced puree 269
  Preserved 314
  Shortcake 232, 233
  Salad 213
  Souffle 261
  Water-ice 263
String-beans 149
Strudel 233
Stuffing.
  Apple 95
  For turkey 94
  Potato 97
Succotash 149
Sugar.
  Sauce 29

PAGE

Sugar—Continued.
  Snaps 229
  Spun 259
Sultana rolls 269
Swans a la Phrygienne
  204
Sweetbread 126
  a la Financiere 126
  a l'Imperatrice 125
  Escallops of 127
  Larded and stuffed. 126
  Timbal of 124
  With mushrooms . 126
Syrup, maple 27
Tapioca.
  Cream 238
  Jelly 528
  Pudding 227, 228
Tarragon vinegar ... 310
Tartare sauce 23
Tartlets, apple 223
Tar, to remove 360
Tarts 223
  Crust for 223
  Fruit, short paste for
    270
  Sand 300
  Sweet-potato 223
Tea 318
  Balls 318
  Beef 327
  Cakes 297
  Dishes 173
  Pot, to clean 361
  Rolls 163
Tenderloin.
  a la Jardiniere ... 134
  Minions of 115
  Of beef 112
Thread-lace, to wash. 363
Timbal.
  a la Belle Eugenie. 201
  a la Christina ... 248
  a la Florence 256
  a la Jardiniere ... 200
  a la Mathild 253
  a la Windsor ... 201
  Chestnuts 244
  Empress Frederick. 267
  Foie gras 199
  Little, of fish..... 56
  Macaroni 154
  Rosamond 254
  Sweetbread 124
Tinware.
  To brighten 362
  To scour 360
Tiptop pickle 305
Toast.
  And water 327
  Cream 181
  Fish 55
  Ham 138, 181
  Milk 181
  Savory 181
  Tomato 147
Tomatoes 146
  Aspic 34
  Baked 147

Tomatoes—Continued.
PAGE

Butter 25, 315
Catsup 306
Custard 147
For garnishing 34
Fritters 147
Mustard 308
Oysters 147
Pickle, green 303
Pie 221
Preserves 315
Puree 34
Salad 212
Sauce 25
Soup 47
Spiced 310
Stew, Indian 146
Stuffed 146
Toast 147

Tongues.

Beef 116
Beef or sheep's 119
Chicken, for 77
Little, and chicken, 79
Little, in chaudfroid
.... 121
Puree 34
Sandwich 197

Tracing-paper 361
Trifle 241
Pineapple 240
Plain 242

Tripe.

Broiled 132
Fried 132
Stewed 131

Trout, fried 55
Tunny-fish 53

Turkey.

Cold 94
Roast 93

Turkey—Continued.
PAGE

Sandwich 195
Scallop 93
Stuffing for 94
Turkish cement 362
Turnips 151
Turtle soup 47

Vanilla.

Bavaroise 241
Sauce 29

Veal.

And ham pie 121
Breast of 120
Broth, brown 47
Broth for invalids, 326
Croquettes 120
Cutlets, broiled 121
Cutlets piques 120
Farce 34
Forcemeat of 36
Hash, egged 122
Jellied 184
Loaf 120
Quenelles of 33
Ragout of 119
Ressoles 120
Roast 122

Vegetables .... 142—156
Veloute sauce 23
Venison soup, brown. 48
Vermicelli soup 48

Vinegar 364

Celery 310
Currant 362
Lemon 310
Nasturtium 310
Pie 220
Raspberry 320, 363
Sauce 29
Spiced 309
Tarragon 310

Vol-au-vent 257
Wafers 300
Mustard 300
Waffles 169, 180
Corn-meal and rice. 169
Flour and Indian .. 169
Rice 180

Washing.

Compound 364
Preparation 364
To make easy 361

Water.

Cologne 361
Crackers 166
Cress 189

Watermelon.

Cake 293
Preserves 312

Wedding fruit-cake.. 280
Weevil, to keep out of
beans 362
Weights and measures
.... 355
Wellington sauce ... 29
Welsh rarebit 183
Wheat, cracked 182
Whey 329
Bread 161
Whitefish 53
Wings of fowls 365

Worcestershire.

Catsup 307
Sauce 19, 24
Yarn, to color yellow, 364

Yeast.

Cakes 172
Dried 172
Jug 171
Wet 172
Without hops 171

Yorkshire buck 186

www.ingramcontent.com/pod-product-compliance
Lightning Source LLC
Chambersburg PA
CBHW030904270326
41929CB00008B/561